# Guide to Housing Be
# Council Tax Benefit 2

*by John Zebedee and Martin Ward*

CHARTERED INSTITUTE OF HOUSING

Shelter

## SHELTER

Shelter is Britain's largest homelessness charity, with a network of 59 housing aid centres and projects providing advocacy and assistance at a local level for people in housing need. Shelter believes that everyone should be able to live in a decent and secure home that they can afford within a mixed neighbourhood where people feel safe, can work and fulfil their potential.

For further information about Shelter, please write to:


Shelter
88 Old Street
London
EC1V 9HU

Telephone: 0845 458 4590

E-mail: info@shelter.org.uk


Visit Shelter's website at www.shelter.org.uk (online ordering of Shelter publications now available).

## CHARTERED INSTITUTE OF HOUSING

The Chartered Institute of Housing is the only professional organisation representing all those working in housing. Its purpose is to maximise the contribution that housing professionals make to the well-being of communities. The Institute merged with the Institute of Rent Officers and Rental Valuers in February 1999. The Chartered Institute has over 17,000 members working for local authorities, housing associations, the Rent Service, educational establishments and the private sector.

For further information, please write to:


Chartered Institute of Housing
Octavia House
Westwood Way
Coventry
CV4 8JP

Telephone: 024 7685 1700
Fax: 024 7669 5110

E-mail: customer.services@cih.org
Web site: www.cih.org

## PUBLICATION DETAILS

*Guide to Housing Benefit,* Peter McGurk and Nick Raynsford, 1982-87 (1st to 9th editions); Martin Ward and John Zebedee, 1988-89 (10th to 12th editions).

*Guide to Housing Benefit and Community Charge Benefit,* Martin Ward and John Zebedee, 1990-92 (13th to 15th editions).

*Guide to Housing Benefit and Council Tax Benefit,* John Zebedee and Martin Ward, 1993-2001 (16th to 24th editions: 1st to 9th of this title).

*Guide to Housing Benefit and Council Tax Benefit 2002-03,* John Zebedee and Martin Ward, 2002 (25th edition: 10th of this title).



## NOTE TO 25TH EDITION

This is the twenty-fifh edition in our series of guides. It is also the tenth edition of the title *Guide to Housing Benefit and Council Tax Benefit.*

This edition covers the rules about housing benefit and council tax benefit as they apply from 1st April 2002, using the information available at that date.

We welcome comments and criticisms on the contents of our guide and make every effort to ensure it is accurate. However, the only statement of the law is found in the relevant Acts and Regulations (chapter 1).

ISBN 1 903208 31 9

Production by Davies Communications
(020 7482 8844)

Printed by Russell Press Ltd, Russell House, Bulwell Lane, Basford,
Nottingham NG6 0BT (0115 978 4505)

## ACKNOWLEDGMENTS

We wish to express our special thanks this year to the Technical Advice and Guidance Unit of the Rent Service for their very valuable comments on chapter 6; and to Sam Lister of the Chartered Institute of Housing for his tireless and expert work introducing the Northern Ireland scheme into this year's Guide. This Guide could not have been written without their work, nor without the help and encouragement of many other people. Early editions were written by Nick Raynsford and Peter McGurk, and much is owed to them. This year we are also glad to acknowledge the contributions of Janet Campbell, Mary Connolly, Mike Harper, Dawn Harris, Judith Paterson, Nick Price, Jim Read, Maureen Sharp, Scott Simpson, Imogen Wilson, Linda Davies and Peter Singer (editing and production) as well as staff from the Department of Work and Pensions. Their help has been essential to the production of this Guide.

## THE AUTHORS

John Zebedee is an independent benefits trainer and writer. He has provided more than 1,400 courses for local authorities, housing associations, advice and law centres and others.

Martin Ward is an independent benefits consultant and trainer (E-mail: mward@info-training.co.uk). He jointly maintains a web-site which gives convenient access to all the relevant legislation and other useful sources – *www.info-training.co.uk.*

They have specialised in housing benefit since the introduction of the 1982-83 scheme and in council tax benefit since it was introduced in 1993.

JOHN ZEBEDEE and MARTIN WARD
APRIL 2002

# Contents

# List of abbreviations

The principal abbreviations used in the guide are given below.

| | |
|---|---|
| AA | The Social Security Administration Act 1992 |
| All ER | All England Law Reports (published by Butterworths) |
| BA | Benefits Agency |
| CA | Court of Appeal |
| CBA | The Social Security Contributions and Benefits Act 1992 |
| CH | Commissioners' decision on HB (normally followed by reference number and year). A letter other than 'H' after the 'C' indicates a Commissioners decision on another benefit e.g. CDLA |
| CTB | council tax benefit |
| CSPSSA | The Child Support, Pensions and Social Secutiry Act 2000 |
| CTBR | The Council Tax Benefit (General) Regulations 1992, SI No. 1814 (as amended) |
| DAR | The Housing Benefit and Council Tax Benefit (Decisions and Appeals) Regulations 2001 SI No. 1002 |
| DAR 99 | The Social Security and Child Support (Decisions and Appeals) Regulations 1999 SI No. 991 |
| DWP | Department for Work and Pensions |
| ECR | European Court Reports |
| EP | extended payment |
| EWCA Civ | Neutral case citation reference. England and Wales Court of Appeal Civil Division. Followed by unique reference number |
| EWHC Admin | Neutral case citation reference. England and Wales High Court (Administrative Court). Followed by unique reference number |
| GM | The DSS Housing Benefit and Council Tax Benefit Guidance Manual, 1993, with several supplements to September 1997 |

| | |
|---|---|
| HB | housing benefit |
| HBR | The Housing Benefit (General) Regulations 1987, SI No. 1971 (as amended) |
| HLR | Housing Law Reports (published by Sweet & Maxwell) |
| HRA | housing revenue account |
| IS | income support |
| JSA | jobseeker's allowance |
| JSA(Cont) | contribution-based jobseeker's allowance |
| JSA(IB) | income-based jobseeker's allowance |
| NIAA | The Social Security Administration (Northern Ireland) Act 1992 |
| NICBA | The Social Security Contributions and Benefits (Northern Ireland) Act 1992 |
| NICSPSSA | The Child Support, Pensions and Social Security Act (Northern Ireland) 2000 |
| NIDAR | The Housing Benefit (Decisions and Appeals) Regulations (Northern Ireland) 2001 SR No. 213 |
| NIDAR99 | The Social Security and Child Support (Decisions and Appeals) Regulations (Northern Ireland) 1999 SR No. 162 |
| NIHBR | The Housing Benefit (General) Regulations (Northern Ireland) 1987 SR No. 487 (as amended) |
| NISR | Statutory Rules of Northern Ireland (equivalent to Statutory Instruments in GB) |
| QBD | Queen's Bench Division |
| s | section(s) |
| sch | schedule |
| SI | statutory instrument |
| SO | subsidy order |
| SR | statutory rules (apply to Northern Ireland) |

# How to use the marginal references

The following examples illustrate how to use the commonest references found on the inside margins of this Guide.

The sections, regulations, paragraphs, etc, shown in marginal references have in many cases been amended by subsequent law. The sources mentioned in paragraph 1.32 set out the law as so amended.

AA 134(5), 139(4) This means sections 134(5) and 139(4) of the Social Security Administration Act 1992 – in other words, sub-section (5) of section 134 and sub-section (4) of section 139 of that Act. *(These give the law about agency arrangements in HB and CTB.)*

CBA 131(9) This means section 131(9) of the Social Security Contributions and Benefits Act 1992 – in other words, sub-section 9 of section 131. *(This gives the law about the 'better buy' calculation in CTB.)*

HBR 31(9)
CTBR 22(9) These mean regulation 31(9) of the Housing Benefit (General) Regulations 1987 and regulation 22(9) of the Council Tax Benefits (General) Regulations 1992 – in other words, paragraph 9 of each of those regulations. *(These give the law about assessing the income of self-employed childminders in HB and CTB.)*

HBR sch 4 para 31
CTBR sch 4 para 32 These mean paragraph 31 of schedule 4 to the Housing Benefit (General) Regulations 1987 and paragraph 32 of schedule 4 to the Council Tax Benefits (General) Regulations 1992. *(These give the law about Pensioners' Christmas Bonus in HB and CTB.)*

SI 1995 No. 1644 This means Statutory Instrument No. 1644 of 1995 (its full name may be found in Appendix 1). *(This gives the law about what counts as an 'exempt case' in HB.)*

# Applying the marginal references to Northern Ireland

Strictly speaking Northern Ireland has a separate social security system from the rest of the United Kingdom founded on its own unique sources of law. A note on the sources of Northern Ireland legislation can be found in the following pages. However, the legislation in Northern Ireland generally mirrors that in Great Britain so as to maintain a UK wide social security system. Not only do the rules mirror those in Great Britain but so does (as far as possible) the text of the Northern Ireland legislation. For each UK Act or statutory instrument there is a Northern Ireland equivalent which is (as far as possible) laid out in a similar manner to the legislation which covers Great Britain. So, for example, Regulation 2(1) of the Housing Benefit Regulations is mirrored in the Northern Ireland Housing Benefit Regulations. Therefore the references for Northern Ireland, except where explicitly stated, are covered by the Great Britain equivalent.

Example: Page 29 reference is:

HBR 8(2)(a), 8(3)

In Great Britain this refers to Regulation 8(2)(a) and 8(3) of the Housing Benefit (General) Regulations 1987, SI 1987 No. 1971 (as amended). For Northern Ireland it refers to Regulation 8(2)(a) and 8(3) of the Housing Benefit (General) Regulations (Northern Ireland) 1987, SR 1987 No. 461 (as amended). Since the reference within the equivalent regulations is identical there is no separate reference.

Occasionally the references are similar but not identical in which case the specific Northern Ireland reference is placed immediately below.

Example: Page 29 reference is:

CBA 130(1)(a)
NICBA 129(1)(a)

In Great Britain this refers to section 130(1)(a) of the Social Security Contributions and Benefits Act 1992. The equivalent Act for Northern Ireland is the Social Security Contributions and Benefits (Northern Ireland) Act 1992. The equivalent reference within the Northern Ireland Act is section 129(1)(a).

Occasionally part of the GB legislation is identical but diverges for some of the references only. In this case there will be a GB reference for the part that is identical, a further GB reference for the part that diverges immediately followed by a Northern Ireland reference for the divergent rules only.

Example: Page 262:

HBR 40(7)

HBR sch 4 paras 64, 66, sch 5 paras 7,53, 55

NIHBR sch 4 paras 66,67, sch 5 paras 51,53

CTBR 31(7), sch 4 paras 64, 66, sch 5 paras 7, 53, 55

Regulation 40(7) is identical in the Northern Ireland regulations. However the equivalent references to sch 4 and 5 are slightly different in the Northern Ireland legislation. There is no council tax in Northern Ireland so these references only ever apply to Great Britain.

There are two main areas of housing benefit policy which are unique to Northern Ireland. These are:

- There is no council tax in Northern Ireland. Occupiers of domestic property are liable for rates instead. Help with domestic rates is provided through housing benefit (as it was in Great Britain prior to 1990).
- Decisions as to the appropriate level of rent for rent allowance claimants are carried out by the Northern Ireland Housing Executive who are also responsible for administering housing benefit for tenants. In effect the Executive carry out the same function as rent officers in England, Wales and Scotland.

The regulations which relate to rent officer functions in Great Britain are broadly reflected in the main Northern Ireland housing benefit regulations (with some differences). Where the rules are similar an equivalent Northern Ireland reference will be included. Some parts of the text relating to rent restrictions applies to Great Britain only and where possible this will be indicated in the title heading. However, there is no separate specific text describing how the rent restriction regime and help with domestic rates is administered in Northern Ireland. The authors, the Chartered Institute of Housing and Shelter are however, committed to the aim of producing a fully comprehensive single UK wide housing benefit guide in the future and we hope to make further progress with this project with the publication of next year's Guide.

# A note on sources of Northern Ireland legislation

Sources of Northern Ireland legislation are more complex than in Great Britain. In Great Britain social security remains a competence of the UK Parliament, so all primary legislation is made by an Act of Parliament whilst powers to make secondary legislation (such as the Housing Benefit Regulations) are devolved to the appropriate social security minister. However, Northern Ireland has had a unique status within the United Kingdom since its creation in 1922. There are three distinct periods in which the legislative process has changed as a result of changes to the governance of the province. These are: devolved government from Stormont 1922-1972; direct rule from Westminster 1972-1999 and from 1999 devolved power sharing Government under the Northern Ireland Assembly. For a wider discussion as to the historical and political background to these three periods and an introduction to the social history of housing in the province see Housing in Northern Ireland (CIH, 2001).

## SOURCES OF PRIMARY LEGISLATION

### 1. Devolved Government from Stormont 1922-1972

Northern Ireland was created by the Government of Ireland Act 1920 which also led to partition of the island of Ireland. The Act set up a devolved government on the Westminster model with its own Parliament based in Stormont. Although the Stormont Government was subservient to, and largely financed by Westminster it had considerable autonomy in terms of local policy making and could enact its own legislation. Although little social security legislation from this period is still in force, occasionally the regulations cross refer to a Stormont statute which is still in force. For example, the definition of 'training allowance' refers to the Employment and Training Act (Northern Ireland) 1950 whereas in Great Britain the equivalent reference is to the Employment and Training Act 1973.

### 2. Direct rule from Westminster 1972-1999

During the period of direct rule the majority of primary legislation was made by Orders in Council. Although these Orders are primary legislation they are actually statutory instruments made by the UK Government under the emergency powers taken by the Crown to enable direct rule (Northern Ireland Act 1972).

Despite direct rule a separate body of law for Northern Ireland has been maintained. The production of separate legislation for Northern Ireland has two objectives: to preserve a separate body of law for the time when devolved government could be restored to the province, whilst ensuring that it remained consistent with the rest of the UK in terms of its legal, political and social institutions. Social security law is a good example of this. The province maintained its own legislation, but it mirrors almost exactly the law in Great Britain. So, for example, the reforms introduced in Great Britain by the Welfare Reform and Pensions Act 1999 were mirrored in Northern Ireland by the Welfare Reform and Pensions (Northern Ireland) Order 1999 (Statutory Instrument 1999 No. 3147). The powers the Great Britain Act gave to UK ministers were duplicated for the Department for Social Development in Northern Ireland by the Northern Ireland Order.

Occasionally during direct rule primary legislation was made by a separate Act of Parliament for Northern Ireland. This was normally reserved for mirroring major pieces of consolidating legislation in Great Britain. So, for example, the principal primary social security legislation for Great Britain is contained within the following Acts:

Social Security Contributions and Benefits Act 1992

Social Security Administration Act 1992

whilst in Northern Ireland it is found in:

Social Security Contributions and Benefits (Northern Ireland) Act 1992

Social Security Administration (Northern Ireland) Act 1992.

As far as possible the layout and the section numbers in the GB Act are mirrored in its Northern Ireland equivalent. During direct rule these Acts of Parliament could be amended by the Order in Council procedure, for example the Welfare Reform and Pensions Order 1999, which mirrored the changes made in Great Britain by the Welfare Reform and Pensions Act 1999.

**3. Devolution and power sharing under the Northern Ireland Assembly 1999**

Devolved government has been restored to Northern Ireland under the power sharing arrangements set out by the Good Friday Agreement. With the exception of a few powers reserved for Westminster, primary legislation for Northern Ireland is now enacted by the Northern Ireland Assembly. However, under the terms of the devolution settlement there is a responsibility on the devolved institutions to maintain a UK wide system of social security (s87 Northern Ireland Act 1998). Mirroring of legislation therefore continues, but its source is now the Assembly rather than the UK Government or Parliament. So, for example, the NI equivalent of the Child Support, Pensions and Social Security Act 2000 (the legislation introducing the new appeals system for housing benefit) is the Child Support, Pensions and Social Security Act (Northern Ireland) 2000, which is an Act of the Northern Ireland Assembly.

# SUMMARY

## KEY PRIMARY LEGISLATION AND SOURCES IN NORTHERN IRELAND

**Acts of the UK Parliament**

Social Security Contributions and Benefits (Northern Ireland) Act 1992

Social Security Administration (Northern Ireland) Act 1992

**Northern Ireland Orders in Council**

The Social Security Administration (Fraud) (Northern Ireland) Order 1997 (SI 1997 No. 1182)

The Social Security (Northern Ireland) Order 1998 (SI 1998 No.1506)

Welfare Reform and Pensions Order 1999 (SI. 1999 No. 3147)

**Acts of the Northern Ireland Assembly**

Child Support, Pensions and Social Security Act (Northern Ireland) 2000

Social Security Fraud Act (Northern Ireland) 2001

## SECONDARY LEGISLATION

As in Great Britain the majority of social security law is made by secondary legislation and in Northern Ireland the process is similar. The power to make regulations is, however, devolved to the Department. The correct terminology for secondary legislation in Northern Ireland is statutory rules (as opposed to Statutory Instruments in Great Britain). Statutory rules are referenced by year and number in a similar way to statutory instruments in Great Britain.

As with primary legislation, as far as possible both the name of the rules and their numbering follow as closely as possible the title and numbering of the equivalent regulations in Great Britain. So for example the principal of housing benefit legislation is the Housing Benefit (General) Regulations (Northern Ireland) 1987 No.461. As in Great Britain this is the principal source of law with any changes to it being made by amendments.

## KEY SECONDARY LEGISLATION IN NORTHERN IRELAND

**The main regulations**

Housing Benefit (General) Regulations (Northern Ireland) 1987, 1987 No.461

**The main decision making regulations**

Housing Benefit (Decisions and Appeals) Regulations (Northern Ireland) 2001, SR 2001 No. 213

Social Security and Child Support (Decisions and Appeals) Regulations (Northern Ireland) 1999, SR 1999 No. 162

Social Security Commissioners (Procedure) Regulations (Northern Ireland) 1999, SR 1999 No.225

**Other key miscellaneous and transitional regulations**

Discretionary Financial Assistance Regulations (Northern Ireland) 2001, SR 2001 No. 216

Social Security (Immigration and Asylum) Consequential Amendments Regulations (Northern Ireland) 2000, SR 2000 No. 71

Social Security (Work-focused Interviews) Regulations (Northern Ireland) 2001, SR 2001 No. 176

Housing Benefit (Supply of Information) Regulations (Northern Ireland) 1988, SR 1988 No. 118.

Housing Benefit (Information from Landlords and Agents) Regulations (Northern Ireland) 1997, SR 1997 No. 453

Housing Benefit (Recovery of Overpayments) Regulations (Northern Ireland) 1997, SR 1997 No. 454

Social Security (Penalty Notice) Regulations (Northern Ireland) 1997, SR 1997 No. 514

Housing Benefit (General) (Amendment No.2) Regulations (Northern Ireland) 1996, SR 1996 No. 111

# 1 Introduction

**1.1** Welcome to this guide. It describes the housing benefit (HB) and council tax benefit (CTB) schemes administered throughout Great Britain from April 2002. Where there are variations in the scheme between England, Scotland and Wales, these are explained in the main body of the text. For space reasons, the guide gives most but not all the Northern Ireland variations. The guide is designed to be used by administrators, advisers, councillors, claimants – indeed anyone with an interest in the schemes.

**1.2** This chapter:

- provides an overview of the HB and CTB schemes;
- explains terminology, references and benefit rates;
- summarises which authorities are responsible for administering the schemes;
- describes how they should go about making their decisions on claims; and
- comments on the legal and other sources of information.

## Overview of the HB and CTB schemes

**1.3** HB and CTB are national welfare benefits administered principally by local councils. The purpose of the HB scheme is to help people on low incomes pay their rent. The CTB scheme provides assistance with council tax and takes two forms. 'Main CTB' is by far the more common. It helps people on low incomes pay their council tax. 'Second adult rebate' (also known as 'alternative maximum CTB') is not based on the claimant's needs or resources but on the income of certain adults in the claimant's household. Claimants eligible for both main CTB and second adult rebate are awarded whichever is the most valuable.

**1.4** HB and CTB follow the structure of the other income-related benefits (which are income support, income-based jobseeker's allowance, working families' tax credit and disabled person's tax credit). The way needs and resources are assessed are similar (but by no means identical) for all of these. Chapter 4 describes which members of the family are taken into account when assessing needs and resources. Chapter 12 explains how the 'applicable amount' (the figure representing the claimant and family's needs) is assessed from this. Chapters 13 to 15 describe the assessment of resources.

**1.5** The maximum amount of HB is 100% of the claimant's 'eligible rent'. The maximum amount of main CTB is 100% of the claimant's 'eligible council tax'. As the claimant's net income increases above his or her applicable amount, HB and main CTB are withdrawn by a percentage of that excess income. The percentage (or 'taper') for HB is 65%; for main CTB it is 20%. Additionally, non-dependant deductions may be made from the claimant's HB and main CTB entitlement further reducing the amount of benefit awarded. Chapters 7 and 8 explain the details of the calculations. Chapters 9 to 11 describe what counts as the claimant's eligible rent and eligible council tax. Chapter 2 gives more details of the council tax scheme itself and chapter 6 explains how the rent officer (an official independent of the council) is involved in deciding whether HB can be awarded on the whole of a private tenant's rent or only on part.

**1.6** Nearly everyone with low income and capital can get HB and/or CTB. However, there are some exceptions – for example many 'persons from abroad' and full-time students cannot get HB or CTB. For those two groups, see chapters 20 and 21 respectively. Chapter 3 gives the general rules about entitlement and some further exceptions.

**1.7** HB and CTB cannot be awarded unless a claim is made and there are numerous procedural rules involved in claiming (Chapter 5). There are specific rules about what claimants must be told and when and how benefit is awarded (Chapter 16). Claimants must also keep the council informed about changes in their circumstances (Chapter 17). Failure to do so is one of the principle causes of overpayments (Chapter 18) – though councils do themselves make mistakes too. Disagreements can lead to a need for more information and to appeals (Chapter 19).

**1.8** HB and CTB are a significant source of help for many claimants. In Great Britain in November 2000, 3.9 million people were in receipt of HB, 4.68 million were in receipt of main CTB, and 32,000 were in receipt of second adult rebate. In each case, about two-thirds of these were also getting income support or income-based jobseeker's allowance, the other one third were getting neither of those. (All figures taken from HB & CTB Quarterly Summary Statistics November 2000, DSS, Analytical Services Division.)

**1.9** Responsibility for running the HB and CTB schemes gives administering authorities a prime role in maintaining the incomes of disadvantaged groups and can reduce rent and council tax arrears. Central government subsidy payments towards the costs of each authority's benefit expenditure are a very significant proportion of authorities' revenue income. Chapter 22 gives more detail about subsidy. AA 134, 139, 191 NIAA 126, 167

**1.10** HB was first introduced in 1982/83 and was replaced with a new HB scheme in 1988. CTB came in with the introduction of council tax in 1993. Table

1.1 summarises changes to the HB and CTB scheme over the past year. A fuller list of changes – going back to April 1988 – may be found in table 2.1 of the 2001-02 edition of this guide.

**TABLE 1.1 SUMMARY OF PRINCIPAL CHANGES AFTER APRIL 2001**

| | | |
|---|---|---|
| SI 2001 No. 487<br>NISR 2001 No. 79 | 21st May 2001 | People renting a home they previously owned are no longer automatically barred from HB entitlement if five years have elapsed since they owned it. |
| | | Clarification of technical points in the rules about eligible rent and rent officer referrals. |
| SI 2001 No. 1002<br>NISR 2001 No. 213 | 2nd July 2001 | Introduction of new decision-making arrangements, including rules about revisions, supersessions, suspensions, terminations, stayings, restrictions on entitlement after a test case, and asking the authority to look at a case again. |
| | | Abolition of review boards, which are replaced by a right of appeal to a social security appeal tribunal and thereafter on a point of law to the Social Security Commissioners. |
| | | Abolition of one year time limit on arrears of entitlement due because of an official error. |
| | | New restrictions on arrears of entitlement when a change of circumstances is notified late. |
| SI 2001 No. 1167<br>NISR 2001 No. 216 | | Abolition of exceptional circumstances payments and exceptional hardship payments. Introduction of a separate discretionary housing payments scheme. |
| SI 2001 No. 1325<br>NISR 2001 No. 238 | | Broadening of rent officer criteria for assessment of the Single Room Rent to reflect the cost of shared accommodation. Similar broadening of Local Reference Rent criteria. |
| SI 2001 No. 1864<br>NISR 2001 No. 259 | 13th August 2001 | Large increase in child care disregard (from £70 to £94.50 in the case of one qualifying child, |

| | | |
|---|---|---|
| | and from £105 to £140 in the case of two or more). Child care disregard can now apply to a woman on maternity leave. | |
| 27th August 2001 | New rules for averaging income from a student loan (and in some cases dependant grants), including cases where the student has a non-standard year and where the student leaves part-way through the course. | SI 2001 No. 2319<br>NISR 2001 No. 278 |
| | New student rules and disregards for travel, books and equipment and child care. Student up-rating. | |
| 24th September 2001 | A volunteer's expenses are now disregarded in assessing income, even if they are paid in advance of the volunteer's incurring them. | SI 2001 No. 2286<br>NISR 2001 No. 258 |
| 1st October 2001 | New limitations on when overpayments can be recovered from a landlord, in cases where the landlord has reported a suspected fraud in writing and certain other conditions are fulfilled. | SI 2001 No. 1190<br>NISR 2001 No. 179 |
| | New rules introduced regarding offences of failing to notify a change of circumstances. | SI 2001 No. 3251<br>SI 2001 No. 3252<br>NISR 2001 No. 416<br>NISR 2001 No. 420 |
| | The Children (Leaving Care) Act 2000 comes into force in England and Wales, excluding certain care leavers from HB entitlement, in whose case support should be provided by the responsible local authority. | |
| 22nd October 2001 | Mini up-rating of dependant additions (up by £1.50 a week for every dependant child/young person). | SI 2001 No. 2980<br>NISR 2001 No. 314 |
| 6th November 2001 | Changes to the areas rent officers should take into account, to partially reverse the effect of the Court of Appeal case, R (Saadat and Others) v the Rent Service (26.10.01). The single legal term 'locality' is replaced with three names for those areas: 'vicinity', 'neighbourhood' and 'locality'. | SI 2001 No. 3561<br>(no NI equivalent) |
| 19th November 2001 | New capital disregard for certain compensation for Second World War forced labour, slave | SI 2001 No. 3481<br>NISR 2001 No. 392 |

| | | |
|---|---|---|
| | | labour, property loss, personal injury or death of a child. |
| SI 2001 No. 668<br>NISR 2001 No. 108 | 1st April 2002 | Annual up-rating.<br>All authorities are required to operate the government's new incentive scheme as a reward for anti-fraud activity. |
| | April 2003 | Proposed introduction of 'Supporting People' – an integrated funding framework for support services; and the end of HB assistance with such costs. |
| | 10th April 2006 | Expiry of bereavement premium. |

## Using this guide

### TERMS

**1.11** A number of different public authorities are involved in the administration of HB/CTB. The term 'authority' is used in this guide to cover them all. The term 'housing benefit' is a generic one that covers the two types of payments which may be made under the scheme, otherwise described as rebates or allowances. It is used in this sense in the guide. Where, however, it is more appropriate, the specific term, i.e. rent rebate or rent allowance, is used. Also the term 'tenant' is used to describe any kind of rent-payer including, for example, licensees. The term 'CTB' is used to refer to both forms of CTB. One of these – 'alternative maximum council tax benefit' – in this guide, in common with DSS guidance and most local authority forms, is referred to as 'second adult rebate'. Where it is more appropriate, the specific term 'main CTB' or 'second adult rebate' is used.

### REFERENCES AND ABBREVIATIONS

AA 134(5), 139(4)
NIAA 126(3)

**1.12** Details of the law and guidance may be found in paragraphs 1.27 onwards, with information on how references are used in this guide in paragraph 1.35. A list of abbreviations, and a summary of how to use the marginal references, are at the front of this guide following the contents page.

## Benefits and tax credits rates

**1.13** In the case of all CTB claims and HB claims the rates quoted are those which apply from 1st April 2002. Other benefit rates are increased during the week commencing 8th April 2002 but must be taken into account of for HB and

CTB purposes from 1st April 2002. Exceptions to this rule concern the uprated amounts of working families tax credit (WFTC) and disabled person's tax credit (DPTC) which apply only to new awards starting on or after 9th April 2002. Awards of WFTC or DPTC that start before 9th April 2002 are not uprated.. Student figures (Chapter 21) apply from September 2001. A summary of the benefit rates for 2002-2003 is printed at the back of the guide (appendix 5). The tax and national insurance (NI) rates quoted are those which apply from 6th April 2002 to 5th March 2003.

## Administration

**1.14** Different arrangements apply in England and Wales and in Scotland. In any individual authority HB/CTB may be administered by one or more departments, usually the housing or treasurer's/finance department or by an external contractor acting on behalf of the council. AA 134, 139, 191 NIAA 126, 167

### ENGLAND AND WALES

**1.15** Claimants in England should obtain HB, and CTB, from the local council in their area, e.g. the council of a district, London borough or the Common Council of the City of London. In Wales claimants should apply to the county or county borough council. In specific areas agency arrangements (para. 1.12) may exist or the ONE service may be in operation (para. 1.15).

### SCOTLAND

**1.16** Tenants of Scottish Homes receive rent rebates from their landlord. All other tenants, whether council, housing association or private should receive rent rebates or allowances from the local council, though agency arrangements (para. 1.12) may exist. Each authority administers CTB on the council tax collected by it.

### NORTHERN IRELAND

**1.17** There is no council tax in Northern Ireland. Tenants wishing to claim HB in Northern Ireland can get a claim form from the nearest office of the Northern Ireland Housing Executive. The phone numbers and addresses are listed in the phone book under Housing Executive. The Rate Collection Agency (an Executive Agency within the Department of Finance and Personnel) is responsible for the collection of rates due to the 26 District Councils in respect of the District Rate and to the Department of Finance and Personnel in respect of the Regional Rate. It receives payment from the Northern Ireland Housing Executive for properties in the public sector. The Agency also administers the HB scheme for owner-occupiers.

## AGENCY ARRANGEMENTS

**1.18** Authorities may make arrangements by which:

- one carries out the functions of the other; or
- functions are carried out jointly or by a joint committee.

For example, agency arrangements sometimes apply to local authority tenants living in property situated outside the landlord authority's boundaries. In such a case they may receive a rent rebate from their landlord authority as opposed to the authority in which they live if agency arrangements have been agreed.

## 'ONE' – THE SINGLE WORK FOCUSED GATEWAY TO BENEFITS

**1.19** The Government has stated its intention to develop a new system for the administration of benefits. The idea is that there should be a single point of access and an interview with a job-finding focus for those who have the potential to work (DSS, *New ambitions for our country: a new contract for welfare,* Cm 3805 and DfEE and DSS *A new contract for welfare: the gateway to work,* Cm 4102). The Welfare Reform and Pensions Act identifies HB and CTB as two of the benefits which may be accessed through the Single Gateway. The work-focused interview may be conducted by the Benefits Agency, the Employment Service, a private/voluntary sector contractor or by the authority.

AA 134, 139, 191 **1.20** From 3 April 2000, most claimants under age 60 not in remunerative work living in ONE pilot areas when making a new HB/CTB claim must, as a condition of receiving benefit, take part in an interview with a Personal Advisor.

**1.21** The ONE service is being piloted in: Essex South East, Warwickshire, Clyde Coast and Renfrew, Lea Roding, Leeds, Suffolk, North Nottinghamshire, North Cheshire, Somerset, Buckinghamshire, Calderdale and Kirklees and South East Gwent. National implementation of the Single Gateway will depend on experience in the pilot areas.

## CONTRACTING OUT ADMINISTRATION AND 'BEST VALUE'

**1.22** Authorities can contract out the administration of HB and CTB to private companies and a number have done so. The Local Government Act 1999 replaced compulsory competitive tendering (CCT) in England and Wales with a duty of obtaining best value for the taxpayer from April 2000. A similar agenda operates in Scotland.

**1.23** The best value initiative focuses on economy, efficiency, effectiveness and quality in local services. Authorities have to conduct performance reviews and publish annual local performance plans. The Government or, in Wales, the National Assembly, have devised performance indicators and national standards for local government activities including benefit administration. The indicators target the priorities of speed; accuracy; security of the benefit delivery; and also value for money and customer-focus.

**1.24** In England as part of its plan to 'modernise' local authorities the Government announced the Beacon Scheme (from April 1999) (DETR Press Release, 9 February 1999, *Beacon councils to lead the way*). This aims to:

- spread best practice (via the Local Government Improvement and Development Agency); and
- allow new freedoms and flexibilities to be tested.

The Government intention is that beacon status will be awarded for excellence in a number of different services including HB/CTB provision. Similar proposals have been put to the National Assembly in Wales.

**1.25** Where an authority has contracted out benefit-related work this does not affect its administrative responsibility. The authority itself remains responsible for the functions and duties placed upon it by the relevant legislation. DSS circular HB/CTB (93)9 emphasised that authorities could not contract out certain functions. These include benefit decision-making, rent officer referrals and the exchange of information with the Benefits Agency. The contracting out of HB/CTB administration does not affect an individual's entitlement or his or her right of appeal to an independent appeal tribunal.

**1.26** The Deregulation and Contracting Out Act 1994 permits contractors to communicate directly with the Benefits Agency but current arrangements result in the double handling of claims by the contractor and the authority and require authorities to maintain in-house teams to carry out the work. A provision in the Local Government Act creates wider powers to contract out functions. It could be used to enable authorities to contract out housing benefit and council tax benefit decision-making.

## Proper decision-making

**1.27** The authority's primary duty is one of proper decision-making. It has to apply the rules of the HB/CTB schemes to the facts of the individual case with the aim of arriving at sound decisions regarding benefit entitlement. The necessary steps in the decision-making process are:

- the identification of the relevant facts in the case;
- proper consideration of the available evidence where the facts are in doubt or in dispute;
- establishing facts 'on the balance of probability' where necessary;
- correct interpretation of the law and its application to the facts of the case; and

◆ arriving at decisions that can be understood in terms of the relevant law and facts.

## DISPUTED FACTS

**1.28** The only facts which are relevant to the authority are those which have a bearing in relation to the application of the specific rules of the HB/CTB schemes. Where there is a disagreement about the facts between the authority and the claimant or other person affected, the authority must consider the available evidence to decide what the true position is. A factual dispute may also be the trigger for a request for revision, supersession or an appeal to an independent appeal tribunal (chapters 19 and 21).

**1.29** The requirement of proof means that a disputed fact must be established to the satisfaction of the authority and, on appeal, the appeal tribunal. This does not, however, mean that the fact must be established with absolute certainty. In civil cases, such as matters involving HB/CTB, the appropriate test is 'on the balance of probability'. In other words, if the greater weight of evidence supports for example the claimant's view of the disputed fact then the claimant has proved the matter on the balance of probability.

AA 5(1) HBR 73 **1.30** In the first instance the burden of proof is on the claimant to support his or her claim by supplying the authority with all the evidence it reasonably requires (para. 7.37). The Department of Social Security's Verification Framework seeks to set out the minimum standards for collecting evidence when a claim is made (para. 7.41). However, where the authority asserts a particular proposition, for example, that a recoverable overpayment has occurred, the authority must have evidence to support its assertion.

**1.31** The burden of proof is only decisive, however, where:

◆ there is no evidence – consequently where the authority asserts a disputed fact it must have evidence to support that assertion; or

◆ the evidence is exactly balanced – in which case the party on whom the burden of proof lies should not succeed.

## ISSUES OF LAW

**1.32** The rules of the HB/CTB schemes are set out in legislation passed by the UK parliament. Issues of law involve the application and interpretation of that legislation. For example, the question as to whether or not the claimant's son counts as a non-dependant for HB/CTB purposes could only be answered by consideration of the definition of 'non-dependant' in the regulations as well as the relevant facts of the case. A dispute over the correct interpretation and application of the legislation may be the trigger for a request for revision, supersession or an appeal to an independent appeal tribunal (chapters 19 and 21). While legal disputes do not fall within the Local Government Ombudsman's remit, negligent reading of the benefit regulations by the authority may constitute maladministration (see for example Complaint 91/B/3223 against Newbury District Council, 26 August 1993).

## THE ACTS

**1.33** The outline rules relating to HB and CTB entitlement are contained in the Social Security Contributions and Benefits Act 1992 (as amended). Section 115 of the Immigration and Asylum Act 1999 provides the outline framework excluding certain persons subject to immigration control from HB and CTB entitlement. The outline rules on the administration of the HB/CTB schemes are contained in the Social Security Administration Act 1992 (as amended). The resulting repeals of earlier legislation and consequential amendments of related legislation are contained in the Social Security (Consequential Provisions) Act 1992. This Act also provides that the substitution of the consolidating Acts for the repealed enactments does not affect the continuity of the law. The Child Support, Pensions and Social Security Act 2000 contains the outline framework for decision-making and appeal arrangements as well as the separate discretionary housing payments scheme.

## DELEGATED LEGISLATION

**1.34** The Acts enable the Secretary of State for Work and Pensions, normally following consultation with the local authority associations, to formulate delegated legislation – 'regulations' and 'orders' – which contain and amend the details of the scheme (appendix 1).

**1.35** The main rules of the HB scheme are contained in SI 1987 No. 1971, the Housing Benefit (General) Regulations as amended by subsequent regulations. The main rules of the CTB scheme are contained in SI 1992 No. 1814, the Council Tax Benefit (General) Regulations as amended. The DWP intention is that the CTB regulations should maintain common provisions with the HB regulations. The details of the HB/CTB decision-making and appeal arrangements are contained in SI 2001 No. 1002, The Housing Benefit and Council Tax Benefit (Decisions and Appeals) Regulations.

## OBTAINING THE LEGISLATION

**1.36** Members of the public have a right to see copies of the relevant legal material together with the details of any local scheme (para. 9.39) at an authority's principal office. CBA 123(3),(4) NICBA 122(3)

**1.37** The many and frequent amendments to the relevant legislation and the government's failure to date to produce a consolidation of the HB and CTB regulations means that it can be quite difficult to keep track of the current rules of the schemes.

**1.38** For those with internet access, all the relevant legislation may be accessed at *www.legislation.hmso.gov.uk* The current provisions relating to social security are also set out in the loose leaf work entitled *The Law Relating to Social Security.* Volume 8 (Parts 1 and 2) contains relevant sections of the Acts and statutory instruments relating to HB/CTB. It is kept up to date with regular supplements. Many main public reference libraries hold this publication. It can be purchased from the Stationery Office by telephone (0870 600 5522) or on the internet at: www.tsonline.co.uk. The Child Poverty Action Group's *Housing Benefit and Council Tax Benefit Legislation* (ISBN 1901698084) also contains all the relevant law at the point of publication plus a useful commentary.

**1.39** The Institute of Revenues, Rating and Valuation produce the *Benefit Legislation Database* CD-ROM. This contains the Acts and delegated legislation relating to HB/CTB. It may be obtained from IRRV, 41 Doughty Street, London, WC1N 2LF, by fax on 020 8831 2048 or by e-mail (enquiries@irrv.org.uk). Ferret Information Systems Ltd produce the CD-ROM *Social Security – Sources and Guidance.* This also contains the relevant law. It may be obtained from Ferret Information Systems Ltd, 4 Coopers Yard, Curran Road, Cardiff CF1 5DF by telephone: 029 2064 4660, fax: 029 2064 4661 or e-mail: sales@ferret.co.uk.

**1.40** Copies of individual pieces of legislation, such as amending regulations, may be obtained from the Stationery Office (see para. 1.32) or viewed free of charge on-line at www.legislation.hmso.gov.uk.

## REFERENCES

**1.41** Where references are made in this guide to the Social Security Contributions and Benefits Act 1992 this is referred to as 'CBA', the Child Support, Pensions and Social Security Act 2000 is referred to as 'CSPSSA' and references to the Social Security Administration Act 1992 are referred to as 'AA'. The number that follows in each instance is the section number of the relevant Act. The Housing Benefit (General) Regulations 1987 as amended are referred to as 'HBR'. The Council Tax Benefits (General) Regulations 1992 as amended are referred to as 'CTBR'. The Housing Benefit and Council Tax Benefit (Decisions and Appeals) Regulations are referred to as 'DAR'. All other regulations and orders (appendix 1) are referred to by their statutory instrument number, e.g. SI 1997 No. 1984. Further guidance on the use of marginal references can be found on the page following the List of Abbreviations at the front of the Guide.

## OTHER RELEVANT LEGISLATION

**1.42** In addition to the Acts and regulations, other pieces of legislation circumscribe the manner in which authorities may administer the schemes. The Local Government Act 1972 or the Local Government (Scotland) Act 1973 contain most of the law relating to the powers and duties of local authorities and the way in which they must carry out their business. The Local Government Finance Act 1982 and Audit Commission Act 1998 cover the auditing of, and public rights of access to, local authority accounts. They also place upon local authorities a duty to secure economy, efficiency and effectiveness in their administration of HB/CTB. The Sex Discrimination Act 1975 and Race Relations Act 1976 make it illegal to discriminate (either directly or indirectly) against someone, or victimise someone, on the grounds of their colour, race, nationality, sex or marital status. The Data Protection Act 1998 controls the use of, and access to, information about an individual held on a computerised system.

**1.43** The Audit Commission Act 1998 enables the Secretary of State to request the Commission to conduct or assist the Secretary of State in conducting studies designed to improve economy, efficiency, effectiveness and quality of performance in the discharge by authorities of functions relating to HB/CTB administration.

## BEST VALUE

**1.44** The Local Government Act 1999 places the duty of best value upon authorities in England and Wales requiring them to make arrangements to secure continuous improvement in the way in which they carry out their functions. Section 4(1) of the Act confers a power on the Secretary of State to specify by Order best value performance indicators and standards.

## BEST VALUE PERFORMANCE INDICATORS – ENGLISH AND WELSH AUTHORITIES

**1.45** For English and Welsh authorities the indicators for 2002-03 are set out in DTLR Best Value Performance Indicators 2002/2003. The indicators are as follows:

- whether the authority has a written and pro-active strategy for combating fraud and error which embraces specified initiatives including those sponsored by the Department of Works and Pensions, which is communicated regularly to all staff
- average time for processing new claims;
- average time for processing notifications of changes of circumstance;
- percentage of renewal claims processed on time;
- percentage of cases for which the calculation of the amount of benefit due was correct on the basis of the information available for the decision for a sample of cases checked post-decision;
- the percentage of recoverable overpayments (excluding Council Tax Benefit) that were recovered in the year.

## STATUTORY INTERPRETATION AND CASE LAW

**1.46** In the first instance, where there is no ambiguity, legislation should be taken to mean exactly what it says. The general rule is that the authority may not look beyond the relevant legislation itself to determine its meaning. However, certain forms of assistance are permissible, or must be considered, such as the precedents contained within case law on the meaning of a word or phrase. For example, where in the past a matter in dispute has gone from a review board to consideration in the High Court, or the Court of Session in Scotland, the interpretation made by a judge in the course of deciding such a case will in particular instances be binding upon all authorities. Relevant cases are identified in appendix 2 and in the appropriate paragraphs of this guide.

**1.47** Decisions in HB cases are often highly persuasive though not binding with regard to CTB and *vice versa*. Equally, many of the words and phrases which were brought forward into the HB/CTB schemes from the old supplementary benefit (SB) scheme, or other parts of social security law, have a body of case law attached. Again, as an aid to interpretation such decisions are of persuasive value though not binding upon authorities.

## COMMISSIONERS DECISIONS

**1.48** Social Security Commissioners are appointed to decide appeals brought by individuals, the Secretary of State for Social Security and, since July 2001, councils, on questions of law from the decision of appeal tribunals.

**1.49** Commissioners' decisions constitute a body of case law. Prior to July 2001, this was not binding upon the Council. It could, however, be considered persuasive where it related to exactly the same wording in the HB/CTB legislation. Since July 2001, relevant Commissioners' decisions are binding upon the Council. They will become increasingly significant as the number of decided HB/CTB cases increases. This should help clarify some previously unclear parts of the legislation.

## THE HUMAN RIGHTS ACT 1998

**1.50** The Human Rights Act 1998 came into force on 2 October 2000. It gives effect in the UK to the rights and freedoms guaranteed under the European Convention for the Protection of Human Rights and Fundamental Freedoms [ECHR]. Authorities and appeal tribunals are under a duty to act compatibly with the Convention rights and all legislation must be read compatibly with the Convention rights as far as it is possible to do so. Also, courts and tribunals have to have regard to the jurisprudence of the European Court of Human Rights and decisions and opinions of the Commission and Committee of Ministers. It is unlawful for the authority to act (or fail to act) in a way which is incompatible with a Convention right.

**1.51** An authority does not act unlawfully if it could not have acted differently as a result of a provision of primary legislation. Nor does the authority act unlawfully where:

- it acts under a provision of secondary legislation;
- that legislation is made under a provision of primary legislation;
- that provision cannot be read compatibly with the Convention rights; and
- the authority is acting so as to enforce or give effect to that provision.

## JUDGMENT

**1.52** There are numerous occasions in the regulations where a decision must be made on the basis of what is 'reasonable' or 'appropriate'. For example, where the claimant has left the home through fear of violence then in specific instances the authority must treat the claimant as occupying two dwelling and consequently potentially entitled to HB on both dwellings 'if it is reasonable' that housing benefit should be paid in respect of both dwellings. There is no single right or wrong answer. In such cases the authority must exercise judgment in the light of the facts of the individual case. For example, if the claimant had brought the threats of violence upon him or herself by engaging in criminal activities it might be considered inappropriate to use public funds to meet the cost of two homes.

## DISCRETION

**1.53** Where an authority has a choice under the regulations to do or not do something, e.g. to make payments of a rent allowance to the claimant's landlord under HB Reg. 94 where there is no mandatory requirement to do so, this is a discretionary power. Such powers individualise the application of the regulations and make them flexible and adaptable to the circumstances of the case.

## CONTROLS ON EXERCISE OF JUDGMENT OR DISCRETION

**1.54** In exercising judgment or discretion, authorities are bound by the established principles of administrative law that the courts have steadily evolved. If they are not in accordance with these principles decisions may be open to legal challenge by way of judicial review (see *Judicial Review Proceedings* by J. Manning and A. Kilpatrick, 2nd Ed (2001), the Legal Action Group; ISBN 0905099966; or for Scotland see *Judicial Review in Scotland,* by T J Mullen and Tony Prosser, Wiley ISBN: 0471966142). For example an authority must consider its discretionary powers in individual cases. It must not fetter its discretion by applying predetermined rules rigidly without giving genuine consideration to the merits of the individual case. The authority cannot decide, for example, that it will never use its power to make direct payments to landlords where it has the discretionary power to do so.

**1.55** A power must be exercised reasonably. An authority will be considered to have acted unreasonably if having regard to the nature of the subject matter:

- it takes into account matters which it ought not to consider; or
- it refuses or neglects to consider matters which it ought to take into account.

An authority will also have acted unreasonably if it comes to a conclusion that no reasonable authority could have come to.

## DWP GUIDANCE MANUAL

**1.56** The Department for Work and Pensions (DWP) is the central government department responsible for housing benefit and council tax benefit policy. It produces the Housing Benefit and Council Tax Benefit Guidance Manual (GM), ISBN: 011-761855-1. This manual advises authorities on how to interpret the regulations and on administrative arrangements. Interesting or contentious parts of the manual are identified in this guide. The DWP also issues guidance on the subsidy arrangements in the form of the Subsidy Guidance Manual. This is re-issued each year to reflect the subsidy arrangements applicable for that year.

## DSS CIRCULARS

**1.57** In addition to the GM, the DWP also issues regular circulars to authorities advising them of forthcoming changes and other important matters. Until April 1994 these were denoted by the initials HB/CTB, followed by the year and the number, e.g. HB/CTB (93)3. In April 1994 the DSS revised the contents and presentation of its circulars. There are now three types of circular distinguished by a prefix – A for adjudication and operations, S for statistics and subsidy and F for fraud. Each type has its own number series and starts from 1/94. Recent circulars are listed in appendix 3.

## STATUS OF DSS ADVICE

CH/3853/2001 **1.58** While the Acts and regulations are binding upon authorities and appeal tribunals, the GM and DWP/DSS circulars are for information and guidance only and do not have the force of law (see Introduction to DSS GM). Authorities do, however, often cite DWP/DSS advice in support of their decisions. The Courts sometimes rehearse the advice contained within the GM with approval whilst recognising that it is not an aid to legal interpretation (see for example R *v* Maidstone Borough Council *ex parte* Bunce, QBD, 23rd June 1994 and R *v* London Borough of Camden *ex parte* W, QBD, 21st May 1999, unreported).

## OBTAINING DSS/DWP GUIDANCE

**1.59** The Guidance Manual can be purchased from the Stationery Office (para. 1.26) and amended by way of supplements. (NB: when ordering this title the purchaser should also order the following supplements, ISBNs 0117620742; 0117621463; 0117623008; 0117624217; 011762442X; 01176255820) but the published version is now seriously out of date and consequently of very little assistance. The DSS (A31/99) has stated its intention to have an updated version of the manual available in the near future. Its aim is that the manual should be available in both its traditional format and on the DSS internet web site: www.dss.gov.uk. The current edition of the Guidance Manual with the existing updates is available on the Ferret Information Systems Ltd CD-ROM *Social Security – Sources and Guidance* (see para. 1.33). Authorities can choose to receive circulars by e-mail (DSS Circulars A9/98, A18/98 and A37/98 refer). The DSS has stated its intention that other organisations will be invited to receive circulars by e-mail once it is satisfied that the initial arrangements with authorities are causing no problems (A9/98 para. 2). DSS circulars are not available from the Stationery Office but it may be possible to obtain them from individual authorities. Some recent DSS circulars are available on the Ferret Information Systems Ltd CD-ROM.

# 2 Council tax

**2.1** This chapter:

- provides an overview of the council tax;
- indicates the dwellings exempt from the tax;
- identifies who must pay the tax; and
- describes other ways of reducing the tax in addition to the award of CTB.

Details of the council tax may be found in Martin Ward's *Council Tax Handbook* (Child Poverty Action Group).

## Overview

**2.2** On 1st April 1993 the council tax replaced the community charge as the means by which local people help meet the cost of local public services. The council tax is a tax on residential properties known as dwellings. Liability for the tax arises on a daily basis.

**2.3** Dwellings include houses and flats, etc. whether lived in or not, as well as houseboats and mobile homes that are used for domestic purposes. Non-residential property is subject to non-domestic rates.

### ADMINISTRATION OF THE TAX

**2.4** There should only be one tax bill for each dwelling but a number of people may be responsible for paying it (para. 2.26). Local councils, known in England and Wales as billing authorities and in Scotland as local authorities, are responsible for the billing and collection of the tax. Scottish authorities are also responsible for collecting the council water charge.

### VALUATION OF DWELLINGS

**2.5** Existing and new dwellings are allocated to one of eight valuation bands on the valuation list according to their assumed market value as at 1st April 1991. The lower the valuation band the lower the tax.

**2.6** General changes in house prices do not lead to a rebanding or give grounds for appeal. Where works to a dwelling have led to a material increase in its value, e.g. the building of an extension, this should lead to a revaluation and the possibility of a rebanding but only following sale or transfer of the property.

**2.7** A revaluation, and possible rebanding, of the dwelling should take place immediately if there has been a material decrease in its value following:

- a partial demolition;
- a change in the physical state of the local area; or
- certain adaptations to make it suitable for a disabled person.

### ROLE OF LISTING OFFICER/LOCAL ASSESSOR

**2.8** In England and Wales the valuation of the dwelling, and the updating of the valuation list, is the responsibility of the listing officer at the local valuation office, an agency of the Inland Revenue. In Scotland it is the responsibility of the local assessor appointed by the council.

**2.9** It is also the listing officer's, or local assessor's, responsibility to decide:

- whether or not a property is a 'dwelling'; and
- what proportion of a property with a mixed residential/non-residential use, such as a house where one room is used as a shop, should be designated as a 'dwelling'.

### ACCESS TO INFORMATION ON BANDING

**2.10** Members of the public may inspect the valuation list. In England and Wales it can be seen at either the local valuation office or the billing authority's main office. In Scotland it may be seen at the local authority's main office. The council tax bill also includes the individual dwelling's valuation band.

## Exempt dwellings

**2.11** Most dwellings on the valuation list are subject to the council tax. Some, however, are exempt from the tax either indefinitely or for a fixed period. Unoccupied dwellings, not covered by any of the exemptions, normally qualify for a 50 per cent discount but certain second homes in Wales may not qualify for such a discount (para. 2.36). The Government proposes in the rural White Paper, published in November 2000, to give English authorities the discretion to charge the full council tax on second homes. A consultation paper will be issued (Hansard Oral Questions 24/04/2001 367 c164-5).

### DWELLINGS EXEMPT WITHOUT A TIME LIMIT

**2.12** The main categories of occupied dwelling exempt indefinitely from the tax are:

- halls of residence mainly occupied by students;
- dwellings where all the residents are students, including in England and Wales where that dwelling is only occupied during term time;

- armed forces accommodation;
- dwellings occupied only by persons under 18 years of age (from April 1993 in Scotland and from April 1995 in England and Wales); and
- dwellings where all occupants who would otherwise be liable for the council tax are severely mentally impaired (from April 1995) including (from April 1999) where the only other occupiers are students.

**2.13** From 1st April 1997 in England and Wales, where an annex or similar self-contained part of a property is occupied by an elderly or disabled relative of the residents living in the rest of it, then it is exempt from the Council Tax. The valuation for 'granny annexes' in Scotland remains unchanged. In Scotland, certain dwellings used as trial flats by registered housing associations for pensioners and the disabled are exempt.

**2.14** The main unoccupied dwellings exempt indefinitely from the council tax are those where the immediately former resident is:

- in prison or detention (except for non-payment of a fine or in England and Wales the council tax); or
- receiving personal care in hospital, a residential care home or nursing home or elsewhere; or
- living in someone else's home in order to provide them with care; or
- a student or certain student nurses studying elsewhere.

**2.15** Other unoccupied dwellings exempt indefinitely include those:

- repossessed by a mortgage lender; or
- reserved for a minister of religion (of any faith) for the performance of his or her duties; or
- where occupation is prohibited by law.

**2.16** In Scotland since the commencement of the scheme an unoccupied dwelling which is part of the same premises as another dwelling and difficult to let separately (such as an empty 'granny flat') or which was last occupied together with agricultural lands is exempt indefinitely. In England and Wales from April 1995 an unoccupied property which cannot be let separately due to planning controls is also exempt.

## DWELLINGS EXEMPT FOR SIX MONTHS

**2.17** The main dwelling types exempt from the council tax for up to six months are unoccupied dwellings that are:

- part of the estate of a deceased person following the date the grant of probate or letters of administration, or grant of confirmation to the estate was made; or
- substantially unfurnished new properties; or

- substantially unfurnished properties which have undergone major repairs or structural alterations; or
- owned by, and used for the purposes of, a charity; or
- substantially unfurnished in any other circumstances.

**Example: Exemptions**

Three full time students share a house. The house is exempt from the council tax. One has left his own property elsewhere to take up the course. That dwelling is also exempt while he is a student.

### OBTAINING AN EXEMPTION

**2.18** The authority is expected to take reasonable steps to ascertain whether particular dwellings are exempt. It may have awarded an exemption on the basis of its existing records. If a dwelling is thought to be exempt, but an exemption not awarded, the owner may write to the authority making the case for an exemption. If the authority refuses to award it an appeal can be made (para. 2.47). There is no time limit on obtaining exemptions.

**2.19** Once an exemption has been awarded the authority should write to the owner providing information on the exempt dwelling's valuation band and what the council tax would be if the dwelling were not exempt. The owner has an obligation to inform the authority if the exemption should be withdrawn. If this is not done a penalty may be applied (para. 2.42).

## Who must pay the tax?

**2.20** The council tax is normally payable by someone resident in the dwelling but in certain instances non-resident owners are liable instead.

### RESIDENTS

**2.21** A resident is someone aged 18 or over, solely or mainly resident in the dwelling. Where there is more than one resident the liable person is the one who comes first in the list in table 2.1.

**2.22** Where there is more than one leaseholder, the liable leaseholder is the person with the inferior lease, that is, for the shortest period of time lasting over six months.

**2.23** Normally a resident owner, a council tenant, a housing association tenant or a private tenant is the liable person. Where, however, the landlord lives with the tenant, the landlord and not the tenant is the liable person.

**Table 2.1 HIERARCHY OF LIABLE RESIDENTS**

- A resident owner.
- A resident long leaseholder (para. 2.22).
- A resident statutory, statutory assured or secure tenant.
- A resident sub-tenant.
- A resident licensee.
- Any other resident (including a squatter).

## LIABLE NON-RESIDENT OWNERS

**2.24** Where a dwelling is empty, or a second or holiday home, and no-one's sole or main residence, the non-resident 'owner' is liable for the council tax. The non-resident owner is also liable for the tax where the dwelling is:

- in multiple occupation, i.e. originally constructed or subsequently adapted for occupation by more than one household, or inhabited by a person who is not liable to pay rent or a licence fee in respect of the dwelling as a whole; or
- a residential care home, nursing home or certain hostels providing a high level of care; or
- occupied by religious communities; or
- occupied by a minister of religion (of any faith) and used for the performance of his/her duties; or
- not the owner's main residence, but the main residence of someone employed in domestic service; or
- accommodation provided under section 95 of the Immigration and Asylum Act 1999 (i.e. for asylum seekers who appear to be destitute); or
- in Scotland certain school boarding accommodation.

**2.25** Since the 'owner' is liable in the above cases, residents who fall into one of the above categories are not liable for the council tax. In many instances, however, the cost of the tax may be passed on to them if the landlord follows the correct procedures. Non-resident owners are not eligible for CTB to help with the council tax (para. 4.89).

## JOINT LIABILITY

**2.26** People who have the same status (resident or non-resident) and the same legal interest in the dwelling as the liable person are jointly liable. For example, two resident owners, or two resident joint tenants where there is no resident

**Examples: Liability**

Two sisters jointly own and live in a property as their sole residence. Their brother also lives with them. Both sisters as joint owners are jointly liable for the council tax. The brother is not liable.

The younger sister allows her male friend to live with her as a partner. The two sisters and the male partner are now jointly and severally liable for the tax. The brother is not liable.

The older sister moves elsewhere on a permanent basis but retains her share in the property. The remaining sister and partner are jointly and severally liable for the council tax. Whilst the older sister has the same legal interest in the property as her younger sister she is no longer resident and therefore no longer liable for the tax. The brother is not liable.

landlord, are normally jointly liable for the tax. The partner of a liable person, whether or not they have the same legal interest in the dwelling, is also jointly liable so long as he or she is living with the liable person as a married or unmarried heterosexual couple. The definition of 'partner' for council tax purposes is similar to that which applies for HB/CTB purposes (para. 6.6).

## JOINT LIABILITY AND SEVERE MENTAL IMPAIRMENT

**2.27** The one exception to these rules on joint liability relates to a severely mentally impaired person (appendix 6). Such a person cannot be held jointly liable if there is someone else with the same status and legal interest in the property who is not severely mentally impaired. Prior to April 1995, a severely mentally impaired person was liable for the tax if he or she was the only liable person, or if all the jointly liable people were severely mentally impaired. Since April 1995 dwellings where all the occupants are severely mentally impaired are exempt. From April 1999 the dwelling would also be exempt if the only other occupiers are one or more students.

## IDENTIFYING THE LIABLE PERSON

**2.28** Many authorities use other records to identify the person liable for the tax on each property. In certain cases households may be sent a form requesting relevant information. Failure to complete and return the form within 21 days renders the individual concerned open to a penalty (para. 2.42). If liability is disputed an appeal may be made (para. 2.47). There is no time limit on the identification of the liable person.

### IMPACT ON CTB

**2.29** Where persons (other than a couple) are jointly liable the amount of council tax used for the purpose of working out a resident's CTB entitlement is based on the total liability divided by the number of jointly liable persons (including the members of a jointly liable couple) (para. 2.26). Changes in the number jointly liable affect their CTB entitlement and may result in under or overpayments of CTB. The authority may seek to recover all of the council tax from one or more of the jointly liable individuals even though that individual may be entitled to CTB on only a share of the liability. From April 1997 where a full-time student is jointly liable with a CTB claimant their presence in the dwelling is ignored in the calculation of CTB.

## Reducing the council tax bill

**2.30** In addition to CTB the council tax bill may be reduced as a result of:

- a disability reduction (para. 2.32); and/or
- the award of a discount (para. 2.35).

In addition to the above, transitional relief was available in England and Scotland in 1993-95 and in England alone in 1995-96. There is no general scheme of transitional relief in or after 1996-97. Transitional relief applied in Wales for 1998-2001. Special transitional relief also applies currently in certain reorganised authorities.

Where both types of help are relevant they are applied in the order discussed above. In addition to these methods some authorities offer a discount for prompt payment of the tax or the adoption of certain payment methods (para. 2.41). Council tax liability may also be reduced or eliminated as a result of an appeal (para. 2.43).

### RELATIONSHIP WITH CTB

**2.31** Any discount related to lump-sum or non-cash payments is ignored in the calculation of CTB. Main CTB is calculated using the liable person's council tax after the deduction of any disability reduction, discount, or transitional relief. Second adult rebate is worked out using the council tax after the deduction of any disability reduction or transitional relief but ignoring any discounts which may apply. The retrospective award of any discount, reduction or relief, or the reduction or elimination of council tax liability following an appeal, may lead to a recoverable overpayment of CTB (para. 20.10).

## Disability reduction scheme

**2.32** The council tax bill may be reduced where the dwelling has certain features which meet the particular needs of a substantially and permanently disabled adult or child.

**2.33** The reduction should be awarded where:

- the dwelling is the sole or main residence of at least one such person; and
- the home provides:
  - an additional bathroom or kitchen for the use of the disabled person;
  - a room, other than a bathroom, kitchen or toilet, used predominantly to meet the disabled person's special needs such as a downstairs room in a two storey house which has to be used as a bedroom by the disabled person; or
  - sufficient floor space to enable the use of a wheelchair required by the disabled person within the dwelling.

In addition the authority must be satisfied that the facility in question is either essential, or of major importance, for the disabled person in view of the nature and extent of the disability.

### OBTAINING A DISABILITY REDUCTION

**2.34** To obtain the disability reduction the liable person should complete the authority's application form. The authority will normally request supporting evidence, such as a letter from a doctor, before awarding a reduction. If the reduction is awarded the tax bill is based on the next valuation band down. For example if the dwelling is in band E the council tax bill is based on that for a band D property. Prior to April 2000 someone with a property in band A - the lowest band - could not receive a disability reduction. From 1st April 2000 the council tax reductions for people with disabilities scheme is extended to dwellings in valuation band A. The reduction for dwellings in band A is 1/9th of band D, i.e. equivalent to that currently given to dwellings in bands B, C and D. Applications for a disability reduction must be renewed each year. If the authority refuses to award a disability reduction the liable person may appeal (para. 2.47). There is no time limit on obtaining a disability reduction.

## Discounts

**2.35** The council tax bill should be reduced by:

- 25 per cent where there is only one resident in the dwelling; or
- 50 per cent in England and Scotland where there are no residents in the dwelling.

The bill does not increase if there are more than two residents in the property.

**2.36** In Wales, dwellings with no residents receive either a 50 per cent discount or, if they fall within a defined class that covers most second homes, a discount of 25 per cent or no discount at all. The individual Welsh authority decides what discount to give such a property.

### DISREGARDED PEOPLE

**2.37** When considering the number of people in the dwelling certain people including students, apprentices, Youth Training trainees and the severely mentally impaired are disregarded. Appendix 6 describes the categories of person who are disregarded. Someone may be disregarded for the purpose of awarding a discount but still liable to pay the tax.

### OBTAINING A DISCOUNT

**2.38** The authority is expected to take reasonable steps to ascertain whether any discount applies to a dwelling. It may have awarded one on the basis of previous information regarding the property or as the result of a canvass. If the bill does not contain a discount the liable person may write to the authority requesting one. The authority may require appropriate evidence in support of the request. If the authority refuses to award a discount the liable person may appeal (para. 2.47). There is no time limit on obtaining a discount.

**2.39** Discounts are awarded on a daily basis. Liable persons have an obligation to inform the authority if a discount which has been applied should be withdrawn or reduced within 21 days. If they fail to do this they may be required to pay a penalty (para. 2.42).

**Example: Discounts**

There are three joint tenants in the dwelling all aged 18 or over. One is a Youth Training trainee under 25, the other a qualifying apprentice, only the third does not meet any of the descriptions of a disregarded person. The council tax bill should be reduced by 25 per cent. There is no resident landlord and the house is not in multiple occupation. The three joint tenants are jointly liable for the council tax.

## Billing and payment

**2.40** A liable person does not have to pay the council tax unless a demand bill has been issued to him or her by the billing or local authority. Where several people are jointly liable, the authority may send the bill in the joint names of all those liable or in the name of one liable person only. Where the authority cannot identify the liable person(s) by name they may address the bill to 'the council tax payer'.

**2.41** Normally payment is in ten monthly instalments, though in certain authorities council tenants for example may pay council tax with their rent. Where liability to pay commences part way through the financial year, or a bill is issued late, the number of instalments is reduced. Authorities may offer a reduction in the council tax bill for lump-sum payments and payments by non-cash methods such as direct debit.

## Penalties

**2.42** A penalty of £50 may be imposed by authorities on people who fail to respond to a request for information relating to the liable person, or fail to notify the authority that the dwelling is no longer exempt, or that they are no longer eligible for a discount. A further £200 penalty can be imposed for each additional failure to provide requested information.

## Council tax appeals

**2.43** Different routes must be taken for appeals relating to:

- the valuation of dwellings;
- tax liability and reductions;
- completion notices; and
- penalties.

In all cases payment of the council tax bill is still due even if an appeal has been made. A penalty does not have to be paid, however, until an appeal against it has been decided.

### VALUATION APPEALS

**2.44** If there is a disagreement over whether or not a property is a dwelling, or the banding of a property, a proposal can be made to the listing officer in England and Wales or the local assessor in Scotland for the valuation list to be altered. Such proposals can be made by:

- the liable person;
- the person who would be liable if the property were not exempt; or
- the owner of the dwelling.

**2.45** Proposals on valuation matters can only be considered if made within six months of:

- someone first becoming liable for council tax on a dwelling but not where the same facts have previously been considered by an appeal body;
- the dwelling first appearing on the valuation list but not where the same facts have previously been considered by an appeal body;
- an appeal decision on a comparable dwelling which gives reasonable grounds for contending that the valuation band for the dwelling should be changed; or
- an alteration being made to the valuation list by the listing officer or assessor.

Proposals can be made at any time where:

- a property should be excluded from the valuation list;
- there has been a material reduction in the value of the dwelling; or
- a change has occurred in the mix between residential and non-residential use.

**2.46** Where the listing officer or assessor disagrees with the proposed alteration, it must be sent, within a six-month period, to a valuation tribunal (VT) in England and Wales or a valuation appeal committee (VAC) in Scotland.

## LIABILITY APPEALS

**2.47** An aggrieved person may appeal in writing to the billing or local authority if it is thought that:

- the authority has identified the wrong person as liable for the tax;
- the dwelling should be exempt; or
- a discount or disability reduction should be awarded.

**2.48** The authority has two months to consider the matter. In England and Wales, if it fails to respond within that period or the aggrieved person is dissatisfied with its decision, an appeal may be made to a VT. This must normally be done within two months of the authority notifying the aggrieved person of its decision; or within four months of the date the initial representation was made if the authority has not responded. In Scotland an appeal to the VAC must be made by writing to the authority within four months of the date the issue was first raised. The authority must pass the appeal on to the relevant VAC.

## APPEALS AGAINST COMPLETION NOTICES

**2.49** In England and Wales the authority, and in Scotland, the assessor, may issue a completion notice that states the date on which a newly erected or structurally altered property is considered to be a dwelling. In England and Wales, an appeal may be made directly to a VT but this must normally be done within four weeks of the notice being sent. In Scotland an appeal to the VAC. must be made by the aggrieved person writing to the assessor within 21 days of receipt of the completion notice. The assessor should pass the appeal to the VAC.

## APPEALS AGAINST PENALTIES

**2.50** These may be made normally within two months direct to a VT in England and Wales or via the local authority to a VAC in Scotland.

## TIME LIMITS FOR APPEALS TO VT OR VAC

**2.51** In England and Wales the President of the VT has power to allow an out-of-time appeal where the time limit has not been met for reasons outside the control of the aggrieved person. In Scotland there is no power to consider out-of-time appeals.

# 3 Who is entitled to benefit?

**3.1** This chapter describes:

- who may be entitled to HB/CTB;
- the circumstance in which someone is or is not considered to be liable to make payments in respect of a dwelling for HB;
- the circumstance in which someone is considered to occupy a dwelling as a home for HB/CTB.

The rules excluding certain 'persons from abroad' from HB/CTB entitlement are described in chapter 20.

## People who may be entitled to HB

CBA 130(1)(a)
NICBA 129(1)(a)

**3.2** A person may be entitled to HB if he or she is liable to make payments in respect of a dwelling in Great Britain which he or she occupies as a home. Certain people, even where they do make such payments, are not entitled to HB. Also HB is not payable on certain types of payments.

**3.3** HB is available to many:

- public sector tenants who live in council or new town accommodation including tenants of Scottish Homes, and also people who are placed by housing authorities in 'bed and breakfast' establishments and hostels;
- private sector tenants, including boarders, who rent accommodation from a private landlord, housing association or co-op, as well as hostel dwellers.

## People and types of payment excluded from the HB scheme

### HOUSING COSTS MET THROUGH INCOME SUPPORT/INCOME-BASED JSA

HBR 8(2)(a), 8(3)

**3.4** Claimants whose accommodation costs are included in the calculation of their income support/income-based JSA are excluded from help via the HB scheme. But where a claimant not in receipt of income support/income-based JSA but in receipt of HB is awarded either benefit, his or her HB continues for the first four weeks after the date he or she becomes entitled to that benefit. The extra HB can be deducted from the appropriate benefit for that period.

## PRIVATE AND VOLUNTARY REGISTERED RESIDENTIAL CARE AND NURSING HOMES

**3.5** Prior to 1st April 1993 many residents in private and voluntary registered residential care and nursing homes had their home fees met through income support. Major changes occurred to these arrangements as a result of the government's community care policy. Individuals who need financial assistance from public funds to enter a residential care or nursing home must now contact their local authority social service or social work department. That department assesses the most suitable type of care and, only if appropriate, helps the individual choose or find a place in a home. The department should meet the home's fees but also assess how much the resident should contribute towards the cost on the basis of a means test.

**3.6** People entering such homes can claim income support on the same basis as they could in their own homes. In addition, they also qualify for an income support residential allowance. This is to help towards the housing element of the home's fees. People entitled to an income support residential allowance are not entitled to HB.

**3.7** Most residents of private or voluntary residential care or nursing homes have been excluded from HB entitlement since 14th January 1991. Prior to that date residents not on income support, for example, those with capital over £8,000 (and therefore excluded from income support entitlement: para. 2.8) but under £16,000, could claim HB on the accommodation element of the home's fee. HBR 7(1)(k)

**3.8** Individuals in the following groups were still able to claim or receive HB on or after 14th January 1991: HBR 7(2)

- people living in registered homes paying rent to a close relative (para. 3.31) – and who therefore could not receive income support to cover their fees – so long as the close relative did not reside in the same dwelling (para. 6.22) and the arrangement was on a genuine commercial basis;
- people entitled to HB in the above accommodation on 29th October 1990;
- people in registered homes in remunerative work (para. 9.33);
- people whose entitlement to HB was subsequently determined to commence on or after 30th October 1990 but whose claim was posted or delivered to the local social security office on or before 29th October 1990;
- people in unregistered small residential homes in England and Wales if income support was not in payment.

The legal status of the amendments to the CTB scheme is questionable given that they are couched in terms of 'occupation as a home' which is not one of the conditions of entitlement to CTB (para. 3.89).

**3.9** Individuals in the first and third groups (in paragraph 3.8) who enter a home on or after 1st April 1993 are not entitled to HB. They may receive income support residential allowances. But if they were entitled to HB on 31st March 1993, or became so as a result of backdating, they retain that entitlement. It only lasts, however, while they remain in the same home. If they move, other than for a temporary period (para. 3.81), or cease to be entitled to HB for some reason, they lose their entitlement and become subject to the same rules as new residents. People who fall into the second or fourth group retain their HB eligibility while in any type of care home.

**3.10** From 1st April 1993, the Registered Homes Act 1984 has been amended so that small homes are now required to seek registration with the local social service authority. This requirement includes accommodation provided under social service adult placement and supported lodgings schemes for less than four residents, but only if both board and personal care is provided. Small homes in Scotland were already subject to registration. Residents in all these homes have potential entitlement to the income support residential allowance. People entering into such homes on or after 1st April 1993 are excluded from HB entitlement. Residents of small homes which are not required to register, or which are refused registration, retain their eligibility for HB. Residents in previously unregistered small homes entitled to HB on 31st March 1993 retain that eligibility for as long as they remain in the same home. If they move, other than for a temporary period (para. 3.81) or cease to be entitled to HB for some reason, they lose this right and become subject to the same rules as new residents.

**3.11** Residential accommodation managed or provided by a body constituted by Act of Parliament or incorporated by Royal Charter such as that provided by the Salvation Army does not have to be registered. New and existing residents in such accommodation retain their HB eligibility.

## LOCAL AUTHORITY 'PART III' RESIDENTIAL ACCOMMODATION

HBR 8(2) **3.12** The local social service authority's powers to provide residential accommodation are contained within sections 21-24 and 26 of the National Assistance Act 1948, in Scotland under section 59 of the Social Work (Scotland) Act 1968 and in Northern Ireland article 15 of the Health and Personal Social Services (Northern Ireland) Order 1972. Amendments made by the National Health Service and Community Care Act 1990 also enable social service authorities to place people in private and voluntary sector accommodation under those powers.

**3.13** Residents of such 'Part III' accommodation are not entitled to HB unless the accommodation is neither owned nor managed by the social service authority, nor registered under the Registered Homes Act 1984 (as amended). The exception to this rule is where the accommodation is owned or managed by the social service authority but the resident does not pay an inclusive charge for the provision of both accommodation and cooked or prepared food. Even if board is not available claimants who were, or are treated as, occupying such accommodation on 31st March 1993 are excluded from HB entitlement. Residents not entitled to HB are potentially entitled to the 'Part III' rate of income support.

## MEMBERS OF CERTAIN RELIGIOUS ORDERS

**3.14** Members of a religious order are excluded from HB if they are maintained fully by that order. Monks and nuns in enclosed orders are excluded under this provision. The DSS (GM para. A3.79) points out that members of religious communities (as opposed to religious orders) are often entitled to HB since they frequently do paid work or retain their own possessions. HBR 7(1)(j)

## MOST STUDENTS

**3.15** Most, but not all, full-time students are excluded from HB entitlement as they are treated as not liable to make payments in respect of their dwelling (para. 20.18). Students who are not excluded from HB entitlement under that provision are in any case not eligible if: HBR 48A, 50

- they live in accommodation provided by the educational establishment they attend (paras. 22.28-30); or
- they are away from their term-time accommodation outside the period of study (para. 22.31).

## OWNER-OCCUPIERS

**3.16** Owner occupiers are not eligible for help via HB on their mortgage repayments. If they are in receipt of income support/income-based JSA, they may receive help with their mortgage interest payments from the Benefits Agency. Under the HB scheme the definition of 'owner' includes those who have the right to sell the freehold only with the consent of other joint owners. This definition invalidates the decision in *R v HB Review Board for Sedgemoor ex parte Weadon, The Times,* 6th May 1986. That decision had allowed such an owner where she had had 'exclusive use and occupation' of the property in return for additional weekly payments to the other joint owners, to receive a rent allowance. HBR 2(1), 10(2)(c) NIHBR 10(2)(a)

## LONG LEASEHOLDERS

**3.17** Long leaseholders (those with a lease which, when granted, was for more than 21 years) are excluded from HB entitlement. But if they are in receipt of income support/income-based JSA they may also receive help with certain housing costs such as ground rent and service charges via the Benefits Agency. Equity sharers buying part of their home from a housing association or housing authority and renting the other part under a shared ownership scheme may receive HBR 2(1), 10(2)(a)

HB on the rental element. If they are in receipt of income support/income-based JSA they may also receive assistance towards their mortgage interest payments from the Benefits Agency.

## PAYMENTS UNDER HIRE PURCHASE, CREDIT SALE OR CERTAIN CONDITIONAL SALE AGREEMENTS

HBR 10(1),(2)(d)
NIHBR 10(1),(2)(b)

**3.18** The following payments are not eligible for help under the HB scheme:

- a hire purchase agreement, for example, paid by individuals purchasing mobile homes;
- a credit sale agreement; or
- a conditional sale agreement.

Payments under a rental purchase scheme (i.e. where all or part of the purchase price is paid in more than one instalment and the purchase is deferred until a specified part of the purchase price has been paid) are eligible for a rent allowance. Conditional sale agreements are agreements for the sale of goods or land under which the purchase price is payable by instalments and the goods or land remain the seller's until the instalments are paid. Where such payments are attributable to land they are eligible for HB.

## PAYMENTS UNDER A CO-OWNERSHIP SCHEME

HBR 2(1), 10(2)(b)

**3.19** People in housing association co-ownership schemes who will be entitled, on ceasing to be a member of the association, to a sum related to the value of the building are excluded from HB entitlement (*R v Birmingham City Council HB Review Board ex parte Ellery and Weir,* 21 HLR 398), but co-operative tenants may get HB for their rent provided they have no more than a nominal equity share in the property.

## CROWN TENANTS

HBR 2(1), 10(2)(e)
NIHBR 10(2)(c)

**3.20** Crown tenants are excluded from HB entitlement. In Northern Ireland the legislation excludes only tenants of Ministry of Defence property. A crown tenant is normally a person renting his or her home from someone managing the property for the Crown or whose landlord is a government department. If the tenant receives income support/income-based JSA he or she may be entitled to an increase in IS/income-based JSA to cover housing costs. If not receiving IS/income-based JSA, crown tenants on low incomes may be entitled to rent rebates under voluntary schemes established by their landlords. Authorities often have a role in the administration of such schemes but the schemes themselves are quite separate from the HB scheme described in this guide (GM chapter A8). Government departments often use housing associations as managing agents to let properties and collect the rent. This does not alter the status of the tenants of such properties who remain excluded from HB entitlement (HB/CTB(93)27).

DSS circular A26/99 updates guidance and gives best practice advice for authorities dealing with claims from Crown tenants.

**3.21** The following persons are not excluded from HB entitlement under the above rule:

- former tenants and licensees whose agreement to occupy a crown property has been terminated but who are liable to pay mesne or violent profits; and
- tenants or licensees of properties either managed by the Crown Estate Commissioners or belonging to the Duchies of Cornwall or Lancaster.

## Liable to pay rent

**3.22** Normally to qualify for HB the claimant should be the person who is liable (has a legal obligation or duty) to pay rent for the home.

CBA 130(1)(a)
NICBA 129(1)(a)
HBR reg 6(1)(a)

### DOUBTS ABOUT LIABILITY

**3.23** Normally liability is not in doubt. Table 3.1 identifies some of the circumstances in which liability may be an issue and the considerations the authority should bear in mind when determining the matter.

**Table 3.1 LIABILITY – SOME CONSIDERATIONS**

| Circumstance | Considerations |
|---|---|
| There is no written agreement | The non-existence of a formal written agreement or the landlord's failure to comply with the duty to issue a rent book is not conclusive (rent liability can arise from a purely oral agreement (GM para. A3.06)) |
| The claimant is not one of the parties to the written agreement | There are circumstances in which someone who is not legally liable may be treated as liable (para. 3.26) |
| The 'landlord' does not have the right to grant occupation | Unless acting as an agent for someone who does have such a right there can be no liability |
| The landlord is a friend/ relative of the claimant | The fact that the landlord is a friend/relative of the claimant does not mean that the claimant is not liable unless the landlord is a close relative residing in the dwelling (para. 3.30) |

| | |
|---|---|
| The landlord would not seek to regain possession of the property or recover any arrears, if the claimant failed to make payments | A possible indicator of a contrivance (para. 3.37) – but is the landlord awaiting the outcome of a decision about benefit entitlement? |
| The claimant was the previous owner of the property | If the claimant has a preserved right to live in the dwelling for life (which could be either explicit or implied) s/he cannot be liable to pay for the dwelling (also see para. 3.52) |
| The claimant has granted the tenancy to him/herself | It is not possible in law to grant a tenancy to yourself but it is possible for a company to grant a lease to either its directors or shareholders (but see para. 3.49) |
| The claimant jointly purchased the property | If the property was purchased freehold the claimant cannot be eligible as he or she falls within the definition of 'owner' (para. 3.16). If the claimant is seeking HB for the share of the dwelling that he or she does not own (e.g. following a relationship breakdown) in most cases he or she will have a right to reside in the property (not just half of it) so the absent joint-purchaser is not in a position to grant a tenancy (also see para. 3.43). |

**3.24** The DSS has reminded authorities (HB/CTB A30/95 para. 12) that certain people, such as those with learning difficulties, may appear unable to enter into a liability but that someone formally appointed to act for them, such as a receiver appointed by the Court of Protection, can enter into a liability on that individual's behalf and that in such circumstances HB may be payable. The question of a child's or young person's liability to pay rent – particularly when assisted by a social services department – is examined in detail in HB/CTB A16/96.

**3.25** In certain circumstances:

- a person who is not liable may be treated as liable;
- someone who is liable should be treated as not liable.

## People who are not liable but who are treated as liable

**3.26** People in the following categories may not be liable to pay rent but can be treated as liable and thus potentially entitled to HB. There are no equivalent provisions for CTB. HBR 6(1)(b)-(e), (2)

- The partner of the liable person;
- A former partner of the liable person who has to make the payments in order to continue to live in the home because the liable person is not doing so;
- Anyone who has to make the payments if he or she is to continue to live in the home because the liable person is not making the payments and the authority consider it reasonable to treat him or her as liable to make those payments;
- A person whose liability is waived by the landlord as reasonable compensation for repairs or redecoration work actually carried out by the tenant – but only up to a maximum of eight benefit weeks in respect of any one waiver;
- The partner of a full-time student excluded from HB entitlement (para 22.24);
- Someone who has actually met his or her liability before claiming;
- Where the rent is varied either during the benefit period or retrospectively, the claimant is treated as liable for the revised amount due.

**Examples: Treated as liable to pay rent**

A claimant has been deserted by her partner. Although she is not the tenant the landlord will allow her to remain in the property if she continues to pay the rent. She should be treated as liable if her former partner is not paying the rent.

A claimant is the son of a council tenant. He takes over responsibility for paying rent while his father is working abroad for two years. The son should be treated as liable if it is reasonable to do so.

## People who are liable but treated as not liable

**3.27** The following paragraphs describe the circumstances in which the authority should treat someone as not liable to make payments in respect of a dwelling and therefore not entitled to HB. These rules were amended and extended for all new and repeat claims made on or after 25th January 1999. Anyone who was in receipt of HB before 25 January 1999 is not subject to the revised rules until they make a repeat claim at the end of their current benefit period. HBR 7(1) SI 1998/No 3257 NISR 1998/No 455

## CLAIMANTS TREATED AS NOT LIABLE PRIOR TO 25TH JANUARY 1999

**3.28** Where a claim for HB was made before 25th January 1999 the claimant should have been treated as not liable to make payments where:

- he or she 'resided with' (para. 6.22) a landlord who is a 'close relative' (para. 3.31); or
- he or she 'resided with' (para. 6.22) the landlord on a 'non-commercial basis' (para. 3.35); or
- he or she was jointly liable and at any time during the eight-week period prior to the creation of the joint liability was a non-dependant of one or more of the other joint occupiers of the dwelling unless the authority is satisfied that the joint liability was not created to take advantage of the HB scheme; or
- it appeared to the authority that the claimant's agreement to make payment in respect of the dwelling had been contrived to take advantage of the HB scheme (see para. 3.37) except someone who was, for any period within the eight weeks prior to the creation of the agreement liable to make payments in respect of the same dwelling.

## CLAIMANTS TREATED AS NOT LIABLE ON OR AFTER 25TH JANUARY 1999

**3.29** Where a new or repeat claim is made for HB on or after 25 January 1999 claimants are treated as not liable to make payments where they fall into any of the categories described in paras 3.30-3.53.

## PEOPLE WHOSE LANDLORDS ARE CLOSE RELATIVES RESIDING IN THE DWELLING

HBR 7(1)(b) **3.30** Where the claimant's landlord is a 'close relative' (para. 3.31) of the claimant, or of the claimant's partner, and the landlord also resides in (para. 3.33) the dwelling, the claimant is not entitled to HB.

## WHO COUNTS AS A CLOSE RELATIVE?

HBR 2(1) **3.31** A 'close relative' is:

- a parent, step-parent or parent-in-law; or
- brother or sister; or
- son, son-in-law, daughter, daughter-in-law, step-son, step-daughter; or
- the partner of any of the above.

**3.32** Arguably the term 'brother' and 'sister' should be taken to include 'half-brothers' and 'half-sisters' (HB/CTB A27/97 para. 3 (following Commissioner's decision R(SB) 22/87)). 'Step-brothers' and 'step-sisters' are not treated as close relatives for HB purposes (HB/CTB A27/97 para. 4).

## WHAT DOES 'RESIDES WITH' MEAN?

**3.33** The equivalent pre-January 1999 rule referred to a claimant who 'resided with' (para. 6.22) the landlord rather than the landlord 'residing in' the dwelling. The DSS policy intention was to retain the same test as operated under the pre-January 1999 form of the rule (DSS Circular A1-99, para. 13). This intention is given weight by the continuing declaration contained within regulation 3(4) (the definition of 'resides with') that it applies to regulation 7(1). An alternative interpretation is that for the claimant to now fall foul of this test his or her liability must be to a close relative who resides in the dwelling, and that the nature of the quality of the relationship between the claimant and landlord (a necessary consideration following *Khadhim v L B Brent Review Board,* CA, 20 December 2000 [200]) is now irrelevant. HBR 3(4)

## NON-COMMERCIAL AGREEMENTS

**3.34** Prior to 25th January 1999 where the claimant 'resided with' (para. 6.22) the person to whom he or she was liable to make payments and the agreement was not on a commercial basis, the claimant was not entitled to HB. Since 25th January 1999 where the agreement under which the claimant occupies the dwelling is not on a commercial basis he or she should be treated as not liable to make payments in respect of the dwelling. For this rule to apply it is no longer necessary that the claimant 'resides with' the landlord. HBR 7(1)(a)

**3.35** What constitutes a 'commercial basis' is not defined in the regulations but from 25th January 1999 the authority is required to have regard to whether the agreement contains terms which are not enforceable at law in determining whether or not it is a commercial one. HBR 7(1A)

**3.36** In *R v Sheffield Housing Benefit Review Board ex parte Smith and others, The Times,* 28th December 1994, QBD, 8th December 1994 it was held that the authority must not only consider the amount payable for the accommodation but also the other terms of the agreement. The important factor is whether the arrangements are at 'arm's length' or more akin to the arrangements that would exist between close relatives who generally only make contributions to their keep or household running costs (HB/CTB A30/95 para. 16). More specifically the DSS advises that an arrangement that involves a former foster child remaining in his or her foster accommodation and paying rent once the fostering allowance ceases, for example, where the foster child reaches the age of 18, should not normally be treated as a non-commercial arrangement (HB/CTB A 30/95 para. 17 iv).

## CONTRIVED LIABILITIES

HBR 7(1)(l) **3.37** Where the authority is satisfied that the claimant's liability was created to take advantage of the HB scheme, the claimant is not entitled to HB. Prior to the 15th January 1999, however, if the claimant was liable to make payments for the same dwelling at any time within the eight weeks period prior to the creation of the arrangement that was said to be contrived, he or she could not be excluded from HB entitlement under this provision.

**3.38** DSS guidance on contrived liabilities can be found in circular HB/CTB A30/95 paras. 18-22 and A 15/97.

**3.39** In *R v Solihull Metropolitan Borough Council Housing Benefit Review Board ex parte Simpson,* 26 HLR 370 QBD) the Court considered that whilst the ability to attract HB could never realistically be the sole purpose of a tenancy, equally, and importantly, anyone eligible for HB must, by definition, have entered into an agreement to pay a rent which he could not afford. The mere fact of having done so could not of itself, except perhaps in extreme cases, be evidence of an arrangement entered in order to take advantage of the scheme. A similar point was made in *R v Housing Benefit Review Board of the London Borough of Sutton ex. p. Keegan,* 27 HLR 92 QBD, 15th May 1992. The judge quashed the review board's decision not to award HB because 'it had attached a wholly disproportionate weight to the fact that the claimant could not meet her liability to pay rent'.

**3.40** In the Sutton case the judge considered that before an agreement could be said to be 'contrived' the means, circumstances and intentions of the claimant and the landlord must be considered. In particular, consideration should be given to the consequences if HB is not to be paid. If it seems likely that the landlord will have to ask the claimant to leave the dwelling so that it can be re-let or sold this is evidence that the liability has not been created to take advantage of the scheme.

**3.41** In the Solihull case it was held that 'an arrangement whereby persons, who would in any event be eligible for HB, were provided with accommodation by a parent or relation who was then to receive rent generated from HB was not of itself an arrangement created to take advantage of the HB scheme' (26 HLR 370). The DSS has advised authorities that mortgage rescue schemes developed by mortgage lenders to enable owner-occupiers in arrears with mortgage payments and facing repossession to convert the mortgage agreement into a tenancy for rent should not be regarded as contrived to take advantage of the scheme (HB/CTB(92)6).

**3.42** *R v Manchester City Council ex parte Baragrove Properties,* 23 HLR 337 QBD, provides an example of the sort of extreme case envisaged in the Solihull judgment. In this case the authority was found to have acted correctly in interpreting the rule as permitting exclusion from HB entitlement cases where landlords were specifically charging higher rents to vulnerable tenants and where the authority could not use its powers to restrict the eligible rent (para. 12.53).

## RENTING A FORMER JOINT HOME FROM AN EX-PARTNER

**3.43** Where a married or unmarried couple separate and the one remaining in the home, or a new partner, makes payments to the one who has left in order to continue living in the dwelling then the person making the payments is treated as not liable. In *R. (on the application of Painter) v Carmarthenshire CC Housing Benefit Review Board,* QBD, May 4, 2001 (*Times,* May 16, 2001) Mr Painter had originally been a lodger renting a bedroom and with the right to use the common parts. He subsequently formed a relationship with his landlady and moved into her room and jointly occupied the accommodation. The relationship ended and Mr Painter reverted back to a tenant and was liable to make payments of rent. The authority decided that Mr Painter should be treated as not liable because he was renting a former joint home from an ex-partner. It was argued that this rule only applied if the dwelling in respect of which the payments were due was the same dwelling which had been occupied during the relationship. Mr Painter submitted that the dwelling was in fact different. It no longer included the landlady's room. Additionally it was argued that if the regulation was applicable, it was incompatible with the Human Rights Act 1998. The Court held that the informal arrangements to occupy separate rooms did not affect the reality of the situation that the dwelling remained the same. It also held that there had been no breach of the Convention rights. Any discrimination was justifiable as a precaution against potential abuse of the housing benefit scheme. HBR 7(1)(c)

## RESPONSIBILITY FOR THE LANDLORD'S CHILD

**3.44** A liable person should be treated as not liable where he or she is responsible, or a partner is responsible, for the landlord's child (i.e. someone under the age of 16). The DSS (A1/99, para. 15) emphasises that 'responsibility for a child' means more than 'cares for'. This is a difficult rule to interpret as it blurs certain established concepts so far as means-tested benefits are concerned. It would appear to apply where the 'landlord' is the biological mother or father of a child, or has adopted a child, but where the child is nevertheless considered to be part of the claimant's family for income support, income-based jobseeker's allowance or HB purposes. The legality of this rule and the argument that it offended the Human Rights Convention was argued in *R v Secretary of State for Social Security, ex parte Sharon Tucker,* QBD, 6th April 2001 (unreported). The Court held that the rule was not ultra vires nor contrary to the European Convention on Human Rights. HBR 7(1)(d)

### RENTING ACCOMMODATION FROM A TRUST OF WHICH THE LIABLE PERSON IS A TRUSTEE OR BENEFICIARY

HBR 7(1)(e) **3.45** A trust is an arrangement under which property is transferred to one or more people known as trustees. Trustees are required to look after the property or deal with it for the benefit of someone else 'the beneficiary' or alternatively for some other purpose such as that of a charity.

**3.46** A person should be treated as not liable to make payments where the payments are to a trustee of a trust of which one of the following is a trustee or a beneficiary:

- the liable person or partner; or
- the liable person's or partner's close relative (para. 3.31) if the close relative 'resides with' (para. 3.33) the liable person; or
- the liable person's, or partner's, former partner.

HBR 7(1B) **3.47** The exception to this rule is where the liable person satisfies the authority that the liability was not intended to take advantage of the HB scheme. In such cases the liable person should be treated as liable.

### RENTING ACCOMMODATION FROM A TRUST OF WHICH THE LIABLE PERSON'S CHILD IS A BENEFICIARY

HBR 7(1)(f) **3.48** A person should be treated as not liable to make payments where the payments are to a trustee of a trust of which the liable person's, or the liable person's partner's child is a beneficiary.

### RENTING ACCOMMODATION FROM A COMPANY OF WHICH THE LIABLE PERSON IS A DIRECTOR OR AN EMPLOYEE

HBR 7(1)(e) **3.49** A person should be treated as not liable to make payments where the payments are to a company of which one of the following is a director or an employee:

- the liable person or partner; or
- the liable person's or partner's close relative (para. 3.31) if the close relative 'resides with' (para. 3.33) the liable person; or
- the liable person's, or partner's, former partner.

The DSS advise (A46/99 para.13) that the reference to a 'company' here is to a registered company. Checks with Companies House will reveal whether or not a company is incorporated.

HBR 7(1B) **3.50** Again the exception to this rule is where the liable person satisfies the authority that the liability was not intended to take advantage of the HB scheme. In such cases the liable person should be treated as liable. Where someone is employed by a company and is liable to make rental payments to a landlord who is a director of the company this liability is not to the company but to the director and as such is not affected by this rule.

## A PERSON WHO WAS PREVIOUSLY A NON-DEPENDANT OF SOMEONE WHO STILL RESIDES WITH THEM

**3.51** If the liable person was at any time prior to the creation of the liability a non-dependant of someone who resided and continues to reside in the dwelling the liable person should be treated as not liable. The exception to this rule is where the liable person satisfies the authority that the liability was not intended to take advantage of the HB scheme. HBR 7(1)(g) HBR 7(1B)

## A PERSON WHO PREVIOUSLY OWNED THE DWELLING

**3.52** If the liable person, or a partner, previously owned the dwelling (from 21 May 2001 – within the last five years) the liable person should be treated as not liable. The exception to this rule is where the liable person is able to satisfy the authority that he or she or a partner could not have continued to live in the dwelling without letting go of ownership. This could be for a variety of reasons. This would be the case, for example, where the liable person is able to provide evidence that a mortgage lender would have sought possession unless the liable person had agreed to the transfer of the property and the establishment of a rental agreement. The DSS has emphasised (A46/99) that inability to repay a lender money borrowed to purchase the property is only one of the possible reasons. It suggests that another example would be where a housing association agrees to take over ownership of the property and take on the ex-owner as a tenant. In each case the authority will need to obtain from the former owner an explanation of his or her reasons for giving up ownership of the property. HBR 7(1)(h)

## TIED ACCOMMODATION

**3.53** A liable person should be treated as not liable if his or her, or a partner's, occupation of the dwelling is a condition of employment by the landlord. The DSS emphasise (HB/CTB A1/99 para. 25) that this test should not be taken to mean 'as a result of the employment'. A retired employee, for example, may continue to live in previously tied accommodation but this would no longer be as a condition of employment by the landlord. The retired employee should consequently be treated as liable unless they fell under some other rule that requires them to be treated as not liable. HBR 7(1)(i)

## Occupation as a home

HBR 5(1) **3.54** HB cannot usually be paid for accommodation that has not been occupied (moved into) by the claimant. HB is only payable where the dwelling is occupied as a home. Accommodation occupied only for a holiday or business purposes is not a home and therefore is not eligible. It is usually only payable on one home.

**3.55** The following paragraphs describe:

- how the home normally occupied may be determined;
- circumstances in which the claimant may be considered to be occupying two homes at the same time and eligible for HB on both;
- circumstances in which the claimant may be treated as occupying the home before moving in;
- in what circumstances a claimant may be treated as occupying the home even though she or he is absent from it.

### DOES THE CLAIMANT OCCUPY THE DWELLING?

**3.56** Doubts about the claimant's occupation of the dwelling can often arise as a result of residency checks by an authority's visiting/fraud officers. If there is any doubt as to whether or not the claimant occupies the dwelling the authority should consider all of the relevant evidence before determining this matter.

### DECIDING WHICH HOME IS 'NORMALLY OCCUPIED'

HBR 5(2) **3.57** In considering which home the claimant normally occupies the authority must have regard to any other dwelling occupied by the claimant or family in, or outside, Great Britain (England, Scotland and Wales). The DSS advises authorities that this requirement is not intended to exclude from entitlement someone who has set up home in this country but whose family, no longer being part of his household, remain abroad. The purpose of taking account of homes outside GB is to avoid simultaneous payments under the HB schemes in Northern Ireland and Great Britain (GM para. A3.16).

### EXCEPTIONS TO THE GENERAL RULE

HBR 5(3)-(4), (7A), (9) **3.58** The exceptions to the rule that the dwelling normally occupied is the one that the claimant is treated as occupying, apply in certain circumstances where:

- the claimant is a single or lone parent student or trainee;
- the normal home has been vacated for essential repairs; or
- the claimant has left a property through fear of violence in the home or from a former member of the family and has no intention of returning to that property.

## DECIDING WHICH HOME A STUDENT OR TRAINEE IS TREATED AS OCCUPYING

**3.59** Following the general rule, the claimant should be treated as occupying the normal home (and no other) if he or she is:

- single or a lone parent; and
- an eligible student or on a government training course; and
- liable to make payments (including mortgage payments) in respect of two homes.

**3.60** If, however, such a claimant only pays for one of the homes, he or she should be treated as occupying the home that he or she pays for, whether or not it is the one in which he or she normally lives. HBR 5(3)

**3.61** The training courses referred to are those provided by, or under arrangements made with or approved by, a government department, any Secretary of State, Scottish Enterprise, or Highlands and Islands Enterprise. This definition includes training courses arranged by a local authority on behalf of one of these entities. The training course may be provided by the local authority itself or the local authority may contract with an external organisation to provide the course. HBR 5(9)

**Example: Occupation as a home**

The claimant normally lives with her parents but rents accommodation whilst on a government training course. In such circumstances she should be considered as normally occupying the rented accommodation during the period she is liable to pay housing costs.

## DECIDING WHICH HOME THE CLAIMANT IS TREATED AS OCCUPYING WHERE THE NORMAL HOME HAS BEEN VACATED FOR ESSENTIAL REPAIRS

**3.62** The claimant should be treated as occupying the home for which payments (including mortgage payments) must be made, where he or she has: HBR 5(4)

- had to leave the normal home whilst it is having essential repairs; and
- has to make payments on either that home or the temporary home, but not both.

If mortgage payments are being made in such circumstances there is no entitlement to HB.

### THE NORMAL HOME WHERE THE CLAIMANT HAS LEFT A PROPERTY THROUGH FEAR OF VIOLENCE IN THE HOME OR FROM A FORMER MEMBER OF THE FAMILY

HBR 5(7A) **3.63** The claimant should be treated as occupying the formerly-occupied home for a maximum period of four weeks if s/he:

- has left and remains absent from it through fear of violence
  - in the home, or
  - by a person who was formerly a member of the claimant's family, and
- has no intention to return to it, and
- has a liability to make payments in respect of that dwelling which is unavoidable.

**3.64** Where this rule applies benefit can only be allowed for the previous home irrespective of whether the claimant also has a new rent liability (but see para. 3.65).

## HB on two homes

HBR 5(5) **3.65** Normally HB is only payable in respect of a rental liability on one home. The following paragraphs set out the circumstances in which the claimant must be treated as occupying two dwellings as a home and thus potentially entitled to HB for both of them.

### FEAR OF VIOLENCE

HBR 5(5)(a) **3.66** The authority must treat the claimant as occupying two dwellings for a maximum period of 52 weeks where the claimant has left and remains absent from the former dwelling through fear of violence:

- in that dwelling; or
- by a former member of the claimant's family.

This duty only applies however if:

- it is reasonable that HB should be paid in respect of both the former dwelling and the present dwelling occupied as the home, and
- the claimant intends to return to occupy the former dwelling as a home.

**3.67** It is estimated that there were about 6.6 million incidents of domestic physical assault in England and Wales in 1995 (Department of the Environment, Transport and the Regions, *Relationship breakdown: a guide for social landlords,* 1999). Actual violence need not have occurred, however, for the above conditions to be met. The claimant has only to be afraid of violence occurring. If the authority to not consider, however, that the fear of violence is one that is reasonably held or that the claimant brought it upon themselves, for example as a result of criminal activity, it may consider it unreasonable that HB should be paid in respect of both homes.

**3.68** The feared violence in the home need not be related to a family or former family member. It could be related to anyone, e.g., a neighbour, so long as it is feared that violence could occur in the home. Where the fear is of violence outside the home it must be a former member of the claimant's family who poses the threat of violence. This would include not only an ex partner but also an adult child.

**3.69** Authorities are advised to check regularly that the claimant intends to return to the previous home (A24/98. para. 10). If the claimant subsequently decides not to return HB on the former home should stop. The HB paid on the former home whilst the claimant had the intention to return will have been properly paid and should not be treated as an overpayment.

## STUDENTS/TRAINEES

**3.70** If the claimant, or partner, is a student eligible for HB (chapter 22) or is on a training course (para 3.61) and it is: HBR 5(5)(b)

- unavoidable that the partners should occupy two separate dwellings; and
- reasonable that housing benefit should be paid in respect of both dwellings,

the authority should treat the claimant as occupying both dwellings as a home and potentially entitled to HB on both of them. There is no time limit on this rule.

## LARGE FAMILIES

**3.71** Where because of the size of the claimant's family they have been housed by a housing authority in two separate dwellings the claimant should be treated as occupying both dwellings as his home. The GM (para. 3.55.3) indicates that both homes should be local authority owned but there would appear to be nothing within the regulation that requires this. The rule would not apply however if the claimant found his or her own dwellings in the private sector. HBR 5(5)(c)

## UNAVOIDABLE OVERLAPPING LIABILITY

**3.72** Where the claimant is liable to make payments in respect of two dwellings, the authority must treat the claimant as occupying the two dwellings as a home where he or she: HBR 5(5)(d)

- has moved into the new dwelling; and
- could not reasonably have avoided liability in respect of both of them.

In such cases the authority should treat the claimant as occupying both dwellings as a home for up to a maximum period of four benefit weeks and thus potentially entitled to benefit on both of them.

**3.73** The rule is extending the period that the claimant is treated as occupying the old dwelling beyond that which would normally be the case and consequently enabling HB to continue to be paid on the liability attributable to both the old and new home for a limited period. There is no explicit requirement for a special or specific claim to be made for the benefit attributable to this overlapping period. An authority may, however, decide that the movement into the new home is a change of circumstance that leads it to end the current benefit period and invite a new claim (para. 19.58-59).

**3.74** The GM (para. 3.55.4) indicates that the rule should only be used in 'exceptional circumstances' but there is no such test within the regulation. If the conditions set out above are met then the authority must treat the claimant as occupying the two dwellings as a home. The authority does, however, need information and evidence that will enable it to identify an overlapping liability and determine whether or not it could reasonably have been avoided.

**3.75** This rule would apply for example where a claimant in housing need is offered at short notice an appropriate new tenancy and is obliged to take up liability for the new tenancy before the period of notice required by the landlord of the old home has expired. HB is only payable on both properties during this period, however, if the claimant has a liability for and has actually moved into the new property whilst having a liability to make payments on the old home. If the claimant is still in fact occupying and liable to make payments on the old home then the fact that he or she has a liability on the new home and may have transferred some items of furniture does not mean that he or she has met the test of having 'moved into' the new home. In such instances HB is only payable on the old home not the new home.

**3.76** For this rule to operate both liabilities need to be eligible for HB. Consequently the rule does not cover periods where the claimant is:

- moving into temporary accommodation with the intention or returning to the former home including circumstances where essential works are being carried out on the normal home;
- moving into owner-occupied property; or
- moving into residential care accommodation (para. 3.5-12).

## DELAYS MOVING-IN DUE TO DISABILITY-RELATED ADAPTATIONS

HBR 5(5)(e) **3.77** A claimant who is liable to make payments in respect of two dwellings should be treated as occupying both dwellings as a home where he or she had to remain in the old home due to a reasonable delay in moving of up to four weeks caused by the requirement to make necessary adaptations to the new home to meet the disablement needs of the claimant or a member of the family (para. 3.79).

### CALCULATION OF BENEFIT ON TWO HOMES

**3.78** A question that is not explicitly addressed in either the regulations or DSS guidance is that of how benefit should be assessed in cases where the claimant is treated as occupying two dwellings as a home. The purpose of the above rules is to treat the claimant as occupying two dwellings as a home. Consequently it would appear that in these cases there is one benefit calculation based on the aggregated eligible rent of the two properties. Where the dwellings are in different areas authorities will need to liaise and/or establish agency arrangements (para. 1.12).

## Entitlement prior to moving in

**3.79** Normally a person is only treated as occupying the dwelling as a home and consequently entitled to HB from the date he or she moves in. The next paragraph sets out the circumstances in which the authority should treat a claimant as occupying the dwelling prior to moving in. This decision can, however, only be made once the claimant has actually moved in to the dwelling. Claimants who meet the described conditions are treated as occupying the dwelling as a home and consequently potentially eligible for HB in respect of a maximum period of up to four week prior to actual occupation. Consequently if the claimant is liable to make payments for alternative accommodation during this period they are not able to receive housing benefit for the accommodation actually occupied during this period, i.e. this is not a rule that generally enables HB to be paid on two homes. The one exception is where the delay in moving is necessary to adapt the new home to meet the disablement needs of the claimant or a member of the family. This is also one of the conditions that enables HB to be paid on two homes (para. 3.77). HBR 5(6)

### THE TESTS

**3.80** The claimant should be treated as occupying the home for up to four weeks prior to moving-in if the following tests are satisfied:

(a) the claimant has moved into the new home; and

(b) was liable to make payments before moving in; and

(c) claims HB before moving in; and

(d) if the authority refused the initial claim (para. 7.76), a further claim is made or treated as made within 28 days of the date the claimant moved into the dwelling; and

(e) the delay in moving was reasonable; and

- the delay was necessary in order to adapt the building to the disablement needs of the claimant or a member of his or her family; or

- the move was delayed pending the outcome of an application for a social fund payment (para. 2.15) to meet a need related to moving into the dwelling, e.g. to meet the cost of removal or an item of household furniture or equipment; and a member of the claimant's family is aged less than six or the claimant satisfies the conditions for one of the age-related or disability-related premiums (chapter 14); or
- the claimant became liable to make the payments whilst an in-patient or in residential accommodation.

For the date such a claim is considered as made in such circumstances see paras. 7.76-77.

## Temporary absence and HB/CTB entitlement

**3.81** The rules of entitlement to HB during periods of temporary absence were amended in April 1995. The same amended rules were introduced into the CTB scheme. Previously CTB had been payable for as long as the claimant was liable for the tax.

**3.82** Claimants who are absent from their homes for a temporary period can only obtain HB/CTB for up to 13 weeks, or in particular circumstances (para. 3.85) 52 weeks, from the first day of absence. In *R v Penwith District Council Housing Benefit Review ex parte Burt,* 22 HLR 292, it was held that the absence must be continuous. Consequently if the claimant (with the exception of prisoners on temporary leave) returns to, and occupies the dwelling as a home, even for a short time, the allowable period of temporary absence starts again. The DSS suggests (GM para. A3.25) that a stay at home lasting, for example, only a few hours may not be acceptable but one that lasts at least 24 hours may be acceptable. Depending upon the facts of the case, however, the authority may decide that the claimant's normal home is elsewhere for HB purposes (para. 3.57). If another person occupying the dwelling starts paying rent in the absence of the claimant, the authority should consider treating that other person as liable and therefore eligible for HB (para. 3.26). In the case of the council tax the authority may, in specific instances, decide that an absent claimant is no longer solely or mainly resident in the dwelling and is therefore no longer liable for the tax (paras. 3.20-25).

**3.83** To be entitled to HB/CTB during a period of absence:

- the claimant must intend to return to live in the dwelling within the 13-week or 52-week period;
- the part of the dwelling normally occupied by the claimant must not have been (sub-)let; and
- the period of absence must be unlikely to exceed 13 or 52 weeks as appropriate.

**3.84** Once it becomes clear that the claimant is going to be away for more than 13 or 52 weeks, HB/CTB entitlement ends. The one exception to this rule concerns those claimants who may be absent for up to 52 weeks and retain entitlement. If their period of absence is unlikely to substantially exceed the 52-week period, and if there are exceptional circumstances, the authority must pay up to the end of the 52nd week of absence. DSS guidance (GM para. A3.31) suggests that the term 'substantially exceed' relates to periods of absence greater than 15 months. It is, however, for the individual authority to interpret the term. The circular illustrates the concept of exceptional circumstances with the examples of:

- someone prevented from returning home by an unanticipated event; and
- a discharge from hospital being delayed by a relapse.

Other circumstances may however be considered.

**3.85** The categories of claimant who may be temporarily absent for up to 52 weeks and retain their HB/CTB entitlement are those:

- on remand including those in bail hostels;
- in hospital as patients;
- undergoing medical treatment or medically approved convalescence but not in 'residential care accommodation' etc (paras. 3.5-13);
- undertaking approved training courses (para. 3.61);
- providing medically approved care;
- providing care for a child whose parent or guardian is receiving medical treatment or medically approved care;
- receiving medically approved care but not in 'residential care accommodation' etc (paras. 3.5-13);
- certain students eligible for HB, e.g. those absent on residential study;
- in fear of violence who are not eligible for HB in the circumstances described in para. 3.66 because, for example, they are staying with close relatives and are not liable to pay rent on two homes but intend to return to occupy their original homes;
- receiving temporary care in residential care accommodation etc (paras. 3.5-13) but not those residing there on a trial basis (para. 3.87).

**3.86** The term 'medically approved' means certified by a medical practitioner. HB/CTB A8/95 para. 18 advises that a medical practitioner could, for example, be a GP or nurse, and that the approval need not necessarily be in the form of a certificate.

**Examples: Temporary absence**

**REMAND AND CONVICTION**

A man has been receiving HB for a while. He is then arrested and detained on remand pending his trial.

- The authority should assume that he will be absent for no more than 52 weeks (para. 3.85). He therefore remains eligible for HB.

Fifteen weeks later he is tried, found guilty, and sentenced to a term of one year's imprisonment.

- Although he may well serve only six months in prison (after remission), and although the 15 weeks he has been on remand will count towards this, his *total* absence from home will now exceed 13 weeks (para. 3.82). So his eligibility for HB ceases, because the fact that he has been sentenced is a change in his circumstances (chapter 17). (But the HB he was awarded for his 15 weeks on remand was nonetheless correctly paid.)

**TRYING OUT A RESIDENTIAL CARE HOME, AND THEN DECIDING TO STAY THERE**

A woman who owns her home has been on CTB for a while. She then goes into a residential care home for a six-week trial period to see if it suits her.

- She remains eligible for CTB (para. 3.87).

In the third week of her trial period, she decides she likes the care home. In the fourth week she tells her family and the managers of the home that this is the case. In the fifth week the managers make her an offer of permanent accommodation in the care home and she accepts this. She tells the authority straight away.

- Her eligibility for CTB ceases once it is clear that she will stay there permanently (para. 3.84), because this is a change in her circumstances. So she is not eligible for CTB from her sixth week in the care home onwards. (But the CTB she was awarded for her first five weeks there was nonetheless correctly paid.)

**3.87** If a claimant enters residential care accommodation etc (paras. 3.5-13) on a permanent basis he or she is no longer entitled to HB or CTB on the former home (but see chapter 3 for other forms of help with council tax). Where a claimant enters such accommodation with the intention of returning home he or she is entitled to benefit for up to 52 weeks (para. 3.85). Some people, however, go into residential care accommodation on a trial basis to see if it suits them. In these circumstances they should continue to receive HB/CTB for up to 13 weeks where:

- they intend to return to their former home if the residential care accommodation etc does not meet their needs; and
- the part of the dwelling normally occupied by them is not (sub-)let.

**3.88** The 13-week period commences from the date the claimant enters the residential accommodation, provided that the total period of absence including, for example any period staying with a relative immediately before entering the residential care accommodation etc, does not exceed 52 weeks.

## People who may be entitled to CTB

**3.89** To be entitled to main CTB, or second adult rebate, the claimant must be: CBA 131(3)

- liable to pay the council tax in respect of a dwelling; and
- a resident of that dwelling.

'Resident' has the same meaning as for council tax purposes (para. 3.21). Non-resident owners are not eligible nor are people under the age of 18 or tenants in houses in multiple occupation. The last two groups may however be entitled to increased HB if the landlord has increased their rents as a result of the introduction of the council tax.

**3.90** The additional rules of entitlement relating to second adult rebate are described in chapter 10. As with HB, many full-time students are excluded from main CTB (para. 22.24). New claims from students also fall under the exclusions described in chapter 5. Eligible students may, however, be entitled to second adult rebate if the qualifying conditions for that form of CTB are satisfied (chapter 10).

**3.91** There may be circumstances where couples are liable for the council tax at different addresses – for example, where one of the partners is working away for long periods from the couple's home. The DSS (HB/CCB(92)34) advises that where the couple are living at different addresses within the same authority only one of the partners must claim CTB for both – but where the two addresses are in different authorities separate claims must be made to each authority. The circular advises that CTB is calculated on the basis of the couple's income, capital and personal circumstances and divided between the partners. CTBR 3(3)

**3.92** Unlike HB, there are no rules that enable those who are not liable for council tax to be treated as liable. However, there are rules relating to certain people, but not the CTB claimant, who fall within the categories described in para. 3.28, but where the intention has been to take advantage of the CTB scheme as well as, or instead of, the HB scheme. In such circumstances those individuals become the claimant's non-dependant for main CTB purposes (para. 6.21).

# 4 The claimant's household

**4.1** This chapter describes:

- the different types of claimant, and different categories of people who may live in the claimant's household;
- the circumstances in which the claimant is considered to be responsible for a child or young person for HB and main CTB;
- the circumstances in which partners and children or young people are treated as members of the claimant's household; and
- other people who may reside with the claimant or live in the same dwelling.

**4.2** Authorities need to identify and define the people who live with the claimant to work out HB/CTB entitlement since:

- only one member of what counts as the claimant's family for benefit purposes can claim HB/CTB;
- in the case of second adult rebate, partners and/or jointly liable persons can affect entitlement;
- in the case of HB/main CTB fixed deductions are made in certain cases for other people who live in the claimant's household who are classified as 'non-dependants';
- second adult rebate is worked out on the basis of the gross income of certain people who reside with the claimant known as 'second adults';
- the amount of HB/main CTB a non-income support/income-based JSA claimant receives is worked out with reference to the combined needs (in the form of the applicable amount) and the income and capital of the claimant's family;
- money from (sub-)tenants and boarders is taken into account in the case of a non-income support/income-based JSA claimant's income for HB/main CTB.

## Household composition

**4.3** The term 'household' is not defined in legislation. It should be given its normal everyday meaning, that is a domestic establishment containing the essentials of home life. People living in one dwelling (for example a house or flat) do not necessarily live together in the same household. The claimant's household may consist of:

- the claimant;
- the claimant's family;
- any other person who lives in the dwelling and who is classified as a 'non-dependant' for HB/main CTB.

In addition to the above, certain other people such as joint occupiers, (sub-)tenants, boarders and carers may live in the same dwelling as the claimant. Those 'non-dependants' and carers aged 18 or over who are not disregarded for the purpose of the council tax (appendix 6) count as 'second adults' for the purpose of second adult rebate.

## CLAIMANT

**4.4** The claimant may be: HBR 2(1) CTBR 2(1)

- single – i.e. a claimant who does not have a partner and is not responsible for a child/young person; or
- a lone parent – i.e. someone who does not have a partner but who is responsible for and is a member of the same household as a child/young person; or
- a member of a married or unmarried couple or polygamous marriage.

## THE FAMILY

**4.5** The claimant's family for benefit purposes consists of: CBA 137(1) NICBA 133(1)

- the claimant's partner(s), if a member of the same household; and
- any children or young persons the claimant is responsible for and who are members of the household (not just sons and daughters).

## PARTNER

**4.6** A partner is included in all instances where he or she is married or polygamously married or, in the case of a couple, unmarried but living together as husband and wife. The partner must be a member of the same household and, except in polygamous marriages, must be of the opposite sex to the claimant. CBA 137(1) NICBA 133(1) HBR 2(1) CTBR 2(1)

## LIVING TOGETHER AS HUSBAND AND WIFE

**4.7** A married couple are treated as one unit as long as they are members of the same household. Either but not both may claim benefit. The same rules apply to an unmarried couple who are 'living together as husband and wife'.

**4.8** Neither the Act nor regulations define the phrase 'living together as husband and wife'. The administration of this particular rule can give rise to serious financial and relationship problems. For example, if a man who has a high income starts living with a woman with a low income and the authority determines that they are 'living together as husband and wife' the woman may lose the whole of her benefit entitlement under this rule though she receives no money from the man. The High Court decision in *Crake and Butterworth v the Supplementary Benefit Commission* (1982) established that the first test when a man and woman appear to be living together as husband and wife is that of the purpose of the parties in living together. The HB/CTB schemes recognise many different ways in which a man and woman could live together in the same household, e.g. joint occupiers, landlady/lodger, etc.

**4.9** If the purpose of the parties is unclear, the question of whether a couple are living together as husband and wife can only be decided by looking at their relationship and living arrangements and asking whether they can reasonably be said to be that of a married couple. Whilst the phrase 'living together as husband and wife' existed in the former HB scheme, it attracted most attention with the former supplementary benefit scheme as the 'co-habitation rule'. A body of case law developed. This suggests that the following factors need to be considered before deciding that a couple are 'living together as husband and wife':

- whether or not they share the same household;
- the stability of the relationship;
- the financial arrangements;
- the presence or absence of a sexual relationship;
- shared responsibility for a child;
- public acknowledgment that they are a couple.

Whilst all these factors should be considered, none individually is conclusive.

## POLYGAMOUS MARRIAGE

HBR 2(1)
CTBR 2(1)

**4.10** A polygamous marriage is any marriage where there is more than one spouse. No marriage that takes place in the UK is valid if one of the partners is already married. Some other countries allow such marriages and these should be taken into account for HB/CTB purposes where they took place under the law of such a country.

## PARTNER'S MEMBERSHIP OF THE SAME HOUSEHOLD

HBR 15(1),(2)
CTBR 7(1)

**4.11** Any partner is normally treated as a member of the same household even when he or she is temporarily living away from the other members of the family. Temporary absence is not defined for the purpose of CTB but for the purpose of HB the partner is no longer counted as a member of the household where he or she is living away from the other members of the family and:

- does not intend to resume living with them; or
- the absence is likely to exceed 52 weeks, unless there are exceptional circumstances where the person has no control over the length of the

absence such as hospitalisation and the absence is unlikely to be substantially more than 52 weeks.

## CHILDREN AND YOUNG PERSONS

**4.12** A child is defined as someone under the age of 16. A young person is someone aged 16 or over but under 19, not on income support or income-based JSA, nor in advanced education, who is treated as a child for child benefit purposes. HBR 2(1), 13 CTBR 2(1), 5

**4.13** To be treated as a child for child benefit the young person must receive 'relevant education', i.e. over 12 hours per week supervised study not above 'A' level, (G)NVQ level 3, OND, Scottish Higher Certificate or equivalent, at a recognised educational establishment or at some other place that the Secretary of State agrees to (the latter circumstance being confirmed by receipt of child benefit). Though child benefit is not payable for any week the young person is in full-time work, he or she is still treated as a child for child benefit purposes after leaving 'relevant education' up to and including the week of the appropriate terminal date or the first Monday before his or her 19th birthday whichever comes first. The terminal date is:

- the first Monday in January; or
- the first Monday after Easter Monday; or
- the first Monday in September. (From 1998, this is the terminal date for all 16-year-old school leavers: circular HB/CTB A45/97.)

**4.14** Child benefit can be paid for an extended period beyond the terminal date where:

- the young person is registered for work/training under Youth Training (YT);
- the young person has not started YT;
- the young person has not reached the age of 18;
- the young person is not in remunerative work (paras. 9.33-36);
- child benefit was payable immediately before the extension period; and
- payment during the extension period has been requested in writing.

The child benefit extension period begins at the terminal date. If the terminal date is in September the extension period ends the week before the first Monday in January. For other terminal dates the extension period ends 12 weeks later.

**4.15** Once the young person is no longer counted as a child for child benefit purposes he or she becomes a non-dependant for HB/main CTB purposes and HB and CTB claims should be re-assessed to exclude the young person's personal allowance and, where appropriate, the family premiums as well as any income the young person had. In the case of HB/main CTB no non-dependant deduction is made for anyone under 18 (table 9.2). Non-dependants, aged 18 or over, who are not disregarded for the purpose of council tax discounts (appendix 6) count as second adults for second adult rebate.

## RESPONSIBILITY FOR A CHILD OR YOUNG PERSON

HBR 14(1), 2(a)
CTBR 6(1), (2)(a)

**4.16** The claimant is considered responsible for any child or young person he or she normally lives with. This is usually straightforward but where the child or young person spends equal amounts of time in different households (e.g. where the parents have separated), or where there is doubt over which household he or she is living in, the child or young person is treated as normally living with the person who gets the child benefit. If no-one gets child benefit, the child or young person is considered the responsibility of:

HBR 14(2)(b)
CTBR 6(2)(b)

- the person who has claimed child benefit; or
- the person the authority considers has 'primary responsibility' if more than one person has made a claim for the child benefit or no claim has been made.

HBR 14(3)
CTBR 6(3)

A child or young person can only be the responsibility of one person in any one benefit week. If the claimant has a child or young person who lives with him or her and that child or young person in turn has a child, for example, the claimant's daughter and the daughter's baby, the authority must decide whether the daughter is dependant on the claimant or forms a family of her own. If the daughter receives income support (or income-based JSA) for herself and her baby she should not be considered part of the claimant's family.

## CHILD/YOUNG PERSON'S MEMBERSHIP OF THE SAME HOUSEHOLD

HBR 15(1),(2)
CTBR 7(1)

**4.17** Where the claimant is treated as responsible for a child or young person, that child or young person is counted as a member of the claimant's family even where he or she is temporarily living away from the other members of the family. Temporary absence is not defined for the purposes of CTB, but for the purposes of HB the child/young person is no longer counted as a member of the household where he or she is living away from the other members of the family and:

- does not intend to resume living with them; or
- the absence is likely to exceed 52 weeks, unless there are exceptional circumstances where the person has no control over the length of the absence such as hospitalisation and the absence is unlikely to be substantially more than 52 weeks.

**4.18** The child/young person is also not counted where he or she is:

HBR 15(4)(a)
CTBR 7(3)(a)

- absent from the claimant's home and being looked after by a local authority, or in Scotland or Northern Ireland is in the care of a local authority or the Department;

- placed with the claimant or partner by a local authority or voluntary organisation, or in Scotland and Northern Ireland boarded out with the claimant or partner; or HBR 15(3)(a),(4)(b) CTBR 7(2)(a),(3)(b)
- placed for adoption or custodianship with the claimant or partner or elsewhere (though once adopted, he or she becomes a member of the household). HBR 15(3)(c),(4)(c) CTBR 7(2)(c),(3)(c)

**4.19** A child or young person in local authority care who lives with the claimant under supervision must be treated as a member of the household. So must a child or young person in care who returns to live with the claimant for part or all of a benefit week if, given the nature and frequency of the visits, it is reasonable to do so. HBR 15(5) CTBR 7(4)

**4.20** A child or young person who is absent in any other circumstance, e.g. attending boarding school, is treated as a member of the claimant's household.

## Non-dependants

**4.21** A non-dependant is someone who normally resides with the claimant such as an adult son or daughter, or other relative, or a person treated as not liable to make payments in respect of the dwelling for HB (para. 4.27) and related provisions for CTB (para. 4.92) but specifically excludes: HBR 3(1),(2) CTBR 2(1)

- members of the claimant's benefit family (para. 4.5);
- a child or young person who lives with the claimant but who is not a member of the claimant's household (paras. 4.17-20), e.g. foster children;
- the persons identified in paras. 4.23-26.

Non-dependants cannot claim HB/CTB for any payments they make for their keep. Such payments are disregarded from the claimant's income (table 15.4) – instead a fixed deduction is usually made from the claimant's HB/main CTB where a non-dependant is present (para. 9.21). If a claimant resides with his or her landlord neither the landlord nor a member of the landlord's family, e.g. a landlady's adult daughter, are treated as non-dependants of the claimant.

**4.22** For HB purposes a person does not count as normally residing with the claimant if that person: HBR 3(4) sch 1 para 7

- only shares a bathroom, lavatory and/or communal area (e.g. halls, passageways and rooms in common use in sheltered accommodation); or
- is visiting the claimant and normally resides elsewhere.

Thus people in self-contained accommodation within the same building as the claimant, e.g. a granny annex, do not count as non-dependants even if they share a bathroom and lavatory with the claimant. Additionally in *Khadhim v L B Brent Review Board,* CA, 20 December 2000 (*Times,* March 27, 2001) it was decided that for A to 'reside with' B, A must not only share accommodation with B (excluding a bathroom, a lavatory or a communal area) but also have some sort of relationship with B that is more than simply sharing specific areas of the accommodation. This effectively reverses the decision reach in *Thamesdown BC v Goonery,* CA, 13 February 1995 (unreported) that held that the simple shared use of the same parts of the dwelling constituted 'residing with'.There is no definition of 'residing with' in the CTB rules.

## Other people who may live in the claimant's dwelling

### BOARDERS

HBR sch 4 para 42
NIHBR sch 4 para 45
CTBR sch 4 para 21

**4.23** A boarder is someone who is liable to pay the claimant an accommodation charge which includes payment for at least some cooked or prepared meals made and consumed in that accommodation or associated premises. A person whose payment does not include an element for some cooked or prepared meals should be treated as a tenant or sub-tenant (para. 4.25). Income from a boarder is taken into account in the assessment of a non-income support/income-based JSA claimant's income in a different way from that of a tenant or sub-tenant (table 15.4). Boarders can claim HB but not CTB in their own right.

### JOINT OCCUPIERS

HBR 3(2)(d)
CTBR 3(2)(d)

**4.24** A joint occupier is someone other than the claimant's partner who is jointly and severally liable with the claimant to pay council tax in respect of the dwelling for CTB purposes; and/or is jointly liable with the claimant to make payments in order to occupy the dwelling for HB purposes, e.g. joint tenants. Joint occupiers may be eligible for the appropriate benefit in their own right. For the purpose of calculating benefit the total council tax and/or rent will be apportioned between them (paras. 11.6-11.10, 12.6).

### TENANTS AND SUB-TENANTS

HBR sch 4 para 20
NIHBR sch 4 para 22
CTBR sch 4 para 20

**4.25** A tenant or sub-tenant is someone who is contractually liable to pay the claimant for the right to occupy part of the claimant's accommodation, but who is not:

- a member of the claimant's family;
- a non-dependant;
- a joint occupier;
- a boarder.

Where the payment includes something for meals the person should be treated as a boarder (para. 4.23). A formal tenancy or sub-tenancy does not have to exist for someone to be treated as a tenant or sub-tenant for HB/CTB purposes, nor does this treatment create or imply the existence of a legal tenancy or sub-tenancy. In this respect the HB/CTB regulations and the landlord/tenant provisions of the Housing and Rent Acts do not accord precisely. A tenant or sub-tenant is able to claim HB in his or her own right. However, where the authority thinks the tenancy or sub-tenancy is contrived, HB is not awarded and instead the tenant or sub-tenant is treated as a non-dependant. For the treatment of the claimant's income from a tenant or sub-tenant see table 15.4.

## A CARER

**4.26** A carer does not count as a non-dependant (or boarder) if he or she is looking after the claimant or partner and engaged by a charitable or voluntary organisation (not a public or local authority) which makes a charge for the service provided, even if the charge is paid by someone else. HBR 3(2) CTBR 3(2)

## SECOND ADULTS

**4.27** Non-dependants and carers, if they are aged 18 or over and are not disregarded for the purpose of council tax discounts (para. 3.37), count as second adults for the purpose of second adult rebate (chapter 10).

# 5 Making a claim

**5.1** This chapter describes how to claim HB and CTB (including both main CTB and second adult rebate), and the various things that happen during the life of a claim. It covers:

- how and where to make a claim;
- what constitutes an effective claim;
- information and evidence;
- the life of a claim;
- the date of claim;
- the first day of entitlement;
- the duration of the benefit period;
- the last day of entitlement;
- renewal claims; and
- backdating.

This chapter does not cover the different rules for getting HB/CTB 'extended payments' – which are in Chapter 17.

## General rules

### CLAIMING HB OR CTB OR BOTH

**5.2** Although HB and CTB are legally distinct benefits, it is usually possible to make a combined claim for both. There are, however, categories of claimant who are eligible to claim only one of these benefits (e.g. CTB only in the case of a home owner) and authorities which administer only one benefit and not the other (paras. 1.10-11). Furthermore it is perfectly possible for someone who is eligible for both benefits to claim only one if that is what he or she wishes.

### CLAIMING MAIN CTB OR SECOND ADULT REBATE OR BOTH

**5.3** CTB is a single benefit. As the DSS points out (GM para. B2.1), a claim for CTB is therefore a claim for both main CTB and second adult rebate. An authority receiving a claim for CTB has a duty to consider entitlement to both. Some claimants qualify for only one: for example, a claimant with no second adults can only qualify for main CTB. Also, some claimants may wish to be considered for second adult rebate only: for example a wealthy claimant with a second adult who has no income. In such cases, the claimant is making a claim for CTB which nonetheless covers both types.

COUPLES

**5.4** In the case of a couple (or polygamous marriage) one partner makes the claim on behalf of both. They may choose between them which partner this is to be. If they cannot agree, the authority must choose. Some authorities ask both partners to sign their claim forms. It would usually be unreasonable for them to reject an otherwise complete claim form signed by only one. HBR 71(1) CTBR 61(1)

**5.5** In some cases a couple may be better off if one partner rather than the other is the claimant. These are identified in this guide as they arise. In general, if the 'wrong' partner claims, the authority ought, as good practice, to return the claim form (having kept a photocopy) inviting the 'right' partner to sign it instead.

APPOINTEES

**5.6** A claim may be made by a third party, known as an 'appointee', if the claimant is unable, for the time being, to act. In such cases, the appointee takes over all rights and responsibilities in relation to the HB/CTB claim. HBR 71(2)-(6) CTBR 61(2)-(6)

**5.7** The authority may accept a claim from:

- a receiver appointed by the Court of Protection;
- an attorney;
- in Scotland, a tutor, judicial factor, curator or other guardian; or
- a person appointed by the DSS to act on the claimant's behalf in connection with some other benefit.

**5.8** In any other case, the authority may accept a written request from anyone over 18 to be an appointee, for example, a friend, a social worker or a solicitor.

**5.9** Either the authority or the appointee can terminate the appointment by giving four weeks' written notice. It has become more common for landlords to request to act as appointees for their tenants. In these and all other cases it is appropriate for the authority to consider any potential conflict of interests before agreeing to the request.

## How and where to make a claim

**5.10** There are three ways of claiming HB/CTB, dealt with in turn in the following paragraphs:

- in parts of the country where the 'One' scheme exists, certain claimants must or may make their HB/CTB claim at a One office;
- in any other case, people making a claim for income support or income-

based jobseeker's allowance may make their HB/CTB claim at the same time via the Benefits Agency or Jobcentre;

- in all cases (except where claiming at a One office is compulsory), people may make their HB/CTB claim direct to the local authority.

## Claims via 'One' offices

### CLAIMING HB/CTB AT A ONE OFFICE

HBR 72(4)(d)(e) NIHBR 72(4)(d) CTBR 62(4)(d)(e)

**5.11** In some parts of the country, attending at a One office, and taking part in a work-focused interview, are an obligatory part of claiming HB/CTB. In others it remains optional.

**5.12** In either case, this applies only to clients who:

- are aged 16 or more but under 60; and
- are not in remunerative work (para. 7.33).

**5.13** The principal aims of the One scheme are to provide a single location for people who could be expected to work, at which they can get help with finding work and claim all relevant benefits on just one form.

**5.14** The details of the 'One' claim procedures differ nationally, but usually claimants are offered an extensive work-focused interview. They complete or are assisted to complete a lengthy claim form, providing information needed for the benefits relevant to their circumstances. A claim made to a One office does not – in its initial stages – have to be in writing (para. 7.36).

**5.15** Further procedural arrangements vary nationally, but generally speaking:

- the One office forwards the above-mentioned claim form (or relevant parts of it, or relevant details) to the authority;
- the One office or the Benefits Agency notifies the authority of whether the claimant is entitled to IS or JSA(IB) and of other matters similar to those in paragraph 5.20;
- on receipt of a claim made via a One office, the authority may or may not need further information, evidence, etc. (para. 5.37), and may or may not have to refer the details to the rent officer (chapter 6).

### ONE OFFICES

HBR 2(1) CTBR 2(1)

**5.16** The Secretary of State nominates which offices are One offices. A One office may be located in a Benefits Agency or Jobcentre office or in an office designated by the local authority. In each case, the authority's HB/CTB claim form (or information attached to it) must give the details and state that this is an office at which HB/CTB may be claimed. One offices may be staffed by Benefits Agency or Jobcentre employees or by staff or contractors of the local authority.

## Claims via the Benefits Agency or Jobcentre

**5.17** Everyone who makes a claim for income support (IS) or income-based jobseeker's allowance – JSA(IB) – is invited to claim HB and CTB at the same time. Special rules apply in areas where the One scheme exists (para. 5.11). The following paragraphs describe how this works in all other areas, and include information on the DSS's guidance on liaison between authorities and Benefits Agency and Jobcentre offices (GM paras. C7.01-30). The official forms (NHB1, etc.) are summarised in table 5.1 (and samples are given in GM chapter C7 annex A). The Jobcentre deals with claims for JSA(IB); the Benefits Agency (BA) deals with claims for IS and also with part of the administration of JSA(IB). In many areas, Jobcentre and BA staff are located in the same office.

### METHOD OF CLAIM

**5.18** With exceptions in areas where the One scheme exists (para. 5.11), everyone claiming IS or JSA(IB) is given three forms: HBR 2(1), 72(4)(a) CTBR 2(1), 62(4)(a)

- a claim form for IS or JSA(IB);
- a claim form for HB – form NHB1(HB); and
- a claim form for CTB – form NHB1(CTB).

**5.19** The HB and CTB forms are known collectively as 'NHB1 forms'. An IS claimant is invited (in the covering notes) to complete all three forms and return them to the BA. A JSA(IB) claimant is invited to complete them and return them to the Jobcentre (which forwards them to the BA). Claimants who want only HB or only CTB need return only the relevant forms.

### BENEFITS AGENCY PROCEDURE ON RECEIPT OF NHB1 FORMS

**5.20** The Benefits Agency keeps the NHB1 forms until the claimant's entitlement to IS or JSA(IB) is decided. The Benefits Agency then forwards them to the authority within two working days or as soon as reasonably practicable. They are sent with a decision form – form NHB(IS) or form NHB(JSA). These forms include: HBR 72(4)(c) SI 1988 No. 662 NISR 1988 No. 118 CTBR 62(4)(c), 92

- the name of the claimant and any partner;
- the address;
- national insurance numbers when known;
- whether HB, CTB or both have been claimed on the NHB1 forms;
- the date of the claim for IS or JSA(IB);
- whether the claimant is entitled to IS or JSA(IB);
- if the claimant is entitled to IS or JSA(IB), the date entitlement begins (and, if known, the date it ends); and

- in some cases, if the claimant is not entitled to IS or JSA(IB), the reason why not.

HBR 2(1), 72(3)
CTBR 2(1), 62(3)

**5.21** To assist with these procedures, authorities are required to notify the Benefits Agency of the address to which it may send forms and correspondence about HB and CTB. This need not be the same as the authority's 'designated office(s)' (para. 5.31). If HB and CTB are administered by two separate departments of the same authority, it is up to the authority to distribute Benefits Agency forms and correspondence as appropriate.

## AUTHORITY PROCEDURE ON RECEIPT OF NHB1 FORMS

**5.22** On receipt of an NHB1 form, the authority may or may not need further information, evidence, etc. (para. 5.37), and may or may not have to refer details to the rent officer (chapter 6). In particular, in the case of private and housing association tenants' claims for HB, the authority is likely to need more information about rent. Sometimes the authority's normal application form is used for this.

**5.23** If the claimant has been awarded IS or JSA(IB), information included on form NHB(IS) or NHB(JSA) (the decision forms) is binding on the authority in two respects:

- as proof of the claimant's entitlement to IS or JSA(IB) at the date shown;
- as proof that (at the date shown) the claimant therefore fulfils the income-related conditions for receiving maximum HB and/or maximum CTB (chapter 7).

**5.24** The second point above was established in *R v Penwith District Council ex parte Menear*, QBD, (1991) 24 HLR 120, a case about HB. In that case the DSS had decided that a man and a woman were not a couple and that the woman was entitled to income support. The authority decided they were a couple and refused the woman maximum HB. The court held that the authority was not entitled to do this.

**5.25** In other respects the authority must make its own determination about entitlement to HB/CTB. Since the Benefits Agency does not screen out ineligible HB/CTB claimants, authorities may receive forms from people not eligible for HB, such as owner-occupiers and non-householders, and from people not eligible for CTB, such as tenants in houses in multiple occupation. (Different considerations apply in the case of claims for HB/CTB 'extended payments': chapter 17.)

## AUTHORITY FOLLOW-UP PROCEDURES

SI 1988 No. 662
NISR 1988 No. 118
CTBR 93

**5.26** To avoid a breach of confidentiality, the authority should notify the Benefits Agency if the claimant is not entitled to HB/CTB at the outset of the claim, or later ceases entitlement. It should also notify the Benefits Agency of any change of circumstances likely to affect entitlement to income support. This should normally be done within five days.

### BENEFITS AGENCY FOLLOW-UP PROCEDURES

**5.27** The Benefits Agency keeps a record of NHB1 forms forwarded to the authority. When the Benefits Agency hears of a change of circumstances likely to affect entitlement to HB or CTB, it sends details to the authority. It also notifies the authority if entitlement to IS or JSA(IB) ends. In both cases, the Benefits Agency uses form NHB(IS) or form NHB(JSA) (para. 5.8). These procedures do not remove the claimant's own duty to notify changes of circumstances to the authority.

SI 1988 No. 662
NISR 1988 No. 118
CTBR 92

**5.28** If a claimant on IS or JSA(IB) moves, the Benefits Agency sends him or her three NHB1A forms (as well as sending the authority a form NHB(IS) or NHB(JSA) notifying it of the move). These three forms are form HHB1A(IS) or NHB1A(JSA), NHB1A(HB) and NHB1A(CTB) – which are invitations to claim IS or JSA, HB and CTB respectively. NHB1A forms for HB and CTB are similar to NHB1 forms, but additionally give the date of the new tenancy (for HB purposes) and the date of the move (for CTB purposes). The claimant is invited to return all the forms to the Benefits Agency. The NHB1A forms for HB and CTB are then dealt with in the same way as NHB1 forms (paras. 5.20 onwards).

## Claims direct to the authority

**5.29** Except for certain people who must claim via a 'One' office (para. 5.13), anyone may claim HB or CTB or both direct from the authority. This is the only method available to claimants who are not also making a claim for income support or income-based jobseeker's allowance. A claim may be made on a form supplied by the authority or in some other format acceptable to the authority. The authority may or may not need further information or evidence and may or may not have to refer details to the rent officer (chapter 6).

### APPLICATION FORMS

**5.30** Authorities design their own application forms. Long forms may put people off claiming. One way of shortening them is by the use of 'trigger questions' (e.g. 'are you self-employed?') with additional information obtained using follow-up letters or forms (e.g. details of income from self-employment). The print should be reasonably large, the language clear and simple, and the design and layout comprehensible. Special forms may be used for various groups of claimants such as linguistic minority groups, students, council tenants, private tenants, those who are eligible only for CTB (e.g. home owners), and so on. Forms should include a question about whether the person has claimed income support or income-based jobseeker's allowance.

**Table 5.1 HB/CTB FORMS FOR IS AND JSA(IB) CLAIMANTS**

| | |
|---|---|
| NHB1(HB) | HB claim form for IS and JSA(IB) claimants |
| NHB1(CTB) | CTB claim form for IS and JSA(IB) claimants |
| NHB1A(HB) | HB claim form for IS and JSA(IB) claimants moving home |
| NHB1A(CTB) | CTB claim form for IS and JSA(IB) claimants moving home |
| NHB(IS)* | Income support decision form for claims, changes and end of IS entitlement |
| NHB(JSA)* | Income-based jobseeker's allowance decision form for claims, changes and end of JSA(IB) entitlement |

* It appears that different names are given to these forms in some areas.

### THE AUTHORITY'S DESIGNATED OFFICE

HBR 2(1) CTBR 2(1) **5.31** The authority's application forms must give the address of its 'designated office(s)'. This is the place to which claims should be sent and changes of circumstances notified. Each authority must have at least one designated office. Designating two offices is possible when HB and CTB are dealt with at different addresses. Designating additional offices, such as the authority's homeless persons unit or a hostel, is often advantageous. The day a claim is received by these can then be the official 'date of claim' (para. 7.54). Forms must also give details of One offices if appropriate (paras. 7.11-12).

### SPOTTING ENTITLEMENT TO IS AND JSA(IB)

**5.32** If the authority considers the claimant may be entitled to income support or income-based jobseeker's allowance, it is good practice to advise him or her to claim it, and to do so promptly, since the IS or JSA(IB) claim will not be treated as having been made when HB or CTB were claimed. However, the authority has no power to require the claimant to do so.

## Is the claim effective?

**5.33** This section explains what constitutes an effective claim for HB/CTB – i.e. a claim which the authority must determine. The rules apply to claims made via a One office, a Benefits Agency office, a Jobcentre or an authority, whether fresh claims or renewal claims. There are two conditions for an effective HB/CTB claim:

- the first condition relates to the manner in which the claim is made;
- the second condition relates to the provision of information and evidence.

**5.34** If both the conditions are fulfilled, the claim is effective from the day it is received. This may either be because both conditions are fulfilled at the outset; or because they are later fulfilled, as described below (paras. 5.36-39).

## MANNER OF CLAIM

**5.35** Except as described in the next paragraph, the first condition for an effective claim is that it must be made in writing. Furthermore it must be:

AA s.1, 5, 6
HBR 72(1),(9)
CTBR 62(1),(9)

- on a form approved by the authority and completed in accordance with the instructions on the form; or
- in some other written form which the authority accepts as sufficient in the circumstances of a particular case or a class of cases.

Authorities' own application forms clearly fall in the first category. Authorities may also regard the Benefits Agency NHB1 and NHB1A forms as doing so. An example of the second category is a letter including a statement that the writer wishes to claim.

**5.36** The exception to the above rule applies only to claims which fulfil all three of the following conditions:

HBR 72(4)(d),(5), 72A
HBR 72B (GB only)
CTBR 62(4)(d),(5), 62A, 62B

- they are fresh claims (i.e. not renewal claims); and
- they are made to a One office (para. 7.11); and
- they are made by a person who is 16 or over but under 60 and who is not in remunerative work (para. 9.33).

In these cases, a 'notification of intention to make a claim' is treated in the same way as a written claim, so long as an actual written claim is received within one calendar month of that notification. It is clear that such a notification can be oral: for example, the words 'I'm planning to claim housing benefit' spoken at a 'One' office.

## INFORMATION AND EVIDENCE: GENERAL

**5.37** The second condition for an effective claim is that the authority may require from the claimant 'certificates, documents, information and evidence' so long as these are 'reasonably required... in order to determine... entitlement'. The exception is that it may not require any information whatsoever about the following types of payment, whether they are made to a claimant, partner, child, young person, non-dependant or second adult. These payments are in any case always disregarded in the assessment of HB and CTB:

HBR AA s.1, 5, 6, 72(1), 73(1),(3), sch A1
CTBR 62(1), 63(1),(3), sch A1

- payments from the Macfarlane Trusts, the Eileen Trust or the Fund, and in certain cases payments of money which originally derived from those sources (para. 13.40);
- payments in kind (i.e. goods not money) of capital from a charity or from the above sources;

◆ payments in kind of income from any source.

AA s1
HBR 2B
CTBR 2B
NISR 1999 No. 372
SI 1999 No. 920

**5.38** A further rule relating to National Insurance ('NI') numbers applies in all cases except for claims for HB made in respect of a hostel (as defined in para. 6.10). It is that (in order for a claim to be effective) the claimant must either provide his or her NI number and the NI number of his or her partner (but not that of any child or young person), along with information or evidence establishing these; or provide information or evidence enabling it to be ascertained; or make an application for an NI number and give information or evidence to assist with this. (This requirement also applies to renewal claims.) DSS circular HB/CTB A16/99 provides a form authorities can use to seek an NI number.

**5.39** Though an authority may require the information, etc, by writing to the claimant for this, it may not require the claimant to attend an interview – though it may request this (*R v Liverpool City Council ex parte Johnson,* QBD, 31.10.94). An authority has no duty to determine a claim if a relevant document has been forged – even if the statements in the forged document are true (*R v Winston*, CA, 15.7.98; *Times Law Report*, 24.7.98). In the special case of refugees who were formerly asylum seekers (para 20.22), the authority may require information, evidence, etc, about any previous period for which they have become entitled to HB/CTB.

**5.40** Apart from the points made earlier in this chapter and in relation to 'extended payments' (chapter 17), the law does not specify what type of proof the authority should require about any particular matter (though see below for DSS guidance under the 'Verification Framework'). It is clear, though, that the authority must not seek unnecessary proof. For example, a self-employed claimant should not be expected to have accounts prepared by someone else. Some information may require detailed proof, for example, if a claimant's capital is close to £16,000. In some cases, the authority may wish to check or confirm information with a third party. For example, authorities often ask claimants to get their landlord to confirm details of rent. If it is necessary for an authority to approach a third party direct, the DSS points out (GM para. C8.11) that 'such enquiries should normally be made only with the claimant's written agreement'. The only exception is that, in the circumstances described in paragraph 13.104 about notional income from a pension scheme, an authority may contact the pension provider direct.

## INFORMATION AND EVIDENCE AND THE VERIFICATION FRAMEWORK

**5.41** DWP's 'Verification Framework' ('VF') for HB and CTB, suggests the types of evidence authorities may seek about the claimant's (and others') identity, residency, rent, household composition, income, capital, etc. This advice is not laid down in law. It is a set of instructions amounting to a voluntary code of practice for authorities. Its objective is to prevent fraud.

**5.42** Several but by no means all authorities have decided to adopt the VF. Those which adopt it in full can get additional subsidy from the DWP towards their set-up and on-going implementation costs. There is nothing to stop an authority from adopting only parts of the VF, if it considers this is reasonable. But only authorities which adopt it in full can get additional subsidy.

**5.43** The legal test for what information and evidence authorities may require in order to determine a claim for HB or CTB is, in broad terms, that this must be 'reasonably required... in order to determine... entitlement' (para. 5.37). The DWP has taken the view that, with appropriate exceptions, the requirements of the VF meet this test. An authority which adopts the VF must inevitably have taken the same view. There may, however, be circumstances in which the requirements of the VF conflict with this legal test (for example, if an authority applies the requirements of the VF as a blanket rule in an inappropriate case: chapter 1).

**5.44** For authorities which adopt the VF, there are instructions about the following main matters:

- what information should be verified before HB/CTB is awarded;
- what evidence is acceptable for this purpose;
- how claimants should be categorised into certain 'risk groups';
- how long benefit periods should be set at – for each such risk group; and
- what checks should be made during the life of a claim – for each such risk group.

**5.45** The DSS's current instructions for authorities adopting the VF are in 'The Verification Framework: Updated Manual', DSS, April 2000 (issued with DSS circular HB/CTB A21/2000) as amended by circulars HB/CTB A26/2000, A31/2000, A34/2000 and A16/2001. Note that the VF does not apply in the case of hostel claims for the first 13 weeks of a claim, and that the DSS has also warned local authorities that over-zealous application of the VF can endanger hostels' work (DSS circular HB/CTB A48/99).

## REMEDYING DEFECTIVE CLAIMS

**5.46** Specific rules apply if a written claim does not comply with one or both of the conditions in paragraph 5.33: HBR 72(6)-(8), 73(1),(2), 76(2) CTBR 62(6)-(8), 63(1),(2), 66(2)

(a) if it is not on an approved form (and the authority does not accept the form it is in as sufficient), the authority should send the claimant an approved form for completion;

(b) if it is on an approved form, but it is incomplete, the authority should return the form to the claimant for completion (and it is good practice to keep a photocopy of the returned form);

(c) if information or evidence is not given or included with the form, the authority must request the claimant to provide this. At the same time, it must also inform the claimant of the duty to notify relevant changes of circumstances which occur, and indicate what these are likely to be.

**5.47** In all three cases, the authority must allow at least four weeks for the claimant to comply with the request, and should allow longer if reasonable to do so. For example, it is good practice to send a reminder, allowing a further period for the reply. If the claimant complies within four weeks (or longer if reasonable) the claim is effective from the original date. Furthermore, the three cases may apply one after the other (as illustrated in the example) or one of the cases may apply more than once (most commonly, a need for yet further information or evidence). Each time, the authority should allow the claimant four weeks to comply (or longer if reasonable).

**5.48** In any of the above cases, the authority has no duty to determine a claim if the claimant takes so much longer than four weeks to comply that the delay becomes unreasonable. (This can arise when a claimant does not provide the information, evidence, etc. reasonably required by the authority – for example, under the Verification Framework.) It is generally accepted that, if the authority does not determine an HB/CTB claim for this reason, there is nothing about which the claimant can appeal using the HB/CTB appeals procedures (chapter 17) – since there has been no decision (para. 19.13). Instead, the claimant's options (not all of which would be appropriate in every case) are:

- to write to the authority asking it to reconsider anyway;
- to complain using the authority's complaints procedure;
- to invite the authority's Monitoring Officer to intervene;
- to complain to the Ombudsman;
- to seek judicial review.

**Example: Remedying a defective claim**

| | |
|---|---|
| Claimant action | A claimant sends the authority a letter saying 'I wish to claim...' |
| Authority action | The letter does not contain sufficient details for the authority to assess the claim. The authority sends the claimant its ordinary application form for completion. |
| Claimant action | The claimant returns the form within four weeks, having omitted to answer some of the questions. |
| Authority action | The claim is now on an approved form, but is incomplete. The authority returns the form to the claimant for completion. |

| | |
|---|---|
| Claimant action | The claimant completes the form, and returns it after five weeks, with a note explaining he has been in hospital. |
| Authority action | The authority accepts that five weeks is reasonable, but needs evidence of income. The authority writes to the claimant requesting this. |
| Claimant action | The claimant returns the evidence within four weeks. |
| Authority action | The authority assesses the claim. The claim is effective from the date when the letter was received. |

**5.49** It is good practice for an authority receiving a claim which is not in writing (e.g. in person or over the telephone) to issue or send out an application form for completion. In this case the claim is not effective before the written application arrives. (Separate rules apply to claims made to One offices: para. 5.11.)

### AMENDING A CLAIM

**5.50** A claimant may write amending a claim at any time before a decision is made on it. The amendment is treated as having been made from the outset of the claim. Once a decision is made, the equivalent of amending a claim is notifying a change of circumstances (para. 17.2). HBR 74(1) CTBR 64(1)

### WITHDRAWING A CLAIM

**5.51** A claimant may write withdrawing a claim at any time before a decision is made on it. The authority is then under no duty to determine the claim. Once a decision is made, there is no provision for withdrawing a claim. HBR 74(2), 76(2) CTBR 64(2), 66(2)

## The life of a claim

**5.52** The remainder of this chapter describes the various things which happen during the life of a claim. The first few sections explain three things which must be established at the beginning of a claim:

- the date of claim;
- the first day of entitlement; and
- the benefit period.

Table 5.2 summarises these and also indicates what can or will happen later on. Rules about the last day of entitlement and renewal claims are explained towards the end of this chapter. Changes of circumstances are dealt with in chapter 17.

### BENEFIT WEEKS

HBR 2(1)
CTBR 2(1)

**5.53** Many of the rules in this chapter refer to a 'benefit week'. For both HB and CTB, benefits weeks are defined as beginning on a Monday and ending on the following Sunday.

## Date of claim

**5.54** This section describes what counts as the 'date of claim' for HB and CTB. The general rule is given first, then the exceptions which may apply. Table 5.3 summarises the main rules. The 'date of claim' is an important concept: it affects the date on which entitlement to HB/CTB actually begins (which may be before, on, or after the date of claim, depending on the other circumstances of the case, as described later in this chapter).

### GENERAL RULE

HBR 72(5)(c)
CTBR 62(5)(d)

**5.55** The general rule is that the date of claim is the day a claim is received at the authority's 'designated office' (para. 5.31). This includes cases where a claim is delivered on a day when the authority's offices are not open. So claims which are 'on the mat' after a weekend or a bank holiday should, if appropriate, be regarded as having been received on the Saturday, Sunday or bank holiday. The claimant may otherwise lose up to two weeks' HB/CTB (paras. 5.78-79).

### SUCCESSFUL IS AND JSA(IB) CLAIMANTS WHO CLAIM HB/CTB WITHIN FOUR WEEKS

HBR 72(5)(a)
CTBR 62(5)(a)

**5.56** This rule applies if:

- a person claims income support (IS) or income-based jobseeker's allowance – JSA(IB); and
- as a result he or she is awarded IS or JSA(IB); and
- the person's or any partner's HB/CTB claim (whether or not on the NHB1 forms) is received by the authority or the Benefits Agency or the Jobcentre no more than four weeks after the IS or JSA(IB) claim was received by the Benefits Agency or Jobcentre.

**5.57** In this case, the date of claim for HB/CTB is:

- the date of first entitlement to IS or JSA(IB). In the case of JSA(IB) this means the first 'waiting day' if the claimant has to wait for his or her JSA(IB) payments to begin. The relevant date for these purposes should be shown on form NHB(IS) or form NHB(JSA) (para. 5.18), though it is sometimes necessary to check that it is correct; or
- if earlier, the date the HB/CTB claim was received by the Benefits Agency or the Jobcentre (because of the rule described in para. 5.61). This would be

## Table 5.2 THE LIFE OF A CLAIM

### THE THREE STEPS TO FOLLOW WHEN A CLAIM BEGINS

Step one: DATE OF CLAIM

The first step is to decide what is the 'date of claim'. Typically this is the day the HB/CTB application form is received by the authority. But there are many other rules. In particular, there are circumstances in which a claim must be backdated.

Step two: FIRST DAY OF ENTITLEMENT

The second step is to work out (from the date of claim) the day on which entitlement to HB/CTB begins – in other words, the first day for which HB/CTB is awarded. Typically this is the Monday following the date of claim. But there are exceptions to this.

Step three: BENEFIT PERIOD

The third step is to decide what the benefit period is to be – in other words, how long the award of HB/CTB will last. This is often 26 or 52 weeks.

### WHAT HAPPENS NEXT

CHANGES OF CIRCUMSTANCES

Once the benefit period has begun the claimant's circumstances may change. Typically if a claimant qualifies for a different amount of HB/CTB because of a change, the new amount is awarded from the following Monday. But there are exceptions to this.

LAST DAY OF ENTITLEMENT

Entitlement to HB/CTB ends at the end of the benefit period, or earlier in the case of some changes of circumstances.

INVITING A RENEWAL CLAIM

When entitlement to HB/CTB ends, the authority must in most cases invite the claimant to make a renewal claim for a further period.

**Table 5.3 DATE OF CLAIM FOR HB/CTB: SUMMARY**

| Rule | Date of claim * |
|---|---|
| **General rule** | The date the HB/CTB claim is received by the authority. |
| **Claimants making a fresh claim for IS or JSA:** | |
| ◆ If IS or JSA(IB) is awarded; and a claim for HB/CTB is received by the Benefits Agency or Jobcentre or the authority within four weeks of the IS or JSA(IB) claim. | The first day of entitlement to IS or JSA(IB). |
| ◆ If IS or JSA(IB) is awarded but the above time limit is not met. | The date the HB/CTB claim is received by the authority. |
| ◆ If IS or JSA(IB) is not awarded. | The date the HB/CTB claim is received by the Benefits Agency or Jobcentre or the authority, whichever is earlier. |
| **Claimants making a claim to a One office** | The above rules apply as though the One office was either the authority, the Benefits Agency or the Jobcentre – whichever would be most beneficial for the claimant. |
| **Claimants on IS or JSA(IB) who become liable for rent or council tax for the first time:** | |
| ◆ If a claim for HB/CTB is received by the authority within four weeks of the start of their new liability for rent/council tax. | The first day of the new liability for rent/council tax.<br>(For rules about people moving home – whether they are on IS or JSA(IB) or not – see para. 5.63 onwards.) |

* If more than one rule applies to a case, use the earliest of the various dates of claim. Further rules apply to renewal claims (as described later in this chapter).

relevant if the claimant's entitlement to IS or JSA(IB) was later than the date they received his or her claim for IS or JSA(IB); or

- if earlier, the date the HB/CTB claim was received by the authority (because of the general rule in para. 5.55).

This rule applies regardless of delays by the Benefits Agency or Jobcentre in providing the details to the authority.

**5.58** The four weeks limit (para. 5.56) may not be extended. However it applies independently from the time limits allowed for the remedying of defective claims (e.g. if NHB1 forms are incomplete, or further information or evidence is required).

**Examples: Date of claim**

**SUCCESSFUL INCOME SUPPORT CLAIMANT**

A claimant applies for income support. The Benefits Agency receives her application on Wednesday 4th September 2002, and later assesses her as entitled to income support from that date.

The date of claim for HB/CTB is also Wednesday 4th September so long as the Benefits Agency or the authority receives a claim for HB/CTB (whether on the NHB1 forms or not) within four weeks of the date of claim for income support (i.e. on or before Wednesday 2nd October 2002).

**UNSUCCESSFUL JSA(IB) CLAIMANT**

A claimant applies for income-based jobseeker's allowance and sends the NHB1 forms with it. The Jobcentre receives his application on Wednesday 4th September 2002, and the Benefits Agency later assesses him as not entitled to JSA(IB).

The date of claim for HB/CTB is Wednesday 4th September.

## SUCCESSFUL IS AND JSA(IB) CLAIMANTS WHO CLAIM HB/CTB AFTER FOUR WEEKS

**5.59** If a person claims and is awarded IS or JSA(IB) but fails to claim HB/CTB within four weeks of making the IS or JSA(IB) claim, the date of claim for HB/CTB is the day the claim is received by the authority. HBR 72(5)(c) CTBR 62(5)(d)

**5.60** The above is confirmed in GM paras. A2.18, B2.37 and C7.17. But it is still sometimes believed that if, for some reason, an HB/CTB claim is sent to the Benefits Agency or Jobcentre more than four weeks after a successful IS or JSA(IB) claim, the day the HB/CTB claim is received by the Benefits Agency or Jobcentre should be regarded as the date of claim for HB/CTB. Whilst this would be beneficial, it is unfortunately incorrect: as stated above, the day the HB/CTB claim is received by the *authority* is the date of claim for HB/CTB. However, in such cases there may be good cause for backdating the HB/CTB claim (para. 5.93).

## UNSUCCESSFUL IS AND JSA(IB) CLAIMANTS, ETC

HBR 72(5)(b)
CTBR 62(5)(b)

**5.61** If a person claims IS or JSA(IB) but is not awarded it, or claims JSA(Cont) regardless of whether he or she is awarded it, the date of claim for HB/CTB is the day the HB/CTB claim is received by the Benefits Agency or Jobcentre or the authority, whichever is earlier.

## CLAIMS MADE TO A ONE OFFICE

HBR 72(5), 72A
HBR 72B (GB only)
CTBR 62(5), 62A, 62B

**5.62** In cases in which a claim for HB/CTB must or may be made to a One office (para. 5.11), the rules mentioned earlier (paras. 5.54-61) apply as though the 'One' office was either the authority's designated office or a Benefits Agency or Jobcentre office, whichever would be most beneficial in any particular claimant's case. This typically means that the date of claim in such cases is either the date the One office received a written claim for HB/CTB, or the date it received the claimant's notification of intention to claim HB/CTB, or the date the claimant is first entitled to income support or JSA(IB).

**Example: Date of claim**

**CLAIM MADE TO A ONE OFFICE**

A claimant visits a One office on Wednesday 4th September 2002 to enquire about his entitlement to state benefits and to seek help with finding work. During his visit he says he intends to claim HB/CTB. He is invited back for a full interview a couple of weeks later. At that interview he is helped to complete an application form covering HB/CTB and other relevant benefits and in due course he is awarded income-based jobseeker's allowance from Wednesday 4th September.

The date of claim for HB/CTB is Wednesday 4th September (because he made his written application for HB/CTB within one month of notifying the One office of his intention to claim.

## IS AND JSA(IB) CLAIMANTS BECOMING LIABLE FOR RENT OR COUNCIL TAX

HBR 72(5)(bb)
CTBR 62(5)(c)

**5.63** This rule makes it easier for a person on IS or JSA(IB) to get HB/CTB from when he or she first becomes liable for rent and/or for council tax. (For related cases, see para. 5.66.) Specifically, the rule applies if:

- a person is receiving IS or JSA(IB); and
- he or she becomes liable for rent or council tax for the first time; and
- the person's or any partner's HB/CTB claim (whether or not on the NHB1 or NHB1A forms) is received by the Benefits Agency or Jobcentre or the authority no more than four weeks after the new liability begins.

**5.64** In this case, the date of claim for HB is the first day of his or her new liability for rent; the date of claim for CTB is the first day of his or her new liability for council tax. Generally speaking this means that the person's HB/CTB will start straight away (paras. 5.79-80).

**5.65** Examples of when this rule applies are when a claimant on IS or JSA(IB):

- inherits the tenancy of his or her home;
- becomes liable for council tax because of the death of someone in his or her home or some other change in circumstances;
- becomes liable for council tax on a dwelling which has been exempt.

**5.66** So long as the claimant (or partner) is receiving IS or JSA(IB) immediately before the event in question, the rule applies regardless of whether he or she continues to receive IS or JSA(IB) afterwards.

## FURTHER RULES ABOUT CLAIMANTS MOVING HOME

**5.67** The following points apply to all claimants who move home within the area of a particular authority – whether they are on IS or JSA(IB) or not:

- If the claimant was receiving HB in respect of the old address, a claim for the new address is dealt with under the rules about renewal claims (para. 5.86). So, as long as the claim for the new address is received by the authority within four weeks of the end of the benefit period for the old address, there will be no break in his or her entitlement to HB. Exactly the same applies in respect of CTB.
- Alternatively in such cases, the authority may treat the move as a change of circumstances, allowing his or her current benefit period to continue (chapter 15), in which case a new claim is not required – though, of course, the claimant will have to give the authority his or her new rent and/or council tax details. (In practice, only some authorities are prepared to take this approach, but it is subject to the ordinary appeal procedures: chapter 19.)

**5.68** It is sometimes argued that the first point above (but not the second) could apply even if the move is from one authority area to another. The law is unclear on this, and it is a matter which has not been tested in the courts. Claimants should certainly not rely on this argument.

## CTB (Rate Rebate in Northern Ireland) CLAIMS IN ADVANCE OF LIABILITY

CTBR 62(10), 66(2) NIHBR 72 (5A) **5.69** A person may claim CTB (or in Northern Ireland HB in respect of rates) up to eight weeks before he or she will become liable for council tax/rates. The rule for dealing with this works as follows:

- The person claims CTB.
- The authority works out the date of claim in the ordinary way.
- He or she is not liable for council tax yet – so, although the claim may be processed, no award of CTB may be made for the time being – but it is anticipated that liability will begin at some point up to eight weeks after the date of claim.
- If liability does actually begin within that period, the authority must change the date of claim to the date liability begins.
- Because of the rule about when entitlement starts in such cases (para. 7.80), the person's CTB will start on that date.

If liability does not begin within the eight weeks mentioned, the claim is of no effect.

**5.70** One aim of this rule is that the person's council tax bill will, when it is issued, be able to show entitlement to CTB. Examples of when the rule applies are when a person:

- plans to move;
- expects that his or her home will cease to be exempt (e.g. if all the occupiers are students and one will soon cease to be a student);
- expects to become liable for council tax because the person currently liable will move out.

**5.71** There is no specific rule in HB similar to the above. However in the case of HB, the following rule may be applied.

## OTHER ADVANCE CLAIMS FOR HB/CTB

HBR 72(11) CTBR 62(12) **5.72** If a claimant is not immediately entitled to HB/CTB, it may be clear that he or she will soon become entitled. The authority may treat the claim as an advance claim. The rule dealing with this works as follows:

- The person makes a claim.
- The authority works out the date of claim in the ordinary way.
- In the benefit week immediately following the date of claim, he or she does not qualify for HB/CTB.
- But the authority considers that he or she will qualify for HB/CTB with

effect from a particular benefit week which is no later than the 13th benefit week after the date of claim.

- The authority may change the date of claim to a date in the benefit week immediately before that particular benefit week.
- Because of the general rule about when entitlement starts (para. 5.79-80), the person's HB/CTB will start in that particular benefit week.

**5.73** Examples of when this rule might be used are if:

- someone in the family will soon have a birthday that will increase the claimant's applicable amount;
- it is known that the claimant's, a partner's, a non-dependant's or a second adult's income will soon go down;
- the claimant plans to move home soon to rented accommodation.

The last example applies in the case of HB only. In the case of CTB a different rule applies (para. 5.67).

## CTB TRANSITIONAL RULES

**5.74** Several transitional rules applied from 1st April 1993 when council tax was introduced. In very rare circumstances (e.g. if someone now receives a first bill for council tax going right back to 1st April 1993), these could still apply. The details are in paras. 5.72-74 of the 2001-2002 edition of this Guide. SI 1992 No. 1909

## DELAYS IN SETTING COUNCIL TAXES

**5.75** Independent of the above rules, a further rule applies when any authority delays setting its council taxes until after 31st March in any year. In such cases, if a CTB claim is received within four weeks after the setting of the council taxes, the date of claim is set so that the claimant's entitlement begins on 1st April in that year (or the week in which the person's entitlement begins if this falls between 1st April and the date the claim is received). CTBR 62(11)

## HB CLAIMS FOR RENT DUE BEFORE THE CLAIMANT MOVES IN

**5.76** In certain cases, claimants can get HB (but not CTB) for a period of up to four weeks when they are liable for rent before moving in to their home (para. 3.67). But the HB due for that period cannot be awarded until the claimant has actually moved in. The rule for dealing with this can be illustrated as follows: HBR 5(7)

- The person makes a claim before moving in.
- The authority notes that it is one of the cases where claimants can get HB for a period before moving in.
- The date of claim for HB is worked out in the ordinary way. No award of HB is made for the time being.

- When the person actually moves in, HB is awarded based on the date of claim as already worked out (unless the person does not satisfy the conditions for getting HB before moving in until a later date, in which case that is the date of claim).

**5.77** There is another way in which this rule can work:

- The person makes a claim before moving in.
- The authority refuses the claim for some reason.
- The person moves in and, no more than four weeks later, makes a further claim (or is treated as doing so under the backdating rules).
- The authority notes that it is one of the cases where claimants can get HB for a period before moving in.
- The date of claim for HB is worked out in the ordinary way but based on the first claim.
- HB is awarded based on the date of claim just worked out (unless the person does not satisfy the conditions for getting HB before moving in until a later date, in which case that is the date of claim).

# First day of entitlement

## GENERAL RULE

HBR 65(1)
CTBR 56(1)

**5.78** The general rule is that:

- HB and CTB are awarded from the Monday following the 'date of claim' (as described earlier), even if the date of claim is a Monday.

Variations to the general rule are given below. Other variations apply for renewal claims (para. 5.86).

## WHEN LIABILITY FOR RENT BEGINS

HBR 65(2)
69(4)(a),(5),(6)
70(2),(4)

**5.79** If the date of claim is in the same benefit week as the claimant becomes liable for rent (or before then), HB is awarded from the benefit week in which the date of claim falls:

- if rent is expressed on a weekly basis (or in multiples of weeks), the full weekly amount of HB is awarded in that week (regardless of when liability began);
- if rent is expressed on a non-weekly basis (e.g. daily or calendar-monthly), entitlement for that week is assessed on a daily basis: divide the ordinary weekly entitlement by seven, then multiply the result by the number of days of liability.

This could arise if the claimant moves to a new home, or inherits a tenancy, or because of a rent-free period. These rules also apply to HB in respect of rates in Northern Ireland if the rates are included in the rent.

## WHEN LIABILITY FOR COUNCIL TAX BEGINS

**5.80** If the date of claim is in the same benefit week as the claimant or a partner becomes liable for council tax (or before then), CTB is awarded from the benefit week in which the date of claim falls: CTBR 56(2)

- entitlement for that week is assessed on a daily basis: divide the ordinary weekly entitlement by seven, then multiply the result by the number of days of liability.

This could arise if, for example, the claimant moves into or within the area, or becomes liable because the previously liable person has died, or his or her dwelling ceases to be exempt because it was formerly occupied wholly by students.

### Examples: First day of entitlement

**GENERAL CASE**

A man claims HB and CTB because his income has reduced. His date of claim is Thursday 18th July 2002. His rent is payable to his landlord each calendar month. He is liable for council tax.

HB and CTB are awarded from the benefit week commencing with the Monday following his date of claim. So Monday 22nd July is the claimant's first day of entitlement. From that week onwards, he is entitled to his normal weekly amount of HB and CTB.

There would be no difference if his rent was due weekly or on any other basis.

**CLAIMANT MOVING TO NEW HOME**

A woman moves into her flat on Thursday 1st August 2002. Her date of claim is Thursday 1st August. Her rent is payable to her landlord each calendar month, and is due from 1st August. She is liable for council tax from 1st August.

HB and CTB are awarded from the benefit week commencing with the Monday in which her date of claim falls, i.e. Monday 29th July. But she is not liable for rent or council tax until the Thursday, so Thursday 1st August is her first day of entitlement. In that first week, entitlement to HB and CTB is four-sevenths of her normal amount (for the Thursday to the Sunday).

If her rent was due weekly (or in multiples of weeks), there would be a difference in HB (only). Her first day of entitlement to HB would be Monday 29th July. From that week onwards she would be entitled to her normal weekly amount of HB. (But she would still only qualify for four-sevenths of the normal amount of CTB.)

## Duration of benefit period

HBR 66(2)
CTBR 57(2)

**5.81** HB and CTB are awarded for a fixed period. This applies to claimants on IS and JSA(IB) and all other claimants. It is up to the authority to decide how many benefit weeks this is to be, taking into account any relevant circumstances which may affect the claimant's future entitlement – for example, if the authority knows that a claimant's income will change shortly. For authorities which have implemented the Verification Framework there is guidance about how long benefit periods should be. They and other authorities typically favour 26 weeks and 52 weeks as standard periods.

HBR 66(1),(3)
CTBR 57(1),(3)

**5.82** Except as described below, the maximum length of a benefit period is 60 benefit weeks, beginning with the first benefit week of entitlement or, if later, the benefit week in which the *authority* (not the Benefits Agency or Jobcentre) receives the claim. For example, if HB or CTB is backdated (para. 5.93), the first week to count towards these 60 weeks is the benefit week in which the claim is actually received by the authority. (For exceptions relating to extensions of the benefit period, see paras. 5.86 and 17.24.)

HBR 66(3)(5)
(GB only)

The one exception to the above 60-weeks maximum arises in HB only and only when there is a 'relevant change of circumstances' (para. 6.11) requiring the authority to re-refer the case to the rent officer. In such cases HB benefit periods are extended by up to 60 weeks.

**Examples: Duration of benefit period**

**CLAIMANT ON INCOME SUPPORT**

A woman claims income support and is awarded it from Monday 7th October 2002. She claims HB/CTB (on the NHB1 forms) via the Benefits Agency at the same time. The Benefits Agency accidentally delays forwarding the NHB1 forms and they do not reach the authority until Wednesday 6th November 2002. She has not recently moved into her home.

- Her date of claim for HB/CTB is Monday 7th October.
- Her first day of entitlement to HB/CTB is Monday 14th October.
- The maximum possible length of her benefit period would be 60 weeks starting on Monday 4th November.

**CLAIMANT WHOSE HB/CTB IS BACKDATED**

A man's claim for HB/CTB is received by the authority on Wednesday 15th May 2002. He is not on IS or JSA(IB) and has not recently moved into his home. The authority agrees that he has proved good cause for failing to claim HB/CTB since Sunday 28th April 2002 (when he went into hospital). He qualifies for HB/CTB for both the backdated period and the current period.

- His date of claim for HB/CTB (because of the backdating rules is treated as being Sunday 28th April.
- His first day of entitlement to HB/CTB is Monday 29th April.
- The maximum possible length of his benefit period would be 60 weeks starting on Monday 13th May.

## Last day of entitlement

**5.83** An award of HB/CTB lasts until:

- the benefit period runs out; or
- the benefit period is brought to an early end.

### BENEFIT PERIOD RUNS OUT

**5.84** One way entitlement to HB/CTB can end is when the benefit period originally set at the beginning of the claim reaches its end. In this case the last day of entitlement is the Sunday at the end of the final benefit week of the benefit period. Except to the limited extent described in paragraph 5.91, there is no power to continue awarding HB/CTB after this, unless a renewal claim is made. HBR 67 CTBR 58

### BENEFIT PERIOD BROUGHT TO AN EARLY END

**5.85** The other way entitlement to HB/CTB can end is when the benefit period is brought to an early end. This can happen if there is a change in the claimant's circumstances. Chapter 17 gives all the rules about changes of circumstances, about which changes can cause a benefit period to end early, and about how the last day of entitlement is calculated in such cases. HBR 67 CTBR 58

**Example: End of benefit period and renewal claim**

A claimant aged over 80 is awarded HB and CTB from Monday 18th June 2001. Her benefit period is set at 52 benefit weeks, due to run out on Sunday 16th June 2002. Throughout this time, she qualifies for a higher pensioner premium.

Some weeks before it is due to run out, the authority writes to the claimant inviting her to make a renewal claim.By Monday 10th June 2002, the claimant has not submitted a renewal claim.

> The authority determines to extend her benefit period by four weeks (para. 5.91), so it is now due to run out on Sunday 14th July 2002. It also sends her a reminder about submitting a renewal claim.
>
> On Friday 9th August 2002, the authority receives a renewal claim from this claimant (and she still qualifies for HB and CTB). This is within four weeks of the end of her benefit period (Sunday 14th July 2002), so the new benefit period for HB and CTB begins on Monday 15th July 2002.

## Renewal claims

**5.86** Whenever a benefit period runs out or is brought to an early end (including cases where this is because the claimant has moved within the authority's area), authorities should invite the claimant to make a claim for a further award of HB/CTB, referred to in this guide as a 'renewal claim' (and sometimes called a 'review' by authority benefit staff). In certain cases, the courts may prevent an authority from evicting its own tenant on the grounds of rent arrears, if the arrears result from the authority's failure to issue an HB renewal claim: *Saint v Barking and Dagenham LBC*, (1999), CA (unreported).

HBR 72(14) NIHBR 72(13) CTBR 62(15)

**5.87** Authorities must invite a renewal claim:

- at some point during the eight weeks before a benefit period is due to run out (unless the benefit period was originally fixed as less than 16 weeks); and
- whenever a benefit period is brought to an early end because the claimant stops being entitled to IS or JSA(IB) or stops receiving payments of IS or JSA(IB).

And whenever benefit stops, even if the above rules do not apply, it is good practice to invite a renewal claim or (if appropriate) remind claimants that they may make a further claim as and when their circumstances change.

HBR 76(2) CTBR 66(2)

**5.88** It is also open to claimants to make a renewal claim at any time. However, if it is made more than 13 weeks before their benefit period runs out, the authority has no duty to act on it.

### FIRST DAY OF ENTITLEMENT IN NEW BENEFIT PERIOD

HBR 72(12)-(14) NIHBR 72(11)-(13) CTBR 62(13)-(15)

**5.89** In all cases, if a renewal claim is received by the authority (for the same or a different address within its area) within 13 weeks before the end of a claimant's benefit period, or within four weeks after it has ended, any new benefit period must run consecutively (so that there is no gap in entitlement). In other words, the first day of entitlement in the new claim must be the day after the last day of entitlement of the old claim. This rule applies equally to a renewal claim from the partner or former partner of a claimant.

**5.90** The four weeks time limit mentioned above cannot be extended (though see chapter 17 in the case of a claimant who is awarded an 'extended payment'). If a renewal claim is received outside this time limit, the only way of avoiding the gap in entitlement is by backdating the renewal claim. It is therefore good practice for authorities to issue reminders well within the four weeks limit (though claimants should not rely on all authorities doing this).

### EXTENSION OF OLD BENEFIT PERIOD

**5.91** If no renewal claim has been received by the last week in the old benefit period, the authority may extend the old benefit period by up to four weeks (but no longer), i.e. award a further four weeks' HB or CTB or both. But this only applies if the claimant (or any partner): HBR 66(4) CTBR 57(4)

- is on IS or JSA(IB); or
- fulfils the conditions for a disability premium, higher pensioner premium or severe disability premium (paras. 12.15, 12.19 and 12.30).

**5.92** This is designed to give the claimant a little more time to make a renewal claim, and to allow the authority to issue a reminder or make a home visit (GM para. A6.10). The four weeks mentioned here is independent from the four weeks allowed for submitting the renewal claim (para. 5.89) as illustrated in the preceding example.

## Backdating

**5.93** HB and CTB must be backdated for up to 52 weeks if the claimant requests this in writing, and 'had continuous good cause for [his or her] failure to make a claim'. It is possible for there to be 'good cause' for backdating HB but not CTB, or *vice versa*. Technically, it is the date of claim which is backdated. So HB/CTB can be backdated even if the claimant is not currently entitled to any HB/CTB. For example, a claimant whose capital has recently increased to over £16,000 could have his or her claim backdated for the period when it was less than £16,000. Benefit during any backdated period must be calculated according to the rules which applied at that time. Many authorities now include a question on their claim forms about whether the claimant wishes to make a claim for backdating. HBR 72(15) NIHBR 72(14) CTBR 62(16)

### 'GOOD CAUSE'

**5.94** Backdating is not discretionary. It is obligatory once the authority decides:

- that the claimant had good cause for failure to make the claim earlier; and
- that his or her good cause lasted throughout the period until the written

request for backdating was actually made (whether for the same reason throughout, or for a combination of successive reasons).

The impact on the authority's financial position (e.g. under the subsidy rules: chapter 19) is irrelevant in deciding whether or not to backdate benefit. This is not affected by the *Brent and Connery* case.

**5.95** However, the question remains of judging just what constitutes 'good cause'. It is clear that authorities should not have an immutable list of what does and does not constitute good cause, but should consider any relevant factor. Many authorities follow, in a general sense, the DSS's advice drawn from its social security 'Adjudication Officers' Guide' (reproduced in GM chapter A2, annex A). Whilst this includes an excellent summary of social security case law, often favourable to claimants, the guidance referred to itself states that the factors it covers 'are not an exhaustive list'. As yet there has been no case law on 'good cause' for backdating HB within the current HB scheme – nor on community charge benefit or CTB. Whilst case law on backdating other state benefits is not binding in HB and CTB, it is in many cases persuasive.

**5.96** Some examples of when claimants may have 'good cause' are listed below.

- If the claimant was ill and had no-one to make the claim on his or her behalf.
- If the claimant could not reasonably have been expected to know his or her rights, e.g. where there have been detailed changes in the law.
- If the claimant did not understand that he or she could claim perhaps because of age, inexperience, language difficulties, difficulty in understanding technical documents or some other reason.
- If the claimant was wrongly advised that he or she was not entitled to HB/CTB.
- If the claimant was unable to manage his or her affairs and did not have an 'appointee'.
- If the claimant has become liable for council tax for a past period because the authority, by its own error, has been attempting to bill a person who is not in fact liable.

## WHAT IS, AND IS NOT, 'BACKDATING'?

**5.97** 'Backdating' only arises when benefit is awarded for a past period for which the claimant has not already claimed HB/CTB. The following do not count as 'backdating' in this sense (and there is no subsidy penalty on authorities in these cases):

- awarding HB/CTB for a past period because other rules require it to be done;

- basing a claim on an application form which was (on the balance of probability) received by the authority or the Benefits Agency, Jobcentre or One office but was then mislaid;
- basing a claim on an application form which the authority originally (and wrongly) regarded as demonstrating that the claimant was not entitled to HB/CTB;
- basing a claim on an application which the authority originally treated as defective but which the authority no longer regards as such because the claimant has now provided relevant information, evidence, etc, within a timescale which the authority now accepts is reasonable;
- increasing entitlement retrospectively for someone who was awarded too little HB/CTB in a past period (chapter 19);
- allowing a claimant to keep underlying entitlement when an overpayment is calculated (para. 18.16).

## LIMIT ON BACKDATING

**5.98** HB and CTB cannot be backdated more than 52 weeks before the date on which the authority received the claimant's written request for backdating (even if this is later than when the claimant made his or her claim for HB/CTB). This does not prevent a claimant from seeking compensation from the authority for earlier periods if the authority itself was at fault.

HBR 72(15)
NIHBR 72(14)

**5.99** If the special rule about asylum seekers who have become refugees applies to a claimant (para. 5.51), his or her date of claim as determined under that rule cannot be backdated.

HBR sch A1 para 2(4),(5)
NIHBR sch A1 para 2(3),(4)

# 6 Referrals to the rent officer

**6.1** Authorities must refer details of many HB cases to the rent officer during the course of assessing a claim for HB (including some renewal claims) or following certain changes of circumstances. This chapter explains the rules and covers:

- which cases are referred to the rent officer and when they should be referred;
- making the referral (this includes details of the information the rent officer requires);
- the rent officer's determinations and how they are made;
- how errors and appeals are dealt with; and
- the rules about pre-tenancy determinations.

In Northern Ireland there is no requirement to refer because the Northern Ireland Housing Executive makes all decisions on housing benefit claims including rent restrictions (Regulation 10A, NI Housing Benefit Regulations).

**6.2** Rent officer referrals can be required in many kinds of rent allowance cases (including claims from private tenants or licensees, hostel residents, people renting a houseboat, mooring, mobile home or caravan site, people with a rental purchase agreement, and – in certain circumstances – housing association tenants). They are never required in rent rebate cases (claims from tenants of the authority administering HB). They relate only to HB: this chapter does not apply at all in relation to CTB.

**6.3** Rent officers are employed by the Rent Service, an independent 'Next Steps' Executive Agency, which has various duties in addition to those relating to HB.

## WHY ARE REFERRALS MADE TO THE RENT OFFICER?

**6.4** As described in this chapter, the rent officer provides the authority with various figures in respect of the cases referred to him or her. These figures are used in different ways depending on whether the HB case in question is an 'Old Scheme' or 'New Scheme' case (as defined in para. 10.7).

- In Old Scheme cases, the rent officer's figures are used to establish whether the authority will receive reduced HB subsidy on any part of the individual claimant's HB (chapter 19). In assessing the HB claim, the authority must make its own determination of eligible rent based on the HB regulations (paras. 9.53 onwards).
- In New Scheme cases, the authority uses the rent officer's figures in

calculating the claimant's 'maximum rent' (paras. 10.29 onwards): they are binding on the authority for this purpose. The claimant's eligible rent, used in assessing the HB claim, is frequently equal to this 'maximum rent' – but can also be higher or lower.

**6.5** The rent officer does not distinguish (in making his or her determinations) between the above types of case: it is the authority that decides which cases fall within which scheme. This is an important duty for the authority, since it can make a substantial difference to the amount of HB a claimant qualifies for.

## Which cases are referred and when?

### GENERAL REQUIREMENTS FOR A REFERRAL (GB only)
### EXECUTIVE REQUIRED TO MAKE A RENT DECISION (NI only)

**6.6** With the exceptions given below, the authority must refer details of all HB cases to the rent officer. In Northern Ireland these are also the circumstances in which the Executive is required to make a rent decision.

HBR 12A(1) (GB only)
NIHBR 10A (NI only)

- whenever it receives a new HB claim (unless the time limit in para. 6.8 prevents this); and
- whenever it receives a renewal HB claim, even if there has been no change in circumstances (unless the time limit in para. 6.8 prevents this); and
- whenever it receives notification of a 'relevant change of circumstances' (as defined in para. 6.11) relating to an existing HB claim.

The authority's duties in making the referral are given in the next section (paras. 6.14-15).

### GENERAL EXCEPTIONS

**6.7** The authority must not make a referral to the rent officer in any of the cases in table 6.1. In Northern Ireland these are the cases in which the Executive must not make a decision about the rent payable. Also, in the special case of refugees who were formerly asylum seekers (para. 20.51), it must not make a referral in respect of any previous periods for which they have become entitled to HB.

HBR 12(2)(b), sch A1, sch 1A
NIHBR 10A(3) sch A1, sch 1B

**Table 6.1 CASES WHICH ARE NEVER REFERRED TO THE RENT OFFICER**

- Rent rebate cases (i.e. council tenants renting from the authority administering their HB, or in Northern Ireland tenants of the NI Housing Executive: para. 1.14).
- Tenancies in England and Wales entered into before 15th January 1989 and tenancies in Scotland entered into before 2nd January 1989 (in other words, 'regulated tenancies': the dates just mentioned are those when the 1988 Housing Acts came into force).
- In Northern Ireland any protected or statutory tenancy subject to the Rent (Northern Ireland) Order 1978, SI 1978 No. 1050.
- Any other 'regulated tenancies' which continue to fall within the Rent Act 1977 or the Rent (Agriculture) Act 1976 (these applied before the 1988 Housing Acts came into force). For example, a tenant whose tenancy began in 1988, but who was later transferred by the landlord to alternative accommodation, may still have a 'regulated tenancy'.
- Housing Action Trust lettings.
- Lettings of former local authority or new towns housing stock which has been transferred to a new owner (for example, a housing association) under the Housing Act 1985 (or equivalent new towns provisions) or the tenants choice provisions of the Housing Act 1988 – unless there has been a rent increase since the date of the transfer and the authority states in the referral that the accommodation is unreasonably large or the rent is unreasonably expensive.
- Lettings where the landlord is a registered housing association or other registered social landlord – unless the authority considers that the accommodation is unreasonably large or the rent is unreasonably expensive, in which case the authority must make a referral and must state in making the referral that the accommodation is unreasonably large or the rent is unreasonably expensive. In such cases, the authority should take into account all relevant factors: for example, in considering whether the accommodation is unreasonably large, the authority must not simply adopt the rent officer's size criteria (paras. 6.24-26).

## TIME LIMITS ON FURTHER REFERRALS

**6.8** In any case which has previously been referred to the rent officer, no further referral must be made unless and until one of the criteria in table 6.2 applies (and in each case one of the general requirements for a referral must also apply: para. 6.6). Note that a change of claimant does not require (or permit) a further referral unless one of the circumstances in table 6.2 (or table 6.3) applies. The current rules result from amendment taking effect from 21st May 2001. They were drawn up in the most impenetrable way, and still seem to leave peculiar loopholes in the law. For example, there can never be a further referral in the case of a claimant who never moves, whose circumstances never change, and who goes on and off HB (so long as none of her times on HB reaches 52 weeks).

HBR 12A(2)(b) sch 1A

NIHBR sch 1B

### TABLE 6.2 WHEN A FURTHER REFERRAL TO THE RENT OFFICER IS REQUIRED

These are the circumstances in which a further referral to the rent officer is required (para. 6.8). The numbers given to the circumstances are purely as an aid to reference (they are not references to the law). 'Benefit period' is defined in paragraph 5.81.

*Circumstance 1*

- The current claimant is the same claimant as at the previous referral (and it is the same address); and
- the current claimant has been (or will have been by the time his or her next benefit period starts) on HB for 52 weeks or more, continuously, since the beginning of the benefit period to which the last referral related (whether one or more benefit periods ago).

*Circumstance 2*

- The current claimant is the same claimant as at the previous referral (and it is the same address); and
- the current claimant's old benefit period was extended (as described in para. 17.74), and the extension period has lasted (or will have lasted by the time his or her next benefit period starts) for 52 weeks or more, continuously.

*Circumstance 3*

- The current claimant's next benefit period will be his or her second (or subequent) consecutive benefit period at this address; and

- the last referral was made in respect of a different claimant (at this address); and
- the current claimant has been on HB for 52 weeks or more, continuously; and
- the old rent officer determination(s) has been used for at least 52 weeks continuously in relation to the current claimant (or will have been by the time his or her next benefit period begins).

*Circumstance 4*

- The current claimant is not the same claimant as at the previous referral; and
- the current HB claim is received by the authority (not, say, the benefits agency, the jobcentre or a 'One' office) more than 12 months (i.e. at least 12 months and 1 day) after the day the last rent officer determination was made (not the day it was notified).

Circumstance 5

- There has been a 'relevant change of circumstances' (para. 6.11) since the day the last rent officer determination was made (not the day it was notified).

## REPRESENTATIVE REFERRALS FOR HOSTEL CASES

HBR 12A(2)(a),(7), sch 1A
NIHBR sch 1B

**6.9** For hostel cases (para. 6.10), no referral is required if a rent officer determination has been made for similar accommodation within the hostel during the previous 12 months, unless there is a 'relevant change of circumstances' (para. 6.11). For these purposes, accommodation must be treated as similar if it provides the same number of bed spaces. It may also be treated as similar in other appropriate cases. The earlier referral applies to any such similar accommodation within the hostel.

## WHAT IS A 'HOSTEL'?

HBR 2(1)

**6.10** A 'hostel' is defined for these purposes as any building (other than a residential care home or nursing home: paras. 3.5-11) to which both the following apply:

- it provides domestic accommodation which is not self-contained together with meals or adequate facilities for preparing food; and
- it is:
  - managed or run by a registered housing association or registered social landlord, or

- run on a non-commercial basis, and wholly or partly funded by a government department or agency or local authority, or
- managed by a registered charity or non-profit-making voluntary organisation which provides care, support or supervision with a view to assisting the rehabilitation of the residents or their resettlement into the community.

**Table 6.3 'RELEVANT CHANGES OF CIRCUMSTANCES'**

- Except in hostel cases (para. 6.10), there has been a change in the number of occupiers.
- Any child or young person in the household has reached the age of 10 or 16 – but only if, at the last referral, the rent officer gave a size-related rent determination (para. 6.24).
- There has been a change in the composition of the household – but only if, at the last referral, the rent officer gave a size-related rent determination (para. 6.24). (One example is when two people have ceased to be a couple.)
- There has been a substantial change or improvement in the condition of the dwelling – regardless of whether there has been an associated change in the rent. (For example, central heating has been installed.)
- There has been a substantial change in the terms of the letting agreement (excluding a change in a term relating to rent alone) – regardless of whether there has been an associated change in the rent. (For example, the landlord has taken over the responsibility for internal decorations from the tenant or vice versa.)
- There has been a rent increase and:
  - the rent increase was made under a term of the letting agreement (which need not be in writing) and that term is the same (or substantially the same) as at the previous referral to the rent officer; and
  - at the previous referral, the rent officer did not make any of the following determinations: a 'significantly high rent determination', a 'size-related rent determination' or an 'exceptionally high rent determination' (paras. 6.23-27).
- At the previous referral to the rent officer, the claimant was not a 'young individual' (para. 6.12), but the claimant in the current case is a 'young individual'.

## WHAT IS A 'RELEVANT CHANGE OF CIRCUMSTANCES'?

HBR sch 1A
SI 1997 No. 1984
SI 1997 No. 1995
NIHBR sch 1B

**6.11** Table 6.3 lists all the changes which count as a 'relevant change of circumstances' for the purposes of the rules described earlier. If there has been a 'relevant change of circumstances' since an HB case was last referred to the rent officer, a further referral must be made to the rent officer as a result of that change (and see also para. 5.82). If the authority does not become aware of such a change straightaway, a referral must be made when it does become aware of it.

## DEFINITION OF 'YOUNG INDIVIDUAL'

HBR 2(1), 11(3B)
SI 1995 No. 1644
NISR 1996 No. 111

**6.12** Every claimant who is a 'single claimant' (para. 4.4) and is under the age of 25 is a 'young individual' (see also para. 6.14) unless he or she:

(a) rents his or her home from the authority, or in Northern Ireland the Housing Executive, itself;

(b) rents his or her home from a registered housing association or registered social landlord;

(c) is under the age of 22 and was formerly in social services care under a court order (under section 31(1)(a) of the Children Act 1989 in England and Wales, or equivalent provisions in Scotland) which applied (or continued to apply) after his or her 16th birthday;

(d) is under the age of 22 and was formerly provided with accommodation by social services (under section 20 of the Children Act 1989 in England and Wales, or equivalent provisions in Scotland) but is no longer in that accommodation or remains in it but the accommodation is no longer provided by social services;

(e) has one or more non-dependant(s);

(f) qualifies for a severe disability premium in the assessment of his or her HB (para. 12.38), income support or JSA(IB);

(g) lives in a residential care home or nursing home (paras. 3.5-11);

(h) lives in certain types of hostel (as defined in para. 6.10).

**6.13** As described in Chapter 10, the rules applying to young individuals take account of the rent officer's 'single room rent determination'. It is the authority (not the rent officer) which decides whether someone is a 'young individual'. Note that (e) above applies only to non-dependants: having a sub-tenant, boarder or joint occupier does not stop someone being a 'young individual'. Technically, it is also worth noting that the law works in a peculiar way in the following cases:

- for claimants who fall in case (a) above, the law defines them as 'young individuals' but then says that no referral may be made to the rent officer in their case: this is the same as saying that they are not 'young individuals';

- for claimants who fall in cases (e) or (f) above, the law defines them as 'young individuals' but then says that the authority must ignore any single room rent determination made by the rent officer in their cases: this is the same as saying that they are not 'young individuals';
- for claimants who fall in cases (g) or (h) above, the law defines them as 'young individuals' but then says that the rent officer may not make a single room rent determination in their cases: this is the same as saying that they are not 'young individuals' (except that it is the rent officer who determines whether they live in the accommodation described in those cases, not the authority).

# Making the referral

## TIME LIMITS AND METHOD OF REFERRAL

**6.14** The referral must be made within three working days of the claim or change of circumstances giving rise to it, or as soon as practicable thereafter. Days when the authority's offices are closed for receiving or determining claims do not count as 'working days' for this purpose. The DWP recommends authorities use a standard form (HBR1). Authorities and rent officers may agree to communicate by electronic means (e.g. by fax) rather than in writing.

## INFORMATION REQUIRED BY THE RENT OFFICER

HBR 12A(1A),(1ZA), (1B), (7A), 106 (GB only)

**6.15** Table 6.3 lists the information the authority should give when making a referral to the rent officer. The law specifically requires certain information to be included (this is indicated in the table) and also generally requires the authority to provide any other information required by the rent officer. This other information can sometimes vary from rent officer to rent officer: the table shows what information is normally required.

### Table 6.4 INFORMATION REQUIRED BY THE RENT OFFICER

IDENTIFICATION AND GENERAL INFORMATION

- A case reference number.
- The claimant's name.
- The address of the property.

- The number of occupiers there.
- The age and sex of those occupiers and their relationship to the claimant (e.g. 'son', 'sub-tenant').
- The date the claimant commenced occupation (which may be approximate if necessary).
- Whether the landlord is a registered housing association or other registered social landlord.
- The details of the letting agreement, including the period of the letting.
- The type of accommodation (e.g. house, bedsit, room).
- In the case of a room, its location within the property (e.g. 'first floor, front').
- Details of all the rooms in the property, the ones the claimant has sole use of, and the ones the claimant has shared use of.

RENT, SERVICES, ETC.

- Whether the claimant is a 'young individual' (para. 6.12) *.
- If the rent includes a charge for any support charges (para. 11.33):
  - the fact that it does*;
  - the authority's valuation of the total value of such items which are eligible for HB*; and
  - the authority's valuation of the total value of such items which are not eligible for HB*.
- The gross actual rent on the property after deducting the authority's valuation of all the above items - whether eligible for HB or not*.
- Whether the rent includes any amount for water charges, fuel or meals (but no valuation of any of these is required)*.
- Details of all other eligible and ineligible services included in the rent, and details of any variable service charges.
- Whether central heating is provided.
- Whether a garage is provided.
- Whether the accommodation is furnished fully, partly or minimally, or is unfurnished.
- Who is responsible for internal decorations (landlord or claimant).
- If the claimant is a joint occupier (para. 6.35) the figures for rent and services mentioned above should be those for the whole property*.

- In the case of combined domestic and business premises, the figures for rent and services mentioned above should relate only to the domestic part.
- The figures for rent and services mentioned above should be given for the period for which rent is due. For example, if the claimant's rent is due calendar monthly, they should be given as calendar monthly figures.

* NOTE: Items marked with an asterisk are those specifically mentioned in the law (para. 6.15).

## The rent officer's determinations

**6.16** The rent officer (in Northern Ireland, the Executive) may provide one or more of the following determinations. More information on each is given in the next few paragraphs: SI 1997 No. 1984 SI 1997 No. 1995 NIHBR sch 1A

- a claim-related rent determination;
- a local reference rent determination;
- a single room rent determination;
- certain determinations relating to service charges.

The rent officer does not make any determinations if the referral is withdrawn by the authority. The rent officer is not required to visit the dwelling but does so in many cases.

### GENERAL RULES AND ASSUMPTIONS ABOUT DETERMINATIONS

**6.17** In making the determinations described below (paras. 6.22-23), the rent officer or in Northern Ireland the Housing Executive: HBR 12A(6) SI 1997 No. 1984 SI 1997 No. 1995 NIHBR sch 1A

- must base these on the facts as they stood on the date on which the authority made the referral, unless the claimant had left the accommodation by that date, in which case they are based on the facts as they stood at the end of the claimant's letting;
- provides these for the same period (e.g. weekly, calendar monthly) as that for which the authority supplied the information to the rent officer (table 6.4);
- must 'assume that no one who would have been entitled to housing benefit had sought or is seeking the tenancy';
- must ignore all rents payable to housing associations, other registered social landlords and registered charities;
- must include the value of any meals provided to the claimant (except that, in

the case of the exceptionally high rent determination, the rent officer may choose whether to include meals or not);

- must exclude the value of all support charges (as defined in para. 11.33) whether eligible or ineligible for HB;
- must exclude the value of all other service charges which are ineligible for HB (chapter 11).

## 'LOCALITY', 'NEIGHBOURHOOD' AND 'VICINITY'

SI 1997 No. 1984
SI 1997 No. 1995
SI 2001 No. 3561
(GB only)
NIHBR sch 1A

**6.18** In the past, the rent officer made all his or her determinations by reference to the 'locality', a concept which was not defined, but which was held in the Court of Appeal (in Regina (Saadat and Others) v the Rent Service, 26.10.01) to mean a relatively limited area. The law was amended as a result on 6th November 2001, eleven days after the judgement. Since then, the rent officer makes his or her determinations by reference to the 'locality', the 'neighbourhood' or the 'vicinity', as defined below. (In all the following, 'area' is not defined in the law and takes its ordinary English meaning.) No amending rules have yet been introduced for Northern Ireland and so the term locality is still in use for all Northern Irish rent decisions.

**6.19** 'Locality' (used in determining local reference rents: para. 6.28; and single room rents: para. 6.31) means an area:

- which comprises two or more neighbourhoods (as defined below), one of which must be the neighbourhood where the dwelling is, and each of which must adjoin at least one other; AND
- where a tenant of the dwelling 'could reasonably be expected to live having regard to facilities and services for the purposes of health, education, recreation, personal banking and shopping which are in or accessible from the neighbourhood of the dwelling, taking account of the distance of travel, by public and private transport, to and from facilities of the same type and similar standard'; AND
- which contains 'residential premises of a variety of types' including ones held on a 'variety of tenancies'.

**6.20** 'Neighbourhood' (used in determining exceptionally high rents: para. 6.27; and in part of the definition of locality: para. 6.19) means:

- in the case of dwelling in a town or city, 'that part of that town or city where the dwelling is located which is a distinct area of residential accommodation';
- in the case of a dwelling not in a town or city, 'the area surrounding the dwelling which is a distinct area of residential accommodation' and where there are dwellings satisfying the size criteria (table 6.5).

**6.21** 'Vicinity' (used in determining significantly high rents: para. 6.23; and size-related rents: para. 6.24) means:

- 'the area immediately surrounding the dwelling'
- however, for size-related rents only (not significantly high rents), if 'the area immediately surrounding the dwelling' contains no dwellings matching the size criteria (table 6.5), 'vicinity' instead means 'the area nearest to the [claimant's] dwelling where there is such a dwelling'.

## CLAIM-RELATED RENT DETERMINATIONS

**6.22** In all cases, the rent officer must make a 'claim-related rent determination.' This is the only, lower or lowest of the following (the latter three are described in the following paragraphs):

SI 1997 No. 1984
SI 1997 No. 1995
NIHBR sch 1A

- the referred rent, adjusted (as regards service charges) in accordance with the general rules and assumptions (para. 6.17);
- the significantly high rent;
- the size-related rent;
- the exceptionally high rent.

## SIGNIFICANTLY HIGH RENT DETERMINATIONS

**6.23** The rent officer determines whether the referred rent for the dwelling is 'significantly higher than the rent which the landlord might reasonably have been expected to obtain'. If it is, he or she makes a significantly high rent determination: this is the amount 'the landlord might reasonably have been expected to obtain' for the dwelling, having regard to 'the level of rent under similar tenancies [or licences] of similar dwellings in the vicinity (or as similar as regards tenancy [or licence], dwelling and vicinity as reasonably practicable'. 'Vicinity' is defined in para. 6.21. Also, the general rules and assumptions apply (para. 6.17). In Northern Ireland 'locality' is still used instead of 'vicinity'.

SI 1997 No. 1984
SI 1997 No. 1995
NIHBR sch 1A

## SIZE-RELATED RENT DETERMINATIONS

**6.24** Except in the case of site rents for caravans or mobile homes and mooring charges for houseboats, the rent officer also determines whether the dwelling exceeds the size criteria given in paragraph 6.25 and table 6.5. If it does, he or she makes a size-related rent determination: this is the amount 'the landlord might reasonably have been expected to obtain' on a dwelling which:

SI 1997 No. 1984
SI 1997 No. 1995
NIHBR sch 1A

- is in 'the same vicinity' (in Northern Ireland 'locality'); and
- is let under a similar tenancy under the same terms as the tenancy of the dwelling in question; and
- matches those size criteria; and

- is in a reasonable state of repair; and
- in other respects, matches the claimant's dwelling 'as closely as reasonably practicable'.

'Vicinity' is defined in para. 6.21. Also, the general rules and assumptions apply (para. 6.17).

**6.25** The size criteria (para. 6.24 and table 6.5) allow for every 'occupier' – which is defined for this purpose as 'a person (whether or not identified by name) who is stated [by the authority], in the application [to the rent officer] for the determination, to occupy the dwelling'. There is no further definition, but the term appears intended to have a degree of flexibility. Note that (as circular HB/CTB A18/97 points out), the authority (not the rent officer) determines whether or not someone is an 'occupier'; and the term is not expressly limited to those whose circumstances are taken into account in the calculation of the claimant's entitlement to HB (though see below). It is clear that all the following should be included as 'occupiers' for this purpose:

- the claimant and members of his or her family (paras. 4.4-20); and
- everyone else who normally lives in the dwelling, such as non-dependants, (sub-)tenants, boarders, joint occupiers, certain carers (para. 4.26), foster children, and certain other children and young persons who do not count as a member of the family (para. 4.19).

**6.26** The Court of Appeal (*R v Swale Borough Council Housing Benefit Review Board ex p Marchant,* 1999) has held that a child who spends time in the homes of each of his or her parents (who live apart) counts as an 'occupier' only in the home of the parent who is 'responsible' for him or her (para. 4.16 – typically the one who receives child benefit). This case does not apply in other difficult situations. One example is that of a grown-up child who lives away from home for part(s) of the year (perhaps as a student) but returns home from time to time (perhaps in the holidays). It is clear that he or she counts as an 'occupier' in weeks in which he or she is treated as a non-dependant. In other weeks (if any), it can be argued that he or she counts as an 'occupier' (since the definition of 'occupier' appears flexible and is unaffected in this situation by the Marchant case), but it is unlikely that all local authorities will agree with this. Matters such as this are open to appeal.

## Table 6.5 THE RENT OFFICER'S SIZE CRITERIA

*These are relevant for size-related rent determinations (para. 6.24), exceptionally high rent determinations (para. 6.27) and local reference rent determinations (para. 6.28). For who counts as an occupier for these purposes, see paragraphs 6.25-26.*

- ◆ One room is allowed as a bedroom for each of the following occupiers, each occupier coming only within the first category which applies to him or her:
  - a married or unmarried couple (paras. 4.4, 4.6);
  - a single person aged 16 or more;
  - two children of the same sex under the age of 16;
  - two children (of the same or opposite sexes) under the age of 10;
  - a child under the age of 16.
- ◆ One, two or three living rooms ('rooms suitable for living in') are allowed as follows:
  - one if there are one to three occupiers;
  - two if there are four to six occupiers;
  - three if there are seven or more occupiers.
- ◆ The size criteria relate to the total number of rooms allowed (under either of the above headings). It is irrelevant whether the claimant actually uses those rooms as bedrooms or living rooms.

**Example: The rent officer's size criteria**

A couple have two children aged 6 and 8. No-one else lives with them. Their dwelling has three bedrooms, one living room, a kitchen, a bathroom, a toilet and several uninhabitable cupboards.

The rent officer's size criteria ignore the kitchen, bathroom and toilet. The criteria allow them four bedrooms/living rooms in all, as follows:

- ◆ one room as a bedroom for the couple;
- ◆ one room as a bedroom for the two children;
- ◆ two rooms as living rooms – because there are four occupiers.

Their four rooms (three bedrooms and one living room) do not exceed the size criteria because bedrooms and living rooms are interchangeable for these purposes.

## EXCEPTIONALLY HIGH RENT DETERMINATIONS

SI 1997 No. 1984
SI 1997 No. 1995
NIHBR sch 1A

**6.27** Except in the case of hostels (para. 6.10) or residential care homes or nursing homes (para. 3.5-11), the rent officer also determines whether either of the figures described above (paras. 6.23-26), or (if he or she has not made a determination in either of those cases) the referred rent for the dwelling, is 'exceptionally high'. If it is, he or she makes an exceptionally high rent determination: this is 'the highest rent, which is not an exceptionally high rent and which a landlord might reasonably have been expected to obtain' on a dwelling which:

- is in 'the same neighbourhood'(in Northern Ireland 'locality'); and
- matches the size criteria (table 6.4); and
- is in a reasonable state of repair.

'Neighbourhood' is defined in para. 6.20. Also the general rules and assumptions apply (para. 6.17).

## LOCAL REFERENCE RENT DETERMINATIONS

SI 1997 No. 1984
SI 1997 No. 1995
NIHBR sch 1A

**6.28** Except in the case of hostels (para. 6.10) or residential care homes or nursing homes (para. 3.5-11), the rent officer also determines whether any of the figures described above (paras. 8.23-27), or (if he or she has not made a determination in any of those cases) the referred rent for the dwelling, is greater than the 'local reference rent' described below. If it is, he or she makes a local reference rent determination (in other words, notifies the authority of the local reference rent). If it is not, he or she notifies the authority that it is not.

**6.29** In determining the 'local reference rent', the rent officer takes account of the range of rents 'which a landlord might reasonably have been expected to obtain' on dwellings which:

- are in 'the same *locality*'(in Great Britain this has been defined, but not in Northern Ireland); and
- match the size criteria (table 6.5) or have the same number of rooms as the claimant's dwelling, if less; and
- in the case of one-room dwellings, are in the same category as the claimant's dwelling (see below); and
- are let on an assured tenancy (or a similar tenancy or licence); and
- are in a reasonable state of repair.

'Locality' is defined in para. 6.19. Also the general rules and assumptions apply (para. 6.17).

The categories (mentioned above) of one-room dwellings are:

- one-room dwellings where a 'substantial' part of the rent is 'fairly attributable' to 'board and attendance' included within the rent;

- other one-room dwellings where the tenant shares a kitchen, toilet, bathroom and living room ('room suitable for living in') with someone who is not a member of his or her household (para. 6.4); and
- other one-room dwellings.

For the purposes of deciding whether it is a one-room dwelling in the first place, the definition of a 'room' is the same as in the note to table 8.6.

**6.30** The 'local reference rent' is then the figure which is half-way between:

- the lowest such rent which is not an 'exceptionally low rent'; and
- the highest such rent which is not an 'exceptionally high rent'.

## SINGLE ROOM RENT DETERMINATIONS

**6.31** Except in the case of hostels (para. 6.10) or residential care homes or nursing homes (para. 3.5-11), and only if the authority states in the referral that the claimant is a 'young individual' (para. 6.12), the rent officer also determines whether the claimant's rent is greater than the 'single room rent' described below. If it is, he or she makes a single room rent determination (in other words, notifies the authority of the single room rent). If it is not, he or she notifies the authority that it is not.

SI 1997 No. 1984
SI 1997 No. 1995
NIHBR sch 1A

**6.32** In determining the 'single room rent', the rent officer takes account of the range of rents 'which a landlord might reasonably have been expected to obtain' on dwellings which:

- provide exclusive use of one bedroom;
- provide no other bedroom;
- provide shared use of a living room ('room suitable for living in');
- provide shared use of a toilet and bathroom;
- provide shared use of a kitchen (and no exclusive use of facilities for cooking food);
- do not provide board and attendance;
- are in 'the same locality';
- are let on an assured tenancy (or a similar tenancy or licence);
- are in a reasonable state of repair.

'Locality' is defined in para. 6.19. Also the general rules and assumptions apply (para. 6.17).

**6.33** The 'single room rent' is then the figure which is half-way between:

- the lowest such rent which is not an 'exceptionally low rent'; and
- the highest such rent which is not an 'exceptionally high rent'.

## SERVICE CHARGES DETERMINATIONS

SI 1997 No. 1984
SI 1997 No. 1995
NIHBR sch 1A

**6.34** Except in the case of a hostel (para. 6.10); the rent officer must determine the value of the ineligible service charges (apart from meals and support charges) he or she excluded in making the claim-related rent determination (unless the amount is negligible).

## JOINT OCCUPIERS

SI 1997 No. 1984
SI 1997 No. 1995
NIHBR sch 1A

**6.35** In the case of accommodation occupied by joint occupiers, the rent officer's determinations (apart from the single room rent determination) relate to the dwelling as a whole. In some areas, the rent officer may suggest an apportionment but this is not binding on the authority.

## NOTIFICATION AND TIME LIMITS (GB only)

SI 1997 No. 1984
SI 1997 No. 1995

**6.36** The rent officer has a duty to notify the authority of the following:

- the claim-related rent (all cases);
- the local reference rent (if any);
- the single room rent (if any);
- except in the case of a hostel (para. 6.10), the value of the ineligible service charges (apart from meals and support charges) he or she has excluded in making his or her claim-related rent determination;
- whether the claim-related rent includes an amount for ineligible meals (as can be the case if it is an exceptionally high rent determination).

**6.37** The rent officer should notify the authority of the above determinations within five working days or, if the rent officer intends to inspect the dwelling, within 25 working days (or, in either case, as soon as reasonably practicable after that). The period begins on the day the rent officer receives the referral from the authority or (if he or she has requested this) on the day he or she receives further information needed from the authority.

**Table 6.6 INDICATIVE RENT LEVELS: THE RENT OFFICER'S CATEGORIES OF DWELLING**

(a) One-room dwellings where a 'substantial' part of the rent is 'fairly attributable' to 'board and attendance' included within the rent.

(b) Other one-room dwellings where the tenant shares a kitchen or toilet with someone who is not a member of his or her household (para. 4.3).

(c) Other one-room dwellings.

(d) Two-room dwellings.

(e) Three-room dwellings.

(f) Four-room dwellings.

(g) Five-room dwellings.

(h) Six-room dwellings.

**Note: Definition of 'room'**

For these purposes, a 'room' is defined as a 'bedroom or room suitable for living in':

- including a room the claimant shares with any member of his or her household, including a non-dependant (para. 4.21), or with a boarder or (sub-)tenant (paras. 4.23, 4.25);
- but (in the case of one-room dwellings: categories (a) to (c)) excluding a room he or she shares with anyone else.

## INDICATIVE RENT LEVELS

**6.38** Separate from the provisions described above, the rent officer provides each authority, on the first working day of each month, with 'indicative rent levels' for its area. The law allows the authority to take these into account in estimating payments on account (para. 16.16), and the subsidy rules encourage this. Indicative rent levels do not apply to site rents for caravans or mobile homes, houseboat moorings or rental purchase agreements. (They also do not take account of the rent officer's size criteria: table 8.5.)

SI 1997 No. 1984
SI 1997 No. 1995
NIHBR sch 1A

**6.39** One 'indicative rent level' is provided for each category of dwelling shown in table 8.6. In determining the indicative rent level for each category, the rent officer takes account of the range of rents 'which a landlord might reasonably have been expected to obtain' on dwellings which:

- are in that category;
- are in the area of the authority (not 'the locality' of the dwelling);
- are let on an assured tenancy (or a similar tenancy or licence); and
- are in a reasonable state of repair;
- adjusted – as regards service charges only – in accordance with the general rules and assumptions (para. 6.17).

**6.40** The 'indicative rent level' for each category is then:

- the lowest such rent which is not an 'exceptionally low rent'; plus
- one-quarter of the difference between that and the highest such rent which is not an 'exceptionally high rent'.

## Appeals and errors (GB only)

### APPEALS BY THE CLAIMANT

HBR 12CA **6.41** If a claimant makes written representations to the authority relating wholly or partly to any determination by the rent officer (and does so within six weeks of notification of the HB decision based on that rent officer determination), the authority must, within seven days of receipt apply to the rent officer for a re-determination for the case in question. The authority must forward the claimant's representations at the same time. This must be done even if the representations are made by a later claimant at the same address. There are however limitations (in the next paragraph).

HBR 12CA **6.42** For any particular claimant and any particular dwelling, only one application to the rent officer may be made in respect of any particular determination (plus one in respect of any particular substitute determination: para. 6.49). This is the case regardless of whether the authority itself has previously chosen to make an application for a re-determination.

**6.43** However, a claimant who considers that a referral should or should not have been made in the first place (e.g. a claimant who disputes whether he or she falls within one of the exceptions described earlier in this chapter) has the right to use the ordinary HB appeals procedure (chapter 19) to challenge this. This is because the determination whether or not to refer a case to the rent officer is made by the authority.

### APPEALS BY THE AUTHORITY

HBR 12B **6.44** The authority may itself choose to apply to the rent officer for a re-determination. For any particular claimant and any particular dwelling, it may do this only once in respect of any particular determination (plus once in respect of any particular substitute determination: para. 6.49); unless a re-determination is subsequently made as a result of an appeal by the claimant (para. 6.41), in which case the authority may do this once more.

### RENT OFFICER RE-DETERMINATIONS

SI 1997 No. 1984
SI 1997 No. 1995 **6.45** In each of the cases described above (paras. 6.41-44), the rent officer must make a complete re-determination. Even if the application for a re-determination relates only to one figure, the rent officer has to reconsider all matters pertaining to the case in question. All the assumptions, etc, applying to determinations (para. 6.14 onwards) apply equally to re-determinations. Re-determinations should be made within 20 working days or as soon as practicable after that. The period begins on the day the rent officer receives the application from the authority or (if he or she has requested this) on the day he or she receives further information needed from the authority.

**6.46** The rent officer making the re-determination (called a 're-determination officer') must seek and have regard to the advice of one or two other rent officers. In England, the rent service (formerly the rent officer service) has set up independent re-determination units and advises that reasons for their re-determinations are always supplied to the claimant and the authority. Similar arrangements are in place in Wales and Scotland. It would certainly be open to challenge if reasons were not given (as happened fairly frequently in the past).

## HOW THE RE-DETERMINATION AFFECTS HB

**6.47** In broad terms, re-determinations affect HB in the same way as determinations (para. 6.4). However, in 'New Scheme' cases (para. 10.7), the following further rules apply:

- If the effect of the re-determination is that the 'maximum rent' increases, this applies from the date of the rent officer's original determination. So the claimant is awarded any resulting arrears of HB (but this applies only to the claimant in question, not to a previous claimant at the same address).
- If the effect of the re-determination is that the 'maximum rent' reduces, this applies from the date of the rent officer's re-determination following the appeal: the reduction is not applied retrospectively. So it does not mean (unless the authority delays applying it) that the claimant has been overpaid HB.

## DEALING WITH ERRORS

**6.48** The rent officer has a duty to notify the authority, as soon as is practicable, upon discovering that he or she has made an error, other than one of professional judgment, in a determination or re-determination (including a substitute determination or substitute re-determination). SI 1997 No. 1984 SI 1997 No. 1995

**6.49** In such cases the authority must apply to the rent officer for a substitute determination (or substitute re-determination). The authority must also do this if it discovers that it made an error in its application to the rent officer as regards the size of the dwelling, the number of occupiers, the composition of the household or the terms of the tenancy. In all such cases, the authority must state the nature of the error and withdraw any outstanding applications for rent officer determinations in that case. HBR 12C, 12D

**6.50** All the assumptions, etc, applying to determinations (para. 6.17 onwards) also apply to substitute determinations/re-determinations. In broad terms, substitute determinations and substitute re-determinations affect HB in the same way as re-determinations (para. 6.47). SI 1997 No. 1984 SI 1997 No. 1995

## Appeals (NI only)

NIDAR 4(1) sch para 1

In Northern Ireland a decision to restrict the rent is made by the Executive so the decision can be revised or superceded in the normal way. Application for a revision must be made wihin one month. However, a decision which restricts the rent cannot be appealed.

## Pre-tenancy determinations

**6.51** People can find out whether their HB would be likely to be restricted if they claimed HB, by asking for a 'pre-tenancy determination' ('PTD').

### HOW TO GET A PRE-TENANCY DETERMINATION

HBR 12A(8) SI 1997 No. 1984 SI 1997 No. 1995 NIHBR 12A(5), sch 1A

**6.52** Any 'prospective occupier' of any dwelling (other than a council letting) may apply to the authority requesting it to refer the rent to the rent officer. So may any current occupier of a dwelling whose current agreement commenced at least 11 months previously and who is contemplating entering a new agreement there (but see para. 6.55). Authorities have standard forms for people who require a PTD.

HBR 12A(1)(c) NIHBR 12A(1)

**6.53** The main conditions for getting a PTD are that the person must:

- indicate on the form that he or she would be likely to claim HB if he or she took up the letting (or took up the new agreement);
- sign the form; and
- obtain a signature on the form from the landlord consenting to a referral. The landlord will be expected to provide the rent officer with necessary information and allow access to the dwelling.

### THE AUTHORITY'S DUTIES

**6.54** With two exceptions (para. 6.55), whenever an authority receives a request for a PTD, it must refer the details to the rent officer within two working days of the date of the request for the PTD. The rent officer's duties in such cases are described in paragraph 6.56.

**6.55** First, if the request for the PTD is invalid (e.g. if the landlord has not consented), the authority must return it to the person along with a notification of why it is invalid. Secondly, if:

- the authority already has a rent officer determination which was made for the dwelling in question; and
- the conditions for making a further referral to the rent officer are not met (table 8.2),

the authority must, within four working days of the request for the PTD, supply details of that determination to the person along with a notification of why a current PTD referral cannot be made.

## THE RENT OFFICER'S DUTIES (GB only)
## HOUSING EXECUTIVE DUTY TO MAKE A DECISION (NI only)

**6.56** When the rent officer receives a referral requesting a PTD, he or she makes the same determinations as in any other case referred to him or her. The rent officer notifies the result to the authority within five working days. In Northern Ireland where the Executive receives a PTD it should make a decision within seven days. SI 1997 No. 1984 SI 1997 No. 1995 NIHBR 12A(3)

## CLAIMS FOR HB FOLLOWING A PRE-TENANCY DETERMINATION

**6.57** With two exceptions (para. 6.58), when the authority receives an HB claim on a dwelling to which a PTD applies, the authority uses the PTD in the same way as if it had been a rent officer determination made following the claim (i.e. no additional referral is required). HBR 10, 11, 12A

**6.58** The PTD does not apply, and a referral must be made to the rent officer, if:

- the PTD was made more than 12 months ago; or
- the circumstances indicated in the claim for HB are different from those indicated in the request for the PTD (i.e. there are differences between them which constitute a 'relevant change of circumstances': para. 6.11).

## CALCULATING 'MAXIMUM RENTS' FROM PRE-TENANCY DETERMINATIONS

**6.59** With the exceptions described in the previous and following paragraphs, whenever the authority is required to calculate a 'maximum rent' in assessing a claimant's eligible rent (chapter 10), it uses the rent officer figures provided in the PTD. HBR 11(6A),(6B) NIHBR 11(7),(8)

**6.60** If the claimant's actual rent at the date of his or her claim for HB is lower than the 'maximum rent' calculated from the rent officer figures provided in the PTD, similar points arise as in paragraph 10.40.

## APPEALS

**6.61** There is no right of appeal relating to a pre-tenancy determination until and unless it is used in connection with the determination of a claim for HB (in which case the ordinary rules about appeals about rent officer determinations apply: paras. 6.36 onwards).

# 7 Calculating HB and main CTB

**7.1** This chapter explains how to calculate HB and 'main CTB'. Chapter 10 describes the other type of CTB known as 'second adult rebate'. This chapter covers:

- how to calculate HB and main CTB;
- non-dependant deductions;
- the discretionary housing payments scheme;
- local schemes;
- reductions in HB/CTB following conviction for certain offences; and
- how figures are converted to weekly amounts.

**7.2** HB and main CTB are dealt with together because they are similar to each other (whereas the method of calculating second adult rebate is completely different). However, it is perfectly possible to be entitled to only one (chapter 3).

**7.3** In general terms, claimants with no income or low income (including all claimants on income support or income-based jobseeker's allowance qualify for maximum benefit – which may be reduced if there are non-dependants in their home. The more income claimants have, the less benefit they get, but there is no general upper limit. The level of income at which benefit entitlement runs out varies from claimant to claimant depending on a wide range of factors.

## The calculation

**7.4** The next few paragraphs explain with examples how to calculate entitlement to HB and main CTB on a weekly basis. Table 7.1 summarises the rules. (Different rules apply to 'extended payments' of HB/CTB: para. 17.88.) Although both benefits are always awarded for specific benefit weeks (para. 5.43), some of the CTB regulations are expressed on a daily basis. For example, the 'taper' mentioned in paragraph 7.14 is given as 2$\frac{6}{7}$ per cent per day (exactly equal to 20 per cent per week). However, this is because of technicalities in the operation of the council tax itself. The 'weekly benefit' approach is adopted in this guide, with variations being described when they arise.

## MAXIMUM BENEFIT

**7.5** The starting point for all calculations of HB and main CTB is the claimant's 'maximum benefit'. On a weekly basis, this is:

CBA 130(1),(4)
NICBA 129 (1),(4)
HBR 61
CBA 131(1),(3),(4),(10)
CTBR 51(1)

- in calculating HB:
  - the whole of the claimant's weekly eligible rent (chapter 10),
  - minus any non-dependant deductions which may apply;
- in calculating main CTB:
  - the whole of the claimant's weekly eligible council tax (chapter 9),
  - minus any non-dependant deductions which may apply.

Note that 'maximum benefit' does not mean the same as 'maximum rent' (para. 10.29).

## CLAIMANTS ON INCOME SUPPORT OR JSA(IB)

**7.6** A claimant qualifies for maximum benefit whilst he or she (or any partner) is:

CBA 130(1),(3),
NICBA 129(1),(3)
HBR sch 4 paras 4, 4A
sch 5 paras 5, 5A
CBA 131(5),(8)
CTBR sch 4 paras 4, 4A
sch 5 paras 5, 5A

- on income support; or
- on JSA(IB); or
- treated as receiving income support or JSA(IB) (as described in the next paragraph).

**7.7** A claimant is treated as receiving income support or JSA(IB) (and so qualifies for maximum benefit) whilst he or she (or any partner) is:

HBR 2(1), (3A)
CTBR 2(1), (3A)

- entitled to JSA(IB) but not receiving it because of a sanction; or
- in the waiting days before his or her JSA(IB) starts – or would start apart from a sanction; or
- subject to a restriction in his or her income support or JSA(IB) as a result of breaching a community order.

## CLAIMANTS NOT ON INCOME SUPPORT OR JSA(IB)

**7.8** In any case other than those described above, if the claimant's capital (valued as in chapters 13 to 15) is over £16,000, then he or she does not qualify for any HB or main CTB at all, and so the remainder of this chapter does not apply. Otherwise, the claimant's income (chapters 13 to 15) is compared with his or her applicable amount (chapter 12).

**7.9** If the claimant has no income; or has income which is less than, or equal to, his or her applicable amount; the claimant is entitled to maximum benefit. In other words, the claimant receives the same amount as if he or she was on income support or JSA(IB). (In some cases, the claimant may actually qualify for income support or JSA(IB), and should be advised of this.)

CBA s.130(1),(3),
NICBA 129(1),(3)

CBA s.130(1),(3), 131(5),(8)
NICBA 129(1),(3)

**7.10** If the claimant's income is more than his or her applicable amount, the difference between the two is known as 'excess income'. The claimant's maximum benefit is reduced by a percentage of this excess income, to give the amount of entitlement.

HBR 62
CTBR 53

**7.11** The percentage used in calculating HB is different from that used in calculating main CTB. For weekly calculations, the percentages are as follows. They are also known as 'tapers':

- 65 per cent in calculating HB;
- 20 per cent in calculating main CTB.

The effect is that for each £1 of excess income a claimant has, his or her maximum benefit is reduced by 65p per week in HB, and by 20p per week in CTB.

## MINIMUM BENEFIT AND ROUNDING

HBR 64(2)

**7.12** If the weekly amount of HB calculated as above is less than 50p, then it is not awarded. There is no equivalent rule in CTB, where there is no minimum award of benefit.

HBR 69(9)
NIHBR 69(8)

**7.13** In HB, the authority may round any amount involved in the calculation to the nearest penny, halfpennies being rounded upwards. In CTB, there is no similar rule: indeed the DSS recommends that entitlement should be calculated to six decimal places (GM para. B3.26). This is to avoid reconciliation errors at the end of the financial year. Notifications sent to claimants about their entitlement may be rounded to the nearest penny.

## MAIN CTB AND THE 'BETTER BUY'

CBA s.131(9)

**7.14** If the amount of a claimant's main CTB calculated as above is lower than his or her entitlement to second adult rebate, he or she will not get main CTB, but will get second adult rebate instead. This is because of the 'better buy' comparison, described in paragraphs 8.29 onwards. Examples are given at the end of chapter 8.

## HB AND RENT-FREE PERIODS

HBR 70(1)

**7.15** The following additional rules apply if a claimant has rent-free weeks or other rent-free periods. They do not apply in cases where a landlord has waived the rent in return for works carried out by the tenant (para. 4.26).

HBR 70(2)

**7.16** No HB is awarded during rent-free periods, including in Northern Ireland rate free periods where rates are paid with the rent. HB is awarded only for periods in which rent is due, during which periods the calculation factors (i.e. applicable amount, income and any non-dependant deductions) are adjusted *pro rata:*

- If rent is expressed on a weekly basis: multiply the calculation factors by 52 or 53, then divide by the number of weeks when rent is due in that year.

- If rent is not expressed on a weekly basis: multiply the calculation factors by 366 or 365, then divide by the number of days when rent is due in that year.

**Table 7.1 AMOUNT OF HB AND MAIN CTB: SUMMARY**

| HOUSING BENEFIT | MAIN COUNCIL TAX BENEFIT |
| --- | --- |
| Weekly eligible rent | Weekly eligible council tax |
| MINUS ↓ | MINUS ↓ |
| Any non-dependant deductions which apply | Any non-dependant deductions which apply |
| MINUS ↓ | MINUS ↓ |
| 65% of excess income (if claimant is not on IS or JSA(IB)) | 20% of excess income (if claimant is not on IS or JSA(IB)) |
| EQUALS ↓ | EQUALS ↓ |
| Weekly entitlement to HB | Weekly entitlement to main CTB |

## Non-dependant deductions

**7.17** HB and main CTB are normally reduced for each non-dependant living in the claimant's home. The next paragraphs explain when a deduction is or is not made, and the additional rules involved. In main CTB, the amounts of the deductions and some of the other rules are different from those applying in HB. The differences are mentioned whenever they arise. HBR 61 CTBR 51(1)

**7.18** Non-dependants are usually adult sons, daughters, other relatives or friends who live in the claimant's household on a non-commercial basis (paras. 4.21-22). Some claimants receive money from their non-dependants to pay for their keep. This may include a contribution towards rent, council tax, food or household expenses. This money is not treated as the claimants' income (table 15.3). Instead deductions are made from the claimant's HB and main CTB. However, these deductions are not related to what the non-dependant actually pays. They are fixed sums which apply even if the non-dependant pays the claimant nothing at all. The level of deductions (table 7.3) is high in some cases, and may cause claimants hardship.

## Examples: Calculating HB and main CTB

### SINGLE CLAIMANT ON INCOME SUPPORT OR JSA(IB)

A single claimant has no non-dependants: she lives alone. Her eligible rent is £55.00 per week. The council tax on her home would be £8.00 per week apart from the fact that she qualifies for a 25% council tax discount, which reduces her liability to £6.00 per week.

Claimants on income support or JSA(IB) get maximum benefit – which is based on their eligible rent and eligible council tax.

| | | |
|---|---|---|
| HB: | Eligible rent | |
| | equals weekly HB | £55.00 |
| Main CTB: | Eligible council tax | |
| | equals weekly main CTB | £6.00 |

### CLAIMANT NOT ON INCOME SUPPORT OR JSA(IB)

A couple have no non-dependants. They are not on income support or JSA(IB). Their joint weekly income exceeds their applicable amount by £20.00. Their eligible rent is £50.00 per week. Their eligible council tax liability is £7.56 per week.

Claimants with excess income get maximum benefit minus a percentage of their excess income.

| | | |
|---|---|---|
| HB: | Eligible rent | £50.00 |
| | minus 65% of excess income (65% x £20.00) | £13.00 |
| | equals weekly HB | £37.00 |
| Main CTB: | Eligible council tax | £7.56 |
| | minus 20% of excess income (20% x £20.00) | £4.00 |
| | equals weekly main CTB | £3.56 |

## CASES IN WHICH NO DEDUCTION IS MADE

**7.19** As described in paragraphs 7.24-26, there are three types of case in which no non-dependant deduction is made. HBR 3(2) CTBR 3(2)

**7.20** No deduction applies in respect of any of the following, because they are defined in the law as not being non-dependants (para. 4.21):

- children aged under 16 and young persons aged 16 to 18 inclusive (whether or not they are counted as a member of the family for HB/CTB purposes);
- boarders, (sub-)tenants and joint occupiers;
- carers provided by a charity or voluntary organisation for whom the claimant or partner are charged;
- the claimant's landlord and members of the landlord's household (this applies only in HB: it is irrelevant in main CTB).

**Table 7.2 NON-DEPENDANTS FOR WHOM NO DEDUCTION APPLIES: SUMMARY**

- Non-dependants on income support or income-based jobseeker's allowance. However in HB (but not main CTB) there is a deduction if they are aged 25 or more.
- Non-dependants under 18.
- Non-dependants who are full-time students. However in HB (but not main CTB) there is a deduction in the summer vacation if they take up remunerative work.
- Non-dependants receiving a Work Based Training Allowance.
- Non-dependants in prison or otherwise detained.
- Non-dependants who have been in hospital for more than six weeks.
- Non-dependants who normally live elsewhere.
- Non-dependants who fall within any of the groups who are 'disregarded persons' for council tax discount purposes. However this applies in main CTB only. In HB there is a deduction (unless they fall within any of the earlier entries in this table).

**Note:**
Appendix 7 gives full information about all the above categories of people. It includes all the 'disregarded persons' mentioned above – such as (in various circumstances) education leavers, students, student nurses, apprentices, people who are severely mentally impaired, and carers.

HBR 2(1), 63(6)
CTBR 2(1), 52(6)

**7.21** There are no non-dependant deductions in either HB or main CTB if the claimant or any partner:

- is registered blind or has ceased to be registered blind within the past 28 weeks because of regaining sight (para. 12.20); or
- receives the care component of disability living allowance payable at any rate (para. 12.22); or
- receives attendance allowance payable at any rate or constant attendance allowance (including the related benefits in para. 12.24).

In such cases, if the claimant has more than one non-dependant, no deduction applies for any of them. (Note that the second and third cases cease to apply when disability living allowance or attendance allowance themselves cease – for example, when the claimant or partner have been in hospital for four weeks.)

HBR 63(1),(7),(8)
CTBR 52(1),
(2),(7),(8)

**7.22** No deduction applies in respect of any non-dependant who falls within certain groups. The main groups are summarised in table 7.2. As indicated there, there are some differences between the groups applying for HB purposes and those applying for main CTB purposes. Appendix 6 defines all the relevant categories of people and gives the detailed rules about whether a non-dependant deduction applies in HB and main CTB.

## CASES IN WHICH A DEDUCTION IS MADE

HBR 63(1),(2)
CTBR 52(1),(2)

**7.23** In cases other than those described above, a non-dependant deduction is made. The amount depends upon whether the non-dependant is in 'remunerative work' (para. 7.33) and, if so, on the level of his or her gross income. The amounts for HB and main CTB are different, and are listed in table 7.3. Additional rules for claimants who are joint occupiers and for non-dependant couples are in paragraphs 7.37-38.

## NON-DEPENDANTS IN REMUNERATIVE WORK

HBR 63(1),(2)
CTBR 52(1),(2)

**7.24** For non-dependants in remunerative work, there are six possible levels of deduction in HB and four in main CTB (table 7.3), depending in either case on the level of the non-dependant's gross income (unless no deduction is appropriate at all: paras. 7.23-26).

HBR 63(9)
CTBR 52(9)

**7.25** It is the non-dependant's gross income, not net income, which is relevant. So long as the non-dependant is in remunerative work, the rule relates to his or her income from all sources. The only exception is that the following types of income are always disregarded:

- disability living allowance (either or both components: para. 12.22);
- attendance allowance and constant attendance allowance (including the related benefits in para. 12.24);

- payments from the Macfarlane Trusts, the Eileen Trust, the Fund or the Independent Living Funds, including payments in kind from these sources and payments of money which originally derived from them (para. 13.40).

**Table 7.3 SUMMARY OF WEEKLY NON-DEPENDANT DEDUCTIONS**

| | Deduction in HB | Deduction in main CTB |
|---|---|---|
| Non-dependants in remunerative work with gross income of: | | |
| £281.00 per week or more | £47.75 | £6.95 |
| between £225.00 and £280.99 per week | £43.50 | £5.80 |
| between £170.00 and £224.99 per week | £38.20 | £4.60 |
| between £131.00 and £169.99 per week | £23.35 | £4.60 |
| between £88.00 and £130.99 per week | £17.00 | £2.30 |
| under £88.00 per week | £7.40 | £2.30 |
| Non-dependants not in remunerative work (regardless of income level) | £7.40 | £2.30 |

**Note:**
'Remunerative work' is defined in paras. 7.33 onwards.

**7.26** As regards any other source of income, there are no rules saying how the gross amount is to be assessed, though none of the disregards in chapter 14 applies. The DSS advises that for non-dependants with savings, the gross actual interest received should be included here (GM para. A5.18).

**7.27** It is up to individual authorities to decide what level of evidence is required about the income of a non-dependant in remunerative work. If there is no evidence, the highest deduction is made (table 7.3). In such cases, if the evidence is later provided, and reveals that a lower deduction should have been made, this means that the claimant has been awarded too little benefit: the claimant must be awarded the arrears (but this is usually subject to a 52 weeks limit on retrospective increases: paras. 17.52-53).

## NON-DEPENDANTS NOT IN REMUNERATIVE WORK

**7.28** For non-dependants not in remunerative work, the lowest level of deduction applies in both HB and main CTB (table 7.3) regardless of the amount – if any – of the non-dependant's income (unless no deduction is appropriate at all: paras. 7.23-26). HBR 63(1) CTBR 52(1)

## 'REMUNERATIVE WORK'

`HBR 4(1)
CTBR 4(1)

**7.29** Remunerative work is work:

- for which payment is made, or expected to be made; and
- which averages 16 hours or more per week.

HBR 4(2)-(4)
CTBR 4(2)-(4)

**7.30** In calculating a weekly average of income, authorities should take into account any recognisable cycle. If there is no such cycle, they should take into account the expected hours of work per week and also (except where the non-dependant is just starting work) the average during the period immediately prior to the claim. This period should be five weeks unless some other period would result in a more accurate estimation in an individual case.

HBR 4(4)
CTBR 4(4)

**7.31** Once it is established that a person is in remunerative work, he or she continues to count as being in remunerative work during any recognised, customary or other holiday, and also during any period of absence without good cause (but not during sick leave or maternity leave: para. 7.35).

HBR 4(2A)
CTBR 4(2A)

**7.32** A further rule applies to people employed in schools, other educational establishments, or anywhere else where their recognisable cycle of work is one year. Their average weekly hours are found by considering only the periods when they work (e.g. school term-times). The result applies both during those periods and during the periods when they do not work (e.g. school holidays). (Note however that changes in income – e.g. between term-time and holidays – are taken into account.)

HBR 2(1), 4(5), (6),(7)
CTBR 2(1),4(5), 5(A), (6),(7)

**7.33** A non-dependant is treated as not being in remunerative work in any of the following cases:

- in any benefit week during which he or she receives income support or income-based jobseeker's allowance for four days or more (regardless of his or her other circumstances);
- on any day on which she is on maternity leave, i.e. is absent from work because she is pregnant or has given birth, and has a right to return to work under her contract or under employment law;
- on any day on which he or she is absent from work because he or she is ill (whether or not receiving statutory sick pay and regardless of whether the employer is making up his or her wages). However, an absence due to illness which falls wholly within a benefit week (Monday to Sunday) will not be taken into account, because of the rules on changes of circumstances (para. 17.16);
- on any day on which he or she is on the 'intensive activity period' of the new deal pilots for those aged 25 or more;
- on any day for which he or she has been or will be paid a Sports Council sports award, so long as he or she is not expected to receive any other payment for that day.

**Examples: Calculating HB and main CTB**

**CLAIMANT ON INCOME SUPPORT WITH WORKING NON-DEPENDANT**

A lone parent is on income support. Her eligible rent is £65.00 per week. Her eligible council tax liability is £8.00 per week. Her 26-year-old son lives with her. He earns £300 per week gross for a 35-hour week.

Claimants on income support get maximum benefit, which in this case involves a non-dependant deduction. The son is in remunerative work with gross income of at least £281 per week, so the highest level of deduction applies in both HB and main CTB.

| | | |
|---|---|---|
| HB: | Eligible rent | £65.00 |
| | minus non-dependant deduction, which in this case is | £47.75 |
| | equals weekly HB | £17.25 |
| Main CTB: | Eligible council tax | £8.00 |
| | minus non-dependant deduction, which in this case is | £6.95 |
| | equals weekly main CTB | £1.05 |

**CLAIMANT ON INCOME SUPPORT WITH NON-DEPENDANT ON INCOME SUPPORT**

The son in the previous example loses his job and starts receiving income support.

The calculation is as above, except that now there is no non-dependant deduction in main CTB and the lowest deduction applies in HB (table 7.2).

| | | |
|---|---|---|
| HB: | Eligible rent | £65.00 |
| | minus non-dependant deduction, which in this case is | £7.40 |
| | equals weekly HB | £57.60 |
| Main CTB: | Eligible council tax | £8.00 |
| | no non-dependant deduction applies | |
| | equals weekly main CTB | £8.00 |

**7.34** The following are also not remunerative work:

- education (since this is not 'work');
- training (since this is not 'work') including attendance on government training schemes and on the 'intensive activity period' of the New Deal (para. 11.41)(but those paid by their employer do not count as trainees);
- voluntary or other work for which the person is paid expenses only (since it is not 'remunerative');
- periods of lay-off (since this is absence with good cause).

## NON-DEPENDANT COUPLES

HBR 63(3),(4)
CTBR 52(3),(4)

**7.35** In the case of a non-dependant couple (or a polygamous marriage), only one deduction applies, being the higher (or highest) of any that would have applied to the individuals if they were single claimants. In appropriate cases, there is no deduction (e.g. if they are both under 18). For the purpose of the various gross income limits in table 7.3, each non-dependant partner is treated as possessing the gross income of both of them.

## NON-DEPENDANTS OF JOINT OCCUPIERS

HBR 63(5)
CTBR 52(35)

**7.36** The following rules apply when a claimant is jointly liable for the rent or council tax on his or her home with one or more other persons who are not his or her partner, and there is also a non-dependant living there. They would arise, for example, if a brother and sister are joint occupiers and have a non-dependant living with them. The law is slightly unclear in some of these cases but the key question is 'whose household is the non-dependant part of?' Having decided that, the rules work as follows:

- If the non-dependant is part of the household of only one of them, then the whole non-dependant deduction is made in any claim for benefit made by that one, and no deduction is made in any claim for benefit made by the others.
- If the non-dependant is part of the household of more than one of them, the amount of the non-dependant deduction is shared between them. Any of them claiming benefit gets his or her resulting share of the non-dependant deduction. In main CTB, the share must be equal between the joint occupiers (but only between the ones who are jointly liable for the council tax on the home: chapter 11). In HB, the share need not be equal: the authority should take into account the number of joint occupiers concerned and the proportion of rent each pays (chapter 12).

# Discretionary housing payments

**7.37** The Child Support, Pensions and Social Security Act 2000 introduced a scheme of Discretionary Housing Payments with effect from 2nd July 2001.

SI 2001 No. 1167
SI 2001 No. 2340
SR 2001 No. 216

**7.38** These payments are an independent scheme administered by authorities who also administer HB/CTB. However, they are not a form of HB or CTB, and so the HB/CTB appeals procedures (chapter 19) do not apply.

**7.39** Discretionary Housing Payments (DHPs) are available to claimants who:

- are entitled to HB and/or CTB; and
- 'appear to [the] authority to require some further financial assistance... in order to meet housing costs'.

**7.40** Discretionary housing payments cannot be awarded towards any of the following:

- ineligible service or support charges (chapter 10);
- any rent liability if the claimant is entitled to CTB only;
- any council tax liability if the claimant is entitled to HB only or to second adult rebate only;
- increases to cover rent arrears which are not eligible for HB (chapter 10);
- reductions in any benefit as a result of Child Support or One sanctions;
- amounts of HB/CTB that have been suspended (chapter 16).

**7.41** Furthermore the total weekly amount of the award, taken together with the claimant's award of HB or CTB, must not exceed:

- the claimant's eligible rent calculated as though he or she were a council tenant (chapter 10);
- the claimant's liability for council tax.

**7.42** So, for example, DHPs could be used for such things as the following:

- to make up for the effect of the hospital down-rating;
- to make up the shortfall in eligible rent in a 'New Scheme' case caused by the rent officer's figures being used;
- to make up the shortfall in eligible rent in an 'Old Scheme' case where the authority considers there is no other way of doing this;
- to make up the shortfall in eligible council tax caused by the restrictions to band E in certain cases;
- to make up for the effect of the 65 per cent HB and 20 per cent CTB tapers used in the calculation of benefit;
- to make up for the effect of non-dependant deductions.

**7.43** Unlike the pre-July 2001 exceptional hardship and exceptional circumstances payments, there is no requirement in the law for the claimant or family's circumstances to be 'exceptional' – nor for there to have to be 'hardship'. The payments are, however, entirely discretionary and authorities vary in their willingness to award them. While it may well be worth enquiring about and/or claiming a DHP, no claimant should rely on his or her authority actually awarding him a payment in the above (or any other) circumstances.

**7.44** The DWP partially subsidises DHPs and its predecessor the DSS issued guidance to authorities in a circular letter (not part of the normal HB/CTB series), 'Discretionary Housing Payments', 16.3.01.

## Local schemes (GB only)

AA s.134(8)-(10) 139 (6)-(8) SI 1996 No. 677 SI 1996 No. 678

**7.45** The HB and CTB schemes as described in this guide are those which authorities are required by law to operate. However, authorities may grant extra benefit under a 'local scheme' – that is, an improved version of the scheme. The only improvement authorities are permitted, however, is to disregard war disablement pensions and war widows' pensions, in whole or part, over and above the fixed disregard required by law (usually £10: para. 15.28). Some, but not all, authorities have decided to do this. The decision to run a local scheme is made by a resolution of the authority. The DSS advises that separate resolutions are required for HB and for CTB (GM para. B3.10). The question of whether or not an authority should run a local scheme is not open to the appeal procedure. Payments under local schemes are not eligible for subsidy.

SI 1996 No. 678

**7.46** For technical reasons, part of the cost of a local scheme is subject to a 'permitted total' of 0.7 per cent of the authority's HB/CTB expenditure. This should have no effect on an authority's power to operate a local scheme (circular HB/CTB A31/95).

## Reductions in HB/CTB following certain convictions

### WHEN THE REDUCTIONS APPLY

SI 2001 No. 4022 NISR 2002 No. 79

**7.47** New regulations come into force from 1st April 2002 under the auspices of the Social Security Fraud Act 2001. That Act provides for disqualifications from and reductions in various state benefits following certain convictions.

**7.48** HB and CTB are reduced in the following circumstances:

- the offender has committed two offences within three years (and neither of those has previously been the cause of a reduction under these rules); and
- the offender if he or she is the claimant, or the claimant whose family the offender is in, is not on income support or income-based jobseeker's allowance.

### AMOUNT AND DURATION OF REDUCTIONS

**7.49** The amounts of the reductions are as shown in table 7.4. They will be up-rated each April at the same time as the other HB/CTB rates. The reductions apply for 13 weeks, beginning on a date (after the second conviction) decided by the Secretary of State (via the benefits agency or jobcentre). In other words, it will not be for the authority to decide the start date; instead the authority will be bound by the decision of the Secretary of State. Note that the term 'seriously ill' is not defined in the Act or the regulations [check this], so it will be for authorities to decide the meaning, applying ordinary English, and will be subject to the appeal procedures.

**Table 7.4 WEEKLY AMOUNTS OF REDUCTIONS TO HB/CTB FOLLOWING CERTAIN CONVICTIONS**

| | Offender aged under 25 | Offender aged 25 or more |
|---|---|---|
| If the claimant, the offender, or any other member of the family is pregnant or seriously ill: | £8.55 | £10.80 |
| Other cases: | £17.10 | £21.60 |

## Conversion to weekly amounts

**7.50** The following paragraphs explain the rules that apply whenever figures involved in the calculation of HB and CTB (including second adult rebate) have to be converted to weekly amounts.

### RENT AND SERVICE CHARGES

**7.51** Whenever a weekly figure is needed for rent or for service charges, the following rules apply: HBR 69(1),(2)

- for rent or service charges due in multiples of weeks, divide the rent by the number of weeks it covers;
- for rent or service charges due daily, multiply the daily amount by seven;
- for rent or service charges due calendar monthly (or at any other intervals which are not multiples of weeks), divide the rent by the number of days it covers to find the daily rent, then multiply the daily rent by seven. This means there are two possibilities for a calendar monthly tenant: 12 months' rent or service charges can be divided by 365 (or 366 in appropriate years) and then multiplied by seven, or a particular month's rent or service charges can be divided by 28, 29, 30 or 31 (as appropriate) and then multiplied by seven.

Further rules apply if the claimant has rent-free periods (para. 7.19).

## COUNCIL TAX

CTBR 51(1)(b) **7.52** Whenever a weekly figure is needed for council tax liability, the following rules apply:

- for annual figures, divide the council tax by 365 (or 366 in financial years ending in a leap year) to find the daily figure, and then multiply the daily figure by seven;
- for figures which do not relate to a whole year, divide the council tax by the number of days it covers to find the daily figure, and then multiply the daily figure by seven.

## INCOME, ETC.

HBR 25(1) CTBR 17(1) **7.53** Whenever a weekly income figure is needed, the following rules apply:

- for an amount relating to a whole multiple of weeks, divide the amount by the number of weeks it covers;
- for an amount relating to a calendar month, multiply the amount by 12 to find the annual figure, then divide the annual figure by 52 or 53. In practice, authorities usually divide by 52 if there are 52 Mondays in the current financial year (as is the case in 2002-2003) or by 53 if there are 53, though the law does not specifically require this;
- for an amount relating to a year (this typically applies only to self-employed income), divide the amount by 365 (or 366 as appropriate) to find the daily figure, and then multiply the daily figure by seven;
- for an amount relating to any other period, divide the amount by the number of days it covers to find the daily figure, then multiply the daily figure by seven.

# 8 Second adult rebate

**8.1** This chapter explains the type of CTB known as 'second adult rebate'. It covers:

- who is eligible for second adult rebate;
- the information needed to establish eligibility;
- how to calculate second adult rebate;
- the information needed to do the calculation; and
- the 'better buy' comparison.

**8.2** In broad terms, second adult rebate is awarded when the claimant has a 'second adult' in his or her home who is on income support or income-based jobseeker's allowance or is on a low income. Although the level of the claimant's own income and capital (and that of the claimant's partner) is irrelevant, certain other circumstances of the claimant and other household members may prevent entitlement to second adult rebate. Also, because of the 'better buy' comparison (para. 8.29), second adult rebate is only awarded if the claimant does not qualify for the other type of CTB known as 'main CTB', or qualifies for more second adult rebate than main CTB. Chapter 7 gives details of how main CTB is calculated.

**8.3** This guide, in common with DSS guidance and most Benefits Agency and local authority forms and other documentation, uses the informal term 'second adult rebate' for what is known in the law as 'alternative maximum council tax benefit'.

## Eligibility for second adult rebate

CBA s.131(1),(3),(6),(7),(9)

**8.4** Several pieces of information are needed to establish whether a claimant is eligible for second adult rebate and, if so, how much it is to be. These are summarised in the flow chart in table 8.1, and described in detail below.

### PRESENCE OF SECOND ADULT

CBA s.131(6)(b),(7)(a),(11) CTBR 55(a),(c)

**8.5** A claimant can only qualify for second adult rebate if there is at least one 'second adult' in his or her home. A person can only be a 'second adult' if he or she:

- is a non-dependant or a particular type of carer (paras. 8.6-7); and
- is not a 'disregarded person' (para. 8.8).

**Table 8.1 SECOND ADULT REBATE FLOW CHART**

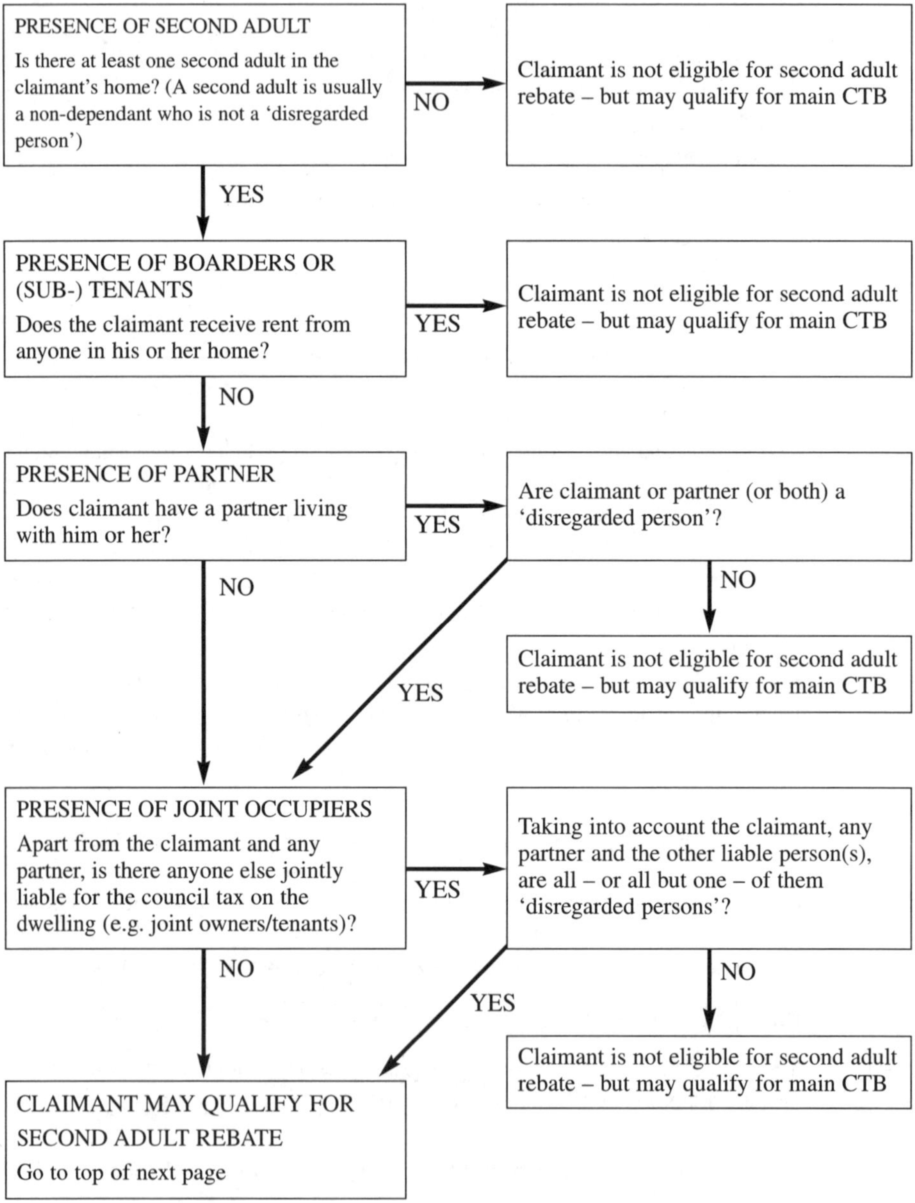

**Table 8.1 continued**

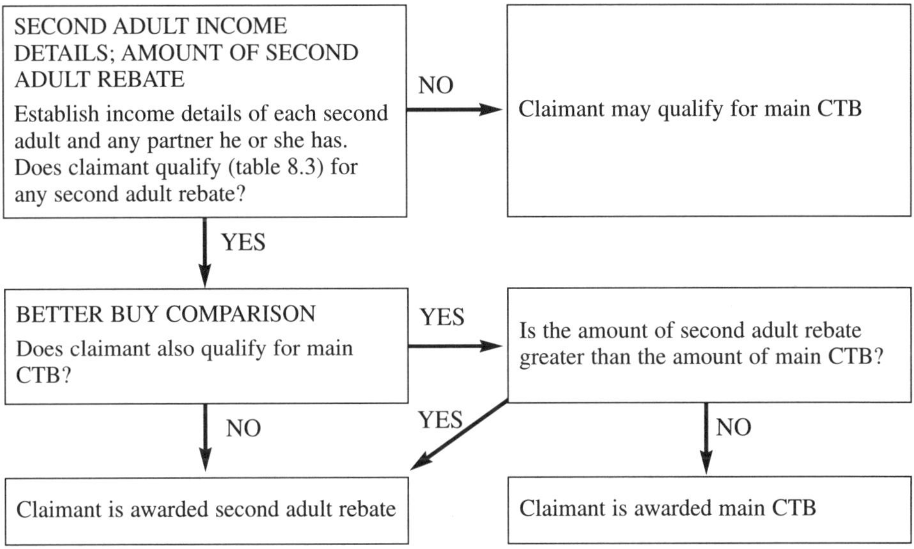


There may be two or more 'second adults' in the claimant's home: the claimant can still qualify for second adult rebate.

**8.6** A non-dependant is by far the most common kind of second adult so long as he or she is not a 'disregarded person'. Typical non-dependants are adult sons, daughters, other relatives or friends who live in the claimant's household on a non-commercial basis (para. 4.21).

**8.7** A person can also be a second adult if he or she is the type of carer who is defined in law as not being a non-dependant (para. 4.26) so long as he or she is not a 'disregarded person'. This kind of second adult is much less common – because many carers are 'disregarded persons'. (For the details, see categories 14 to 17 in appendix 6.)

**8.8** A 'disregarded person' cannot be a second adult. This means a person who falls within any of the groups who are disregarded for council tax discount purposes (para. 2.37). The main groups are summarised in table 8.2. Appendix 6 defines all the relevant categories of people and gives the detailed rules about whether they are 'disregarded persons'.

**Table 8.2 'DISREGARDED PERSONS': SIMPLIFIED SUMMARY**

- People under 18, or aged 18 if child benefit is payable.
- Education leavers under 20.
- Various students, foreign language assistants and student nurses.
- Youth Training trainees under 25.
- Apprentices on NCVQ/SVEC courses.
- People who are severely mentally impaired.
- Carers.
- People in prison or other forms of detention.
- People who normally live elsewhere.
- Members of religious communities.
- Diplomats and members of international bodies or of visiting forces.

## PRESENCE OF BOARDERS OR (SUB-)TENANTS

**8.9** A claimant who receives rent from any resident in his or her home is not eligible for second adult rebate (even if all the other conditions are fulfilled). Typically, this means that home-owner claimants with boarders or tenants, and tenant claimants with boarders or sub-tenants, cannot get second adult rebate. CBA s.131 (6)(a),(11) CTBR 2(1)

**8.10** The exclusion from entitlement applies only if the person paying rent is 'resident' in the claimant's dwelling. A 'resident' means a person aged 18 or more who has 'sole or main residence' there. Therefore, rent received from an under-18-year-old or a holiday maker does not prevent entitlement.

**Example: A couple who have a tenant**

A couple are liable for council tax on their home. The only people living with them are their adult son and a tenant. The tenant's letting agreement was signed by the woman in the couple, who takes all the responsibility for the letting and receives all the income from it.

They should ensure that the man is the claimant. No-one is liable to pay rent to him. So he may qualify for second adult rebate, so long as all the other conditions apply (and there are several in a case like this: table 8.1).

**8.11** The exclusion appears in the Act of Parliament rather than the regulations. The Act does not, however, define 'rent'. The regulations give a definition of 'rent' for other purposes as being (in broad terms) a payment which could be met by HB, and this definition seems appropriate here.

**8.12** The exclusion is worded in such a way that it applies only if someone is liable to pay rent to the claimant. It does not apply if someone is liable to pay rent to the claimant's partner (or any other resident).

## CLAIMANT'S INCOME AND CAPITAL

**8.13** None of the rules about eligibility for second adult rebate takes into account the amount of a claimant's (or partner's) income or capital in any way.

**8.14** The £16,000 capital limit (which applies for HB and main CTB) does not apply when second adult rebate is being considered. Millionaires can get second adult rebate (so long as they fulfil the appropriate conditions).

## CLAIMANT'S AND PARTNER'S OTHER CIRCUMSTANCES

CBA s.131(7)(b) **8.15** If the conditions mentioned earlier are satisfied, the final condition about eligibility for second adult rebate depends on whether the claim is made by:

- a single claimant or a lone parent (with no joint occupiers);
- a couple (with no joint occupiers); or
- a claimant who has joint occupiers.

## SINGLE CLAIMANTS AND LONE PARENTS

**8.16** There is no further condition if the claimant is single or a lone parent. It does not matter whether he or she is or is not a 'disregarded person'. But if the claimant is jointly liable for council tax, see paragraph 8.18.

## COUPLES

CTBR 55(b) **8.17** There is a further condition if the claimant is in a couple. Couples are eligible for second adult rebate only if at least one partner is a 'disregarded person' (para. 8.8). It does not matter whether this is the claimant or the partner – and so long as one of them is a 'disregarded person' it does not matter whether the other one is or is not a 'disregarded person'. But if the couple are jointly liable for council tax with some other person, see paragraph 8.18. A polygamous marriage is eligible for second adult rebate if all – or all but one – of the partners are 'disregarded persons'.

## JOINT OCCUPIERS

**8.18** There is also a further condition if the claimant is jointly liable for the council tax on his or her home with at least one other person (other than just his or her partner if the claim is made by a couple). In such cases, information is needed about all of these joint occupiers. Each one who makes a claim is eligible for second adult rebate so long as either: CTBR 55(d)

- all the joint occupiers are 'disregarded persons'; or
- all but one of the joint occupiers are 'disregarded persons'.

**8.19** This rule typically applies to joint owners and joint tenants. For example, if two sisters jointly own their home (and they have a second adult), each of them is eligible for second adult rebate so long as at least one of them is a 'disregarded person' (para. 8.8). Or if three single people jointly rent their home (and they have a second adult), each of them is eligible for second adult rebate so long as at least two of them are 'disregarded persons'.

**8.20** In all such cases, each joint occupier who makes a claim qualifies for his or her share of the total amount of second adult rebate. This share must always be equal between all the joint occupiers, including any who are students. CTBR 54(2),(3)

## CALCULATING SECOND ADULT REBATE

**8.21** Having established that the claimant is eligible for second adult rebate, the authority needs the following information in order to calculate the amount on a weekly basis:

- the claimant's weekly eligible council tax liability (para. 8.23); and
- details of the second adult's income or, if the claimant has more than one second adult, details of all the second adults' incomes (paras. 8.24 onwards).

**8.22** As shown in table 8.3, the amount of second adult rebate may be 25 per cent, 15 per cent or 7½ per cent of the claimant's weekly eligible council tax – depending on the income of the second adult(s). No matter how many second adults a claimant has, the claimant can only get one amount of second adult rebate. CTBR 2(3A), 54(1) sch 2 para 1(1)

**8.23** The amount of a claimant's eligible council tax liability is described in chapter 9. As described in that chapter, a claimant's eligible council tax can be lower than his or her actual council tax liability if his or her dwelling is in valuation band F, G or H. Paragraph 7.49 explains how to convert council tax figures to a weekly amount. Examples of the calculations follow. The last example illustrates how a 25 per cent discount is dealt with in calculations. The example at the end of this chapter illustrates the calculation of second adult rebate for joint occupiers.

## Table 8.3 THE PERCENTAGE OF COUNCIL TAX MET BY SECOND ADULT REBATE

FOR CLAIMANTS WITH ONE SECOND ADULT

| | |
|---|---|
| If the second adult is on income support or JSA(IB)* | 25% |
| If the second adult is not on income support or JSA(IB) and his or her income** is: | |
| £170.00 per week or more | nil |
| between £131.00 and £169.99 per week | 7½% |
| under £131.00 per week | 15% |

FOR CLAIMANTS WITH TWO OR MORE SECOND ADULTS

| | |
|---|---|
| If all the second adults are on income support or JSA(IB)* | 25% |
| If at least one of the second adults is not on income support or JSA(IB) and the combined gross income of all the second adults*** is: | |
| £170.00 per week or more | nil |
| between £131.00 and £169.99 per week | 7½% |
| under £131.00 per week | 15% |

**Notes**

* For these purposes, a person is treated as receiving JSA(IB) (income-related jobseeker's allowance) if he or she is:

- entitled to JSA(IB) but not receiving it because of a sanction; or
- in the waiting days before his or her JSA(IB) starts – or would start apart from a sanction.

** If the second adult has a partner, the partner's income is added into the second adult's income.

*** For each second adult who has a partner, the partner's income is added into the combined income of the second adults. The income of any second adult who is on income support or JSA(IB) (or whose partner is) is disregarded.

### ASSESSING SECOND ADULTS' GROSS INCOME

CTBR sch 2 paras 2,3

**8.24** To calculate the amount of second adult rebate (table 8.3), it is necessary to assess the gross income of any second adult who is not on income support or JSA(IB) (or treated as receiving JSA(IB): table 8.3). If the second adult has a partner, the partner's income is added in with the second adult's income (even if the partner is a 'disregarded person' and so could not be a second adult in his or her own right). If the gross income is £170.00 per week or more, the claimant does not qualify for second adult rebate.

**Examples: Calculating second adult rebate**

**SINGLE CLAIMANT WITH SECOND ADULT ON JSA(IB)**

A single claimant is the only person liable for council tax on his home. The only person living with him is his adult daughter, who is on JSA(IB). Neither the claimant nor his daughter is a 'disregarded person'. His eligible council tax liability is £8.00 per week.

*Eligible for second adult rebate?*

As a single claimant, he is eligible for second adult rebate because:

- he has a second adult living with him (his daughter); and
- he does not receive rent from a boarder or (sub-)tenant.

*Amount of second adult rebate*

His daughter is on JSA(IB) so the weekly amount is:

25% of weekly eligible council tax (25% x £8.00) £2.00

**COUPLE WITH TWO SECOND ADULTS**

A couple are the only people liable for council tax on their home. The only people living with them are their two adult sons. One son is on JSA(IB). The other son is working and his gross pay is £128 per week. He also has savings which generate a weekly gross interest of £5 per week. One partner in the couple is a full-time mature university student. The other partner and the sons are not 'disregarded persons'. The couple's eligible council tax liability is £10.00 per week.

*Eligible for second adult rebate?*

As a couple, they are eligible for second adult rebate because:

- they have at least one second adult living with them. In fact they have two second adults (the sons); and
- they do not receive rent from a boarder or (sub-)tenant; and
- at least one of the couple is a 'disregarded person' (the student).

*Amount of second adult rebate*

If there is more than one second adult, their gross incomes are combined. But in this case the income of the son on JSA(IB) is disregarded. So only the other son's income counts. That son's gross weekly income is £128 (from the job) plus £5 (interest), which amounts to £133, so the weekly amount of second adult rebate is:

7½% of weekly eligible council tax (7½% x £10.00) £0.75

**DISCOUNT PLUS SECOND ADULT REBATE**

A single woman is the only person liable for council tax on her home. The only other person living with her is her father, who is on income support. The woman is a student nurse, and is a 'disregarded person'. Her father is not a 'disregarded person'. The council tax for the dwelling (before any discount is granted) is £730 per year – which is £14 per week.

*Discount*

When calculating council tax discounts, 'disregarded persons' are ignored (appendix 7). So for discount purposes, this dwelling has one resident. The woman qualifies for a 25% discount which, on a weekly basis, is:

25% of the weekly amount for the dwelling (25% x £14.00) £3.50

*Eligible for second adult rebate?*

As a single claimant her own circumstances are immaterial. She is eligible for second adult rebate because:

- she has a second adult living with her (her father); and
- she does not receive rent from a boarder or (sub-)tenant.

*Amount of second adult rebate*

Her father is on income support so she qualifies for second adult rebate of 25% of her weekly eligible council tax. This means 25% of liability for council tax before the discount is subtracted, which is:

25% of weekly eligible council tax (25% x £14.00) £3.50

She qualifies for both the discount and the second adult rebate, the total of the two being £7.00 per week.

*Better buy*

It turns out in this particular case that, because of her own low income, the woman qualifies for main CTB of £4.00 per week. Since her main CTB is greater than her second adult rebate, she gets only her main CTB. The final result is that she qualifies for main CTB of £4.00 plus the discount of £3.50, so in total her council tax bill is reduced by £7.50 per week.

**8.25** If a claimant has more than one second adult, it is necessary to combine the income of all of them, apart from any who are on income support or JSA(IB) (or treated as receiving JSA(IB): table 8.3) – adding in the income of the partner of each second adult. Once it is clear that the gross income of some of them has reached £170 per week, there is no need to go any further (because of course it is impossible that the gross income of all of them would be lower).

**8.26** It is gross, not net, income which is relevant, and it is calculated in exactly the same way as a non-dependant's income is calculated for the purposes of main

CTB, as outlined in paragraphs 7.29-30. However, the DSS points out (GM para. B3.10) that the authority may adopt a 'local scheme' (para. 7.39) whereby a second adult's income from a war disablement pension or war widow's pension is wholly or partly disregarded. The authority is entitled to require the same level of evidence, proof, etc. as when it assesses a claimant's income (para. 5.37).

**8.27** Providing details of second adults' income (and that of their partners) can pose several difficulties for claimants. They may not be able to obtain these details, or may not wish to ask. However, if the authority does not know how much the gross income is, it cannot award a second adult rebate.

### DISCRETIONARY HOUSING PAYMENTS

**8.28** If a claimant qualifies for second adult rebate no discretionary housing payment (para. 7.37) may be awarded.

## The 'better buy'

**8.29** A claimant cannot be awarded both main CTB and second adult rebate at the same time. Deciding which one the claimant is actually awarded is often called a 'better buy' comparison. As indicated in table 8.1: CBA s.131(9)

- a claimant who only qualifies for main CTB is awarded that;
- a claimant who only qualifies for second adult rebate is awarded that;
- a claimant who qualifies for both is awarded whichever of the two is higher or, if the two are the same, main CTB. This is decided entirely according to the amounts themselves and entirely by the authority. A claimant cannot choose to have the lower figure.

Some examples of the better buy calculation are given below.

### JOINT OCCUPIERS AND THE BETTER BUY

**8.30** If a dwelling has one or more joint occupiers and one or more of them claims CTB, each joint occupier's entitlement to main CTB and second adult rebate is assessed separately, and the better buy comparison is done separately for each joint occupier. This can mean that one joint occupier is awarded main CTB, another second adult rebate. The second of the examples below illustrates this. CBA s.131(9) CTBR 54(2),(3)

### A RULE OF THUMB

**8.31** If a claimant qualifies for a large amount of main CTB, it is unlikely that he or she will qualify for a larger amount of second adult rebate. As a rule of thumb, this is the case if the claimant's main CTB meets around 35 per cent or more of his or her council tax liability.

**Example: Better buy**

**LONE PARENT WITH ONE NON-DEPENDANT/SECOND ADULT**

A lone parent is the only person liable for the council tax on her home. She is not on income support and has excess income for main CTB purposes of £25.00. The only people living with her are her daughter of 15 and her son of 21. The son works 12 hours per week for a gross pay of £135 per week (and has no other income). Only the daughter (because of being under 18) is a 'disregarded person'. The lone parent's eligible council tax liability is £10.00 per week. Her circumstances means that she is eligible for second adult rebate (the son is her second adult) as well as main CTB (taking the son into account as a non-dependant).

*Main CTB*

| | |
|---|---|
| Weekly eligible council tax | £10.00 |
| minus non-dependant deduction for son (although the son's income is over £131 he is not in remunerative work, so the lowest deduction applies: table 7.3) | £2.30 |
| minus 20% of excess income (20% x £25.00) | £5.00 |
| equals weekly main CTB | £2.70 |

*Second adult rebate*

The level of the son's gross income means that the claimant qualifies for a 7½% second adult rebate:

| | |
|---|---|
| weekly second adult rebate (7½% x £10.00) | £0.75 |

*Better buy comparison*

Her entitlement to main CTB is greater than her entitlement to second adult rebate, so she is awarded main CTB only.

**Example: Better buy for joint occupiers**

**TWO JOINT HOME-OWNERS WITH ONE NON-DEPENDANT/SECOND ADULT**

The only residents of a (d)well(ing) are three sisters, Elsie, Lacie and Tillie. Elsie and Lacie jointly own it, and are jointly liable for the council tax there. Tillie lives there rent-free. She is their non-dependant. The eligible council tax for the whole dwelling is £20.00 per week.

Elsie is a full-time university student (learning, as it happens, to draw) and is therefore a 'disregarded person'. She has capital of £20,000.

Lacie is working (as a treacle operative, in fact). She is not a 'disregarded person'. For main CTB purposes she has excess income of £30.00 (and capital under £3,000).

Tillie is on income support. She is not a 'disregarded person'. She is therefore a second adult.

*Elsie's claim for CTB*

Elsie is not eligible for main CTB – she has too much capital (and, in any case, most full-time students are not eligible for main CTB, though they are eligible for second adult rebate: chapter 21).

Elsie is eligible for second adult rebate (para. 8.18). Tillie is on income support, so the second adult rebate for the whole dwelling is 25 per cent of the council tax. Because there are two joint occupiers, Elsie qualifies for half of this,

| | |
|---|---|
| which is (½ of 25% x £20.00) | £2.50 |

*Lacie's claim for CTB*

Lacie is eligible for main CTB. Because there are two joint occupiers, it is worked out on half the council tax for the dwelling. Because Tillie is on income support, there is no non-dependant deduction for her.

Lacie's entitlement to main CTB is:

| | |
|---|---|
| weekly eligible council tax (½ x £20.00) | £10.00 |
| minus 20% of excess income (20% x £30.00) | £6.00 |
| which is | £4.00 |

Lacie's entitlement to second adult rebate is the same as Elsie's,

| | |
|---|---|
| which is (½ of 25% x £20.00) | £2.50 |

*Better buy comparisons*

| | | |
|---|---|---|
| Elsie: | No better buy comparison is required. | |
| | She is awarded second adult rebate of | £2.50 |
| Lacie: | A better buy comparison is required. | |
| | Her main CTB (£4.00) is greater than her second adult rebate (£2.50). | |
| | She is awarded main CTB of | £4.00 |
| The total weekly CTB awarded on the dwelling is therefore | | £6.50 |

# 9 Eligible council tax

**9.1** CTB is worked out by reference to the claimant's 'eligible council tax'. This chapter explains this term, and gives the details of how to work out eligible council tax in all cases. It covers:

- eligible council tax for the purposes of main CTB;
- eligible council tax for the purposes of second adult rebate; and
- CTB restrictions.

### COUNCIL TAX OVERVIEW

**9.2** The amount of council tax due on a dwelling (unless the dwelling is exempt) depends first on the valuation band in which that dwelling is placed. There are eight bands: band A (the lowest) to band H (the highest). It also depends on whether the claimant qualifies for a disability reduction, a council tax discount, a council tax transitional reduction and/or CTB. Chapter 3 gives further details of these and of the council tax scheme in general.

### 'ELIGIBLE COUNCIL TAX'

**9.3** A claimant's 'eligible council tax' is the figure used in calculating his or her entitlement to main CTB (para. 7.8) and/or second adult rebate (para. 8.23). The eligible council tax figure used in calculating main CTB can differ from that used in calculating second adult rebate; and in each of those cases it can be lower than the claimant's actual liability for council tax: the details are given in this chapter.

## Eligible council tax for main CTB purposes

### GENERAL RULES

CTBR 51(1),(2) **9.4** For the purposes of calculating main CTB (para. 7.8), a claimant's weekly eligible council tax is calculated as follows:

- start with the council tax due on his or her home. The means the amount due after deductions have been made for any disability reduction, transitional reduction, or council tax discount granted to the claimant (but no deduction is made for any entitlement to second adult rebate);

- then, for certain claimants whose dwelling is in band F, G or H, multiply the result by the fraction referred to in the following paragraph;
- then apportion the result if the claimant is a joint occupier (paras. 9.6-9) and convert it to a weekly figure (as described in para. 7.49).

See also paragraph 9.10 about other items which can affect a council tax bill.

## CTB RESTRICTIONS

**9.5** Except as described below, a claimant's eligible council tax is restricted if his or her dwelling falls in valuation band F, G or H. This is done by multiplying it by the fraction shown in table 9.1. The effect of the fractions is that claimants with dwellings in bands F, G or H are awarded CTB as though their dwelling was in band E: in other words they get less CTB. Unlike the rules about HB restrictions, the authority has no discretion to award an addition compensating for these restrictions.

CTBR 2(1), 51(2A),(2B)
SI 1997 No. 1841

The restrictions do not apply to any claimant ('**A**') if:

- **A** was entitled to CTB on 31st March 1998; or
- **A** resided on 31st March 1998 with a partner ('**B**') who was entitled to CTB on that day and continuously thereafter for the same dwelling, and either:
  - **A**'s entitlement to CTB for that dwelling begins no more than 12 weeks after the date on which **B**'s entitlement ceased (regardless of why **B**'s entitlement ceased and regardless of whether **A** and **B** are now partners), or
  - **A**'s claim for CTB is made no more than 12 weeks after the date on which **B** died or ceased to reside in the dwelling – but in this case only if **B** was on that date a 'welfare to work beneficiary' (table 13.3).

However, in the above cases, the restrictions start to apply if:

- **A** moves to a new dwelling; or
- there is a break in **A**'s entitlement to CTB of more than 4 weeks (52 weeks if **A** is a 'welfare to work beneficiary': table 13.3).

## Table 9.1 COUNCIL TAX RESTRICTIONS: FRACTIONS USED

| | FRACTION |
|---|---|
| *Claimants who do not qualify for a disability reduction* | |
| ◆ Dwellings in valuation band F | 11/13ths |
| ◆ Dwellings in valuation band G | 11/15ths |
| ◆ Dwellings in valuation band H | 11/18ths |
| *Claimants who qualify for a disability reduction* * | |
| ◆ Dwellings in valuation band F | N/A * |
| ◆ Dwellings in valuation band G | 11/13ths |
| ◆ Dwellings in valuation band H | 11/15ths |

**Notes**

* For claimants who qualify for a disability reduction (para. 2.32), these fractions apply after the disability reduction has been deducted. There is no restriction in such cases for dwellings in band F.

**Example: Council tax restrictions**

CALCULATIONS IN MAIN CTB

In a particular council's area, the annual council tax for dwellings in band E is £550 for the year, for dwellings in band F is £650 for the year, and for dwellings in band G is £750 per year. A claimant moves into a dwelling in the area which is valued as falling in band G. She claims CTB and qualifies for main CTB (but not for second adult rebate). She also qualifies for a disability reduction (para. 2.32). She does not qualify for a discount or for a transitional reduction. She is not a joint occupier.

Her eligible council tax for main CTB purposes is calculated as follows:

| | |
|---|---|
| ◆ annual council tax for a dwelling in band G | £750.00 |
| ◆ minus disability reduction | – £100.00 |
| ◆ which equals | £650.00 |
| ◆ her annual eligible council tax for main CTB purposes is found by multiplying the last figure by the fraction 11/13ths (table 9.1): £650 x 11/13 = | £550.00 |

◆ to convert this to a weekly figure, divide by 366 and multiply by 7: £550.00 ÷ 365 x 7 (to the nearest 1p) = £10.55

If she is on income support or income-based jobseeker's allowance and has no non-dependants, her annual entitlement to main CTB (£550.00) is £100.00 less than her annual liability for council tax (£650.00).

THE RULES FOR A 'WELFARE TO WORK BENEFICIARY'

On 31st March 1999, Mr and Mrs Twoshoes resided in a house and Mr Twoshoes was getting CTB there. He continued to get CTB there until July 2000, when he became a 'welfare to work beneficiary' (and his CTB stopped as a result). In late November 2001, Mr Twoshoes (still at that time a 'welfare to work beneficiary') died. Mrs Twoshoes claims CTB for the same house in early January 2002.

The CTB restrictions did not apply to Mr Twoshoes' CTB throughout his entitlement to CTB. They also do not apply to Mrs Twoshoes' CTB from when she claims. This is because she meets the criteria in paragraph 9.5: in particular, her claim is made within 12 weeks of Mr Twoshoes' death, and at the date of his death he was a 'welfare to work beneficiary'.

## APPORTIONMENT FOR JOINT OCCUPIERS

**9.6** A joint occupier (also known as a joint tenant or joint owner) is one of two CTBR 51(3),(4) or more people who are jointly liable to pay the council tax on a dwelling, other than just a couple or polygamous marriage (para. 4.24). In such cases, the figures used in calculating eligible council tax are apportioned between the joint occupiers for main CTB purposes.

**9.7** This apportionment is found by dividing the total council tax liability (para. 9.4) by the number of people who are jointly liable, ignoring any person who is both:

◆ a student as defined under CTB law (para. 22.3); and

◆ ineligible for main CTB (i.e. does not fall within one of the eligible groups for students listed in table 21.1).

For example, if three single friends jointly rent a house and are jointly liable for council tax there, but (only) one of them is a student who is ineligible for main CTB, each of the other two is eligible for CTB on one-half of the council tax liability.

**9.8** If amongst several jointly liable people some are a couple or polygamous marriage, the law is unclear. The DSS advises (GM para. B2.14) that if there are three jointly liable people, two of whom are a couple, then the couple are eligible for main CTB on two-thirds of the council tax liability and the other person on one-third.

**9.9** It is also worth noting here that, in certain cases, people who are severely mentally impaired are not jointly liable for council tax (para. 2.27) so the apportionment ignores them.

### OTHER ITEMS AFFECTING A COUNCIL TAX BILL

CTBR 51(2) **9.10** The following additional rules apply to main CTB and also to second adult rebate:

- in the case of an authority which offers discounts against its council taxes for people who pay in a lump sum or by a method other than cash (e.g. direct debit), CTB is calculated on liability before those discounts are subtracted;
- when lower council taxes are set as a result of council tax 'capping' procedures, these apply from the beginning of the financial year, and CTB is worked out (throughout the financial year) on the lower amount;
- if a council tax bill is increased to recover an earlier overpayment of CTB or of community charge benefit, CTB is calculated before those amounts are added;
- if a penalty is added to a council tax bill, CTB is calculated as if that penalty was not included.

## Eligible council tax for second adult rebate purposes

### GENERAL RULES

CTBR 54(1), sch. 2 para. 1(2) **9.11** Except as described in the following paragraph, for the purposes of calculating second adult rebate (para. 8.23), a claimant's weekly eligible council tax is calculated as follows:

- start with the council tax due on his or her home. The means the amount due *after* deductions have been made for any disability reduction or transitional reduction has been granted to the claimant, but *before* any council tax discount is deducted (and no deduction is made for any entitlement to main CTB);
- then, for certain claimants whose dwelling is in band F, G or H, multiply the result by the fraction referred to in table 9.1;
- then convert the result to a weekly figure (as described in para. 7.49) – but do not at this stage apportion it if the claimant is a joint occupier (para. 4.25).

See also paragraph 9.10 about other items which can affect a council tax bill.

## CTB RESTRICTIONS

**9.12** The rules about CTB restrictions are the same for second adult rebate as they are for main CTB (para. 9.5).

CTBR sch. 2 para. 1(3),(4) SI 1997 No. 184

### Example: Council tax restrictions in second adult rebate

In a particular council's area, the annual council tax for dwellings in band G is £750 per year. A claimant moves into a dwelling in the area which is valued as falling in band G. He claims CTB and qualifies for second adult rebate (but not for main CTB). He also qualifies for a 25% council tax discount (para. 2.35). He does not qualify for a disability reduction or for a transitional reduction. He is not a joint occupier.

His eligible council tax for second adult rebate purposes is calculated as follows:

- annual council tax for a dwelling in band G — £750.00
- although he qualifies for a discount, it is ignored here
- his annual eligible council tax for second adult rebate purposes is found by multiplying the above figure by the fraction 11/15ths (table 9.1): £750 x 11/15 = — £550.00
- to convert this to a weekly figure, divide by 366 and multiply by 7: £550.00 ÷ 365 x 7 (to the nearest 1p) = — £10.55

It turns out that the above claimant has one second adult who is on income support or income-based jobseeker's allowance. So his annual entitlement to second adult rebate is 25% of £550.00 (table 8.3) – which is £137.50; and his resulting annual liability for council tax is then calculated as follows:

- annual council tax for a dwelling in band G — £750.00
- minus his annual council tax discount: 25% of £750.00 — - £187.50
- minus his annual second adult rebate: 25% (table 8.3) of £550 (as above) — - £137.50
- so his resultant liability (after both the above have been granted) is — £425.00

## NOTE ON COUNCIL TAX DISCOUNTS

CTBR 54(1), sch. 2 para. 1(2)

**9.13** For second adult rebate purposes, as indicated in paragraph 9.11, a claimant's eligible council tax is calculated as though he or she did not qualify for any council tax discount. This is mainly for mathematical reasons: as illustrated in the following example, a claimant who qualifies for a discount does not lose it (and see also para. 8.23).

## NOTE ON JOINT OCCUPIERS

CTBR 52(2),(3)

**9.14** As indicated in paragraph 9.11, second adult rebate is always calculated on council tax liability for the whole dwelling. If there are joint occupiers (para. 4.25), the amount of second adult rebate is apportioned between them after the calculation is otherwise complete (as described in para. 8.20).

**Example: Entitlement to CTB and liability for council tax**

(1) INFORMATION

In a particular council's area, the annual council tax for dwellings in band D is £450 per year. A claimant in the area resides in a dwelling valued as falling in band D. He is single and qualifies for a council tax disability reduction (para. 2.32). He is also a 'disregarded person' for the purposes of calculating council tax discounts (para. 2.37 and appendix 6) (but is not a student or severely mentally impaired). The only other person in his home is his adult daughter (who is his non-dependant for main CTB purposes: chapter 7, and also counts as a 'second adult' for second adult rebate purposes: chapter 8). For these reasons, he qualifies for a 25% council tax discount. It is also the case that both the claimant and his daughter are on income support or income-based job-seeker's allowance.

(2) ANNUAL LIABILITY FOR COUNCIL TAX IF HE DID NOT CLAIM CTB

If he did not claim CTB his annual liability for council tax would be:

| | |
|---|---|
| ◆ annual council tax for a dwelling in band D | £450.00 |
| ◆ minus disability reduction: this would be | – £50.00 |
| ◆ which leaves | £400.00 |
| ◆ minus discount (25% of £400.00) | £100.00 |
| ◆ so his annual liability would be | £300.00 |

## (3) ELIGIBLE COUNCIL TAX FOR MAIN CTB PURPOSES

| | |
|---|---|
| His annual eligible council tax for main CTB purposes is the amount of his liability after both the disability reduction and the discount have been deducted; which is | £300.00 |
| Converted to a weekly amount this is (to the nearest 1p) | £5.75 |

## (4) ELIGIBLE COUNCIL TAX FOR SECOND ADULT REBATE PURPOSES

| | |
|---|---|
| His annual eligible council tax for second adult rebate purposes is the amount of his liability after the disability reduction has been deducted but before the discount has been deducted; which is | £400.00 |
| Converted to a weekly amount this is (to the nearest 1p) | £7.67 |

## (5) CALCULATION OF MAIN CTB

| | |
|---|---|
| ◆ Weekly amount of eligible council tax for main CTB purposes (see (3) above) | £5.75 |
| ◆ Minus non-dependant deduction (nil in this case) | – £0.00 |
| ◆ So his weekly entitlement to main CTB is | £5.75 |

## (6) CALCULATION OF SECOND ADULT REBATE

| | |
|---|---|
| ◆ Weekly amount of eligible council tax for second adult rebate purposes (see (4) above) | £7.67 |
| ◆ Multiplied by 25%, equals (to the nearest 1p) | £1.92 |
| ◆ So his weekly entitlement to second adult rebate is | £1.92 |

## (7) THE 'BETTER BUY' AND HIS ENTITLEMENT TO CTB

| | |
|---|---|
| Because of the 'better buy' (para. 8.29), he is granted weekly main CTB of | £5.75 |

## (8) ANNUAL LIABILITY FOR COUNCIL TAX AFTER CTB HAS BEEN AWARDED

On an annual basis this is:

| | |
|---|---|
| ◆ The figure shown at the end of (2) above | £300.00 |
| ◆ Minus the annual equivalent of his entitlement to CTB: £5.75 per week as in (7) above, converted to an annual figure is | – £300.00 |
| ◆ So his annual liability for council tax (after the disability reduction, the discount and CTB have all been granted) is | NIL |

# 10 Eligible rent

**10.1** HB is worked out by reference to the claimant's 'eligible rent'. This chapter explains this term, and gives the details of how to work out 'eligible rent' in all cases. It covers:

- what counts as 'rent' for HB purposes and how this differs from 'eligible rent';
- eligible rent for council tenants;
- eligible rent for housing association tenants;
- eligible rent for private tenants under the 'New Scheme';
- eligible rent for private tenants under the 'Old Scheme';
- eligible rent for registered rent cases; and
- eligible rent for other cases.

**10.2** The next chapter deals in more detail with the service charges and other items that may be included in a claimant's rent, and how these affect the claimant's eligible rent. Paragraph 10.69 gives further information on how marginal references work in this and the next chapter.

## 'Rent' and 'eligible rent'

### 'RENT'

HBR 8(1), 10(1) **10.3** The term 'rent' has various meanings in different branches of the law. As far as HB is concerned, all the types of payment shown in table 10.1 count as rent. In this chapter, the term 'actual rent' is used to mean the total of all the payments shown in that table which a claimant is liable to pay on his or her normal home.

**10.4** As may be seen from the table, charges for services are included as 'rent' for HB purposes. This does not means that HB will necessarily pay for them (chapter 11). Note that in certain types of dwelling a claimant cannot get HB even if he or she pays rent (paras. 3.4 onwards); that some housing costs which do not count as rent for HB purposes can be met through income support or income-based jobseeker's allowance (para. 3.4); and that further rules apply in relation to increases to cover arrears of rent, garages and land, and business premises (paras. 11.30-32).

## TABLE 10.1 PAYMENTS COUNTED AS RENT FOR HB PURPOSES

- Rent in its ordinary sense, whether under a tenancy or licence, including board and lodgings payments and payments for 'use and occupation'.
- 'Mesne profits' in England and Wales or 'violent profits' in Scotland (paid after a tenancy or right to occupy is terminated).
- Houseboat mooring charges and berthing fees and caravan and mobile home site charges (even if owned by the claimant, and in addition to rental if not owned).
- Payments made by residents of charitable almshouses.
- Payments under rental purchase agreements.
- Payments for crofts and croft land in Scotland.

## 'ELIGIBLE RENT'

**10.5** A claimant's 'eligible rent' is the figure used in calculating his or her entitlement to HB (para. 7.8). It could be exactly equal to his or her actual rent (this happens in some council tenant cases, for example), but it is much more common for it to be different. The three main reasons for this are: HBR 10(3)

- many service charges cannot be met by HB (for example water charges, meals and most fuel and, in Northern Ireland, any rates included in the rent);
- in the case of much privately rented accommodation (and some housing association and similar accommodation), the rent officer's valuations are used to work out the eligible rent rather than the landlord's figures;
- in some cases the eligible rent may be restricted to a lower figure.

This chapter explains all the rules about working out 'eligible rent'. A summary of the main points may be found at the end of the chapter (table 10.5).

## APPORTIONMENT FOR JOINT OCCUPIERS

**10.6** In the case of a claimant who is a joint occupier (para. 4.24), many of the figures used in calculating eligible rent are apportioned between the joint occupiers. In doing this, the authority must determine how much of the actual rent on the dwelling is fairly attributable to each of the joint occupiers, taking into account the number of people paying towards the rent, the proportion of rent paid by each, and any relevant other circumstances – such as the size and number of rooms each occupies, and whether there is any written or other agreement between them. The authority must then apportion the figures used in calculating the claimant's eligible rent on the same basis. If one joint occupier leaves and is HBR 10(5) not replaced, it is normally reasonable to re-apportion the figures between the remaining joint occupiers (see example).

**Example: Joint occupiers**

TOM, DICK AND HARRY

Three unrelated friends in their thirties, Tom, Dick and Harry, jointly rent a two-bedroom housing association house, where the rent for the whole house is £150 per week (and this does not include any service charges). Dick and Harry have a bedroom. Tom uses the living room as a bedroom. They share the kitchen and all other facilities. They have each contributed one-third of the rent in the past. Harry loses his job and claims HB, saying that his share remains one-third.

Harry's eligible rent is very likely to be regarded as £50 per week. It is possible that a fairer split would be something other than one-third each, but unlikely based on the information given.

TOM MOVES OUT

Tom moves out. He is not replaced. Dick and Harry keep their own bedrooms and begin to share the living room. They agree between them that they should contribute equally to the rent.

Harry's eligible rent is now very likely to be regarded as £75 per week – unless the authority considers that the new rent is unreasonable and has the power to restrict it (as described in later parts of this chapter).

## Definitions

### 'OLD SCHEME' CASES VS 'NEW SCHEME' CASES

SI 1995 No. 1644
NISR 1996 No. 111

**10.7** Especially in the private rented sector, the amount of a claimant's eligible rent depends very much on whether his or her case falls within the 'Old Scheme' or the 'New Scheme'. (Strictly speaking, the distinction applies to all types of HB case – including council tenants and housing association tenants – but the greatest impact is on private sector tenants.) 'Old Scheme' and 'New Scheme' are defined below. In broad terms, all claimants who have been on HB since before 2nd January 1996 (and some claimants who have more recently taken over an HB claim from someone who has been on HB since before then) fall within the 'Old Scheme'. So do claimants in certain kinds of accommodation where care, support or supervision is provided.

**10.8** Terminology varies widely across the country. 'Old Scheme Cases' are also known as 'Old Regulation 11 Cases', 'Old Cases' or 'Exempt Cases' (because they were exempt from the January 1996 changes). 'New Scheme Cases' are also known as 'New Regulation 11 Cases', 'New Cases' or 'Non-exempt cases'.

**10.9** As described below, a person falls within the Old Scheme if he or she:

- is (personally) an 'exempt claimant'; or
- has had exemption transferred to him or her; or
- is claiming HB in respect of 'exempt accommodation'.

Otherwise, he or she falls within the New Scheme.

## 'EXEMPT CLAIMANTS'

**10.10** A claimant is an 'exempt claimant' (and therefore falls within the 'Old Scheme') if he or she: SI 1995 No. 1644 NISR 1996 No. 11

- was 'entitled to' HB on Monday 1st January 1996 (including cases where this is because HB was backdated to include this date); and
- has remained 'entitled to and in receipt of' HB continuously since that date (disregarding breaks in HB entitlement/receipt of up to 52 weeks in the case of a 'welfare to work beneficiary': table 13.3; or in any case disregarding breaks of four weeks or less): this includes renewal claims so long as they run continuously or are backdated to run continuously (disregarding breaks as just mentioned); and
- has not moved to occupy a new dwelling as his or her home since that date, or has moved only because a fire, flood, explosion or natural catastrophe made his or her former home uninhabitable.

**10.11** Also, in the special case of a refugee who was formerly an asylum seeker (para. 20.34), the refugee is an 'exempt claimant' (and therefore falls within the 'Old Scheme') in respect of any previous period for which he or she has become entitled to HB. HBR sch. A1

## TRANSFERRING EXEMPTION: DEATH, DEPARTURE AND DETENTION

**10.12** Exemption is transferred in the following three ways from one claimant ('A') to another claimant ('B') (who therefore falls within the 'Old Scheme'). 'Partner' and 'member of the household' have their specific HB meanings (paras. 4.3 onwards): SI 1995 No. 1644 NISR 1996 No. 11

- A dies; and B was (until then) his or her partner or any other member of the household;
- A leaves the dwelling; and B was (until then) his or her partner;
- A is 'detained in custody pending sentence upon conviction or under a sentence imposed by a court' (and is not entitled to HB under the rules about

absences from home: chapter 3); and B is (or was until then) his or her partner.

**10.13** Additionally, in all three cases:

- At the date of his or her death, departure or detention, A must be in receipt of HB (or a 'welfare to work beneficiary': table 13.3, who was in receipt of HB no more than 52 weeks previously);
- B must occupy the dwelling as a home on that date (or be treated as occupying it: chapter 3);
- B's claim for HB must be made within four weeks of that date (or backdated to fall within those four weeks: para. 5.86);
- B's claim is then treated as having been made on that date;
- B then continues to be exempt for as long as he or she:
  - remains 'entitled to and in receipt of HB' continuously (disregarding breaks in HB entitlement/receipt of up to 52 weeks in the case of a 'welfare to work beneficiary': table 13.3; or in any case disregarding breaks of four weeks or less): this includes renewal claims so long as they run continuously or are backdated to run continuously (disregarding breaks as just mentioned), and
  - does not move to occupy a new dwelling as his or her home, or moves only because a fire, flood, explosion or natural catastrophe makes his or her home uninhabitable;
- B's exemption is then transferred to any other claimant in the same way as described above (para. 10.12). There is no limit to the number of transfers of exemption so long as the above conditions are complied with in each case.

**Example: Old Scheme cases: exempt claimants and transferring exemption**

(1) Mrs Sawable is a part-time magician's assistant. She is in receipt of HB, on behalf of herself and her husband, on 1st January 1996.

So she is an exempt claimant from 2nd January 1996.

(2) Her HB claim becomes due for renewal on various dates over the next few years. She renews it on time in each case, so there is no break in her entitlement to HB.

So she continues to be an exempt claimant.

(3) Mrs Sawable (still on HB) dies in May 2002, due to an accident at work. Mr Sawable makes a claim for HB within four weeks of her death.

So, because of the rules about 'transferred exemption', he is an exempt claimant.

'EXEMPT ACCOMMODATION'

**10.14** Any claimant in 'exempt accommodation' falls within the 'Old Scheme', no matter when his or her claim for HB is made. 'Exempt accommodation' is: SI 1995 No. 1644 NISR 1996 No. 111

- any accommodation 'provided by':
  - a housing association, whether registered or unregistered,
  - a registered charity,
  - a non-profit-making voluntary organisation,
  - a non-metropolitan county council, or
  - any other registered social landlord,

  where (in each of the cases) 'that body or a person acting on its behalf also provides the claimant with care, support or supervision'; or
- any resettlement place provided by a local authority or non-profit-making voluntary organisation which has received a grant under section 30 of the Jobseekers Act 1995.

**10.15** For the purposes of the first type of exempt accommodation, there is no definition of 'care', 'support' or 'supervision': these terms take their ordinary English meanings and are open to appeal (chapter 19). Also, what it means for a accommodation to be 'provided by' the body concerned is open to debate, though it is not restricted to cases where the claimant pays rent to that body. (For example, if a registered charity makes arrangements with a private landlord to use accommodation owned by him for its clients, and the landlord collects the rent but the charity retains the right to say who will live in the accommodation, it may be argued that the accommodation is 'provided by' the charity.)

## Eligible rent for council and NIHE tenants

**10.16** The eligible rent of a council tenant (or in Northern Ireland a tenant of the NIHE) is simply: HBR 10(3)

- the actual rent;
- minus amounts for service charges which are ineligible for HB (chapter 11).

**10.17** This applies in all rent rebate cases (para. 1.11): it applies whether it is the claimant or a partner (or both) who rents from the council. (Different rules apply to people renting from county councils: paras. 10.66.)

**10.18** In all these cases:

- non-weekly rents need to be converted to a weekly figure (para. 7.50);
- adjustments must be made in the case of joint occupiers (para. 10.6);
- it is always the authority (not, say, the rent officer) which determines how much the eligible rent is and deals with all matters relating to service charges.

HBR 10(6B), HBR Old 11 **10.19** In theory at least, it is possible for the authority to reduce the eligible rent below the figure described above, depending on whether the case falls within the Old Scheme or New Scheme (para. 10.7). For an Old Scheme case, the same rules and protections apply as for a private sector Old Scheme case (para. 10.46.) For a New Scheme case, the general power in paragraph 10.41 applies. In practice, council tenants' eligible rents are rarely if ever restricted.

> **Example: Eligible rent for a council tenant**
>
> A claimant rents a council flat. His actual rent is £50 per week. This figure includes £3 per week for the cleaning and lighting of communal areas, £1 per week for use of the communal TV aerial, and £2 per week for an emergency alarm system.
>
> His eligible rent is calculated as follows. The charge for the communal areas is eligible for HB, and it turns out that the emergency alarm system is eligible for HB in his case (chapter 13). However, the TV aerial is not eligible, so this has to be deducted from his actual rent to find his eligible rent. His eligible rent is therefore £49 per week.

## Eligible rent for housing association tenants, etc

**10.20** A housing association tenant's eligible rent depends first on whether the claimant falls within the Old Scheme or the New Scheme (paras. 10.7).

HBR 2(1) **10.21** This applies in all cases in which the landlord is a housing association, whether or not the housing association is a registered housing association, or registered social landlord: it applies whether it is the claimant or a partner (or both) who rents from them.

Housing associations sometimes act as managing agents for private landlords ('HAMA' schemes – short for 'Housing Association as Managing Agent'). In these cases the housing association is not the tenant's landlord, the private landlord is instead, and the rules in paragraph 10.26 apply. Housing associations sometimes also lease accommodation from private landlords and rent it in turn to tenants ('HAL' schemes – short for Housing Association Leasing). In these cases the housing association is the tenant's landlord and the following rules apply.

### OLD SCHEME CASES

HBR Old 11 **10.22** In Old Scheme cases, the claimant's eligible rent is worked out in the same way as for a private sector Old Scheme case (para. 10.46). For example:

- the authority could restrict the eligible rent on grounds of unreasonableness (but must have comparables demonstrating this and cannot rely on figures provided by the rent officer);

- however, there are rules preventing all or part of such a restriction in the case of certain protected groups.

NEW SCHEME CASES

**10.23** In New Scheme cases, everything depends on whether the authority refers the rent to the rent officer on the grounds that it considers the rent or size to be unreasonable (table 6.1). In Northern Ireland, if the Housing Executive considers the rent or size unreasonable it is obliged to apply the rent restriction rules in the same way that rent officers do in Great Britain. HBR 2(1), 10(3), sch 1A para 3 NIHBR sch 1B para 3

**10.24** If the authority does make a referral to the rent officer, the claimant's eligible rent is worked out in the same way as for a private sector New Scheme case (para. 10.28). For example: HBR 11(1) HBR 12A (GB only) NIHBR 10A

- the rent officer's figures are binding and a 'maximum rent' will apply – which often results in the eligible rent being restricted;
- however, there are rules preventing all or part of such a restriction in the case of certain protected groups.

**10.25** If the authority does not make a referral to the rent officer, the claimant's rent is worked out in the same way as for a council tenant (para. 10.16) – but the resulting eligible rent cannot be restricted in any way (because if the authority considers the rent to be unreasonable, it must refer the rent to the rent officer – table 6.1 – and the previous paragraph will then apply). HBR 10(3)

# Eligible rent for private tenants

**10.26** There are two main ways of working out a private tenant's eligible rent, depending on whether the claimant falls within the New Scheme or the Old Scheme (as defined in paras. 10.7-15). Rules for those two types of cases are dealt with in turn below, and are followed by some further rules which apply in registered rent cases and other special cases.

**10.27** This applies in all cases in which the landlord is a private individual or company: it applies whether it is the claimant or a partner (or both) who rents from them.

**TABLE 10.2 ELIGIBLE RENT FOR PRIVATE TENANTS: KEY FEATURES**

New Scheme cases

- The rent officer figures are binding
- Some people get a '50% top-up' whereas others don't
- There are two protected groups

Old Scheme cases

- The rent officer figures are not binding (but may be used with other evidence)
- The eligible rent may be restricted if unreasonably large, expensive, etc.
- The authority must have evidence if restricting eligible rent
- There are three protected groups

## Eligible rent for New Scheme private sector cases

HBR 11(1)
HBR 12A (GB ONLY)
NIHBR sch 1A

**10.28** In New Scheme private sector cases (para. 10.26), the claimant's eligible rent is always the 'maximum rent' applying in his or her case (as described in the following paragraphs), unless:

- the claimant and/or other occupiers could formerly afford the accommodation (para. 10.33); or
- the claimant has had a bereavement (para. 10.36); or
- the claimant's rent details change during his or her benefit period (para. 10.40); or
- the authority reduces the eligible rent to below the maximum rent in certain cases (para. 10.41); or
- the claimant has a registered rent (para. 10.61).

### MAXIMUM RENT: THE GENERAL RULE

HBR 2(1), 11

**10.29** The claimant's 'maximum rent' is the lowest of the figures provided by the rent officer (chapter 6) in his or her case (or the only figure if the rent officer provides only one). But before deciding which is lowest, the figures must be adjusted in certain cases. Table 10.3 describes the rent officer's figures and shows how to calculate maximum rent.

**10.30** There are two exceptions: different rules can apply to claims continuing from before 6th October 1997 (para. 10.31), and to lettings begun in or before January 1989 (para. 10.62).

## TABLE 10.3 CALCULATING 'MAXIMUM RENT' FOR NEW SCHEME CASES

### 1. START WITH THE RENT OFFICER'S FIGURES

The authority needs all the figures provided by the rent officer, which could be one or more of the following:

- a claim-related rent determination,
- a local reference rent determination,
- a single room rent determination (only in the case of a 'young individual': para. 6.12).

Convert these to a weekly figure at this stage (para. 7.50). Work through Step 2 separately for each figure.

### 2. ADJUSTMENTS MADE BY THE AUTHORITY *

*(a) Deduction for meals*

Deduct an amount for meals – but only if the claimant's actual rent includes meals. Use the amounts shown in table 11.3. There are two exceptions:

- do not deduct anything for meals in the case of the single room rent;
- do not deduct anything for meals in the case of the claim-related rent if the rent officer has notified the authority that it does not include meals.

*(b) Addition for eligible support charges*

Add an amount for all eligible support charges (paras. 11.43 onwards) – but only if the claimant's actual rent includes these. Use the authority's valuation for these.

*(c) Apportionment for joint occupiers*

If the claimant is a joint occupier, apportion the resulting figures (para. 10.26). Do not, however, apportion the single room rent.

### 3. CALCULATE MAXIMUM RENT

The claimant's 'maximum rent' is the lowest of the resulting figures (or if there is only one figure, it is that one).

** Note: No adjustment is made for water charges, fuel or any service charges other than those in this table: if those are included in the claimant's actual rent, the rent officer takes this into account when fixing his or her figures (chapter 6).*

**Examples: Calculating maximum rent**

**EXAMPLE ONE: A STRAIGHTFORWARD CASE**

A private tenant over the age of 25 makes a first claim for HB. Her actual rent is £80 per week including water charges and fuel charges. She is not a joint occupier. The rent officer has provided the following figures:

- a claim-related rent determination of £70 per week;
- a local reference rent determination of £65 per week;
- no single room rent determination (because the claimant is not a 'young individual')

Because none of the adjustments in table 10.3 apply in this case, her maximum rent is simply the lower of the above two figures, i.e. £65 per week.

**EXAMPLE TWO: A JOINT OCCUPIER AGED UNDER 25**

A private tenant under the age of 25 makes a first claim for HB. He is a joint occupier with two others: they share their rent equally. The actual rent for the whole property is £180 per week including water charges and fuel charges. The rent officer has provided the following figures:

- a claim-related rent determination of £150 per week;
- a local reference rent determination of £135 per week;
- a single room rent determination of £42 per week.

The only adjustment in table 10.3 which applies is the apportionment for joint occupiers:

- the adjusted claim-related rent is (£150 ÷ 3 =) £50 per week;
- the adjusted local reference rent is (£135 ÷ 3 =) £45 per week;
- the single room rent is not adjusted; it is £42 per week.

The claimant's maximum rent is the lowest of the resulting figures, i.e. £42 per week.

**EXAMPLE THREE: SUPPORT CHARGES INCLUDED**

A private tenant under the age of 25 makes a first claim for HB. Her actual rent is £115 per week including water charges, fuel charges, meals charges and eligible support charges (because she has a community care assessment: para. 11.43). She is not a joint occupier. The authority determines that the figure for meals is £18.95 per week (table 11.3), and has valued the eligible support charges as worth £20 per week. The rent officer has provided the following figures:

- a claim-related rent determination of £70 per week (including meals);
- no local reference rent determination;
- a single room rent determination of £40 per week.

The adjustments in table 10.3 apply as follows:

- the adjusted claim-related rent:

| | |
|---|---|
| rent officer figure | £70.00 |
| minus meals charge | – £18.95 |
| plus support charges | + £20.00 |
| total | £71.05 |

- the adjusted single room rent:

| | |
|---|---|
| rent officer figure | £40.00 |
| (no adjustment for meals) | |
| plus support charges | + £20.00 |
| total | £60.00 |

The claimant's maximum rent is the lower of the resulting figures, i.e. £60 per week.

## MAXIMUM RENT: THE '50% TOP-UP' FOR CERTAIN OLDER CLAIMS

**10.31** As described in the next paragraph, the calculation of a claimant's maximum rent is different in the case of any claimant who meets the following conditions: SI 1997 No. 852 SI 1997 No. 1975 SI 1999 No. 2734 NISR 1997 No. 17 NISR 1997 No. 37 NISR 1998 No. 41

- the claimant was 'entitled to and in receipt of' HB on Sunday 5th October 1997; and
- the claimant has remained 'entitled to and in receipt of' HB continuously since that date (disregarding breaks of up to 52 weeks in the case of a

'welfare to work beneficiary': table 13.3; but in any other case with no breaks whatsoever): this includes renewal claims so long as they run continuously or are backdated to run continuously (disregarding breaks as just mentioned); and

- the claimant has not moved to occupy a new dwelling as his or her home since that date (regardless of the reason for the move); and
- the claimant has qualified for a '50% top-up' continuously since his or her first renewal claim beginning after that date; and
- the rent officer has provided a local reference rent in the claimant's case.

**10.32** If a claimant meets all the above conditions, he or she must be considered for a 50% top-up, calculated by working through the following steps:

- Start with the rent officer's figures and make all the adjustments exactly as in steps 1 and 2 in table 10.3.
- The claimant's maximum rent is then the average of (i.e. half-way between) the local reference rent and the claim-related rent; unless the single room rent is lower than that, in which case the maximum rent is that single room rent.

**Example: Maximum rent with a '50% top-up'**

A private tenant over the age of 25 makes a renewal claim for HB. She was on HB on 5th October 1997. She has not moved since then and she meets all the other conditions to be considered for a 50% top-up. Her actual rent is £100 per week including water charges and fuel charges. She is not a joint occupier. The rent officer has provided the following figures:

- a claim-related rent determination of £90 per week;
- a local reference rent determination of £70 per week;
- no single room rent determination (because she is not a 'young individual).

Because she qualifies for a 50% top-up (paras. 10.31-32), and because none of the adjustments in table 10.3 applies, her maximum rent is the average of (i.e. half-way between) the local reference rent and the claim-related rent, which is £80 per week.

## MAXIMUM RENT: PROTECTION FOR PEOPLE WHO COULD FORMERLY AFFORD THEIR ACCOMMODATION

**10.33** This is the first of the two 'protected groups' – people who are protected against the effect of the rules about maximum rents (and various other rent restrictions: para. 10.53). A claimant falls within this protected group if: HBR 11(9),(10) NIHBR 11(12),(13)

- he or she or any combination of the occupiers of his or her home (para. 10.38) could afford the financial commitments there when the liability to pay rent was entered into (no matter how long ago that was); and
- the claimant has not received HB for any period in the 52 weeks prior to his or her current claim. Receipt of CTB during those weeks is ignored.

**10.34** In such a case, the protection lasts for the first 13 weeks of his or her entitlement to HB. During those weeks, his or her eligible rent is worked out in the same way as for a council tenant (para. 10.16) – but the resulting eligible rent cannot be restricted in any way.

**10.35** This protection gives the claimant time to move, without the additional pressure of having insufficient HB. In the case of a couple, so long as the claimant has not received HB during the past 52 weeks, it is immaterial whether his or her partner has. In some cases it therefore makes a substantial difference which person in a couple makes the claim for HB (para. 5.5).

## MAXIMUM RENT: PROTECTION FOR PEOPLE WHO HAVE HAD A BEREAVEMENT

**10.36** This is the second of the two 'protected groups' – people who are protected against the effect of the rules about maximum rents (and various other rent restrictions: para. 10.53). A claimant falls within this protected group if: HBR 11(7),(8) NIHBR 11(9),(10)

- any of the occupiers of his or her home (para. 10.38) has died within the last 12 months (including occupiers who were temporarily absent); and
- the claimant has not moved home since the date of that death.

**10.37** In such a case, the protection lasts until 12 months after that death. During that period it works as follows. If the claimant was on HB at the date of the death, his or her eligible rent must not be reduced to below whatever was his or her eligible rent immediately before that date (it is, however, increased if any rule requires this). If the claimant was not on HB at the date of the death, his or her eligible rent is worked out in the same way as for a council tenant (para. 10.16) – but the resulting eligible rent cannot be restricted in any way.

## DEFINITIONS: 'OCCUPIER' AND 'RELATIVE'

**10.38** For the purposes of the above two protected groups, the only 'occupiers' taken into account are: HBR 11(11),(12) NIHBR 11(14),(15)

- the claimant;
- any member of his or her family (partner, child, young person: paras. 4.5-20);
- any 'relative' (para. 10.39) of the claimant or partner (including non-dependants, boarders, tenants, sub-tenants and joint occupiers) who has no separate right to occupy the dwelling.

HBR 2(1) **10.39** A 'relative' is defined for the above (and all other HB) purposes as:

- a parent, parent-in-law, daughter, son, daughter/son-in-law, step-daughter/son, sister or brother; or
- a partner (married or unmarried: para. 4.6) of any of the above; or
- a grandparent, grandchild, aunt, uncle, niece or nephew.

**Examples: The protected groups**

**EXAMPLE ONE: BEREAVEMENT**

A claimant makes a claim for HB shortly after the death of her husband (and the council agrees to backdate the claim: para. 5.93). She has not moved since her husband's death. Her actual rent is rather high.

Because of the protection for people who have had a bereavement, her eligible rent must not be restricted in any way until the first anniversary of her husband's death. Until then, her eligible rent is her actual rent minus amounts for any ineligible services.

**EXAMPLE TWO: REDUNDANCY**

A claimant makes a claim for HB a few weeks after he is made redundant (and he does not request backdating). His actual rent is high. He moved to this address when he was in a well-paid job and could easily afford the rent and outgoings. He has not been on HB in the last year.

Because of the protection for people who could formerly afford their accommodation, his eligible rent must not be restricted in any way for the first 13 weeks of his entitlement to HB. During those weeks, his eligible rent is his actual rent minus amounts for any ineligible services.

## MAXIMUM RENT IF THE CLAIMANT'S RENT CHANGES

HBR 11(5),(6A),(6B),(13)
NIHBR 11(5),(6A),(8),(16)

**10.40** Once a claimant's maximum rent has been calculated as above, it applies until the end of his or her benefit period (para. 5.81) – except as described in the following two paragraphs.

**10.41** If the claimant's details have to be re-referred to the rent officer (paras. 6.6-11), a new maximum rent must be calculated as above and used for the remainder of his or her benefit period (whether it is higher or lower than – or the same as – the initial maximum rent). Not all rent increases (indeed very few) trigger a re-referral to the rent officer.

**10.42** If the claimant's actual rent reduces to below the maximum rent, the law is a little unclear. It appears to mean that, over-riding all the above rules, the most a person's eligible rent can ever be is what he or she actually pays minus the authority's valuation of amounts for ineligible service charges. If this is not the effect of the law, it would seem reasonable for the authority to use its general power to restrict the eligible rent (10.41) to that figure.

### REDUCING MAXIMUM RENT IN CERTAIN CASES

**10.43** In private sector New Scheme cases, the authority has a general power to reduce any claimant's eligible rent to below the 'maximum rent' calculated as above if 'it appears to the authority that in the particular circumstances of the case the eligible rent… is greater than it is reasonable to meet by way of housing benefit.' (The same power applies in council tenant New Scheme cases: para. 10.19, but not in housing association cases: para. 10.25.) In such a case, the eligible rent is reduced to 'such lesser sum as seems to that authority to be an appropriate rent in that particular case.' HBR 10(6B)

**10.44** In practice, reductions under this provision are uncommon. They can be made only if the authority makes a proper judgment about the above matters (para. 1.27). This means (as pointed out in circular HB/CTB A7/96) that the authority 'should have evidence and an objective justification' before making a reduction.

### INCREASING MAXIMUM RENT FOR EXCEPTIONAL HARDSHIP

**10.45** Increases for exceptional hardship were abolished in July 2001 and replaced with discretionary housing payments (para. 7.37).

## Eligible rent for Old Scheme private sector cases

**10.46** In Old Scheme private sector cases (para. 10.26), the claimant's eligible rent is worked out in the same way as for a council tenant (para. 10.16) unless:

- the authority restricts the eligible rent to a lower figure (paras. 10.47 onwards); or
- the claimant has a registered rent or other fixed rent (paras. 10.61-64).

HBR Old 10, 11, 1
SI 1996 No. 1644 (GB)
SI 1997 No. 852 (GB)
NISR 1996 No. 11
NISR 1997 No. 17

## ELIGIBLE RENT RESTRICTIONS

**10.47** The rules about eligible rent restrictions in Old Scheme cases are summarised in table 10.4. In applying them, authorities:

- must not take a blanket approach (GM para. A4.99): each step must be considered in the individual circumstances of each case and each step is open to appeal;
- must not restrict a claimant's eligible rent just because of the subsidy rules (chapter 21). The requirements of the HB regulations (described below) are the only test that is relevant in deciding whether or not benefit should be restricted.

There has been much case law about these matters, well explained in CPAG's *Housing Benefit and Council Tax Benefit Legislation,* by Lorna Findlay and others, published annually by the Child Poverty Action Group. The key points are referred to below.

### TABLE 10.4 HB RESTRICTIONS FOR OLD SCHEME CASES: A SIMPLIFIED SUMMARY

#### STEP ONE: IS THE RENT OR SIZE UNREASONABLE?

The claimant's HB can be restricted only if, compared with suitable alternative accommodation:

- the rent is unreasonably high; or
- the dwelling is unreasonably large; or
- a rent increase is unreasonable.

#### STEP TWO: IS THE CLAIMANT IN A PROTECTED GROUP?

Protections against HB restrictions can apply for claimants:

- who could afford their accommodation when their letting began; or
- who have had a death in their home; or
- who have children or young persons, or are aged 60 or more, or are sick or disabled.

#### STEP THREE: SHOULD THE ELIGIBLE RENT BE RESTRICTED?

If the rent is unreasonable (step one) and none of the protections applies (step two), the authority must decide how much (if at all) the claimant's eligible rent should be reduced.

## DECIDING WHAT IS 'UNREASONABLE' BY FINDING COMPARABLES

**10.48** The first question is whether: HBR Old 11(2), 12(1)

- the rent is unreasonably high, or
- the accommodation is unreasonably large for all the occupiers, or
- a rent increase is unreasonably high, or
- a rent increase is unreasonably soon after another increase during the previous year.

**10.49** As regards size, the question of who counts as an occupier is open to interpretation (since 'occupier' is not further defined for these purposes) and appeal (chapter 19), but it is not limited to the groups listed in paragraph 10.38. Though the Swale and Marchant case (para. 6.20) may affect how some authorities interpret 'occupier' for these purposes, there is an argument that that case was about the definition of 'occupier' in a different context and so is not binding here.

**10.50** In all the above cases, authorities:

- must make a comparison (as regards the rent, size or rent increase, as appropriate) with suitable alternative accommodation (paras. 10.51-52);
- may additionally take account of figures provided by the rent officer (if the case was referred to the rent officer: chapter 6) – and the DSS advises that they 'ought' to do this (GM para. A4.99), bearing in mind that the rent officer's function is different;
- must not, at this stage, take into account the impact of the subsidy rules on their own finances (para. 10.59).

**10.51** Authorities should make the comparison by working through the following questions:

(a) what is the rent (including all eligible and ineligible services) for the claimant's dwelling?

(b) what type of alternative accommodation is suitable for the claimant? and, in order to determine this, what services are requisite in order to regard the alternative accommodation as suitable and what other factors need to be taken into account (para. 10.52)?

(c) what rent (including all eligible and ineligible services) would be payable for such accommodation?

(d) is the rent in (a) unreasonably high by comparison with the rent in (c)?

The above is based on *R v East Yorkshire Borough of Beverley Housing Benefits Review Board ex p Hare,* (1995), QBD, The Times 28.2.95. As regards (d) above, 'unreasonably high' means more than just 'higher': *Malcolm v the Review Board for Tweeddale District*, Court of Session, August 1991.

HBR Old 11(6)(a),(7),(8)

**10.52** In deciding what alternative accommodation would be suitable for the claimant (question (b) above), authorities:

- must take account of the nature of the alternative accommodation and the exclusive and shared facilities provided, having regard to the age and state of health of all the occupiers (as defined in paras. 10.38-39). 'For example, a disabled or elderly person might have special needs and require more expensive or larger accommodation than would otherwise be the case' (GM para. A4.112);
- must only take into account alternative accommodation with security of tenure which is reasonably equivalent to what the claimant currently has;
- 'must have a sufficiency of information to ensure that like is being compared with like… Unless that can be done, no safe assessment can be made of the reasonableness of the rent in question or the proper level of value': *Malcolm v the Review Board for Tweeddale District, Court of Session,* August 1991;
- may take account of alternative accommodation outside the authority's own area if there is no comparable accommodation within it. But if this is necessary, it is unreasonable to 'make comparisons with other parts of the country where accommodation costs differ widely from those which apply locally' (GM para. A4.114).

## PROTECTED GROUPS

HBR Old 11(3)-(5), 12(2),(3)

**10.53** Three groups of claimants are protected against the effect of the above rules about HB restrictions. The first two groups, and the rules applying to them, are the same as those described in paragraphs 10.33-37; the details of the third group, and the rules applying to it, are described below.

## THE PROTECTION FOR CERTAIN VULNERABLE PEOPLE

HBR Old 11(3),(6)(b)

**10.54** A claimant falls within this protected group if any of the occupiers of his or her home (as defined in paras. 10.38-39) is:

- aged 60 or more; or
- responsible for a child or young person in the household (paras. 4.12-20); or
- incapable of work for social security purposes (though the person need not have claimed a relevant social security benefit).

In such a case, the authority must not reduce the claimant's eligible rent unless there is suitable alternative accommodation available (para. 10.55) and it is reasonable to expect the claimant to move (para. 10.56).

HBR Old 11(3)

**10.55** What counts as suitable alternative accommodation was described earlier (para. 10.52). The point here is that it must be available. For example, accommodation the claimant has recently left, or an offer of accommodation the claimant has refused, may be available – but only whilst it actually remains available to the claimant, and not after it has been let to someone else. The DWP advises that 'it is not necessary for an authority to be able to identify specific properties' but emphasises that 'authorities should regard accommodation as not available if, in practice, there is little or no possibility of the claimant being able to obtain it, for example because it could only be obtained on payment of a large deposit which the claimant does not possess' (GM para. A4.121). In *R v HB Review Board of East Devon Council ex p Gibson,* (1993), 25 HLR 487, CA, the judge emphasised that the authority was not an accommodation agency, and said: 'It is... quite sufficient if an active market rent is shown to exist in houses in an appropriate place at the appropriate level of rent to which the [eligible] rent is restricted. There must, however, be evidence at least of that... otherwise the recipient, if he had to move, would have nowhere to go. It is, however, sufficient, as I wish to stress, to point to a range of properties, or a bloc of property, which is available without specific identification of particular dwelling houses'.

**10.56** In deciding whether it is reasonable to expect the claimant to move, authorities must take into account: HBR Old 11(6)(b)

- the claimant's prospects of retaining employment; and
- the effect on the education of a child or young person who would have to change school (this means any child or young person mentioned in para. 10.38).

In *R v Sefton Metropolitan Borough Council ex p Cunningham,* (1991), 23 HLR 534, QBD, the judge emphasised the authority's duty to take individual circumstances into account when considering 'suitability', 'availability' and 'reasonableness'. In that case, the Review Board's decision was overturned because there was no evidence that it had considered the effect of a move on the claimant's eight-year-old child's education.

## RESTRICTING THE ELIGIBLE RENT

**10.57** The final question (if it applies at all, considering the above points) is of how much to restrict the eligible rent. In considering this, the authority must work through the following questions: HBR Old 11(2), 12(1) SI 1999 No. 2734 (GB) NISR 2000 No. 74

(a) is it appropriate to make a reduction in the claimant's eligible rent?
    and if it is

(b) what is the appropriate amount for the reduction? and

(c) how was that appropriate amount arrived at?

The above is based on the judgments in *Mehanne v Housing Benefit Review Board of the City of Westminster,* (1999), CA, *The Times* 5.3.99, and *R v East Yorkshire Borough of Beverley Housing Benefits Review Board ex p Hare,* (1995),

QBD, *The Times* 28.2.95. As regards (b) above, the authority must not reduce the claimant's eligible rent below the cost of comparable alternative accommodation: *R v Brent London Borough Council ex p Connery,* (1989) 22 HLR 40 QBD.

**10.58** As regards all the above questions, authorities must consider what is appropriate in the individual circumstances of each case. There are cases in which no reduction is appropriate. There are also cases in which no reduction is appropriate for the time being but may become appropriate later on. In practice in such cases, some authorities still tend to restrict claimants' eligible rents to what the rent officer has recommended (in cases which have been referred to the rent officer: chapter 6). However, the rent officer's figures do not take into account personal circumstances at all, whereas the question of what is 'appropriate' places a duty on authorities to do so.

## THE IMPACT OF SUBSIDY

**10.59** In *R v Brent London Borough Council ex p Connery,* (1989), 22 HLR 40, QBD, it was held that: 'An authority was entitled, except when acting in those cases where an absolute duty was to be fulfilled, to take into account the implications for its own financial situation [e.g. subsidy] when exercising its discretion' (*The Times,* 25.10.89, reproduced in GM ch. A4, annex A). As described earlier, there are three main questions to be considered in applying the rules about HB restrictions:

- whether the rent, size or rent increase is unreasonable;
- whether people fall within the protected groups; and
- whether to reduce the eligible rent or disallow a rent increase and, if so, by how much.

**10.60** The first two are questions of fact. Subsidy considerations cannot therefore play a part in answering them. The DSS's opinion is that the authority may take subsidy into account in answering the third question, though not as the only consideration (GM para. A4.115).

## IF A RENT HAS BEEN FIXED AS BINDING ON THE LANDLORD

HBR Old 11(1)
BR Old 11(1A)(GB)

**10.61** In addition to the other Old Scheme rules, if a claimant's rent has been fixed by a rent officer, rent tribunal or rent assessment committee (so that it is binding on the landlord), the claimant's eligible rent must not exceed that fixed figure. This applies for one year from the date on which the fixed figure takes effect. (If, however, the letting began in or before January 1989, see below.)

# Eligible rent for registered rent cases

**10.62** The following rules apply to: HBR 10(3) HBR Old 11(1) HBR Old 11(1A)(GB HBR sch 1A NIHBR sch 1B

- tenancies in England and Wales which were entered into before 15th January 1989;
- tenancies in Scotland which were entered into before 2nd January 1989;
- tenancies in Northern Ireland which are protected or statutory tenancies to which article 3 of the Housing (Northern Ireland) Order 1978 applies, i.e. their rent is fixed by a rent officer;
- tenancies granted on or after those dates in which the landlord is required to preserve the tenant's rights (typically because the landlord has moved a tenant whose tenancy began before those dates).

These are referred to in this Guide as 'registered rent cases'. They are sometimes also called protected tenancies, regulated tenancies, fair rent tenancies, Rent Act tenancies, and even the 'Old, Old Scheme'.

**10.63** In registered rent cases, the claimant's eligible rent is worked out as follows (but see also the next paragraph):

- if the claimant's rent has been fixed by a rent officer, rent tribunal or rent assessment committee (so that it is binding on the landlord), the claimant's eligible rent equals that figure minus any ineligible service charges included within it;
- in any other case, it is worked out in the same way as for a council tenant (para. 10.16).

**10.64** In either of the above cases, it is possible for the authority to restrict the rent – though this is in practice rare. The rules are as follows: HBR 10(6B) HBR Old 11

- if the case falls within the 'Old Scheme' (para. 10.7), it is dealt with in the same way as any other Old Scheme private sector case (paras. 10.46 onwards);
- if the case falls within the 'New Scheme', then a maximum rent cannot apply (because the case is not referred to the rent officer: chapter 6). The only way in which the rent can be restricted is if the authority uses its general power described in para. 10.41.

# Eligible rent for other cases

## TENANTS OF CHARITIES AND VOLUNTARY ORGANISATIONS

**10.65** The eligible rent of a claimant renting from a registered charity or a non-profit making voluntary organisation is worked out in the same way as for private sector cases (paras. 10.26 onwards); unless the charity or voluntary organisation is a registered housing association or other registered social landlord, in which case the rules for housing association tenants apply (paras. 10.20-25).

TENANTS OF NON-METROPOLITAN COUNTY COUNCILS

**10.66** The eligible rent of a claimant renting from a non-metropolitan county council (a typical example would be when a claimant rents from a county social services department) is worked out in the same way as for private sector cases (paras. 10.26 onwards).

TENANTS IN RESETTLEMENT PLACES

**10.67** The eligible rent of a claimant renting a resettlement place (defined as in para. 10.14) is worked out in the same way as for a private sector Old Scheme case (paras. 10.46 onwards) – unless it is a rent rebate case, in which case it is dealt with as such (para. 10.16).

TENANTS IN HOSTELS AND NIGHT SHELTERS

**10.68** There are no rules specifically for hostels or night shelters. The various rules given in the rest of this chapter apply. For example, a hostel might also be a registered housing association, a registered charity, etc; in which case the rules for that type of accommodation apply.

## Note on marginal references

SI 1995 No. 1644 **10.69** In this and the following chapter, marginal references to:

ISR 1996 No. 111 SI 1996 No. 965

- 'HBR 10' and 'HBR 11' are to regulations 10 and 11 of the main regulations (para. 1.29) as they currently apply – i.e. as they apply to 'New Scheme' cases;

SR 1996 No. 181

- 'HBR Old 10', 'HBR Old 11' and 'HBR Old 12' are to regulations 10 to 12 of those regulations as they stood immediately before 2nd January 1996 – i.e. as they continue to apply to 'Old Scheme' cases.

In the following chapter, references to 'HBR 10' and 'HBR 11' should be regarded as including references to 'HBR Old 10' and 'HBR Old 11'.

**TABLE 10.5 ELIGIBLE RENT: SUMMARY OF THE MAIN TYPES OF CASE**

COUNCIL TENANTS

| | | |
|---|---|---|
| General rule: | Old Scheme cases: | Actual rent minus ineligible service charges. |
| | New Scheme cases: | Actual rent minus ineligible service charges. |
| Rent restrictions: | Old Scheme cases: | Only by the use of comparables (para. 10.47). |
| | New Scheme cases: | Restrictions are possible only by using the rules in para. 10.41. |

HOUSING ASSOCIATION TENANTS

| | | |
|---|---|---|
| General rule: | Old Scheme cases: | Actual rent minus ineligible service charges. |
| | New Scheme cases: | Actual rent minus ineligible service charges. |
| Rent restrictions: | Old Scheme cases: | Only by the use of comparables (para. 10.47). |
| | New Scheme cases: | Is referred to the rent officer and is then the same as a private sector New Scheme case; otherwise no restriction is possible. |

MOST PRIVATE SECTOR TENANTS

| | | |
|---|---|---|
| General rule: | Old Scheme cases: | Actual rent minus ineligible service charges. |
| | New Scheme cases: | Use the lowest of the rent officer's figures (as adjusted by authority if appropriate). |
| Rent restrictions: | Old Scheme cases: | Only by the use of comparables (para. 10.47). |
| | New Scheme cases: | Restrictions are already 'built in' by the use of rent officer figures. Further restrictions are possible only by using the rules in para. 10.41. |

# 11 Service charges

HBR 10, 11, sch. 1 **11.1** This chapter deals with service charges (and related charges) which may be included in a claimant's actual rent, or payable as well as the rent. It applies to all HB claims and explains which charges are eligible for HB and which are not. The chapter covers:

- which service charges are and are not eligible for HB;
- whether the authority or the rent officer is responsible for valuing the various kinds of services; and
- the special rules for support charges and supported accommodation.

This chapter is relevant only in the calculation of HB (not CTB). Paragraph 10.69 gives further information on how marginal references work in this chapter.

## Overview

### THE IMPORTANCE OF SERVICE CHARGES

**11.2** Many tenants pay for services either in with their rent (in which case it is immaterial whether they are mentioned in their letting agreement) or separately. As illustrated in the examples, there are two main methods of showing service charges in letting agreements:

- a claimant's rent may be shown as so much per week (or month, etc.) including certain services; or
- it may be shown as so much per week (or month, etc.) with an amount for service charges being due on top of the rent.

**Examples: Service charges**

1. A council tenant claimant's rent is expressed as being £100 per fortnight including £20 per fortnight for fuel for the claimant's own room and £10 per fortnight for heating, lighting, cleaning and maintaining communal areas. In this case the eligible rent is £80 per fortnight (£40 per week). The ineligible charge for fuel for the claimant's own room is deducted.

2. A housing association claimant's rent is expressed as being £70 per fortnight plus £20 per fortnight for fuel for the claimant's own room and

£10 per fortnight for heating, lighting, cleaning and maintaining communal areas. In this case the eligible rent is £80 per fortnight (£40 per week). The eligible charge for the communal areas is added.

*Notes*

- The facts in the two examples are the same but are expressed differently.
- Information about the service charges illustrated is given later in this chapter.
- The terms 'net rent' and 'gross rent' are sometimes used to distinguish between different methods of expressing a rent figure. But they are used in different ways nationally and are best avoided for HB purposes.

**11.3** Whether a service charge is eligible for HB affects the amount of a claimant's eligible rent, which in turn affects the amount of his or her HB. Eligible rent was described in general terms in chapter 10.

- If a charge is 'eligible for HB', this means that it is in principle a charge which can be included in a claimant's eligible rent. With certain exceptions (mentioned below as they arise), it does not need to be valued; and no deduction is made for it at any stage in deciding the amount of a claimant's eligible rent unless the charge for it is excessive (para. 11.22).
- If a charge is 'ineligible for HB', this means that it is in principle a charge which cannot be included in a claimant's eligible rent. With certain exceptions, it needs to be valued and deducted at some point in deciding the amount of a claimant's eligible rent (para. 11.4).

Councils, housing associations and many other landlords provide details of service charges to their tenants (and in many cases, tenants have a right to this information: for good information on this, see *Housing Rights Guide* by Geoffrey Randall, published by Shelter). It is in their interests as well as their tenants' to bear in mind the detailed rules when deciding what services to provide and how much to charge for them.

## WHO DEALS WITH SERVICE CHARGES

**11.4** Service charges may be dealt with by the authority or the rent officer (or both of them) in assessing a claimant's eligible rent. Fuller details are given in the remainder of this chapter and in chapter 10, but in general terms:

- when a 'maximum rent' applies in assessing the claimant's eligible rent (as in many private tenant cases, for example), the rent officer provides the council with figures which are already adjusted to take account of most service charges: in effect, the rent officer values them;
- when a 'maximum rent' does not apply (as in all council, most housing association and some private tenant cases), it is the authority which assesses all matters relating to service charges.

'Maximum rent' is explained in paragaph 10.29. Details of which rules apply for various service charges are given at the relevant places throughout this chapter.

### DEFINITION OF 'SERVICES'

HBR 10(7) **11.5** The law defines 'services' as 'services performed or facilities... provided for, or rights made available to, the occupier...' and 'service charge' as any periodical charge for any such service.

## Eligibility: general rules

HBR 10(1),(3),(7) **11.6** Service charges are eligible for HB, so long as they:

- have to be paid as a condition of occupying the dwelling as a home; and
- are not listed in the regulations as ineligible (as described in the following paragraphs); and
- are not excessive in relation to the service provided (para. 11.12).

**11.7** The first of these conditions need not have applied from the date the letting agreement began. A service charge is eligible for HB (subject to the other conditions) whenever the claimant agreed to pay it, if the only alternative would have been to lose his or her home. (Note also that a different rule applies in the case of charges for garages, land etc: para. 11.31.)

**11.8** Details of which service charges are eligible for HB (subject to the above points) follow, and are summarised in table 11.1. Helpful advice on services is given by the DWP (GM paras. A4.57-95).

**11.9** Sometimes services are provided free to a claimant. The DWP points out in relation to hostel residents (thought the point is relevant to all claims) that 'Authorities should... ensure that they ascertain which services are included within the hostel charge. Authorities should not attempt to deduct the value of ineligible items funded from other sources' (GM para. A4.69).

## VALUING INELIGIBLE SERVICE CHARGES

**11.10** When the authority has the duty of valuing ineligible service charges (paras. 11.4), this is done as follows: HBR 10(3), sch. 1 para. 2

- if the amount can be identified from the letting agreement or in some other way, the authority uses the amount so identified as the value;
- but if this identified amount is unrealistically low for the service provided, or if the amount cannot be identified, the authority must decide what amount is fairly attributable to the value;
- however, different rules can apply for water charges, fuel and meals (paras. 11.14-23).

## VALUING ELIGIBLE SERVICE CHARGES

**11.11** It is not usually necessary to value eligible service charges. The main exception is support charges. In general terms the authority values them as follows: HBR 10, sch. 1, HBR sch. 1B (GB) NIHBR sch. 1C

- if the amount can be identified from the letting agreement or in some other way, the authority uses the amount so identified as the value;
- but if this identified amount is excessive, or if the amount cannot be identified, the authority must decide what amount is fairly attributable to the value.

## EXCESSIVE ELIGIBLE SERVICE CHARGES

**11.12** In deciding whether an eligible service charge is excessive, the authority must take account of the cost of comparable services. If it is excessive, the authority must decide how much would be reasonable for that service and disallow the excess. HBR 10(6B), sch. 1 para. 3

### Table 11.1: SERVICE CHARGES SUMMARY

As described throughout this chapter, further details apply in many of the following cases.

| Type of service charge | Is it a 'support charge'? | Eligible for HB in 'supported accommodation?' | Eligible for HB elsewhere? |
|---|---|---|---|
| Water charges | NO | NO | NO |
| Provision of a heating system | NO | YES | YES |
| Fuel for communal areas | NO | YES | YES |

| Type of service charge | Is it a 'support charge'? | Eligible for HB in 'supported accommodation?' | Eligible for HB elsewhere? |
|---|---|---|---|
| Other fuel | NO | NO | NO |
| Meals | NO | NO | NO |
| Furniture/household equipment | NO | YES | YES |
| Communal window cleaning | NO | YES | YES |
| Other exterior window cleaning which the occupier(s) cannot do | NO | YES | YES |
| Other interior window cleaning which the occupier(s) cannot do | YES | YES | NO |
| Other window cleaning | YES | NO | NO |
| Communal cleaning | NO | YES | YES |
| Other cleaning which which the occupier(s) cannot do | YES | YES | NO |
| Other cleaning | YES | NO | NO |
| Emergency alarm systems in certain accommodation | YES | YES | NO |
| Emergency alarm systems otherwise | YES | NO | NO |
| General counselling and support which meets the conditions in paragraph 11.39 | YES | YES | NO |
| General counselling and support otherwise | YES | NO | NO |
| Specific counselling and support | YES | NO | NO |
| Medical/nursing/personal care | YES | NO | NO |
| Day-to-day living expenses | NO | NO | NO |
| Most communal services relating to the provision of adequate accommodation | NO | YES | YES |

## Which service charges are eligible?

**11.13** The remainder of this chapter deals with the following two types of charges:

- 'support charges' (dealt with in paras. 11.33 onwards); and
- other service charges and related charges (dealt with below).

### WATER CHARGES

**11.14** Water charges (including any sewerage or environmental charges) are not eligible for HB. So if such charges are included in a claimant's rent, an amount must be deducted for them. (No deduction is made at any stage if the claimant pays water charges direct to the water company, since in such a case the water charges are not included in the claimant's rent). In Northern Ireland water charges are covered by the rates element of HB. However the rates element is deducted from the rent as in Great Britain.

HBR 2(1) (GB)
HBR 10(3),(6)

**11.15** In cases in which a maximum rent applies, the rent officer deducts an amount for such charges (table 10.3). In other cases, the authority decides the value as follows:

- if the water charge varies according to consumption, either the actual amount or an estimate;
- otherwise, if the claimant's accommodation is a self-contained unit, the actual amount of the water charge;
- otherwise, a proportion of the water charge for the self-contained unit. The proportion should equal the floor area of the claimant's accommodation divided by the floor area of the self-contained unit (but in practice, authorities sometimes use different, simpler methods).

### FUEL, ETC.

**11.16** Charges for fuel (such as gas, electricity, etc. and also any standing charges or other supply costs) are not eligible for HB. So if such charges are included in a claimant's rent, an amount must be deducted for them. (No deduction is made at any stage if the claimant pays fuel charges direct to the fuel company, since in such a case the fuel charges are not included in the claimant's rent.)

HBR 10(3)
HBR sch. 1
paras. 4, 5, 7 (GB)
NIHBR sch. 1
paras. 4, 5, 8

**11.17** There are two exceptions to the above:

- a charge for the provision of a heating system is eligible for HB, but only if it is separate from the fuel charge;
- a fuel charge for communal areas is eligible for HB, but only if is it separate from the fuel charge for the claimant's own accommodation. Communal areas are areas of common access (e.g. halls, stairways, passageways) and,

in sheltered accommodation only, they also include common rooms (e.g. a dining room or lounge).

**11.18** In cases in which a maximum rent applies, the rent officer deducts an amount for such charges (table 10.3). In other cases, the rules depend on whether the amount of the fuel charge is known to the authority, as described below.

**11.19** If the amount of a fuel charge is identifiable, the authority uses this figure as the value of the fuel charge. However, if this is unrealistically low or includes an element for communal areas which cannot readily be separated out, the fuel charge is treated as unidentifiable.

**11.20** If the amount of a fuel charge is not identifiable (or not 'readily identifiable'), the authority decides its value by reference to standard amounts depending on what the fuel is for, as shown in table 10.2. As shown there, the standard amounts are lower for claimants who occupy one room only: the DWP advises that this includes cases where a claimant has shared used of only one room; and that communal areas should be disregarded (GM para. A4.90). If the authority uses these standard amounts, it must invite the claimant to provide evidence on which the 'actual or approximate' amount of the actual charge may be estimated; and, if reasonable evidence is provided, the authority must estimate the value of the fuel charge.

**Table 11.2 STANDARD WEEKLY FUEL DEDUCTIONS**

***Amounts are added together if fuel is provided for more than one of the purposes shown.***

IF THE CLAIMANT AND ANY FAMILY OCCUPY MORE THAN ONE ROOM

| | |
|---|---|
| Fuel for heating | £9.40 |
| Fuel for hot water | £1.15 |
| Fuel for lighting | £0.80 |
| Fuel for cooking | £1.15 |
| Fuel for any other purpose | NIL |
| Fuel for all the above | £12.50 |

| IF THE CLAIMANT AND ANY FAMILY OCCUPY ONE ROOM ONLY | |
|---|---|
| Fuel for heating | £5.68 |
| Fuel for hot water: | |
| if fuel for heating is also provided | NIL |
| if fuel for heating is not also provided | £1.15 |
| Fuel for lighting: | |
| if fuel for heating is also provided | NIL |
| if fuel for heating is not also provided | £0.80 |
| Fuel for cooking | £1.15 |
| Fuel for any other purpose | NIL |
| Fuel for all the above: £5.68 for heating + £1.15 for cooking (+ NIL for hot water and lighting) | £6.83 |

## MEALS (INCLUDING FOOD)

**11.21** Charges for meals are not eligible for HB. So if such charges are included in a claimant's rent, an amount must be deducted for them. HBR sch. 1 para. 1(a), 1A

**11.22** For these purposes, 'meals' includes the preparation of meals (e.g. where meals are prepared somewhere else and then delivered) and also the provision of unprepared food (e.g. cereal, bread still in its wrappings).

**11.23** In cases in which a maximum rent applies, the rent officer does not deduct an amount for such charges, though there are uncommon exceptions to this (table 12.3). So both in these cases and in all other cases, the authority decides the value by reference to standard amounts depending on what meals are provided, as shown in table 11.3. Those amounts cannot be varied; the actual amount the landlord charges for meals is never used. As shown in the table, one deduction applies for each person whose meals are paid for in the claimant's rent (whether this is the claimant, a member of the family or some other person such as a non-dependant). No deduction applies for anyone whose meals are not included (for example, a baby). When appropriate, deductions are calculated separately for each person (for example fewer meals may be provided for someone who goes out to work than for someone who does not).

**Table 11.3 STANDARD WEEKLY MEALS DEDUCTIONS**

***A separate amount is assessed and deducted for each person whose meals are provided.***

| | |
|---|---|
| IF AT LEAST THREE MEALS ARE PROVIDED EVERY DAY | |
| For the claimant, and each other person from the first Monday in September following his or her 16th birthday | £19.25 |
| For each other person | £9.70 |
| IF BREAKFAST ONLY IS PROVIDED | |
| For the claimant, and each other person of any age | £2.35 |
| ALL OTHER CASES | |
| For the claimant, and each other person from the first Monday in September following his or her 16th birthday | £12.80 |
| For each other person | £6.45 |

FURNITURE AND HOUSEHOLD EQUIPMENT

HBR 10(3), sch. 1 para. 1(b)

**11.24** Charges for the use of these are eligible for HB, unless there is an intention that they will become part of the claimant's personal property, in which case they are ineligible. Ineligible amounts are valued by the rent officer in maximum rent cases, otherwise by the authority.

CERTAIN CLEANING AND WINDOW CLEANING

HBR 10(3), sch. 1 para. 1(a)(iv) HBR sch. 1B para. 3 (GB) NIHBR sch. 1C para. 3

**11.25** Charges for the following are eligible for HB:

- cleaning of communal areas;
- communal window cleaning; and
- cleaning the outsides of windows which no-one in the household can do.

Other cleaning and window cleaning falls within different rules, as described in paragraph 11.37.

## OTHER COMMUNAL SERVICES, ETC.

**11.26** Charges for the following are eligible for HB: HBR 10(3), sch. 1 para. 1(a)

- children's play areas;
- TV and radio relay (though not normally of satellite or cable services);
- other services which are related to the provision of adequate accommodation.

**11.27** The DWP advises (GM paras. A4.71, A4.85) that the last item includes:

- portering and refuse removal;
- lifts, communal telephones and entry phones; and
- communal laundry facilities (e.g. a laundry room).

## OTHER DAY-TO-DAY LIVING EXPENSES, ETC.

**11.28** Charges for the following are not eligible for HB. So if charges for them are included in a claimant's rent, an amount must be deducted for them. The amount is valued by the rent officer in maximum rent cases, otherwise by the authority: HBR 10(3), sch. 1 para. 1(g)

- laundering (e.g. washing sheets, etc, for the claimant);
- transport;
- sports facilities;
- TV and radio rental and licence and (in most cases) satellite service charges;
- any other leisure items or day-to-day living expenses; or
- any other services which 'are not related to the provision of adequate accommodation'.

## OTHER OVERHEADS INCLUDING MANAGEMENT COSTS AND COUNCIL TAX

**11.29** Whether the landlord's normal overheads (such as maintenance, insurance and repair costs) count as 'services' or simply as part of the claimant's rent is an arguable point. But in either case they are eligible for HB. In particular, this includes any part of the rent towards the landlord's liability for council tax (e.g. if the claimant has a resident landlord or lives in a house made up of bedsits). No amount is deducted for these items at any stage, so they do not normally need to be valued.

### INCREASES TO COVER ARREARS OF RENT

HBR 8(2A) **11.30** If a claimant's rent has been increased in order to recover arrears of rent or other charges, that part of the rent is ineligible for HB. This rule applies only if an individual claimant's rent is increased to cover his or her own arrears on a current or former home. It does not apply when landlords increase rents on all their properties as a result of arrears generally.

### GARAGES, LAND, ETC.

HBR 2(4)(a) **11.31** The rent on a garage (or any other buildings, gardens or land included in the claimant's letting agreement) is eligible for HB, but only if:

- they are used for occupying the dwelling as a home; and
- the claimant acquired them at the same time as the dwelling; and
- the claimant has no option but to rent them at the same time.

Otherwise, they are eligible for HB only if the claimant has made or is making reasonable efforts to end liability for them.

### BUSINESS PREMISES

HBR 10(4) **11.32** Rent on any part of a property which is used for business, commercial or other non-residential purposes is not eligible for HB. For example, if a claimant rents both a shop and the flat above it, only the rent relating to the flat is eligible for HB. If the rent on the business premises is not specified separately from the rent on the home, it is necessary for the authority to decide how much relates to each. For self-employed claimants who work from home, see paragraph 13.22.

## Support charges

### DEFINITION AND OVERVIEW

HBR 11(5A)-(5F)
HBR 12A(1ZA)(GB)
HBR sch. 1B (GB)
NIHBR sch. 1C

**11.33** 'Support charges' are a special type of service charge. The following count as 'support charges':

- cleaning and window cleaning (apart from communal cleaning, communal window cleaning, and cleaning the outsides of windows which no-one in the household can do: para. 11.25);
- emergency alarm systems;
- counselling and support;
- medical, nursing and personal care.

**11.34** Some of these are eligible for HB only in 'supported accommodation' (para. 11.43); others are never eligible for HB. The following paragraphs give the current rules, which apply from April 2000 until April 2003 and are therefore sometimes called the 'transitional scheme'. From April 2003, the DWP plans that help with these charges will instead be available from 'Supporting People', a body administered jointly by housing services, social services and probation services.

**11.35** In cases in which a maximum rent applies, the authority decides the value of eligible support charges and adds this (table 12.3). In other cases, the authority decides the value of ineligible support charges and deducts this (chapter 10).

## CERTAIN CLEANING AND WINDOW CLEANING

**11.36** Charges for some kinds of cleaning and window cleaning are always eligible for HB and do not count as 'support charges': they are given in paragraph 11.25.

HBR 10(3), sch. 1 para. 1(a)(iv)
HBR sch. 1B para. 3 (GB)
NIHBR sch. 1C para. 3

**11.37** Charges for any other cleaning and window cleaning are eligible for HB only in 'supported accommodation' (para. 11.43), and only if no-one in the claimant's household is able to do it. Examples would include cleaning the inside of a claimant's home in sheltered accommodation. Otherwise they are ineligible for HB.

## EMERGENCY ALARM SYSTEMS

**11.38** Charges for these are eligible for HB only in 'supported accommodation' (para. 11.43) which (in addition to the definition referred to) is designed or adapted for elderly, sick or disabled persons, or particularly suitable for them as regards size, heating systems and other major features or facilities. Otherwise they are ineligible for HB.

HBR 10(3), sch. 1 para. 1(c), HBR sch. 1B para. 4 (GB)
NIHBR sch. 1C para. 4

## GENERAL COUNSELLING AND SUPPORT

**11.39** Charges for these are eligible for HB only if all the following criteria are met:

HBR 10(3), sch. 1 para. 1(f), HBR sch. 1B para. 2 (GB)
NIHBR sch. 1C para. 2

- it is 'supported accommodation' (para. 11.43); and
- the charges are for time spent on 'general counselling' (compare para. 11.41) or 'other support services'; and
- the services are provided by the landlord personally or by a person on the landlord's behalf; and
- the services fall within the list in the following paragraph.

Otherwise they are ineligible for HB.

HBR sch 1B para. 2
NIHBR sch. 1C para. 2

**11.40** The services which are eligible for HB under the above rule are general counselling and support which:

- assists the claimant with maintaining the dwelling's security; or
- assists the claimant with maintaining the dwelling's safety (including arranging for checking the claimant's own appliances if they could be a safety hazard); or
- is directed at assisting the claimant with complying with the terms of his or her letting agreement relating to nuisance, rent liability, maintenance of the interior and/or the period of the letting – including in each case assisting the claimant with contacts with individuals or professional or other bodies with an interest in ensuring the claimant's welfare; or
- is for any other general counselling and support provided by a resident or on-call warden – but in this case only in accommodation which is one of a group of dwellings which the landlord lets as a matter of practice to people in need of general counselling and support.

## SPECIFIC COUNSELLING AND SUPPORT

HBR 10(3), sch. 1 para. 1(d)

**11.41** Charges for counselling and support which is of a specific nature (i.e. is not 'general' as described in paras. 11.39-40) are not eligible for HB in any kind of accommodation. Examples (from circular HB/CTB A10/2001) would include counselling to meet an identified need such as alcohol or drug dependency.

## MEDICAL, NURSING AND PERSONAL CARE

HBR 10(3), sch. 1 para. 1(e),(f)

**11.42** Charges for the following are not eligible for HB in any kind of accommodation:

- 'medical expenses (including the cost of treatment or counselling relating to mental disorder, mental handicap, physical disablement or past or present alcohol or drug dependence)'; or
- 'the provision of nursing care or personal care (including assistance at meal-times or with personal appearance or hygiene)'.

## THE DEFINITION OF 'SUPPORTED ACCOMMODATION'

HBR 2(1), sch. 1 para. 7

**11.43** For the purposes of the above rules (paras. 11.33-41), 'supported accommodation' is:

- any accommodation 'provided by':
    - a housing authority or in Northern Ireland the Housing Executive, Health and Social Services Board or HSS Trust,
    - a registered housing association,
    - a registered charity,

- a non-profit-making voluntary organisation,
- a non-metropolitan county council, or
- any other registered social landlord,

where (in each of the cases just listed) 'that body or a person acting on its behalf also provides the claimant with care, support or supervision'; or

- ◆ any resettlement place provided by a local authority or non-profit-making voluntary organisation which has received a grant under section 30 of the Jobseekers Act 1995; or
- ◆ any accommodation occupied by a person for whom the social services (in Scotland, social work) department has made a community care assessment (CCA) stating that the person needs the services in question (paras. 11.33-41), and that the landlord is capable of providing these services or of arranging for them to be provided.

The comments in paragraph 10.15 apply equally here.

**11.44** If the social services (or social work) department makes a retrospective CCA, it also has full effect retrospectively for HB purposes, with the following two time limits. Support charges become eligible retrospectively for HB: HBR 68(1),(8), sch. 1 para. 7

- ◆ only if, and to the extent that, they were provided to the claimant continuously up to the date the CCA was made; and
- ◆ only back to 1st or 3rd April 2000 at the earliest.

**11.45** A retrospective CCA may have the effect of increasing someone's entitlement, in which cases the arrears must be awarded; or it may have the effect that someone who claimed HB and was thought not to qualify for it now qualifies, in which case the HB claim they made must be reconsidered. These cases do not count as 'backdating' (para. 5.86), so there is no test of 'good cause'. Also, these cases are not undermined by the rule on late notified changes of circumstances (para. 17.33; because the claimant has no duty to notify the council of a retrospective CCA until it has been made).

**11.46** A retrospective CCA may mean that someone who did not claim HB now realises he or she would have qualified. To get HB awarded retrospectively in this case, it is necessary for the claimant to ask for backdating and to satisfy the test of 'good cause' (para. 5.86 onwards).

# 12 Applicable amounts

**12.1** An applicable amount is the figure used in calculating HB and main CTB to reflect the basic living needs of the claimant and family. People on income support or income-based jobseeker's allowance have already had their applicable amount worked out for the purpose of assessing entitlement to those benefits. This chapter does not apply to them. This chapter covers:

- personal allowances;
- general rules about premiums;
- the detailed rules for each premium in turn; and
- further rules and special cases.

CBA 135
NICBA 131
HBR 16
CTBR 8

**12.2** A claimant's applicable amount is the same for both HB and main CTB purposes. It is the total of any personal allowances and premiums which apply in his or her case.

## Personal allowances

HBR 16(a),(b), sch 2 paras 1,2
CTBR 8(a),(b) sch 1 paras 1,2

**12.3** Personal allowances are awarded for the claimant and any other family members (para. 4.5). There are different amounts for single claimants, lone parents and couples. Additions are made for children and young persons (sometimes known as dependants' allowances). The amounts, which vary with age, are given in table 12.1.

### ADDITIONS FOR CHILDREN AND YOUNG PERSONS

HBR sch 2 para 2
CTBR sch 1 para 2

**12.4** The two possible levels of addition for children and young persons are listed in table 12.1. The claimant qualifies for one addition for each child or young person:

- the lower addition applies from the Monday following the day on which the child is born;
- the higher addition applies from the second Monday in September following his or her 16th birthday. (Although the law mentions the first Monday in September, the rules about changes of circumstances mean that the higher amount is taken into account from the second Monday: para. 17.65.)

## Table 12.1 WEEKLY APPLICABLE AMOUNTS

| | | |
|---|---|---|
| **PERSONAL ALLOWANCES** | | |
| Single claimant | aged under 25 | £42.70 |
| | aged 25 or over | £53.95 |
| Lone parent | aged under 18 (HB only) | £42.70 |
| | aged 18 or over | £53.95 |
| Couple | both aged under 18 (HB only) | £64.45 |
| | at least one aged 18 or over | £84.65 |
| Child/young person addition (see para. 12.4) | lower rate | £33.50 |
| | higher rate | £34.30 |
| **PREMIUMS** | | |
| *Premiums that can apply regardless of the claimant's or partner's age* | | |
| Family premium | protected rate | £22.20 |
| | basic rate | £14.75 |
| Disabled child premium | child/young person | £35.50 |
| Enhanced disability premium * | child/young person | £11.25 |
| Severe disability premium | single rate | £42.25 |
| | double rate | £84.50 |
| Carer premium | claimant or partner or each | £24.80 |
| *Premiums that can apply only if the claimant is (or in the case of a couple, either partner is) aged 60 or more* | | |
| Pensioner premium *or* Enhanced pensioner premium *or* Higher pensioner premium | single claimant or lone parent | £44.20 |
| | couple | £65.15 |
| *Premiums that can apply only if the claimant is (or in the case of a couple, both partners are) aged under 60* | | |
| Disability premium | single claimant or lone parent | £23.00 |
| | couple | £32.80 |
| Enhanced disability premium * | single claimant or lone parent | £11.25 |
| | couple | £16.25 |
| Bereavement premium | single claimant | £21.55 |

** The enhanced disability premium appears twice in this table – once for a child/young person, once for the claimant and/or partner.*

**Examples: Applicable amounts**

Except for the lone parent in the fourth example, none of the following qualifies for any of the premiums for disability or for carers.

SINGLE CLAIMANT AGED 23

| | |
|---|---|
| Personal allowance: | |
| single claimant aged under 25 | £42.70 |
| No premiums apply | |
| Applicable amount | £42.70 |

COUPLE WITH TWO CHILDREN AGED 13 AND 17

The older child is still at school so still counts as a dependant of the couple.

| | |
|---|---|
| Personal allowances: | |
| couple at least one over 18 | £84.65 |
| child aged 13 (lower addition) | £33.50 |
| child aged 17 (lower addition) | £34.30 |
| Premium: family premium (basic rate) | £14.75 |
| Applicable amount | £167.20 |

COUPLE AGED 58 AND 65

| | |
|---|---|
| Personal allowance: | |
| couple at least one over 18 | £84.65 |
| Premium: pensioner premium (couple rate) | £65.15 |
| Applicable amount | £149.80 |

DISABLED LONE PARENT WITH BABY

The lone parent is in receipt of the highest rate of the care component of disability living allowance and so qualifies for a disability premium and an enhanced disability premium. Because of this, she cannot get the protected rate of the family premium.

| | |
|---|---|
| Personal allowances: | |
| lone parent aged over 18 | £53.95 |
| child (lower addition) | £33.50 |
| Premiums: | |
| Family premium (basic rate) | £14.75 |
| disability premium (lone parent rate) | £23.00 |
| enhanced disability premium (lone parent rate) | £11.25 |
| Applicable amount | £136.45 |

# Premiums

**12.5** Many claimants – but not all – qualify for one or more premiums. Table 12.1 lists the premiums available and gives their amounts. A premium is awarded if its conditions of entitlement are satisfied. Some of the conditions are straightforward, some more complicated and less well known. Also, some of the rules have changed this year. Claimants may therefore miss entitlement unless authority staff are fully trained and claim forms are carefully designed. In particular, receipt of various state benefits affects many premiums, and general points about these are given in paragraphs 12.39-41. The next few sections give the conditions for each premium.

HBR 16(c),(d)
sch 2 paras 3-6, 1!
CTBR 8(c),(d)
sch 1 paras 3-6, 1!

## HOW MANY PREMIUMS AT ONCE?

**12.6** Generally speaking, there are no limits on how many premiums a claimant can be awarded at the same time as each other. In the law, some limitations follow from the conditions relevant to the premiums in question. In this Guide, the premiums are described in such a way that all limitations are given as conditions for the premiums.

HBR sch 2
CTBR sch 1

**12.7** As shown in table 14.1 (and in the descriptions below for each premium), some premiums depend on whether the claimant or partner has or has not reached the age of 60. This in itself limits the number of premiums that can be awarded at the same time, as is illustrated in the following examples. For further points relating to couples, please see the description of the relevant premium(s) given below.

### Examples: Overlapping premiums

OVER 60 AND DISABLED

A claimant is aged 63. She lives alone. She is also disabled in one of the ways relevant to the disability premium.

She gets one of the pensioner premiums (in fact it will be the higher pensioner premium). But she cannot get a disability premium as she is aged 60 or more.

OVER 60 WITH A DISABLED SON

A claimant is aged 63. He is not disabled in any way but his son aged 15 gets the highest rate of the care component of disability living allowance. No-one else lives with them.

He gets one of the pensioner premiums (in fact it will be the (ordinary) pensioner premium). He also gets a disabled child premium and an enhanced disability premium for his grandson. He also gets a family premium.

UNDER 60, DISABLED AND BEREAVED

A single claimant aged 57 has had a bereavement and fulfils the conditions for the bereavement premium. He also gets the highest rate of the care component of disability living allowance.

He gets a disability premium and an enhanced disability premium. But he cannot get a bereavement premium at the same time.

## FAMILY PREMIUM

**12.8** The condition for this premium is that there is at least one child or young person in the claimant's family - whether the claimant is in a couple or is a lone parent. The terms 'child', 'young person', 'family', 'couple' and 'lone parent' are used in the specific senses defined for HB and CTB (paras. 4.5-20). In particular, a child or young person need not be the natural child of the claimant but could, for example, be a grandchild living as part of the claimant's family.

**12.9** There are two rates of this premium:

- lone parents who satisfy the conditions in paragraph 12.10 get the protected lone parent rate (which is higher than the basic rate);
- other lone parents get the basic rate;
- couples (with at least one child or young person) get the basic rate.

**12.10** A lone parent qualifies for the protected lone parent rate of the family premium if, and for as long as, all the following conditions apply:

- on 5th April 1998, he or she was entitled to HB or CTB and satisfied the conditions for the lone parent rate of the family premium or would have done so but for the fact that 5th April 1998 fell within a rent-free period;
- he or she has remained entitled to HB or CTB continuously since that date (ignoring breaks due only to rent-free periods);
- he or she has not ceased to be a lone parent at any time since that date;
- he or she has not become entitled to income support or to income-based jobseeker's allowance, or ceased to be entitled to both those benefits, at any time since that date; and
- he or she has not reached the age of 60 or become entitled to a disability premium at any time since that date.

**12.11** As soon as any of the last four conditions ceases to apply, the person ceases permanently to qualify for the protected lone parent rate (but may still qualify for the basic rate).

## THE THREE PENSIONER PREMIUMS

**12.12** The condition for getting one of the three pensioner premiums is that the claimant (or in the case of a couple, either partner) is aged 60 or more. In the case of a couple, the couple rate is awarded even if only one partner is aged 60 or more.

HBR sch 2 paras. 9, 9A, 10
CTBR sch 2 paras 9, 10, 11

**12.13** Although there are three different pensioner premiums, the amounts are (since April 2001) the same as each other. For completeness the conditions for each of the three premiums follow.

**12.14** *Pensioner premium:* The condition for this premium is that the claimant (or in the case of a couple, the older partner) is aged between 60 and 74 inclusive.

**12.15** *Enhanced pensioner premium:* The condition for this premium is that the claimant (or in the case of a couple, the older partner) is aged between 75 and 79 inclusive.

**12.16** *Higher pensioner premium:* There are three possible ways of qualifying for this premium. They are that:

- the claimant (or in the case of a couple, the older partner) is aged 80 or more; or
- the claimant (or in the case of a couple, at least one partner) is aged 60 or more and counts as 'disabled or long-term sick' in one of the ways described in paragraph 12.20 (in the case of a couple, it is sufficient if one is over 60 and the other counts as 'disabled or long-term sick'); or
- the 'automatic transfer rule' (but see the following paragraph).

**12.17** The 'automatic transfer rule' no longer has any value. This is because all the pensioner premiums are now worth the same, and so there is no advantage to be gained by qualifying for the higher pensioner premium rather than the (ordinary) pensioner premium or the enhanced pensioner premium.

HBR sch 2 para 10
CTBR sch 1 para 11

**12.18** The full details of the automatic transfer rule may be found in paragraphs 12.16-18 of the 2001-02 edition of this Guide. In general terms it provides that if a person qualifies for HB/CTB with a disability premium at or around the date of his or her 60th birthday, then he or she qualifies for a higher pensioner premium thereafter, for as long as he or she remains on HB/CTB, without ever having to show that he or she is disabled or long term sick.

HBR sch 2 para 11
CTBR sch 1 para 12

## DISABILITY PREMIUM

**12.19** There are two conditions for this premium. They are that:

- the claimant is (or in the case of a couple, both partners are) aged under 60; and
- the claimant (or in the case of a couple, either partner) counts as 'disabled or long-term sick' in one of the ways described in paragraph 12.20.

In the case of a couple, the couple rate is awarded even if only one partner fulfils the conditions.

## 'DISABLED OR LONG-TERM SICK'

HBR 2(1) sch 2 para 12(1),(2) CTBR 2(1) sch 1 para 13(1),(2)

**12.20** The following are the ways of counting as 'disabled or long-term sick' in order to qualify for a disability premium (para. 12.19; or in certain cases for a higher pensioner premium: para. 12.15). They are that the claimant or any partner:

- is registered or certified blind (this means with the social services or social work department, in Northern Ireland with the Health and Social Services Board); or
- ceased to be registered or certified blind within the past 28 weeks because of regaining sight; or
- receives disability living allowance (either component payable at any rate); or
- disabled person's tax credit; or
- attendance allowance; or
- any increase for attendance or mobility paid with an industrial disablement benefit or war disablement benefit (including constant attendance allowance, 'old cases' attendance payments, mobility supplement, severe disablement occupational allowance and exceptionally severe disablement allowance); or
- has part or all of his or her disability living allowance paid to the Motability fund; or
- has an invalid vehicle supplied by the NHS or gets DSS payments for car running costs; or
- is incapable of work and fulfils the further conditions in either of the next two paragraphs.

HBR sch 2 para 12(1),(4),(7) CTBR sch 1 para 13(1),(4),(6A) SI 1995 No. 626 (GB) ISR 1995 No. 129

## PEOPLE WHO ARE INCAPABLE OF WORK: THE MAIN RULE

**12.21** For the purposes of qualifying for a disability premium (or higher pensioner premium), the claimant or any partner counts as 'disabled or long-term sick' if he or she:

- receives incapacity benefit payable at the long-term rate (which starts after 52 weeks of incapacity for work), or is terminally ill and receives it at the short-term higher rate (which starts after 28 weeks of incapacity for work); or

- transferred from incapacity benefit (or the former invalidity benefit) to retirement pension whilst he or she was on HB or CTB (or community charge benefit), and has since remained on HB or CTB (or community charge benefit) with no breaks in entitlement to both of more than eight weeks.

People who are disqualified from incapacity benefit do not satisfy the rule.

## PEOPLE WHO ARE INCAPABLE OF WORK: THE '28/52-WEEK RULE'

**12.22** Additionally, for the purposes of qualifying for a disability premium (but not a higher pensioner premium), the claimant counts as disabled or long-term sick if he or she:

- is incapable of work; and
- has been incapable of work for a 'waiting period' (calculated as described below) of:
  - 28 weeks if he or she is terminally ill, or
  - 52 weeks in any other case.

After the waiting period is completed, there are further 'linking rules' (described below).

**12.23** This way of qualifying for a disability premium 'fills the gap' for people who are incapable of work but do not get incapacity benefit. For couples, it must be the claimant – not his or her partner – who fulfils this rule. It can therefore be important which partner makes the claim (para. 5.5).

**12.24** 'Incapable of work' means the same here as it does for incapacity benefit purposes. Broadly, during the first 28 weeks the person must satisfy an 'own occupation test', and thereafter (or from the outset if he or she has no normal occupation) an 'all work test'. Broadly, a person is 'terminally ill' if his or her death can be expected within six months. Circular HB/CTB A42/98 enclosed a form which authorities may use to obtain information from the Benefits Agency relevant to whether someone is 'incapable of work'.

## THE 'WAITING PERIOD' AND THE 'LINKING RULES'

**12.25** In the following, a 'gap' means a period during which the person either is capable of work or is disqualified from incapacity benefit. The waiting period (para. 12.22) need not be continuous. Any number of periods are added together so long as the gap between each is eight weeks or less.

Once a person has completed the waiting period, there are linking rules as follows:

- the claimant does not qualify for a disability premium during a gap;

- after a gap of eight weeks or less, the person qualifies for a disability premium straight away;
- after a gap of more than eight weeks, the person does not qualify for a disability premium until he or she has completed a fresh waiting period.

Breaks in entitlement to HB or CTB during the waiting period or after it have no effect on this rule.

## DISABLED CHILD PREMIUM

HBR sch 2 para 14
CTBR sch 1 para 15

**12.26** The condition for this premium is that a child or young person in the family:

- is registered or certified blind (this means with the social services or social work department); or
- ceased to be registered or certified blind within the past 28 weeks because of regaining sight; or
- receives disability living allowance (either component payable at any rate).

A disabled child premium is awarded for each child or young person to whom this applies.

## ENHANCED DISABILITY PREMIUM

HBR sch 2 para 13A
CTBR sch 1 para 13A

**12.27** This premium can be awarded in respect of the claimant or partner and/or in respect of a child or young person in the family. Two or more of these premiums are awarded if appropriate – for example, if a claimant or partner qualify and also one or more child(ren) or young person(s).

**12.28** The condition in the case of the claimant or partner is that:

- the claimant is (or in the case of a couple, both partners are) aged under 60; and
- the claimant (or in the case of a couple, either partner) receives the highest rate of the care component of disability living allowance. (The mobility component of disability living allowance is not sufficient, nor are the lower or middle rates of the care component.)

In the case of a couple, the couple rate is awarded even if only one partner fulfils the second condition.

**12.29** The condition in the case of a child or young person is that he or she receives the highest rate of the care component of disability living allowance. (The mobility component of disability living allowance is not sufficient, nor are the lower or middle rates of the care component.)

## SEVERE DISABILITY PREMIUM

**12.30** There are three conditions for this premium: HBR 2(1) sch 2 para 11 CTBR 2(1) sch 1 para 12

- the person must be receiving:
  - the middle or highest rate of the care component of disability living allowance, or
  - attendance allowance, or
  - any increase for attendance or mobility paid with an industrial disablement benefit or war disablement benefit (including constant attendance allowance, 'old cases' attendance payments, mobility supplement, severe disablement occupational allowance and exceptionally severe disablement allowance);

  and
- the person must have no non-dependants (with the exceptions mentioned below);

  and
- no-one must be receiving invalid care allowance to care for the person (though it does not count if someone ceased to receive invalid care allowance only because the person has been in hospital for four weeks or more). A backdated award of invalid care allowance is ignored for this purpose as regards any period before the award was made: in other words the backdated part does not cause an overpayment.

**12.31** A single claimant or lone parent who fulfils all three conditions gets the single rate of severe disability premium.

**12.32** In the case of a couple, a severe disability premium is awarded as follows:

- if both partners fulfil all three conditions, they get the double rate;
- if both partners fulfil the first two conditions but only one fulfils the third condition, they get the single rate;
- if the claimant fulfils all three conditions, and his or her partner is registered or certified blind or ceased to be within the past 28 weeks, they get the single rate. In this case, if the 'wrong' partner makes the claim, they should be advised to 'swap the claimant role';
- if they have been getting the double rate, but one partner then ceases to fulfil the first condition because of having been in hospital for four weeks, they get the single rate from that point.

**12.33** For the purposes of the above rule, the following non-dependants do not count (i.e. do not prevent the award of a severe disability premium):

- non-dependants under 18;

- non-dependants who are registered or certified blind or who ceased to be within the past 28 weeks;
- non-dependants receiving:
  - the middle or highest rate of the care component of disability living allowance, or
  - attendance allowance, or
  - any increase for attendance or mobility paid with an industrial disablement benefit or war disablement benefit (including constant attendance allowance, 'old cases' attendance payments, mobility supplement, severe disablement occupational allowance and exceptionally severe disablement allowance).

It should also be borne in mind that a number of categories of people are excluded from the definition of a non-dependant (para. 4.21).

**Example: Severe disability premium, etc**

A husband and wife are both under 60 and both receive the middle rate of the care component of disability living allowance. Neither of them is or has recently been registered or certified blind. Their daughter of 17 is in full-time employment and lives with them. Their son lives elsewhere and receives invalid care allowance for caring for the husband. No-one receives invalid care allowance for the wife.

**Disability premium:** Because of receiving disability living allowance, they are awarded the couple rate of disability premium.

**Enhanced disability premium:** Because they get the middle (not the highest) rate of the care component of diability living allowance this cannoit be awarded.

**Severe disability premium:**

- Both receive the appropriate type of disability living allowance.
- Although their daughter is a non-dependant, she is under 18.
- Someone receives invalid care allowance for caring for only one of them.

So they are awarded the single rate of severe disability premium (for the second reason in para. 12.32).

## CARER PREMIUM

**12.34** The condition for this premium is that the claimant (or in the case of a couple, either partner): HBR sch 2 para 14ZA CTBR sch 1 para 16

- is entitled to invalid care allowance; or
- ceased to be entitled to invalid care allowance within the past eight weeks.

A single claimant who fulfils the condition gets one carer premium. A couple get one or two carer premiums, one if only one of them fulfils the condition, two if both do.

**12.35** It is worth noting that although a claim for invalid care allowance means the award of a carer premium for the carer, the person cared for may lose a severe disability premium (though not retrospectively: para. 12.30).

## BEREAVEMENT PREMIUM

**12.36** This premium is awarded to a claimant who meets all the following conditions: HBR sch 2 para 8A CTBR sch 1 para 8A SI 2000 No. 2239 (GB) NISR 2000 No. 26

- on 9th April 2001, the claimant was aged 55 or over but under 60 (in other words, his or her date of birth falls between 10th April 1941 and 9th April 1946 both dates included); and
- the claimant is still under 60; and
- the claimant does not qualify for a disability premium (or enhanced disability premium); and
- the claimant's spouse (i.e. husband or wife, not an unmarried partner) has died on or after 9th April 2001; and
- the claimant has been receiving bereavement allowance (a new state benefit) in respect of that death but has ceased to do so; and
- the claimant is either on HB or CTB at the time bereavement allowance stops, or claims HB or CTB within eight weeks of the last day on which he or she was entitled to it; and
- at that date, the claimant is a single claimant (i.e. has neither a partner, married or unmarried, nor a child or young person in the family).

**12.37** A claimant who meets the above conditions qualifies for a bereavement premium continuously. Once it has been awarded, the claimant again qualifies for a bereavement premium following:

- a break in entitlement to both HB and CTB of no more than eight weeks, or
- a break in counting as a single claimant of no more than eight weeks (e.g. because of trying out a new partner or gaining a child or young person in the family).

**12.38** Although this premium was introduced in April 2001, it is unlikely to be awarded until about April 2002 (because it can be awarded only after the new bereavement allowance – which normally lasts for one year – has expired). The premium ceases to exist on 10th April 2006 (by when all beneficiaries will have reached 60).

## General rules

### BEING 'IN RECEIPT' OF A BENEFIT

HBR sch 2 para 14B
CTBR sch 1 para 18

**12.39** Receipt of a state benefit forms part of the condition for many of the premiums. For these purposes, a person is 'in receipt' of a benefit only if it is paid in respect of himself or herself, and only during the period for which it is awarded.

### DSS CONCESSIONARY PAYMENTS

HBR sch 2 para 14A
CTBR ch 1 para 17

**12.40** For the purpose of entitlement to any premium, a DSS concessionary payment compensating for non-payment of any state benefit is treated as if it were that benefit.

### OVERLAPPING SOCIAL SECURITY BENEFITS

HBR sch 2 para 7
CTBR sch 1 para 7

**12.41** If any benefit is not paid to the claimant because of the rules about overlapping social security benefits, it is nonetheless treated as received for the purpose of entitlement to any premium. For example, a widow's pension is sometimes paid instead of incapacity benefit. The claimant is nonetheless treated as receiving incapacity benefit.

## Special cases

### POLYGAMOUS MARRIAGES

HBR 17 sch 2
CTBR 9 sch 1

**12.42** The applicable amount for a claimant in a polygamous marriage (para. 4.10) is the sum of the following. If the following could combine to produce more than one result, the result which is most favourable to the claimant applies:

- a personal allowance of £84.65, unless (in HB only) all the members of the polygamous marriage are under 18, in which case £64.45;
- £33.50 for each spouse in excess of two;
- additions to the personal allowance for any child or young person as in any other case plus, if appropriate, disabled child premium and enhanced disability premium for them;
- the basic rate of the family premium if there is at least one child or young person in their family;

- the double rate of severe disability premium if all members of the marriage fulfil all three conditions in paragraph 12.32; the single rate if all members of the marriage fulfil the first two of those conditions but someone receives an invalid care allowance for caring for at least one of them; and the single rate if the claimant fulfils all three conditions and all the other members of the marriage are registered or certified blind or ceased to be within the past 28 weeks;
- up to two carer premiums (but not more) if the ordinary conditions are satisfied;
- the couple rate of any other premium if the ordinary conditions are satisfied.

## CHILDREN AND YOUNG PERSONS WITH CAPITAL

**12.43** If in the claimant's family there is a child or young person with capital of his or her own amounting to over £3,000 (assessed under the rules described in chapters 13-15):

HBR 16(b) sch 2 paras 13A(2), 14(a

CTBR 8(b) sch. 1 paras 14A(2), 15(a

- no addition is made in the calculation of the claimant's personal allowance for that child or young person;
- no disabled child premium or enhanced disability premium is awarded for that child or young person;
- but the claimant's entitlement to a family premium (whether the basic rate or protected lone parent rate applies) is not affected (i.e. this is awarded regardless of any child's or young person's capital).

**Example: Child with capital of her own**

A lone parent qualifies for the protected lone parent rate of the family premium and has a daughter of 13. Neither has any disability. The daughter has capital of over £3,000, so no addition is made for her in the personal allowances. Her capital does not affect the award of a family premium.

| | |
|---|---|
| Personal allowance: | |
| lone parent aged over 18 | £53.95 |
| Premium: | |
| family premium (protected lone parent rate) | £22.20 |
| Applicable amount | £76.15 |

## PEOPLE ON TRAINING COURSES

**12.44** Once a person qualifies for any of the premiums for disability or for carers, if he or she goes on a government-run or approved training course (table

HBR sch 2 paras 7, 12(5)

CTBR sch 1 paras 7, 13(5)

15.2), the premium does not cease just because entitlement to a state benefit has ended or the person no longer fulfils the rule about being incapable of work. The objective of this rule is that otherwise there would be a disincentive to join such courses.

## PEOPLE IN HOSPITAL

**12.45** The following rules apply only in the case of a stay in an NHS hospital (including an NHS trust hospital). They do not apply at all to those serving a custodial sentence, nor to private patients whose fees cover all their costs.

HBR sch 2 aras 12(1), (4), 14
CTBR sch 1 aras 13(1), (4), 15

**12.46** If a claimant or any member of the family goes into hospital, and disability living allowance or attendance allowance (including the equivalents in para. 12.20 and also including cases where it is paid within a war disablement pension) stops being paid as a result (which normally happens after four weeks in hospital), this by itself does not mean that the claimant loses entitlement to a disability premium, higher pensioner premium or disabled child premium. However, the claimant's entitlement to a severe disability premium does stop after four weeks for this reason (except as described at the end of para. 12.32). And a carer's entitlement to a carer premium stops after the disabled person he or she is caring for has been in hospital for four weeks.

HBR 18
CTBR 10

**12.47** Applicable amounts are, however, normally reduced after the claimant or any partner has been in hospital for six weeks (table 12.2). There is no reduction under this rule if a child or young person goes into hospital. For the purposes of counting the six-week period, two stays in hospital are added together if the break between them is four weeks or less. However, the DSS advises (GM para. C4.54) that this 'linking rule' should not be applied (and so there is no reduction in the claimant's applicable amount) if 'a claimant [or presumably any partner] is regularly discharged from hospital during the week, for example, to accustom [him or her] to being at home'. An income support commissioner's decision (CIS/571/1997) is persuasive for HB/CTB. It held that the day someone goes into hospital does not count as a day in hospital, whereas the day someone comes out does count as a day in hospital.

**12.48** If the claimant is in hospital for 52 weeks or more, HB and CTB may cease altogether (chapter 3). If any partner, child or young person is in hospital for 52 weeks or more, he or she may cease to count as part of the family (paras. 4.11, 4.17).

**12.49** Whilst day-to-day living expenses may reduce after a period in hospital, liability for rent and council tax usually do not. The reduction in applicable amounts after six weeks in hospital can cause hardship. Authorities should consider making a discretionary housing payment in such cases (para. 7.44).

**Table 12.2 APPLICABLE AMOUNTS AFTER SIX WEEKS IN HOSPITAL**

| | |
|---|---|
| (a) Single claimant | Applicable amount reduces to £18.90 only. |
| (b) Lone parent | Applicable amount reduces to £18.90 plus:<br>◆ additions for children and young persons;<br>◆ family premium;<br>◆ any disabled child premium(s). |
| (c) Couple where one only has been in hospital for six weeks or more* | Applicable amount is the same as if neither were in hospital minus £15.10. |
| (d) Couple where both have been in hospital for six weeks or more** | Applicable amount reduces to £37.80 plus any of the following which apply:<br>◆ additions for children and young persons;<br>◆ family premium;<br>◆ any disabled child premium(s). |
| (e) Polygamous marriage where not all have been in hospital for six weeks or more* | Applicable amount is the same as if none were in hospital minus £15.10 for each one who has been in hospital for six weeks or more. |
| (f) Polygamous marriage where all have been in hospital for six weeks or more** | Applicable amount reduces to £18.90 for each member of the marriage plus any of the following which apply:<br>◆ additions for children and young persons;<br>◆ family premium;<br>◆ any disabled child premium(s). |

* *In these cases entitlement to a premium remains even if the person in hospital fulfils the condition for it.*

** *For couples, there may be two succeeding reductions in the applicable amount. Case (c) applies six weeks after the first partner goes into hospital. Case (d) applies six weeks after the second partner goes into hospital. A similar phased reduction may apply for polygamous marriages.*

# 13 Income and capital

**13.1** This and the following two chapters describe how income and capital are dealt with in the assessment of HB and main CTB. Chapters 14 and 15 give additional information relating to employed earners and the self-employed. This chapter covers:

- general matters;
- benefits, pensions, and other state help;
- the home, property and possessions;
- savings and investments;
- other items of income and capital;
- notional income and capital; and
- aggregation of income and capital.

Income and capital are assessed in the same way for HB and for main CTB purposes. They are assessed differently for all purposes relevant to second adult rebate (para. 10.24) and to non-dependant deductions (paras. 7.29-30); this chapter does not apply in such cases.

HBR sch 3 para 10, sch 4 para 4, sch 5 para 5 CTBR sch 3 para 10, sch 4 para 4, sch 5 para 5

**13.2** If a claimant is entitled to income support or income-based jobseeker's allowance (or his or her partner is), this chapter does not apply. Such claimants have already had their income and capital assessed for the purposes of those benefits and their income and capital is not taken into account in the assessment of their HB/main CTB (paras. 7.4-6). Moreover, the law spells out that 'Where a person is on income support or [JSA(IB)], the whole of [his or her] earnings [and] income other than earnings [and] capital [is] to be disregarded' for HB/CTB purposes. (It is therefore strange that a few authorities have begun of late to seek proof of income and capital from such claimants – and almost always inappropriate.)

## General matters

### WHOSE INCOME AND CAPITAL COUNTS

HBR 19, 39 CTBR 11, 30

**13.3** In assessing entitlement to HB and main CTB, a claimant is treated as possessing any income and capital belonging to:

- the claimant himself or herself;
- any partner he or she has; and

- in certain cases, his or her children and young persons.

*All references in this chapter to the income or capital of a claimant should be read as also referring to the income and capital of a partner.* Paragraph 13.105 describes how a child's or young person's income and capital is taken into account.

## WHEN A CLAIMANT IS TREATED AS HAVING A NON-DEPENDANT'S INCOME AND CAPITAL

**13.4** A special rule applies if: HBR 20 CTBR 12

- it appears to the authority that the claimant and non-dependant have entered into arrangements to take advantage of the HB or CTB scheme; and
- the non-dependant has both more income and more capital than the claimant; and
- the claimant is not on income support or income-based jobseeker's allowance.

**13.5** The rule in such cases is that:

- the claimant is treated as having the income and capital of the non-dependant; and
- the claimant's own income and capital is completely disregarded.

For the purposes of considering the amount (if any) of the non-dependant deduction (para. 7.28), the non-dependant is treated as having his or her own income and capital (not the income and capital of the claimant).

## DISTINGUISHING CAPITAL FROM INCOME

**13.6** HB and CTB law does not give a general definition of 'income' and 'capital'; though the regulations do define how certain types of payment should be treated: those rules are given as they arise in this and the next two chapters. Examples are given in table 13.1. The DWP gives good general advice (GM para. C2.08):

> 'Capital can take a variety of forms. A payment of capital can normally be distinguished from income because it is:
>
> *i.* made without being tied to a period; and
>
> *ii.* made without being tied to any past payment; and
>
> *iii.* not intended to form part of a series of payments.
>
> As a general rule, capital includes all categories of holdings which have a clear monetary value…'

## Table 13.1 EXAMPLES OF CAPITAL AND INCOME

**Capital which is (wholly or partly) taken into account for HB/main CTB purposes**

- Savings in a bank, building society, etc.
- National Savings Certificates, stocks and shares
- Property (unless it falls within one of the numerous disregards)
- Redundancy pay (with some exceptions)
- Tax refunds

**Capital which is disregarded for HB/main CTB purposes**

- The home a claimant owns and lives in
- A self-employed claimant's business assets
- Arrears of certain state benefits
- Certain compensation payments
- A life insurance policy which has not been cashed in

**Income which is (wholly or partly) taken into account for HB/main CTB purposes**

- Earnings from a job or from self-employment
- Pensions
- Certain state benefits (e.g. contribution-based jobseeker's allowance, retirement pension)
- Rental received from a sub-tenant or boarder in the claimant's home
- Tariff income from capital

**Income which is disregarded for HB/main CTB purposes**

- Reimbursement of expenses wholly incurred in the course of a job
- Certain state benefits (e.g. disability living allowance, attendance allowance)
- Certain charitable or voluntary payments
- Payments (e.g. 'keep') received from a non-dependant
- Fostering payments

*These examples are simplified. In many cases further disregards apply. The detailed rules are given later in this chapter.*

## WHICH TYPES OF INCOME AND CAPITAL COUNT

**13.7** As described in the later parts of this chapter, some types of income and capital are wholly disregarded; some are partly disregarded; and some are counted in full. Examples are given in table 13.1. Also, in some cases a claimant can be treated as having income or capital he or she does not in fact possess: this is known as 'notional' income or capital (para. 13.96).

## WHY CAPITAL IS ASSESSED

**13.8** A claimant's capital is first assessed under the rules in this chapter, then taken into account as follows: HBR 37, 45 CTBR 28, 37

- the first band (which is any amount up to the 'lower capital limit': para. 13.10) is completely ignored in the assessment of HB and main CTB;
- the next band (which is from the 'lower capital limit' to £16,000) is treated as generating 'tariff income' (para. 13.9);
- if it amounts to more than £16,000, the claimant is not entitled to HB or main CTB at all.

**13.9** 'Tariff income' is assessed as follows (and this is illustrated in the example):

- deduct the appropriate 'lower capital limit' from the total amount of assessed capital;
- then divide the remainder by 250;
- then, if the result is not an exact multiple of £1, round the result up to the next whole £1. This is the claimant's weekly tariff income.

**13.10** The 'lower capital limit' (below which capital is ignored) is:

- £10,000 in some kinds of residential accommodation (para. 13.11: this applies in HB only);
- £6,000 in any other case if the claimant (or in the case of a couple, the older partner) is aged 60 or more;
- £3,000 in all other cases.

**13.11** The kinds of accommodation in which the £10,000 lower capital limit applies are:

- a residential care home or nursing home where the claimant has pre-1993 preserved rights (para. 3.9);
- local authority Part III accommodation so long as board is not provided (para. 4.13);
- an unregistered Abbeyfield Home (para. 3.10);
- accommodation which is not treated as a nursing home, but is provided

together with both board and personal care under an Act of Parliament or Royal Charter. This can apply, for example, to accommodation provided by the Salvation Army or the Royal British Legion (para. 3.11).

In CTB there is never a £10,000 lower capital limit (doubtless because a resident in the above types of accommodation cannot be liable for council tax).

**Example: Calculating tariff income**

CLAIMANT AGED UNDER 60

A single claimant (who does not live in residential accommodation: para. 13.11) has capital, assessed under the rules in this chapter of £8,085.93.

The first £3,000 is disregarded, leaving a remainder of £5,085.93. Divide the remainder by 250 and round the answer up to the next whole £1. The claimant has tariff income of £21.

CLAIMANT AGED 60 OR OVER

The same claimant reaches 60 and the amount of his capital is exactly the same.

The first £6,000 is disregarded, leaving a remainder of £2,085.93. Divide the remainder by 250 and round the answer up to the next whole £1. The claimant has tariff income of £9.

## HOW CAPITAL IS ASSESSED

HBR 38 CTBR 29 **13.12** The whole of a claimant's capital is taken into account, including certain types of income which are counted as capital, but excluding capital which is disregarded. The general rules about how capital is valued are given below. Other rules about this, about which types of income are counted as capital, and about which types of capital are disregarded, are mentioned in the relevant places in this chapter. Authorities may seek the assistance of the Valuation Office Agency in valuing capital items such as dwellings or other property. Forms authorities may use for this purpose were issued with circular HB/CTB A55/98.

## VALUING CAPITAL IN GENERAL

HBR 41(a) CTBR 32(a) **13.13** The following rule applies whenever a property, shares, or anything else (except for national savings certificates: para. 13.72) has to be valued for HB/main CTB purposes. Other parts of this chapter mention considerations that also have to be taken into account for specific items. The rule has three steps:

- take the current market or surrender value of the capital item;
- then disregard 10 per cent if selling it would involve costs;
- then disregard any mortgage or other 'incumbrance' (e.g. a loan) secured on it.

In practice, a claimant's capital is usually valued at his or her date of claim and revalued only if there is a reasonably large change. But it should be revalued whenever there is a change which affects tariff income.

## VALUING JOINTLY HELD CAPITAL

**13.14** To assess a particular person's share of capital which is held jointly: HBR 44 CTBR 36

- first assume that all the joint owners own an equal share in the capital item – even if they actually own it (or regard themselves as owning it) in differing proportions;
- then value the person's resulting share using the rules in the previous paragraph.

An example is given below. (The above rules are taken into account by the Valuation Office Agency when authorities seek its assistance.)

## WHY INCOME IS ASSESSED

**13.15** A claimant's earned and unearned income, assessed under the rules described in this chapter and chapters 14 and 15, is compared with his or her applicable amount in calculating how much HB or main CTB he or she is entitled to (paras. 7.11-15).

### Examples: Valuing capital

#### SHARES WHOLLY OWNED BY A CLAIMANT

A claimant owns 1,000 shares in a company. The sell price is currently £0.50 each.

For HB/main CTB purposes, from the current market value (1,000 x £0.50 = £500) deduct 10% (£50) giving £450. Assuming no loan or other incumbrance is secured on the shares, the value for HB/main CTB purposes is therefore £450.

#### A JOINTLY OWNED PROPERTY

A claimant and her sister inherit some land from their father. In his Will, he stipulated that the claimant is to have two-thirds of the value of the land and her sister is to have one-third. The land has recently been valued by the Valuation Office Agency, and the authority accepts their valuations, which are as follows:

- if the whole of the land was sold, it would fetch £10,000;
- if a half-share in the land was sold, the half-share would fetch only £4,000 (because of certain covenants which affect the use of the land).

The claimant has recently taken out a loan for £2,000 using the land as security (and none of the loan has yet been repaid).

For HB/main CTB purposes, the claimant's share of the capital in the land is valued as follows:

- first the claimant is treated as owning half of the land;
- then this half share is valued. Using the Valuation Office Agency's figure, the authority values the half share as being £4,000;
- then 10% is deducted towards sales costs: £4,000 minus £400 leaves £3,600;
- then the claimant's loan is deducted: £3,600 minus £2,000 leaves £1,600.

So for HB/main CTB purposes, the claimant has capital of £1,600 (plus any other capital she may have).

## HOW INCOME IS ASSESSED

HBR 21, 24, 33, sch 4 para 1
CTBR 13, 16, 24, sch 4 para 1

**13.16** The whole of a claimant's income is taken into account, including tariff income from capital (para. 13.9) and certain types of capital which are counted as income, but excluding income which is disregarded. General points about income are given below. Other rules about this, about which types of capital are counted as income, and about which types of income are disregarded in whole or in part, are mentioned in the relevant places in this chapter. The income tax payable on any kind of income is disregarded in the assessment of that income. Otherwise, no income can be disregarded unless a specific rule requires this.

The HB and main CTB rules distinguish earned income (i.e. earnings received by employed earners or by the self-employed) from unearned income (e.g. pensions, benefits, rent received by the claimant, and so on). Chapter 14 deals with earnings from a job, chapter 15 with self-employed earnings. The rules about unearned income are in this chapter.

### DECIDING WHICH WEEKS INCOME BELONGS TO

**13.17** The general objective for HB/main CTB purposes is 'estimating the amount which is likely to be [the claimant's] average weekly income over [his or her] benefit period' (para. 5.81). However, there are many specific rules and these are given in this and the next two chapters as they arise. Where there is no specific rule, it is usually straightforward to decide according to the facts of the case which week or weeks a claimant's income belongs to for HB/main CTB purposes. HBR 21(1) CTBR 13(1)

### ARREARS OF INCOME

**13.18** In broad terms, it is usually the case that if a claimant receives arrears of income, then those arrears should be treated as being income belonging to the week or weeks to which they relate (except to the extent that they are income which is disregarded). Exceptions to this and further specific rules are given in this and the next chapter as they arise. HBR 68 CTBR 59

### CONVERTING INCOME TO A WEEKLY FIGURE

**13.19** For HB/main CTB purposes, income must be converted (if necessary) to a weekly figure. The details are given in paragraph 7.50.

## Benefits, pensions, and other state help

**13.20** The following section of this chapter gives the rules about the assessment for HB/main CTB purposes of state benefits, state pensions, other pensions, and other payments from state, local authority and related sources.

### STATE BENEFITS: GENERAL RULE FOR CURRENT PAYMENTS

**13.21** Except when indicated in the following paragraphs, state benefits and pensions are counted in full as unearned income. For example, all the following are counted in full (as are many others): HBR 33(1) CTBR 24(1)

- child benefit;
- contribution-based jobseeker's allowance;
- incapacity benefit;
- bereavement allowance
- industrial injuries benefit;
- maternity allowance;
- retirement pensions.

## STATE BENEFITS: GENERAL RULE FOR ARREARS

HBR 68(7)
CTBR 59

**13.22** Except when indicated in the following paragraphs, arrears of state benefits and pensions are counted:

- as unearned income for the period they cover, if they are for periods on or after 6th March 1995; or
- as current capital (and never as income) if they relate to periods before that.

> **Example: Arrears of incapacity benefit**
>
> A claimant, who has been receiving HB and main CTB for many years, has been receiving incapacity benefit since January 2001. It has been taken into account as her income for HB/main CTB purposes from that date. In June 2002, following a successful appeal, she is paid arrears of incapacity benefit for the period from September 2000 to January 2001.
>
> The arrears are her income for the period from September 2000 to January 2001. The authority may therefore reassess her entitlement to HB/main CTB for that period, which may result in an overpayment (chapter 18).

## REDUCED STATE BENEFITS

HBR 33(3)
CTBR 24(3)

**13.23** If the amount of a state benefit received by a claimant has been reduced due to a Child Support Agency 'reduced benefit direction', the net amount (i.e. after the reduction) is counted as unearned income. But it it has been reduced for any other reason (typically in order to recover a previous overpayment), the gross amount (i.e. before the reduction) is counted as unearned income.

## INCREASES IN STATE BENEFITS FOR DEPENDANTS

BR sch 4 para 52
NIHBR sch 4 para 55
CTBR sch 4 para 51

**13.24** With some state benefits, an amount may be awarded for a dependent adult or dependent child(ren). Count the increase as unearned income if the benefit it is paid with counts as unearned income – unless the dependant is not a member of the family (para. 4.5), in which case disregard it.

## RULES FOR PARTICULAR BENEFITS, PENSIONS, ETC.

**13.25** The following paragraphs give the rules about particular benefits, pensions and other forms of state help – whether they are paid currently or in arrears.

## DISABILITY LIVING ALLOWANCE, OTHER BENEFITS FOR ATTENDANCE AND MOBILITY, AND GUARDIAN'S ALLOWANCE

**13.26** Current payments of the following are disregarded in full as unearned income:

HBR sch 4 paras 5-8, 50 sch 5 para 8
NIHBR sch 4, paras 5-8, 53 sch 5 para 8
CTBR sch 4 paras 5-8, 49 sch 5 para 8

- disability living allowance;
- attendance allowance and constant attendance allowance;
- exceptionally severe disablement allowance;
- severe disablement occupational allowance;
- 'old cases' attendance payments;
- mobility supplement;
- payments compensating for non-receipt of the above;
- guardian's allowance.

Arrears of the above are disregarded in full as income. They are also disregarded as capital for 52 weeks from the date of payment.

**Example: Arrears of disability living allowance**

A claimant, who has been receiving HB and main CTB for many years, has been receiving disability living allowance since January 2001. It has been disregarded in the assessment of his income for HB/main CTB purposes from that date. In June 2002, following a successful appeal, he is paid arrears of disability living allowance for the period from September 2000 to January 2001.

Because disability living allowance is income which is disregarded, the arrears have no effect on his income for the period from September 2000 to January 2001. If he still has any money derived from those arrears as at June 2003 (52 weeks after the arrears were paid), they will from that point begin to count as part of his capital.

## 'PRE-1973' WAR WIDOW'S PENSIONS

HBR sch 4 paras 43, 53-55 sch 5 paras 8, 38
NIHBR sch 4 para 46, 56-58 sch 5, paras 8, 3
CTBR sch 4 paras 42, 52-54 sch 5 paras 8, 37

**13.27** Current payments of the special pensions paid to 'pre-1973' war widows are disregarded in full as unearned income. From April 2002, the current amount is £59.95 per week. Arrears of such payments are disregarded in full as income. They are also disregarded as capital for 52 weeks from the date of payment, as are payments compensating for non-receipt of such pensions.

## OTHER WAR WIDOW'S AND WAR DISABLEMENT PENSIONS

**13.28** From current payments of any other war widow's or war disablement

HBR sch 4 para 14
NIHBR sch 4 para 13
CTBR sch 4 para 14

pensions, disregard £10.00 (subject to the rules on aggregation in para. 13.109). In Northern Ireland the whole of the payment is disregarded, not just £10. Also disregard any amount included within the pension for attendance or mobility or for dependants who are not a member of the family. The above rule applies to:

- war widow's and war disablement pensions;
- payments to compensate for non-payment of those;
- analogous payments from Governments outside the UK;
- Nazi persecution compensation payments.

Arrears of the payments described above fall within the general rule (para. 13.22) – except that the £10.00 disregard mentioned above applies when they are income.

Note that many councils operate a 'local scheme' whereby the whole of the above payments are disregarded currently and/or in arrears (para. 7.39); and also see the rules for second world war payments (para. 13.82).

## WIDOWED MOTHER'S ALLOWANCE AND WIDOWED PARENT'S ALLOWANCE

HBR sch 4 para 14A
CTBR sch 4 para 14A

**13.29** From current payments of these benefits, disregard £15 (subject to the rules on aggregation in para. 13.109). Arrears of these payments fall within the general rule (para. 13.22) – except that the £15 disregard just mentioned applies when they are income (but only for periods back to 1st/2nd April 2001).

IBR sch 4 para 31
NIHBR sch 4 para 33
BR sch 4 para 32

## PENSIONER'S CHRISTMAS BONUS

**13.30** This is disregarded in full as unearned income.

## WORKING FAMILIES' TAX CREDIT AND DISABLED PERSON'S TAX CREDIT

HBR 2(1), 21(1), (1ZA)
HBR sch 4 paras 57, 58
sch 5 para 8 (GB)
NIHBR sch 4 paras 60,61
sch 5 para 8
CTBR 2(1), 13(1),(1ZA)
h 4 paras 56, 57
sch 5 para 8

**13.31** The general rule is that current payments of working families' tax credit (WFTC) and disabled person's tax credit (DPTC) are counted in full as unearned income (even though they are often administered by employers). However, there are two circumstances in which an amount is disregarded from either of these:

- Certain recipients of WFTC/DPTC qualify for a disregard from their earnings of £11.65 per week (para. 14.17). If (uncommonly) their earnings are insufficient for this £11.65 disregard to be made in full from them (as described in para. 16.19), £11.65 is instead disregarded from their WFTC/DPTC (or £11.45 for awards of WFTC/DPTC which began before 9th April 2002).
- Certain claimants with child care costs qualify for a disregard from their earnings (para. 14.12). If (uncommonly) their earnings are insufficient for this disregard to be made in full from them, any balance of the disregard is made from their WFTC/DPTC.

**13.32** Arrears of WFTC and DPTC are dealt with as follows:

- As income, these arrears fall within the general rule (para. 13.22) – so they usually count as past income, after making the disregards mentioned above if appropriate (though the way these worked was different in the past). Having said that, the DWP has sometimes advised authorities to fully disregard these arrears as income, and some authorities do this.
- As capital, the value of these arrears is disregarded for 52 weeks from the date of payment.

The same points apply to arrears of predecessor benefits (family credit, disability working allowance and family income supplement) and to payments compensating for non-receipt of any of the above.

## INCOME SUPPORT, INCOME-BASED JOBSEEKER'S ALLOWANCE, HB AND CTB

**13.33** Current payments of these benefits are disregarded in full as income, as are transitional payments awarded with some payments of the first two. Arrears are dealt with as follows:

HBR sch 4 paras 51, 61, 62
sch 5 paras 5, 8 45, 50, 51
NIHBR sch 4 paras 4, 44, 48
sch 5 paras 5, 8 44, 48, 49
CTBR sch 4 paras 4, 36, 60,
sch 5 paras 34, 44, 50, 51

- As income, arrears of all of these benefits are disregarded in full, including arrears of HB/CTB paid under the special provisions relating to refugees who were formerly asylum seekers (para. 20.51).
- As capital, arrears of these benefits (and of payments compensating for non-receipt of any of them) are disregarded for 52 weeks from the date of payment in all cases, and thereafter without time limit in the case of arrears of HB and CTB.

Similar rules apply to discretionary housing payments (para. 13.44).

As income arrears of predecessor benefits to IS, HB and CTB (community charge benefit, housing benefit, housing benefit supplement and supplementary benefit) are disregarded in full. As capital arrears (including payments compensating for non-payment of them) are disregarded for 52 weeks in all cases and thereafter without time limit in the case of predecessor payments for HB.

HBR sch 4 paras 35, 36, 40, 48
NIHBR sch 4 par 6, 38, 39, 43, 5
HBR sch 5, paras 28, 29, 35, 42
CTBR sch 4 para 6, 37, 38, 47, 5
sch 5 paras 8, 2 29, 35, 41

## COUNCIL TAX REDUCTIONS

**13.34** Disregard in full (both as income and capital) disability reductions, discounts and transitional reductions (chapter 2). In other words, the fact that the claimant gets one of these does not mean that it counts as his or her income or capital.

HBR sch 4 para
NIHBR sch 4, pa
HBR sch 5 para
CTBR sch 4 para
sch 5 para 35

## SOCIAL FUND PAYMENTS AND LOANS

**13.35** Disregard payments and loans from the social fund (chapter 1) in full (both as income and capital) – including Winter Fuel Payments.

HBR sch 4 para
NIHBR sch 4 par
HBR sch 5 para
CTBR sch 4 para
sch 5 para 19

HBR sch 4 paras 26, 67 sch 5 para 18 NIHBR sch 4 paras 28, 65 sch 5 para 18 CTBR sch 4 paras 37, 62 sch 5 para 18

## SOCIAL SERVICES PAYMENTS

**13.36** Disregard in full (both as income and capital) any social services payment made for the purposes of avoiding taking children into care and any such payment made to children leaving care. Also disregard in full as income any social services payment made in lieu of providing community care.

## FOSTERING, BOARDING OUT AND RESPITE CARE PAYMENTS

HBR sch 4 paras 24, 25 NIHBR sch 4 paras 26, 27 CTBR sch 4 paras 25, 26

**13.37** Disregard these payments in full (as income) if they are received from a local authority or voluntary organisation or (in the case of respite care payments) a primary care trust. In the case of respite care payments, contributions required under the National Assistance Act 1948 from the person cared for are also disregarded as income.

## ADOPTION AND CUSTODIANSHIP ALLOWANCES

HBR 2(1), sch 4 para 23 NIHBR sch 4 para 25 CTBR 2(1), sch 4 para 24

**13.38** If these payments are received from a local authority (in Great Britain or Northern Ireland), disregard any amount in excess of the dependant's allowance and any disabled child premium for the child or young person concerned. Count any balance as unearned income. However, if the child or young person concerned has capital valued at over £3,000 disregard the whole amount.

## OCCUPATIONAL AND PERSONAL PENSIONS

HBR 28(2), 33(4), sch 5 para 30 CTBR 19(2), 25(4), sch 5 para 30

**13.39** These count in full as unearned income, after deducting tax. However, disregard the capital value of any amount held in a pension scheme and of the right to receive money from it.

## THE MACFARLANE TRUSTS, THE FUND, THE EILEEN TRUST, THE INDEPENDENT LIVING FUNDS, THE VCJD TRUST

HBR sch 4 para 34, sch 5 paras 23, 32, 60 NIHBR sch 4 para 37 sch 5 paras 23, 32, 61 CTBR sch 4 para 35 sch 5 paras 23, 32, 60

**13.40** The Macfarlane Trust, the Macfarlane (Special Payments) Trust, the Macfarlane (Special Payments) (No. 2) Trust, 'the Fund', and the Eileen Trust were all set up to assist certain people with HIV. The Independent Living Fund, the Independent Living (Extension) Fund, and the Independent Living (1993) Fund were all set up to enable severely disabled people to live independently. Any payment from any of these is disregarded in full (both as capital and income). Payments in kind from any of these are also disregarded. If money from any of these is passed on to a third party, it is usually also disregarded in the assessment of the third party's income and capital.

Most payments to sufferers of variant Creutzfeldt-Jacob disease (vCJD) and their families are disregarded as capital. Full details are in circular HB/CTB A19/2001.

## THE NEW DEAL, WELFARE TO WORK, AND DWP SCHEMES GENERALLY

**13.41** The following is about payments received by people on the New Deal or on other schemes run by the DWP. Options available on the New Deal include:

HBR 2(1), 40(7), sch 4 paras 11, 49, 64, 66, 68-73 sch 5 paras 7, 33, 43, 44, 53-61 NIHBR 2(1), 40(7) sch 4 paras 11, 52, 66-71 sch 5 paras 7, 33, 43, 51-61 CTBR 2(1), 31(7) sch 4 paras 11, 48, 64-72, sch 5 paras 7, 33, 42, 43, 53-6 SI 1998 No. 217 NISR 1998 No 12[illegible]

- the 'full-time education and training option';
- the 'voluntary sector option';
- the 'environment task force option';
- the 'employed earner's route' of the 'employment option';
- the 'self-employment route' of the 'employment option'; and
- joining a 'qualifying course of study'.

Most people on the New Deal remain entitled to income support or JSA(IB), so their income and capital are disregarded. In all other cases, their income and capital is assessed as in table 13.2. That table also deals with other DWP schemes. (See also paras. 13.99-102 for points about notional income and capital for some of these schemes.) Table 13.3 goes on to give the definition of 'welfare to work beneficiary' used for all HB and CTB purposes.

### Table 13.2 THE NEW DEAL AND OTHER DWP SCHEMES: TREATMENT OF PAYMENTS FOR HB/CTB PURPOSES

**1. THE NEW DEAL**

The following points apply to all options (para.13.41) unless stated otherwise.

*Mandatory and discretionary 'top-up' payments:* The general rule is as follows:

- disregard these in full as unearned income;
- disregard these in full as capital for 52 weeks from the date of payment.

An exception applies to people on a 'qualifying course of study'. In their case, the above points apply – except that discretionary 'top-up' payments for travel expenses are not disregarded if an amount is disregarded for travel under the normal student rules (table 21.3).

*Payments towards child care costs:* Disregard these as unearned income.

*The 'intensive activity period':* The above points apply to people on pilot 'intensive activity periods' of the New Deal in the same way as for anyone else on the New Deal. If they are trying to become self-employed, they are treated in the same way as those on the 'self-employed route' (see above). (There are also special rules for non-dependants in these cases: para. 7.36.)

*Training allowances:* The general rule is as follows:

- disregard as income any travel or living away from home allowance;
- count any maintenance and/or meals allowance as unearned income;
- disregard as capital the first £200 of any training bonus.

The exceptions are that the above points do not apply to the income of employees on the 'employed earner's route'; to the trading receipts of people on the 'self-employment route' (see below); or to people undertaking an 'intensive activity period' (see above).

*Training grants under the 'New Deal 50-plus Employment Credit Scheme':* Disregard as capital for 52 weeks from the date of payment.

*People on the 'self-employed route' of the employment option:* In addition to the above points, there are several further rules: see paragraph 13.39.

*People undertaking a 'qualifying course of study':* In addition to the above points, such people count as students: see paragraphs 21.7-8.

**2. WELFARE TO WORK**

*Welfare to work beneficiaries:* For the definition, see table 13.3. There are several concessions in the HB and CTB schemes for welfare to work beneficiaries: these are mentioned in this Guide as they arise (in chapters 10 and 12). Their earnings are assessed in the normal way (chapter 16).

**3. EMPLOYMENT ZONE (EZ) PROGRAMMES**

*Employment Zone (EZ) programmes: subsistence allowance:* The following rules apply:

- EZ subsistence allowances are disregarded as income – but only to the extent that the amount of the subsistence allowance exceeds what he or she would receive as JSA(IB) minus 50p. (Imagine a person's JSA(IB) entitlement would be £42.70 and her EZ subsistence allowance is £49.70. £7.50 of the EZ subsistence allowance is disregarded. If she has no other income, she qualifies for 50p of JSA(IB), which is the minimum award. Otherwise, £42.20 of her EZ subsistence allowance is counted as unearned income.)
- Arrears of EZ subsistence allowances are disregarded in full as income, and disregarded as capital for 52 weeks from the date of receipt of the payment.

*Employment Zone (EZ) programmes: discretionary payments:* Any such payment from an EZ contractor (whether a fee, grant, loan, or otherwise) is disregarded in full as both income and capital.

*Employment Zone (EZ) programmes: assistance with self-employment:* People on an EZ programme who are assisted with self-employment are treated in the same way as people on the 'self-employed route' of the employment option of the New Deal (see above).

**4. OTHER SCHEMES**

*Access to work:* Disregard (both as income and capital) all payments under this scheme, which is available to certain disabled people.

*Work Based Training for Young People, Work Based Training for Adults (in England and Wales), Training for Work (in Scotland), Community Action:* If the person is receiving payments from any of these as an employed earner, count these as earnings in the normal way (chapter 14). In any other case:

- disregard as unearned income any travel or living away from home allowance and any training premium;
- count any maintenance and/or meals allowance as unearned income;
- disregard as capital the first £200 of any training bonus.

*Jobfinder's grant:* Count this in full as capital.

*Jobmatch payments:* Count these in full as unearned income.

## Table 13.3 DEFINITION OF 'WELFARE TO WORK BENEFICIARY'

For all HB/CTB purposes, this means a person who:

- has been incapable of work for at least 28 weeks (196 days); and
- has stopped (on or after 5th October 1998) receiving a benefit or advantage which was dependent on his or her being incapable of work (the relevant benefits and advantages for HB/CTB purposes are indicated as they arise in chapters 10 and 12 of this Guide); and
- has – within 7 days of ceasing to be incapable of work – started:
  - remunerative work (in broad terms, 16 hours or more per week: para. 7.33), or
  - Work Based Training for Adults (in England and Wales), or
  - Training for Work (in Scotland); and
- has notified the benefits agency of the fact that he or she has started work, and has done so within one month of the date on which he or she ceased to claim that he or she is incapable of work (or, in certain cases, has won a social security appeal relating to this).

Such a person counts as a welfare to work beneficiary for 52 weeks only. The Benefits Agency should inform authorities if someone is a welfare to work beneficiary (circular HB/CTB A41/98).

## CAREER DEVELOPMENT LOANS (GB ONLY)

HBR 34(4) sch 4 para 63 CTBR 25(4) sch 4 para 63

**13.42** Career development loans are paid under arrangements between the DWP and national banks (circular HB/CTB A1/97). They are dealt with as follows:

- any amount which (over the period of the education or training to which the loan applies) relates to the claimant's or a member of the family's food, ordinary clothing or footwear (excluding school uniform and sportswear), household fuel, eligible rent (apart from any non-dependant deduction), council tax, or water charges, is counted in full as income;
- any amount relating to any other purposes (such as for course fees and course-related expenses) is disregarded in full (as both income and capital).

HBR sch 4 paras 37, 44, 45 HBR sch 5 paras 39, 40 NIHBR sch 4 paras 40, 47, 48 CTBR sch 4 paras 39, 44, 45 sch 5 paras 38, 39

## HEALTH BENEFITS AND PRISON VISITS PAYMENTS

**13.43** The following are disregarded in full as unearned income. The last two items are also disregarded as capital for 52 weeks from the date of payment:

- hospital resettlement benefit;
- payments for travel for hospital visits;
- health service supplies or payments in lieu of free milk and vitamins.

BR sch 4 para 46, HBR sch 4 para 49 HBR sch 5 para 41 sch 5 para 8(d) BR sch 4 para 45, sch 5 para 40

Disregard in full as unearned income any Home Office payment for travel for prison visits. Disregard it as capital for 52 weeks from the date of payment.

## DISCRETIONARY HOUSING PAYMENTS

BR sch 4 para 74, sch 5 para 8(e) NIHBR sch 4 para 73 CTBR sch 4 para 73, sch 5 para 8(f)

**13.44** Discretionary housing payments (para. 7.46) are disregarded in full as unearned income. They are also disregarded as capital for 52 weeks from the date of payment. (The same points apply to arrears of the former HB/CTB exceptional circumstances additions and HB exceptional hardship additions, since these count as arrears of HB/CTB: para 13.33.)

# The home, property and possessions

**13.45** The following section of this chapter is about how things the claimant owns affect his or her entitlement to HB and main CTB. It covers:

- when the value of the home and other property is ignored and when it is taken into account;
- how property which is rented out is dealt with;
- possessions and miscellaneous items.

## WHEN THE VALUE OF THE HOME AND PROPERTY IS DISREGARDED

**13.46** The claimant's current, former or future home can be disregarded and so can a home or other property (including non-domestic property) which the claimant has never occupied, if the conditions in the next few paragraphs apply. The disregards described below can apply one after another, so long as the relevant conditions are met (as illustrated in the example following para. 13.58).

## THE CLAIMANT'S CURRENT HOME

**13.47** Disregard the capital value of the dwelling normally occupied as the claimant's home, and any land or buildings which are part of it or are impracticable to sell separately. There is no time limit. This disregard is limited to one home per claim but see the other headings below.

HBR sch 5 para 1
CTBR sch 5 para

## THE HOME OF AN ELDERLY OR INCAPACITATED PERSON

**13.48** Disregard the capital value of the home of a partner or relative of anyone in the claimant's family, if that partner or relative is aged 60 or more or incapacitated. There is no time limit. The property may be occupied by others as well as the partner or relative. Any number of properties may be disregarded under this rule. 'Relative' is defined in paragraph 10.39. 'Incapacitated' is not defined for this purpose; in particular, it is not linked to premiums or state benefits.

HBR sch 5 para 4(a)
CTBR sch 5 para 4(a)

## THE CLAIMANT'S INTENDED HOME

**13.49** Disregard the capital value of a property which the claimant intends to occupy as a home as follows:

HBR sch 5 paras 2, 26, 27
CTBR sch 5 paras 2, 25, 26

- in all cases, for 26 weeks from the date of acquisition or such longer period as is reasonable; and/or
- if the claimant is taking steps to obtain or regain possession (e.g. if there are squatters or tenants), for 26 weeks from the date the claimant first seeks legal advice or begins legal proceedings, or such longer period as is reasonable; and/or
- if the property requires essential repairs or alterations, for 26 weeks from the date the claimant first takes steps to render it fit for occupation or reoccupation as his or her home, or such longer period as is reasonable. This could apply for example to the normal home of a claimant in temporary accommodation.

## THE CLAIMANT'S FORMER HOME

**13.50** There is no disregard of the capital value of a claimant's former home as such. However, a former home may well fall within one of the following headings (which also apply to other property): if it does not, then it is taken into account as capital.

## PROPERTY THE CLAIMANT INTENDS TO DISPOSE OF

HBR sch 5 para 25
CTBR sch 5 para 25

**13.51** Disregard the capital value of any property the claimant intends to dispose of, for 26 weeks from the date when the claimant first takes steps to dispose of it, or for such longer period as is reasonable. This can apply to a former or second home or any other property. It can apply to more than one property.

## DIVORCED OR ESTRANGED COUPLES AND POLYGAMOUS MARRIAGES

HBR sch 5 para 24
CTBR sch 5 para 24

**13.52** If a claimant has actually divorced or become estranged from a former partner, disregard the whole capital value of the claimant's former home (and any land or buildings which are part of it or are impracticable to sell separately) as follows:

- for any period when it is occupied by the former partner if he or she is now a lone parent. This could begin straight after the divorce/estrangement, or later on, and there is no time limit in this case;
- in any other case, for 26 weeks from the date of divorce or estrangement (e.g. if the former partner is not a lone parent at the time, or the property is empty). The time limit in this case cannot be extended, but the property may fall within one of the other disregards afterwards.

Note that (unlike in the next paragraph) the claimant must have formerly lived there as his or her home for this disregard to apply. 'Estranged' is not defined in the law and so carries its ordinary English meaning that the people in question no longer regard themselves as a couple or as being in a polygamous marriage.

## SEPARATED OR SPLIT COUPLES AND POLYGAMOUS MARRIAGES

HBR sch 5 para 4(b)
CTBR sch 5 para 4(b)

**13.53** If a claimant has not actually divorced or become estranged from a former partner, but the HB/CTB rules treat him or her as no longer being in a couple or polygamous marriage (e.g. because of the rules about absence of a partner: para. 4.11), disregard the whole capital value of any property currently occupied as a home by the former partner. There is no time limit. Note that (unlike in the previous paragraph) it is irrelevant who used to live there.

## DISPUTED ASSETS WHEN A RELATIONSHIP ENDS

**13.54** When a relationship ends, ownership of a property may be in dispute. This can sometimes mean the current market value of the property is nil until ownership of the property is settled.

## HOUSING ASSOCIATION DEPOSITS

HBR sch 5 para 10
CTBR sch 5 para 10

**13.55** Disregard in full as capital any amount deposited with a housing association in order to secure accommodation.

**Example: The capital value of a property following relationship breakdown**

- A married couple jointly own the house they live in. They do not own any other property. They have one child at school. They claim CTB. The man is the claimant.

  The value of the house is disregarded as capital: it is their normal home (para. 13.47). However, they turn out not to qualify for CTB because they have too much income.

- The coupler separate (but are not estranged).The man leaves and rents a room in a shared house. He does not intend to return (and so they no longer count as a couple: para. 4.11). He claims HB and CTB for the flat.

  In the man's claim, his share of the house is disregarded: it is the home of his former partner from whom he is separated (para. 13.53).

- They divorce. The terms of the divorce are that the man retains a one-third share in the house; but that the house cannot be sold until their child is 18. The man notifies the council of this.

  In his claim, his share of the house is disregarded: it is his former home and is occupied by his former partner from whom he is divorced and who is a lone parent (para. 13.52).

- More than 26 weeks after their divorce, their child leaves school. The house is not put up for sale and the man does not seek his share of its value.

  In his claim, his interest in the house must now be taken into account (para. 13.52). As a joint owner, he is treated as possessing one-half of its value (and the other points in para. 13.14 are taken into account in valuing it).

- The house is put up for sale.

  In the man's claim, his interest in the house is now disregarded as capital for 26 weeks (or longer if reasonable: para. 13.51).

- The house is sold, and the man puts his share into a building society account and starts trying to raise a mortgage using the money. It seems likely that he will be able to buy somewhere within the next two or three months.

  In his claim, this money is disregarded: it is the proceeds of the sale of his former home and he plans to use it to buy another property within 26 weeks (para. 13.56).

## HOME SALE PROCEEDS, ETC.

HBR sch 5 para 3
CTBR sch 5 para 3

**13.56** Disregard in full as capital:

- money from the sale of the claimant's former home, including in Northern Ireland any compensation paid resulting from compulsory purchase; and
- money refunded by a housing association with whom it was deposited (para. 13.55),

but only if it is intended for purchasing another home within 26 weeks, or such longer period as is reasonable. (However, interest accrued on the money is counted as capital in the normal way: para. 13.71.)

## VALUING PROPERTY GENERALLY

**13.57** The general rules about valuing capital apply to a property which has to be taken into account as capital for HB/main CTB purposes (paras. 13.13-14). In such cases, an authority can get a free valuation of property from the Valuation Office Agency (circular HB/CTB A55/98 – which also enclosed forms for authorities to use for this purpose).

## VALUING PROPERTY WHICH IS RENTED OUT

HBR sch 5 para 6
CTBR sch 5 para 6

**13.58** Unless it forms part of the capital assets of a business (or in certain circumstances a former business: para. 17.5), property a claimant owns and has rented out is is valued as described earlier (paras. 13.13-14). However, the fact that it is rented out will affect its market value; for example, the presence of a sitting tenant can reduce it. For information about rental income see the following paragraphs.

## RENTAL INCOME RECEIVED BY THE CLAIMANT

HBR sch 4
paras 19, 20, 42
NIHBR sch 4
paras 4, 21, 22, 45
HBR sch 5 para 31
CTBR sch 4
paras 19, 20, 21,
sch 5 para 31

**13.59** Table 13.4 shows how rental income received by the claimant from people living in his or her home is taken into account. See also the example after that table. Paragraphs 13.60-61 deal with rent from property other than the claimant's home. Also, the value of the right to receive rent (para. 13.68) is disregarded as capital.

## Table 13.4 RENTAL INCOME RECEIVED FROM PEOPLE IN THE CLAIMANT'S HOME

**Rent, keep, etc. from household members**

- Disregard the whole of any rent, 'keep', etc. received from a child or young person in the family (paras. 4.12-20) or from a non-dependant (para. 4.21).

**Rent from boarders (as defined in para. 4.23)**

- Disregard the first £20.00 of that rent;
- count only half the rest as unearned income;
- a separate £20.00 is disregarded for each individual boarder who is charged for – even if a child – regardless of whether they have separate agreements.

**Rent from tenants/sub-tenants (as defined in para. 4.25)**

- Always disregard the first £4.00 of that rent;
- disregard a further £9.70 if the rent covers heating;
- count the rest as unearned income;
- a separate £4.00 (and, if appropriate, £9.70) is disregarded for each (sub-) tenant liable to pay rent for living in the claimant's home.

### Example: Letting out a room

A couple on HB/CTB have a spare room. First they let it out to a man for £50 per week inclusive of gas, electricity and water charges. He is their sub-tenant.

For the purposes of their HB/CTB, their income from this sub-tenant is £50 minus the standard £4 and the additional £9.70 because they provide heating; which is £36.30.

Later the same couple agree with the man that if he incrreases what he pays them to £65 per week, they will feed him. He is now their boarder.

So now, for the purposes of their HB/CTB, their income from this boarder is £65 minus the standard £20 – which is £45; the result being divided by two – which is £22.50.

Note that the rules therefore mean that a claimant is usually better off renting out a room to a boarder than to a (sub-)tenant.

### RENT ON DISREGARDED PROPERTY WHICH IS NOT THE CLAIMANT'S HOME

HBR sch 4 para 15(2) NIHBR sch 4 para 17(2) CTBR sch 4 para 15(2)

**13.60** The following applies if the claimant receives rent (or some other payment) on a property which is not his or her home, but is one of the types of property whose capital value is disregarded under the above rules (paras. 13.48-54) or the rules about the assets of the self-employed (para. 15.5). In such cases:

- take the amount of the rental income for an appropriate period (e.g. a month, a year);
- disregard any payment towards mortgage repayments (both interest and capital repayments) or any council tax or water charges the claimant is liable to pay during that period on the property (note that other outgoings cannot be disregarded);
- count the balance (converted to a weekly figure) as the claimant's unearned income.

### RENT ON NON-DISREGARDED PROPERTY

HBR 40(4), sch 4 para 15(1) NIHBR 40(4), sch 4 para 17(1) CTBR 31(4), sch 4 para 15(1)

**13.61** The following applies if the claimant receives rent (or some other payment) on a property whose value is taken into account as capital (even if for some reason the capital value is nil for HB/main CTB purposes). In such cases:

- take the amount of the rental income for an appropriate period (e.g. a month, a year);
- deduct any outgoings incurred in respect of the letting (e.g. estate agents' fees, tax due on the income, repairs, council tax, water charges, repayments of mortgages/loans, etc.);
- the balance (if any) is not income for HB/main CTB purposes: it is taken into account in deciding the amount of the claimant's capital. As with any other capital received by the claimant, he or she may use it all for living or other costs, in which case it does not affect his or her capital for HB/main CTB purposes (unless the deprivation rule applies: para. 13.97).

### PAYMENTS FOR ESSENTIAL REPAIRS AND IMPROVEMENTS TO THE HOME

HBR sch 5 para 9 CTBR sch 5 para 10

**13.62** Loans or gifts for these purposes are disregarded as capital for 26 weeks from the date paid, or such longer period as is reasonable. This disregard applies, for example, to home improvement grants, loans from a bank or similar institution, or from a friend or relative, etc.

### PORTABLE DISCOUNTS

BR sch 5 para 37 CTBR sch 5 para 36

**13.63** Grants from a local authority to purchase, alter or repair a property to be used as a home, are disregarded as capital for 26 weeks from the date of the grant, or such longer period as is reasonable. An example is when a council tenant gets a grant to buy another property.

### TAX REFUNDS FOR MORTGAGE INTEREST

**13.64** Tax refunds for interest on a mortgage taken out for purchasing or acquiring a share in the home, or for carrying out home repairs or improvements, are disregarded in full as capital.

HBR sch 5 para 2
CTBR sch 5 para 20

### INSURANCE PAYMENTS UNDER A MORTGAGE OR LOAN PROTECTION POLICY

**13.65** The following applies if a claimant has taken out insurance against being unable (perhaps because of sickness) to pay his or her mortgage or some other loan (for example a car loan), and is now receiving payments under that insurance policy. In such cases, payments the claimant receives under that insurance policy are disregarded as unearned income – but only insofar as they cover the cost of:

HBR sch 4 para 2
NIHBR sch 4 para 30
CTBR sch 4 para 29

- the repayments on the mortgage or other loan; and
- any premiums due on the policy in question; and
- (only in the case of a mortgage protection policy) any premiums on another insurance policy which was taken out to insure against loss or damage to the home and which was required as a condition of the mortgage.

### COMPENSATION AND INSURANCE PAYMENTS FOR THE HOME OR POSSESSIONS

**13.66** Such payments are disregarded as capital if they are for repair or replacement following loss of, or damage to, the claimant's home or personal possessions. They are disregarded for 26 weeks from the date paid, or such longer period as is reasonable.

HBR sch 5 para 9
CTBR sch 5 para

### PERSONAL POSSESSIONS

**13.67** Disregard in full as capital the value of the claimant's personal possessions – unless they were purchased for the purpose of obtaining or increasing entitlement to HB/CTB (in which case they should be valued as in paras. 13.11-13).

HBR sch 5 para 1
CTBR sch 5 para 11

## Savings and investments

### SUMMARY AND DEFINITIONS

**13.68** The following paragraphs deal with the assessment of the claimant's savings and investments. When these are taken into account, they are valued as described in paragraphs 13.13-14. (But for national savings certificates, see para. 13.72.) The following terms are used below:

- the 'surrender value' (of an insurance policy, for instance) means what the claimant would be paid (by the insurance company, for instance) if he or she cashed it in now (rather than waiting for it to mature, for instance);
- the 'value of the right to receive income' (from an annuity, for instance) means what the claimant would be paid in return for transferring the right to receive the income to someone else.

### SAVINGS AND CASH

HBR 38(1)
CTBR 29(1)

**13.69** These count in full as capital. For example, money in a bank or building society account is counted as capital (but see the next paragraph).

### INCOME PAID REGULARLY INTO AN ACCOUNT

**13.70** Regular payments of income (e.g. earnings, benefits, pensions) into a claimant's bank, building society or similar account should not be counted as capital for the period they cover (see e.g. Commissioners' decisions R(SB) 2/83 and R(IS) 3/93). For example, if earnings are paid in monthly, only what is left at the end of the month is capital. In practice, authorities rarely do this unless claimants specifically ask them to do so.

### INTEREST AND OTHER INCOME DERIVED FROM CAPITAL

HBR 40(4)
CTBR 31(4)

**13.71** Interest or other income derived from capital is dealt with as follows:

- if it is from non-disregarded capital, it is counted as capital from the date it is due to be credited to the claimant (examples include interest on a bank or building society account, and rent received on certain property: para. 13.61);
- if it is from the claimant's normal home (e.g. rent: table 15.4), or from self-employed business assets (para. 15.5), or from trust funds for personal injury (para. 13.83), it is counted as capital (as described in those paras.) from the date it is due to be credited to the claimant;
- if it is from any other form of disregarded capital, it is classified as capital and is itself then disregarded (examples include interest on house sale proceeds for 26 weeks: para. 13.56; and rent received on certain property: para. 13.60).

### NATIONAL SAVINGS CERTIFICATES

HBR 41(b)
CTBR 32(b)

**13.72** These count as capital, but the following applies instead of the normal rules about valuing capital. From 1st July in any year to 30th June in the next year, the capital amount for HB/main CTB purposes is their value as at 1st July in the first of those years. For current issues, this means their purchase price. The DWP issues a circular with valuation tables each year – usually in July.

## INVESTMENTS

**13.73** These count as capital. They are valued as described in the general rules (paras. 13.13-14), with the effect that:

- *shares* are valued at their 'sell' price. Then disregard 10 per cent towards the cost of their sale;
- *unit trusts* are valued at their 'sell' price. Normally this already allows for notional sales costs. If it does not, disregard 10 per cent for this;
- *income bonds* count in full.

## LIFE INSURANCE POLICIES

**13.74** Disregard as capital the surrender value of a life insurance policy, and also the value of the right to receive income from it (para. 13.68). But count as capital any money actually received from it (e.g. if the claimant actually cashes all or part of it in).

HBR sch 5 para 16
CTBR sch 5 para 16

## ANNUITIES

**13.75** If the claimant has an annuity, it means he or she has invested an initial lump sum with an insurance company who, in return, pay the claimant a regular income. Count this income in full as unearned income. Disregard as capital the surrender value of the annuity, and also the value of the right to receive income from it (para. 13.68).

HBR 34(2), sch 5 para 12
CTBR 25(2), sch 5 para 12

## HOME INCOME PLANS

**13.76** If the claimant has a home income plan, it means he or she raised a loan using his or her home as security, has invested the loan as an annuity and, in return, gets a regular income: part of this income is used to repay the loan, part may be used to repay the claimant's mortgage, and part may be left over for the claimant to use. Count the income received by the claimant as unearned income, but only after deducting (if they have not been deducted at source):

- any tax payable on that income;
- any repayments on the loan which was raised to obtain the annuity; and
- any mortgage repayments made using the income (using the figures for the repayments which apply after tax has been deducted from them).

Disregard as capital the surrender value of the annuity, and the value of the right to receive income from it (para. 13.68).

HBR 34(2), sch 4 para 16
NIHBR 34(2), sch 4 para 18
CTBR 25(2), sch 4 para 16

## LIFE INTEREST OR LIFERENT

**13.77** If a claimant has a life interest or (in Scotland) liferent, it means he or she has the right to enjoy an asset during his or her or someone else's lifetime, after

HBR sch 5 para 1
CTBR sch 5 para 14

which it will pass to someone else. The actual value to the claimant (if any) of the life interest or liferent is counted as capital; and any actual income the claimant receives from it is counted as earned or unearned income as appropriate. Disregard as capital the value of the right to receive income from it (para. 13.68).

### REVERSIONARY INTEREST

HBR sch 5 para 6
CTBR sch 5 para 6

**13.78** If a claimant has a reversionary interest, it means he or he has an interest in property but will not possess it until some future event (for example, the death of a relative). Disregard in full the capital value of a reversionary interest. For HB and main CTB purposes, however, a property the claimant has rented out is not disregarded as a reversionary interest: the rules for dealing with such property are explained in paragraphs 13.60-61.

## Other items of income and capital

### MAINTENANCE RECEIVED

HBR sch 4 para 47
NIHBR sch 4 para 50
CTBR sch 4 para 46

**13.79** If there is at least one child or young person in the claimant's family, disregard £15 of any maintenance received or due to be received from:

- the claimant's former partner; or
- the claimant's partner's former partner; or
- the parent of any child or young person in the claimant's family (so long as that parent is not in the claimant's family)

The definitions of 'partner', 'child', 'young person', 'family' are in chapter 4. The £15 disregard applies whether the maintenance is payable to the claimant or to a child or young person. If two or more maintenance payments are received in any week, the maximum disregard is £15 per week.

### CHARITABLE AND/OR VOLUNTARY PAYMENTS

HBR 40(6)
HBR sch 4 paras 13, 21
sch 5 para 32
NIHBR sch 4 paras 15, 23,
sch 5 para 32
CTBR 31(6), sch 4 paras 13, 22,
sch 5 para 32

**13.80** The following rules apply if the claimant receives payments which are charitable and/or voluntary. A lump sum payment counts as capital, as does a payment which is neither made nor due to be made at regular intervals. The following apply to a payment which is made or due to be made at regular intervals:

- if it is intended and used for the claimant's (or a member of the family's) food, ordinary clothing or footwear (excluding school uniform and sportswear), household fuel, eligible rent (apart from any non-dependant deduction), council tax, or water charges; disregard £20.00 (subject to the rules on aggregation: para. 13.105). Count the rest as unearned income;
- if it is for any other item, disregard it in full.

However, the above rules do not apply to payments in kind (i.e. goods not money) from a charity, which are always disregarded in full; nor to maintenance received (para. 13.79), nor to payments from the Trusts and Funds described in paragraph 13.40.

## PAYMENTS IN KIND; CASH IN LIEU OF CONCESSIONARY COAL

**13.81** Payments in kind (i.e. goods not money – apart from those in paras. 13.80 and 14.26) count in full as unearned income. Cash in lieu of concessionary coal which is paid to a current employee of the British Coal Board counts as part of his or her earnings. If it is paid to an ex-miner or a miner's widow, it counts in full as unearned income.

## SECOND WORLD WAR EX GRATIA AND COMPENSATION PAYMENTS

**13.82** Disregard in full as capital, without time limit, the ex gratia payments of £10,000 made by the Secretary of State in respect of imprisonment or internment of the claimant or his or her deceased partner, or the claimant's or partner's deceased spouse, by the Japanese during the Second World War. The DWP (circular HB/CTB A1/2001) has recommended that authorities need not attempt to identify the particular £10,000, but that £10,000 should simply be disregarded from the capital the claimant has.

HBR sch 5 para 64
NIHBR sch 5 para 59
CTBR sch 5 para 64

Disregard in full as capital, without time limit, any payment (apart from a war pension) made to compensate for the fact that, during the Second World War, the claimant or partner or either's deceased spouse:

HBR sch 5 para 67
NIHBR sch 5 para 63
CTBR sch 5 para 6

- was a slave labourer or a forced labourer; or
- had suffered property loss or personal injury; or
- was a parent of a child who had died.

## GALLANTRY AWARDS

**13.83** Disregard in full (as capital and income):

HBR sch 4 para 9
HBR sch 5 para 4
NIHBR sch 5 para 46
CTBR sch 4 para
sch 5 para 48

- Victoria Cross and George Cross payments;
- the lump sum payments of up to £6,000 for those who have agreed not to receive any further payments of income from those; and
- analogous awards for gallantry from this country or another country.

## TRUST FUNDS FOR PERSONAL INJURY, OTHER TRUST FUNDS, AND INFANT FUNDS IN COURT

**13.84** The general principle is that any amount in a trust fund is capital and is counted in full. The two exceptions are as follows:

HBR sch 5 paras 13, 46, 47
NIHBR sch 5 paras 13, 45
CTBR sch 5 paras 13, 46, 47

- In all cases, money held in a trust fund for personal injury is disregarded in full as capital without time limit – as is the value of the right to receive income from it (para. 13.68). Only payments actually received from the trust are counted – as unearned income or capital as appropriate.

- In any other case, money held in a discretionary trust (one which the claimant has no absolute right to take money from) is disregarded. Only payments actually received from the trust are counted – as unearned income or capital as appropriate.

Compensation to children and young persons for personal injury or the death of a parent, if paid into a court on their behalf, is disregard in full as capital without time limit.

## PARENTAL CONTRIBUTIONS TO STUDENTS

HBR sch 3 para 9 sch 4 paras 17, 18 NIHBR sch 3 para 9, sch 4 paras 19, 20 CTBR sch 3 para 9 sch 4 paras 17, 18

**13.85** The following rules apply to contributions made by claimants to a student son or daughter ('student' is defined in chapter 21):

- If a claimant has been assessed by a grant-awarding body as being able to make a contribution to the student's grant, and it is not a discretionary grant, the whole amount of the assessed contribution is disregarded in the assessment of the claimant's income.
- If a claimant contributes towards the maintenance of a student under the age of 25, who has a discretionary grant or no grant, the amount of the contribution is disregarded in the assessment of the claimant's income – but only up to a maximum weekly figure. The maximum weekly figure is £42.70 minus the amount of any discretionary grant.

So far as possible the above are disregarded from unearned income, then any balance is disregarded from earned income. There is no disregard specifically for parental contributions towards student loans, but a contribution towards a loan could fall within the second point above.

## EDUCATION MAINTENANCE ALLOWANCES

HBR sch 4 para 10, sch 5 para 60 CTBR sch 4 para 10, sch 5 para 60

**13.86** Disregard Education Maintenance Allowances or Awards (including Assisted Places Allowances) in full as unearned income. These could include bursaries for 16-to-18-year olds in non-advanced education or payments towards a child's travel to school.

Disregard Education Maintenance Allowance bonuses in full as capital for 52 weeks from the date of payment.

HBR 2(1) HBR sch 4 para 71, sch 5 para 59 NIHBR sch 4 para 72, sch 5 para 57 CTBR 2(1), sch 4 para 70, sch 5 para 59

## SPORTS AWARDS

**13.87** Sports Council sports awards are dealt with as follows:

- any amount awarded in respect of the claimant's or a member of the family's food (excluding vitamins, minerals or other special performance-enhancing dietary supplements), ordinary clothing or footwear (excluding school uniform and sportswear), household fuel, rent, council tax, or water charges, is counted in full as income or capital as appropriate;

- any amount awarded for any other purpose is disregarded in full as unearned income, and as capital for 26 weeks from the date of payment.

## COURT OF PROTECTION

**13.88** If money is held on the claimant's behalf by the Court of Protection, count it in full as capital.

## JURORS' ALLOWANCES

**13.89** Disregard these in full except in so far as they compensate for loss of earnings or loss of a social security benefit.

HBR sch 4 paras 38, 41 CTBR sch 4 para 40

## LOANS

**13.90** The general principle is that if a claimant receives a genuine loan it increases his or her capital (until and to the extent that he or she spends it, perhaps on the thing it was lent for): the loan is not income. A pretended loan (for instance, a payment which is described as a loan but which will not be repaid) is not a loan: it is treated as capital or unearned income as appropriate. Whether a payment is a genuine loan or a pretended loan can itself be a difficult question of fact. Completely different rules apply to student loans (chapter 21) and career development loans (para. 13.42).

## OUTSTANDING INSTALMENTS OF CAPITAL

**13.91** If, at the claimant's date of claim for HB/CTB (or at the date of any subsequent reconsideration of the claim), he or she is entitled to outstanding instalments of capital (i.e. instalments due after that date), the authority must consider whether the sum of the outstanding instalments and the claimant's other capital exceeds £16,000:

HBR 19(2), 34(1), sch 5 para 17 CTBR 11(2), 25(1) sch 5 para 17

- if it does, the outstanding instalments are ignored as capital but are counted as income. The law does not lay down any particular way of doing this;
- if it does not, the outstanding instalments are counted in full as capital from the date of claim (or reconsideration).

**13.92** When the above rule is applied to outstanding instalments of capital to which a child or young person is entitled (para. 13.106), the only difference is that £3,000 is substituted for £16,000.

## OVERSEAS CAPITAL

HBR 42, sch 5 para 22
CTBR 33, sch 5 para 22

**13.93** The following rules apply if a claimant possesses capital in a country outside the UK:

- if there is no prohibition in that country against bringing the money to the UK, value it at its market or surrender value in that country; then disregard 10 per cent if selling it would incur costs; then disregard any mortgage or other incumbrance secured on it; then disregard any charge which would be incurred in converting it into sterling; and count the remainder as capital;
- if there is such a prohibition, value it at what a willing buyer in the UK would give for it; then disregard 10 per cent if selling it would incur costs; then disregard any mortgage or other incumbrance secured on it; and count the remainder as capital.

## OVERSEAS INCOME

HBR sch 4 paras 22, 32, sch 5 para 15
NIHBR sch 4 paras 24, 34, sch 5 para 15
CTBR sch 4 paras 23, 33, sch 5 para 15

**13.94** The following rules apply if a claimant is entitled to income payable in a country outside the UK:

- if there is no prohibition in that country against bringing the money to the UK, treat it as income in the normal way, allowing any disregard which may apply (including any earnings disregard in the case of earned income); also disregard any charge for converting it into sterling;
- if there is such a prohibition, disregard it in full; also disregard as capital the value of the right to receive income from it (para. 13.68).

## OUTGOINGS; EXPENSES

**13.95** The only outgoings which can affect a claimant's income for HB/CTB purposes are payments for child care costs (para. 14.12) and payments by parents and spouses towards a student's maintenance (para. 13.85 and chapter 21). No allowance is made in the case of a person who makes any other kind of payment to someone else (though see para. 13.24 in the case of certain additions within state benefits).

Expenses in unpaid work are disregarded (para. 14.30; for work expenses see para. 14.29).

# Notional income and capital

HBR 35(6),(7), 43(6)
CTBR 26(6),(7), 34(6)

**13.96** In the situations described below a claimant is treated, for HB/main CTB purposes, as possessing income and/or capital he or she does not in fact possess – known as 'notional' income and/or capital. The notional income or capital is assessed as if it was actual income or capital and any relevant disregards must be applied.

## DEPRIVATION

**13.97** If a claimant deliberately deprives himself or herself of capital or income in order to qualify for HB (or for more HB), he or she is treated as still having it for HB purposes. The same applies independently for CTB. It is the claimant's intention which must be taken into account (not the item he or she spent the money on). HBR 35(1), 43(1) CTBR 26(1), 34(1)

## DIMINUTION OF NOTIONAL CAPITAL

**13.98** If a claimant is treated as having notional capital for the above reason, the amount of notional capital taken into account is reduced each week, broadly speaking, by the amount of any HB, CTB, income support, income-related job-seeker's allowance, working families' tax credit and disabled person's tax credit lost as a result of the claimant being treated as having notional capital. The rules for doing this are complicated, and in practice not all authorities follow them. For further details, please see GM paras. C2.79-102. HBR 43A CTBR 35

## AVAILABLE ON APPLICATION

**13.99** Any income or capital which a claimant could have on application (in other words, simply by applying for it) is treated as possessed by him or her from the date it could be obtained. This rule does not apply to income which could be obtained in the form of a DSS rehabilitation allowance; nor does it apply to any payments (of income or capital) made to a provider of a New Deal arrangement (para 13.41); nor does it apply to income or capital which could be obtained from a discretionary trust or a trust for personal injury (para. 13.85), or a personal pension scheme or retirement annuity contract; nor does it apply to any kind of disregarded capital. Also, the DWP advises that this rule should not be applied in the case of income from any social security benefit unless the authority is sure about the amount the person could receive (GM para. C3.118). This rule is, for example, commonly used in the case of unclaimed child benefit. HBR 35(2), 43(2) CTBR 26(2), 34(2)

## PAYMENTS TO OR FOR THIRD PARTIES

**13.100** If income or capital is paid in A's name but used by B for food, household fuel, clothing or footwear (other than school uniform and sportswear), eligible rent (apart from any non-dependant deduction), council tax, or water charges, it is treated as belonging to B. This rule does not apply to concessionary coal (para. 13.81) or to payments under the New Deal (including those to a provider of a New Deal arrangement) (para. 13.41). It does, however, apply to payments to a third party of occupational or personal pensions; unless the intended beneficiary is bankrupt or subject to sequestration, payment is made to the trustee (or similar) and the beneficiary and any family have no other income. HBR 35(3),(8), 43(3),(3A),(7) CTBR 26(3),(8), 34(3),(3A),(7)

### UPRATINGS

HBR 35(4)
CTBR 26(4)

**13.101** If the April uprating date for social security benefits is slightly different from that for HB/CTB, they are generally treated as uprated on the same date as HB/CTB.

### WORK PAID AT LESS THAN THE GOING RATE

HBR 35(5),(5A),(5B)
CTBR 26(5),(5A),(5B)

**13.102** If a claimant is paid less than the going rate for a job, he or she can be treated as having whatever additional pay is reasonable in the circumstances. The means of the employer must be taken into account; and this rule does not apply to voluntary work, to claimants provided with a New Deal arrangement (para. 13.41) or to claimants on an 'approved work' training programme (e.g. Work Trials or work placements). When this rule is used, disregard notional tax and national insurance contributions (Appendix 4) and apply the earnings disregards (chapter 12).

### RELATIONSHIP TO A COMPANY

HBR 43(4),(5)
CTBR 34(4),(5)

**13.103** This applies to a claimant who is not the sole owner of, or a partner in, a company, but whose relationship to that company is analogous to somconc who is. In such cases, the claimant's share of the capital of that company may be assessed as though he or she was the sole owner or partner (para. 14.28) and, if this is done, any actual share of the company he or she possesses is disregarded.

### PENSION SCHEMES

HBR 35(2A)-(2C)
CTBR 26(2A)-(2C)

**13.104** If a claimant aged 60 or more could get income from his or her pension scheme, but has failed to do so or chosen not to do so, then he or she is treated as having that income. Further details are given in circular HB/CTB A25/95.

## Aggregation of income and capital

**13.105** As described at the beginning of this chapter, in assessing HB and main CTB, a claimant is treated as possessing any income and capital which belongs to himself or herself, any partner and, in certain cases, children and young persons. The details for children and young persons are dealt with below. (Paragraph 13.4 explains the rules which apply when a non-dependant's income and capital is treated as belonging to a claimant. Paragraph 13.109 explains a final rule about aggregation.)

### CHILDREN'S AND YOUNG PERSONS' CAPITAL

HBR 19, 39
CTBR 11, 30

**13.106** Except for the rule described in paragraph 13.92 (about outstanding instalments of capital), a child's or young person's capital is calculated in the same way – and with the same disregards – as for the claimant. But a child's or young person's capital is never counted as part of the claimant's capital.

**13.107** Instead, for any child or young person who has capital of over £3,000, the claimant is not awarded a personal allowance for him or her, nor any disabled child premium or enhanced disability premium (paras. 12.43). However, no matter how many children/young persons in the family have capital over £3,000, the claimant keeps his or her family premium – whether this is payable at the basic rate or the protected lone parent rate.

## CHILDREN'S AND YOUNG PERSONS' INCOME

**13.108** A child's or young person's income is calculated in the same way – and with the same disregards – as for the claimant. But the following variations apply: HBR 19, 36 CTBR 11, 30

- Payments of maintenance made to a child or young person are treated as if they were paid to the claimant (and dealt with as in para. 13.79).
- If a child or young person has capital over £3,000, his or her income is completely disregarded (apart from maintenance as just described).
- If a child or young person has left school and is in remunerative work (work averaging 16 hours per week or more: para. 7.29), count any unearned income and earnings he or she has. Note that the earnings disregard is £15.00 if the claimant gets a disabled child premium for the child or young person in question; otherwise it is £5.00.
- For any other child or young person, count unearned income only.
- The child's or young person's income, calculated as above, is counted as part of the claimant's income – but only up to the amount of the dependant's allowance and any disabled child premium and enhanced disability premium for the child or young person in question. Anything beyond that is disregarded.

Details of the allowances and premiums referred to above are in chapter 12.

## THE OVER-RIDING £20 DISREGARD FROM CERTAIN INCOME OF THE FAMILY

**13.109** In any particular claim for HB/main CTB, the maximum weekly disregard per claim is £20 from any or all of the following: HBR sch 4 para 33 NIHBR sch 4 para 35 CTBR sch 4 para 34

- certain charitable and voluntary payments (para. 13.80);
- student loan, access fund and covenant income (chapter 21);
- certain war widow's and war disablement pensions (para. 13.28);
- widowed mother's allowance and widowed parent's allowance (para. 13.29).

If two (or more) members of the family get any of these types of payment, the maximum weekly disregard is £20 for the whole family. In such cases, the disregard is used in whatever way is most favourable to the claimant.

**13.110** Nothing in the above prevents an authority from running a local scheme whereby more than £10 (or all) of a war widow's or war disablement pension is disregarded (para 7.45).

# 14 Employed earners

**14.1** This chapter describes the rules for assessing income (and capital) received by employed earners in connection with their employment. The rules apply to both HB and main CTB. The distinction between an employed earner and a person who is self-employed is described in paragraphs 15.3-4. The following matters are explained in this chapter:

- the assessment of earnings;
- earned income disregards generally;
- the child care disregard;
- the 30 hours per week disregard;
- particular kinds of earnings and expenses;
- starting work;
- absences from work and ending work.

HBR 28
CTBR 19

**14.2** This chapter applies equally to the employed earnings of the claimant, a partner or a child or young person in a claimant's family. *References to 'a claimant' should be read accordingly.* It does not apply to the employed earnings of a non-dependant or a second adult: the law does not lay down any particular way of assessing employed earnings in such cases (although it must be gross income, not net).

## The assessment of earnings

HBR 21, 22, 28
CTBR 13, 14, 19

**14.3** The key steps for assessing employed earnings for HB/main CTB purposes are:

- averaging or estimating the gross earnings;
- deducting tax and national insurance contributions;
- deducting half of any approved pension contribution;
- converting the result, if necessary, to a weekly figure;
- deducting a fixed 'earned income disregard' and, if appropriate, amounts for child care costs and for certain people working 30 hours or more per week.

In certain circumstances, notional (rather than actual) earnings are used (para. 11.102).

### AVERAGING OR ESTIMATING GROSS EARNINGS

HBR 22
CTBR 14

**14.4** The general rule is that earnings are averaged over the five weeks immediately preceding the date of claim if the claimant is paid weekly; or the two months immediately preceding the date of claim if the claimant is paid monthly. But if averaging the earnings over some other period would produce a more accurate estimate of what will be the claimant's earnings during his or her benefit period, they should be averaged over that period. (See also para. 15.102 in the case of work paid at less than the going rate.)

**14.5** If the claimant has not been employed for long enough to assess earnings on the above basis, earnings should be estimated. This might be done by asking the claimant to provide an estimate from his or her employer: most authorities have standard forms which can be used for this.

**14.6** If the claimant's earnings change during the course of the benefit period, an estimate should then be made of what they will be during the remainder of the benefit period.

### DEDUCTING INCOME TAX AND NATIONAL INSURANCE CONTRIBUTIONS

**14.7** If the claimant's actual earnings were averaged as described above, any income tax or class 1 national insurance contributions actually paid (or made from them) must be deducted from those earnings. HBR 29 CTBR 20

**14.8** If the claimant's earnings were estimated as described above, a notional amount for income tax and class 1 national insurance contributions must be deducted from those estimated earnings (appendix 4).

Where, in Northern Ireland, the claimant works in the Republic, the amounts deducted are those which the NIHE estimates would have been deducted if they worked in Northern Ireland. NIHBR 29(5)

### DEDUCTING HALF OF PENSION CONTRIBUTIONS

**14.9** Whether the claimant's earnings were averaged or estimated, half of any contributions he or she makes to an occupational or personal pension scheme must be deducted from his or her earnings. HBR 29 CTBR 20

### CONVERSION TO A WEEKLY FIGURE

**14.10** If a claimant's earnings are paid other than weekly, they must be converted to a weekly figure as described in paragraph 7.50.

## Earned income disregards generally

**14.11** A fixed earned income disregard must be deducted from each claimant's earnings. The amount depends on the type of case: the figures are given in table 14.1 (which also applies to self-employed earners). As shown in that table, only one of the amounts shown there is deducted from the combined earnings of a couple or polygamous marriage. (In certain cases, there are further disregards: paras. 13.85, 14.12 and 14.17.) HBR 29, sch 3 CTBR 20, sch 3

## TABLE 14.1 WEEKLY EARNED INCOME DISREGARDS

### LONE PARENTS

The weekly disregard is £25 for all lone parents.

### CERTAIN PEOPLE WHO ARE DISABLED OR LONG-TERM SICK

The weekly disregard is £20 (per single claimant or per couple) in all the following cases:

- Single claimants who count as disabled or long-term sick (as described in paras 12.20 onwards) and couples where at least one partner does so. This applies in all cases until the claimant (or in the case of a couple, the older partner) reaches the age of 60. It then applies only if the claimant (or in the case of a couple, either partner):
  - qualified for the £20 disregard (or the former £15 disregard) at any time in the 8 weeks up to and including the claimant's (or partner's) 60th birthday; and
  - has continued on HB or CTB or community charge benefit since then (regardless of breaks of up to eight weeks in entitlement to any or all of these); and
  - has continued in employment since then (regardless of breaks of up to eight weeks in employment).
- Any other single claimants or couples who are awarded a severe disability premium.

### CERTAIN CARERS AND CERTAIN PEOPLE IN THE EMERGENCY SERVICES

Except where the preceding disregards of £25 or £20 apply, the weekly disregard is £20 (per single claimant or per couple) in the following cases:

- Single claimants and couples who are awarded a carer premium.
- Single claimants and couples employed in the emergency services listed in paragraph 14.24.

This £20 disregard applies only to the earnings of the partner(s) to whom either of those conditions applies. If those earnings are less than £20, then up to £10 (for couples) or £5 (for single claimants) of the balance is applied to any other earnings they have.

OTHER SINGLE CLAIMANTS AND COUPLES

In any case not mentioned above, the weekly disregard is:

- £10 per couple;
- £5 per single claimant.

CHILDREN AND YOUNG PERSONS

The weekly disregard per child or young person is:

- £15 if he or she qualifies for a disabled child premium;
- £5 in any other case.

*Notes*

Other earned income disregards are described in paragraph 14.12 and 14.17.

For the details of the premiums referred to in the table, see chapter 12.

## The child care disregard

**14.12** In addition to the disregards in table 14.1, up to £70 or £105 per week per HB/main CTB claim is disregarded for child care costs in the circumstances described below. 'Remunerative work' means the same as it does in paragraphs 7.33 onwards, except that for the following purposes a woman on maternity leave from remunerative work still counts as being in remunerative work (however, she cannot get the child care disregard in respect of the child she is on maternity leave for). HBR 21, 21A CTBR 13, 13A

WHO CAN QUALIFY?

**14.13** The following groups qualify for the child care disregard in the circumstances described in the next two paragraphs:

- lone parents who are in remunerative work;
- couples if both are in remunerative work;
- couples if one of them (claimant or partner) is in remunerative work and the other one:
  - counts as disabled or long-term sick (as described in paras. 14.20 onwards); or
  - would meet either of the above conditions apart from the fact that he or she has been in hospital etc. (para. 12.49) for more than six weeks, or
  - would meet any of the above conditions apart from the fact that he or she is disqualified from incapacity benefit;

- couples if the partner is in remunerative work and the claimant:
  - is incapable of work, AND
  - has been incapable of work for a waiting period of 28 weeks. The waiting period may be made up of any number of periods of incapacity for work, so long as the gaps between them are no greater than 8 weeks long. 'Incapable of work' means satisfying the conditions for any rate of incapacity benefit (or its Northern Ireland equivalent).

## IN WHAT CIRCUMSTANCES DO THEY QUALIFY?

**14.14** The above groups qualify for the disregard if the claimant or partner pays one or more of the following to care for at least one child in his or her family (so long as that child satisfies the age condition – see below):

- a registered child-minder; or
- a child-minding scheme for which registration is not required (e.g. run by a school or local authority); or
- child care approved for tax credit purposes; or
- any other out-of-school-hours scheme provided by a school on school premises or by a local authority – but, in this case only, the child must be aged 8 or more.

The disregard does not, however, apply to payments in respect of compulsory education, nor to payments made by a claimant to his or her partner (or *vice versa*) if the child is the responsibility of at least one of them (para. 4.16).

## THE AGE CONDITION

**14.15** A child satisfies the age condition until the first Monday in September after his or her 15th birthday or, in the case of a child who meets the conditions for a disabled child premium (chapter 12), the first Monday in September after his or her 16th birthday.

## AMOUNTS, ETC.

**14.16** The amount of the disregard equals what the claimant or partner pays, up to a maximum of:

- £94.50 per week per HB/main CTB claim for claimants with one child who meets the above criteria (paras. 14.14-15); or
- £140 per week per HB/main CTB claim for claimants with two or more children who meet those criteria.

The disregard is made as far as possible from the earnings (from employment or self-employment) of a claimant and/or partner who satisfies the conditions in paragraph 14.13. Any balance, if the earnings are insufficient, is disregarded from any Working Families' Tax Credit or Disabled Person's Tax Credit the claimant or partner receives (para. 13.31). Apart from that, it cannot be disregarded from unearned income.

The amount the claimant or partner pays is averaged over whichever period, up to a year, gives the most accurate estimate of the charges during the benefit period, taking account of information provided by the person providing the care.

## The 30 hours per week disregard

**14.17** In addition to the earned income disregards mentioned above, a disregard of £11.45 per week is made if at least one of the following conditions is met (but see the following paragraph for the exception to this rule):

HBR sch 3 para. 1[illegible] CTBR sch 3 para 16

- the claimant (or his or her partner) receives working families' tax credit (WFTC) or disabled person's tax credit (DPTC) which includes the addition for working 30 hours or more per week on average (although the amount of the addition to WFTC/DPTC is £11.45 for certain older awards, the earned income disregard is always £11.65); or
- the claimant's applicable amount includes a family premium (chapter 12) – but only if the claimant (or his or her partner) works 30 hours or more per week on average;
- all the following conditions are met in a particular case:
  - (a) the claimant (or his or her partner) counts as disabled or long-term sick (as described in paras. 12.20 onwards) or is aged 80 or over, and
  - (b) the claimant (or his or her partner) (not necessarily, in the case of a couple or polygamous marriage, the same one as in (a)) works 30 hours or more per week on average; and
  - (c) in the case of a couple or polygamous marriage, at least one partner both meets the condition in (a) and works 16 hours or more per week on average.

**14.18** For the above purposes, the question of whether anyone works 16 hours or more per week on average is decided as in paragraphs 7.33 onwards; and the question of whether anyone works 30 hours or more per week on average is decided in the same way (apart from the different number of hours).

**14.19** The above £11.65 earned income disregard is not made if it (along with the other earned income disregard(s) which apply in any particular case) would result in a negative earned income figure. In such a case, a similar disregard is instead made from Working Families' Tax Credit or Disabled Person's Tax Credit (para. 13.31).

# Particular kinds of earnings and expenses

## BONUSES, TIPS AND COMMISSION

HBR 28(1)
CTBR 19(1)

**14.20** All forms of bonuses, tips and commission are included in the assessment of earnings.

## ARREARS OF EARNINGS

HBR 68
CTBR 59

**14.21** Pay arrears count as earnings for the period they cover if they relate to periods on or after 6th March 1995. They count as capital if they relate to periods before then.

## TAX REFUNDS

HBR 40(2)
CTBR 31(2)

**14.22** Tax refunds on earnings count as capital (not earnings) including in Northern Ireland any analogous payments from the Irish Republic.

## EARNINGS PAID IN A LUMP SUM

HBR 34(3)
CTBR 25(3)

**14.23** If earnings are paid in a lump sum (or in any other form which could in broad terms be characterised as capital), they are nonetheless counted as earnings. They are averaged over the period they cover.

## EMERGENCY SERVICES ANNUAL BOUNTY

HBR 40(1)
CTBR 31(1)

**14.24** Annual bounty paid by the emergency services counts as capital (not earnings) if it is paid annually or at longer intervals. For these purposes the 'emergency services' means part-time fire-fighters, auxiliary coast guards, part-time life-boat workers, and members of the Territorial Army or similar reserve forces.

## NON-CASH VOUCHERS

HBR 28
CTBR 19

**14.25** If an employee receives non-cash vouchers which are taken into account for the purposes of calculating his or her National Insurance contributions, their value is counted as employed earnings. The value of such vouchers should appear on pay slips (circular HB/CTB A17/99).

## PAYMENTS IN KIND

HBR 28
CTBR 19

**14.26** With the exception of certain non-cash vouchers (para. 14.25) and concessionary coal (para. 13.81), payments in kind (i.e. payments of goods rather than money) are completely disregarded in the assessment of earnings. The DWP advises (circular HB/CTB A6/98) that credits received via Local Exchange Trading Schemes ('LETS') do not count as payments in kind, but should be given a cash value as earnings.

### COUNCILLORS' ALLOWANCES

**14.27** Councillors' allowances, apart from expenses payments, count as employed earnings. (For general advice on these, see GM para. C3.10).

### COMPANY DIRECTORS

**14.28** In the case of a claimant who is a diretor of a company registered with Companies House:

- the income paid by the company to the director is assessed as earned income under the usual rules;
- his or her interest (or share of it) in the company is assessed as capital.

### WORK EXPENSES

HBR 28, sch 4 para 3
CTBR 19, sch 4 para 3

**14.29** Work expenses met by an employee may not be disregarded against the employee's earnings (but see paragraph 14.12 as regards child care expenses). The treatment of work expenses met by an employer is as follows:

- if they are for travel to work, or for the cost of caring for a child or other dependant, these must be added in as part of the employee's earnings;
- if they are for other items necessary for performance of the job, these are disregarded in full.

### EXPENSES IN UNPAID WORK

HBR sch 4 para 2
CTBR sch 4 para

**14.30** Expenses received by a person doing unpaid work are disregarded in full if they are paid by a charitable organisation or non-profit-making voluntary organisation.

## Starting work

**14.31** Although in HB and main CTB there are no specific rules about the period to which earned income should be attributed, the general principle is that, when a claimant starts work, his or her earnings should be taken into account from the beginning of his or her job – not (if different) the first pay day. (However, for Access to Work and similar schemes, see para. 13.41; for 'extended payments', see para. 17.54; and for the general rules about when changes of circumstances are taken into account, see chapter 17.)

### ADVANCES OR LOANS FROM AN EMPLOYER

HBR 40(5)
CTBR 31(5)

**14.32** Advances and loans from an employer do not count as earnings. They count as capital if (and for as long as) the person has the money.

## Absences from work and ending work

HBR 28
CTBR 19

**14.33** The general rules are described below. More details are in tables 14.2 and 14.3. These rules may appear complicated. This is because (for example) during a holiday a person may get sick pay, or while on sick leave a person may get holiday pay. (For the general rules about when changes of circumstances are taken into account, see chapter 17.)

### HOLIDAY PAY

HBR 40(3)
CTBR 31(3)

**14.34** Holiday pay counts as earnings (but see tables 14.2 and 14.3). The exception is that it counts as capital (for as long as the person has the money) if it is payable more than four weeks after:

- the beginning of an absence or break from work (table 14.2), or
- ending work (table 14.3).

### SICK PAY AND MATERNITY PAY

HBR 28(1)(i)
CTBR 19(1)(i)

**14.35** Statutory sick and maternity pay and employer's sick and maternity pay count as earnings (but see tables 14.2 and 14.3).

### RETAINERS

HBR 28(1)(e)
CTBR 19(1)(e)

**14.36** Retainers (e.g. payments made in the holidays to employees of school meals services) count as earnings (but see tables 14.2 and 14.3).

### STRIKE PAY

**14.37** Strike pay does not count as earnings. It counts as unearned income (but see tables 14.2 and 14.3).

### REDUNDANCY PAYMENTS

**14.38** Redundancy payments (including those paid periodically rather than in a lump sum) do not count as earnings. They count as capital if (and for as long as) the person actually has the money (but see table 14.3 for the treatment of other payments which may be made on redundancy – such as payments in lieu of notice and compensation payments).

## Table 14.2 ABSENCES FROM WORK

SHORT ABSENCES

- Because of the ordinary rules about changes of circumstances (para. 17.13), do not reassess earnings in any of the cases mentioned below unless the absence or break spans at least one Sunday/Monday midnight.

PERIODS WHILST SOMEONE RECEIVES A RETAINER

- Reassess earnings if they change (for example, if the person is paid less during the summer holidays).

HOLIDAYS, ABSENCES WITHOUT GOOD CAUSE, AND STRIKES

- Reassess earnings if they change (for example, if the person is paid less during holidays, or nothing during a strike). (See also the general rule about holiday pay: para. 14.34.)

SICK LEAVE, MATERNITY LEAVE, LAY OFF, SUSPENSION AND OTHER ABSENCES WITH GOOD CAUSE

The following rules apply so long as the employment has not terminated.

- *If the absence for any of these reasons began before the person's 'date of claim' (para. 5.54).* Count only the following as earnings (and only if they are received during the absence):
  - retainers;
  - statutory or employer's sick or maternity pay;
  - holiday pay – but only if it is an absence from remunerative work (paras. 7.33 onwards). (See also the general rule about holiday pay: para. 14.34.)
- *If the absence for any of these reasons begins on or after the person's 'date of claim' (para. 5.54).* Reassess earnings if they change (for example if the person receives a lower rate of pay for any of these reasons). (See also the general rule about holiday pay: para. 14.34.)

**Table 14.3 ENDING WORK**

*'Remunerative work' is described in paragraphs 7.33 onwards.*

RETIRING FROM REMUNERATIVE WORK AT OR AFTER THE AGE OF 60/65

- If the person retires and is entitled to a state pension immediately afterwards (including someone who has deferred entitlement to a state pension for up to five years), or is not entitled only because the necessary national insurance contributions have not been paid, all his or her earnings are disregarded during any period following the date of retirement.

ENDING REMUNERATIVE WORK IN OTHER CASES

- *If the termination occurred before the person's 'date of claim' (para. 5.54).* During any period following the date of termination, disregard all earnings except:
  - retainers;
  - payments in lieu of remuneration (but periodic redundancy payments count as capital: para. 14.38);
  - payments in lieu of notice or compensating for loss of income;
  - holiday pay (see also the general rule about holiday pay: para. 14.34);
  - compensation awards made by industrial tribunals for unfair dismissal. Other compensation payments count as capital (not earnings).
- *If the termination occurs on or after the person's 'date of claim' (para 5.54).* Reassess to take changes and ending of earnings into account. There are no special rules.

ENDING WORK WHICH IS NOT REMUNERATIVE WORK

- *If the termination occurred before the person's 'date of claim' (para. 5.54).* Disregard all earnings apart from retainers.
- *If the termination occurs on or after the person's 'date of claim' (para. 5.54).* Reassess to take changes and ending of earnings into account. There are no special rules.

# 15 The self-employed

**15.1** This chapter describes the rules for assessing income (and capital) received by the self-employed. The rules apply to both HB and main CTB. It describes the necessary steps for assessing income from self-employment, which are:

- deciding who is self-employed;
- deciding what assessment period to use;
- assessing the total income during that period;
- assessing allowable expenses during that period;
- calculating pre-tax profit (chargeable income) for that period;
- allowing for tax and national insurance;
- allowing for half of any pension contributions;
- calculating net profit.

HBR 19
CTBR 11

**15.2** This chapter applies equally to the self-employed income of the claimant, a partner or a child or young person in a claimant's family. *References to a 'claimant' should be read accordingly.* It does not apply to the self-employed income of a non-dependant or second adult: the law does not lay down any particular way of assessing income from self-employment in such cases (although it must be gross income, not net).

The special rules for self-employed people on the New Deal are given at the end of this chapter (paras. 15.39-41).

## Who is self-employed?

CBA 2(1)(b)
HBR 2(1), 30(2)
CTBR 2(1), 21(2)
HBR sch 5 para 7
CTBR sch 5 para 7

**15.3** A 'self-employed earner' means someone who is gainfully employed in Great Britain (or in Northern Ireland gainfully employed in NI or the Republic) except anyone employed under a contract of service (i.e. an employee) or employed in an office (e.g. a company director). A person may be a sole trader or in a business partnership (para. 15.27), and therefore be a self-employed earner. But someone who has set up a company, and is a director of it, counts as an employed earner (para. 14.28). The DWP advises that the claimant's word should generally be accepted as to whether he or she is self-employed unless there are grounds for uncertainty (GM para. C3.37).

**15.4** The following are not self-employed income: fostering payments and 'respite care payments' (para. 13.37); receipt of a Sports Council award (para. 13.87); rent received from someone living in the claimant's home (table 13.3);

and rent received on other property (paras. 13.60-61); unless, in the last case, the renting of property constitutes gainful self-employment.

### A NOTE ON CAPITAL

**15.5** Assets of a business wholly or partly owned by a claimant are disregarded in the assessment of capital if he or she: HBR sch 5 para 7 CTBR sch 5 para 7

- is self-employed; or
- has ceased to be self-employed. In this case the assets are disregarded for as long as reasonably needed to dispose of them; or
- is not self-employed because of sickness or disability, but intends to be afterwards. In this case the assets are disregarded for 26 weeks from the date of any claim, including a renewal claim; or for such longer period as is reasonable to enable him or her to return to self-employment.

**15.6** It is sometimes necessary to decide whether capital is personal or part of the business. The DWP advises that the test depends on whether the capital is (part of) 'a fund employed and risked in the business' (circular HB/CTB(93)16).

## The assessment period

**15.7** The income and expenses of a self-employed person are estimated by reference to an 'assessment period'. This is whatever period is appropriate to enable an accurate estimation of average weekly earnings in the benefit period. It must not be longer than one year. The general principle is that income and expenses in the past (in the assessment period) are used to calculate HB and CTB in the future (in the benefit period). HBR 21(1), 23 CTBR 13(1), 15

### PEOPLE WHO HAVE BEEN SELF-EMPLOYED FOR SOME TIME

**15.8** For people who have been self-employed for some time, the assessment period is almost always in the past. For example, the DWP advises that the assessment period should normally be that of the last year's trading accounts, but that a shorter or different period may be used if appropriate (GM para. C3.40).

**15.9** If claimants have not kept accounts, it is necessary for them to provide whatever evidence is reasonable in order to establish what their income and expenses were in the assessment period. In some cases their drawings from their business (what they have paid themselves) may provide some evidence. Drawings must not be used, however, where there is evidence of their actual business income.

### PEOPLE SETTING UP IN BUSINESS

**15.10** For people claiming HB or CTB at the point of setting up in business, the assessment period cannot be in the past: it must be in the future. To avoid delays for claimants, the DWP recommends that authorities should estimate income and expenses based on information from the claimant, and that HB or CTB should be awarded for only a short period, perhaps 13 weeks (GM para. C3.40).

## IF THE NATURE OF A BUSINESS CHANGES

**15.11** If the nature of a claimant's business changes, the authority should deal with it as though it was a new business from the point of change (para. 15.10). One example would be if a claimant changes from full-time to part-time self-employment.

## CAN THE FIGURES BE ALTERED LATER?

**15.12** Once the various figures have been assessed as described (paras. 15.8, 15.10), they can be altered later if they were based on a mistake of fact or law or there was an official error, or if there has subsequently been a relevant change of circumstances (e.g. as in para. 15.11). It is incorrect in any other case to revise the figures.

## A NOTE ON ACCOUNTING METHODS

**15.13** Self-employed people commonly account for their income (and expenses) using one of the following methods:

- a 'cash' basis – counting income as being received on the day they receive the money (and counting expenses as being incurred on the day they pay the money out); or
- an 'on paper' basis – counting income as being received on the day they issue their bill or invoice for it (and counting expenses as being incurred on the day they receive a bill or invoice for them); or
- the basis required (roughly speaking) for income tax purposes – counting income as being received on the day they issue their bill or invoice or the day they receive the money, whichever happens first (and counting expenses as being incurred on the day they receive a bill or invoice or the day they pay the money out, whichever happens first).

**15.14** On the one hand, there is a body of opinion that HB and CTB should reflect a claimant's cash flow – the first method above. On the other hand, there is evidence that the HB and CTB regulations were originally written on the assumption that claimants use (or should use) the second or third method above. (For example, the rules about debts referred to in items (k) and (l) of table 15.1 would not be needed for claimants operating accounts on a purely cash flow basis.) It is probably reasonable to say that the method chosen by the claimant does not matter for HB/CTB purposes – so long as he or she operates that method consistently over the years.

# Assessing total income

**15.15** The total income (or 'gross earnings') of the employment means all the income coming into the business during the assessment period. There are two general points to bear in mind. HBR 30(1), 31(1),(3) CTBR 21(1), 22(1),(3)

- Only payments of income are taken into account. A payment of capital into a business is not a payment of income. It is disregarded under the general rule about disregarded capital (para. 15.5).
- Only income 'derived from' the employment is taken into account. Income from some other source (e.g. as described in para. 15.16) falls under whatever rules apply to that kind of income (chapter 13).

## GRANTS, LOANS AND THE ACCESS TO WORK SCHEME

**15.16** The following additional points apply:

- Typically, but not always, grants are not 'derived from' self-employment. If not, they should be regarded as a separate source of income or capital – typically voluntary or charitable (para. 13.80).
- Genuine loans are not income (para. 15.90). Money from a loan forms part of the claimant's capital. If it is a loan to the business it is therefore disregarded (para. 15.5).
- Disabled people setting up in self-employment can get payments under the government's Access to Work scheme: these are disregarded as income (para. 15.41).

## BUSINESS START-UP ALLOWANCES

**15.17** Any payments of a business start-up allowance received by the claimant during the assessment period (except for capital payments) must be counted as part of the total income of the employment. They must not be counted as a separate source of income. But they are not included as income if payments ceased before the date of claim for HB or CTB. HBR 30(1) CTBR 21(1)

**15.18** Business start-up allowances are still sometimes called enterprise allowance. They may in some cases be used up completely to pay for business expenses (with the effect that the self-employed person has no profit at all).

**Example: Business start-up allowances**

The authority decides that a claimant's assessment period is the last year for which she has accounts. In that year she received a total of 52 payments of a business start-up allowance of £40 per week (total

£2,080), plus other gross earnings of £4,000; and her allowable business expenses were £2,000.

If at her date of claim she is still receiving business start-up payments, then her total income is £8,080. After deducting her expenses, she has a pre-tax profit of £6,080.

But if she ceased receiving business start-up payments before her date of claim, then her total income is £4,000. After deducting her expenses, she has a pre-tax profit of £2,000.

## Assessing allowable expenses

HBR 31(3),(7)
NIHBR 31(3), (7), (12)
CTBR 22(3),(7)

**15.19** Having worked out the total income in the assessment period, the next step is to allow for the expenses incurred in running the business during the assessment period. In Northern Ireland, if the claimant is employed in the Republic the authority will deduct what it considers would have been deducted had they worked in Northern Ireland. The two general principles are:

- expenses are allowed for so long as they are 'wholly and exclusively incurred' for the purpose of the business;
- but the authority cannot allow for an expense if it is not satisfied, given the nature and the amount, that it has been 'reasonably incurred'.

**15.20** Subject to those points, typical examples of expenses which would be allowable are:

- staff costs;
- rent, rates and mortgage payments on business premises;
- the purchase of stocks and supplies;
- fuel costs (see also para. 15.22);
- cleaning and protective clothing;
- transport connected with the business;
- advertising, telephone, postage and stationery;
- carriage and delivery costs;
- hire and leasing charges;
- legal and accountancy fees;
- bank charges;
- insurance; and
- subscriptions to trade and professional organisations.

**15.21** The law contains rules about special kinds of expenses. These are summarised in table 15.1. HBR 31(4)-(6),(8) CTBR 22(4)-(6),(8)

**Table 15.1 SPECIAL TYPES OF EXPENSES**

| | Allowable? |
|---|---|
| (a) Interest payments on any business loan | yes |
| (b) Sums (other than interest payments) employed or intended to be employed in setting up or expanding the business | no |
| (c) Income spent on repairing an existing business asset (except to the extent that any sum is payable under an insurance policy for this) | yes |
| (d) Capital repayments on loans for repairing an existing business asset (except to the extent that any sum is payable under an insurance policy for this) | yes |
| (e) Capital repayments on loans for replacing business equipment or machinery | yes |
| (f) Capital repayments on any other business loans | no |
| (g) Any other capital expenditure | no |
| (h) Depreciation of any capital asset | no |
| (i) Losses incurred before the beginning of the assessment period | no |
| (j) Excess of VAT paid over VAT received in the assessment period | yes |
| (k) Proven bad debts | yes |
| (l) Other debts | no |
| (m) Expenses incurred in the recovery of any debt | yes |
| (n) Business entertainment | no |
| (o) Any sum for a domestic or private purpose | no |

**Example: Expenses**

A self-employed technical writer's accounts include the following expenditure. Before the purchase of her computer and laser printer, she used to do all her writing by hand. The references (a), (b), etc, are to table 15.1.

| | |
|---|---|
| A cash payment to buy her computer. | Not allowable (g). |
| Repayments on the loan she took out to buy her laser printer. | The capital element of the repayments is not allowable (f). The interest element is allowable (a). |
| Repayments on a smaller loan covering half the cost of repairing her laser printer, which was not insured. | Capital and interest elements are both allowable (d), (a). |
| A cash payment covering the other half of the cost of the laser printer repair. | Allowable (c) |
| Repayments on a general purpose business loan to help with her cash-flow. | The interest element of the repayments is allowable (a). The capital element is not (f). |
| A figure for depreciation in the value of the computer and laser printer. | Not allowable (h). |

## WORKING FROM HOME

**15.22** A rent-paying claimant who works from home may regard part of his or her rent as a business expense. Whether it is an allowable expense depends on the circumstances of the case. It is clear that if part of the home is exclusively used for the business (e.g. an annexe), then the rent on this is an allowable expense but is also disregarded in the assessment of the claimant's eligible rent (chapter 10). In all cases, however, an allowance should be made for a reasonable proportion of heating the home and of similar overheads.

## DRAWINGS TAKEN BY THE CLAIMANT FROM THE BUSINESS

**15.23** Claimants may take 'drawings' from their business as a kind of wages or salary for themselves. These must not be allowed as a business expense.

## EMPLOYING A HUSBAND, WIFE OR UNMARRIED PARTNER

HBR 31(8) CTBR 22(8) **15.24** If the claimant pays his or her husband, wife or unmarried partner to work for the business, this is allowable as a business expense. It will then count as the partner's earnings. The rules are different if the couple are in a business partnership (para. 15.27).

### SELF-EMPLOYED CHILDMINDERS

**15.25** For claimants who are self-employed childminders, instead of working out what their actual expenses are, two-thirds of their total income is disregarded in lieu of expenses. No actual expenses can be allowed for. HBR 31(9) CTBR 22(9)

**Example: A self-employed childminder**

A claimant earns £120 per week from working as a self-employed childminder. She is a lone parent with no other form of earned income. She does not make pension contributions. She does not use a childminder for her own children. Her income from childminding is assessed as follows:

- From the gross amount, two-thirds (£80) is disregarded. The remaining amount is £40.00
- £40 per week is too low for a deduction to be made for notional tax and national insurance (tables 15.2, 15.3).
- She qualifies for an earned income disregard. For a lone parent (table 14.1) this is £25.00
- So her assessed weekly earned income for HB/main CTB purposes is £15.00

## Pre-tax profit

**15.26** The next step is to work out the claimant's 'pre-tax profit' (referred to in the regulations as 'chargeable income'): HBR 31(1)(a),(3) CTBR 22(1)(a),(3)

Total income (paras. 15.13-18)

MINUS

- allowable expenses (paras. 15.19-25)

= pre-tax profit.

### BUSINESS PARTNERSHIPS

**15.27** If the claimant is self-employed in a partnership, the pre-tax profit (as defined above) should be assessed for the partnership and then split between the business partners. This split should reflect how the business partners actually split their income. Similar rules apply to 'share fishermen'. This split is required even if the business partners are a couple because it will ensure the correct calculation of notional tax and national insurance (para. 15.32). The rules are different if one partner in a couple employs the other (para. 15.24). HBR 31(1)(b),(4) CTBR 22(1)(b),(4)

### NIL INCOME FROM SELF-EMPLOYMENT

**15.28** If the claimant's allowable expenses exceed his or her total income, then pre-tax profit is nil. So his or her income from the self-employment is nil.

### MORE THAN ONE EMPLOYMENT

HBR 31(10) CTBR 22(10)

**15.29** If a self-employed claimant is engaged in any other employment or self-employment, the losses from one cannot be set against the income from the other.

### IF THE PRE-TAX PROFIT APPEARS UNREPRESENTATIVE

HBR 23(1) CTBR 13(1)

**15.30** If the pre-tax profit appears unlikely to represent income during the benefit period, the authority should consider whether selecting a different assessment period would produce a more accurate estimate of this (para. 15.7).

## Notional income tax and notional NICs

HBR 32 CTBR 23

**15.31** Allowances are made for income tax and national insurance contributions ('NICs'). However, the authority must work these out itself, based on the claimant's pre-tax profit. The figures calculated by the authority are known as 'notional income tax' and 'notional NICs'. They usually differ from the actual income tax and NICs paid by the claimant. One reason for the difference is that an amount for depreciation and certain expenses which are allowed by the Inland Revenue cannot be allowed for HB/CTB purposes.

### THE CALCULATIONS

HBR 26, 32 CTBR 18, 23

**15.32** The calculations are given in tables 15.2 and 15.3. An example is given near the end of this chapter. The tables apply to annual amounts of pre-tax profit. If a claimant's assessment period was a different length (e.g. three months), convert pre-tax profit into an annual figure before doing the calculations (para. 7.59). In the case of a couple, work through the calculations separately for each one who has self-employed income.

**15.33** Tables 15.2 and 15.3 give the figures for the tax year from 6th April 2002 to 5th April 2003. Authorities must use the figures applying at the date of claim for HB/CTB (para. 5.44). However they may disregard for up to 30 benefit weeks any change in tax and NICs caused by a change in the law (typically the Budget). So 2001-02's tax and NI figures may continue to be used if the date of claim occurs on or before Sunday 3rd November 2002.

**Table 15.2 CALCULATING NOTIONAL INCOME TAX (2002-03 TAX YEAR)**

(a) Start with the annual pre-tax profit figure.

(b Subtract £4,615*.

(c) If there is a remainder:
multiply the first £1,920 (or all, if it is under £1,920) by 10%;
multiply the rest (if any) by 22%, and add to the result of the above.**

(d) The result is the amount of notional tax.

**Notes**

* £4,615 is the personal allowance.

** The 40% tax rate is not used in assessing notional income tax, nor are any allowances taken into account other than as above. (The regulations have in fact referred to apparently out-of-date tax law for some years. The above is nonetheless believed to be the case.)

## Pension contributions

**15.34** An allowance is made for half of any pension contributions payable by self-employed claimants towards: HBR 31(11),(12) NIHBR 31(11),(11 CTBR 22(11),(12)

- a self-employed personal pension scheme if they are payable on a periodical basis (e.g. monthly). No allowance is made for the lump sum payments some self-employed people make (often for tax purposes); or
- an annuity for a retirement pension for the claimant or a dependent (including husbands, wives and unmarried partners) – if the scheme is approved by the Inland Revenue as eligible for tax relief. People can no longer enter such schemes, but those who entered them in the past may still be in them.

### Table 15.3: CALCULATING NOTIONAL NI CONTRIBUTIONS (2002-03 TAX YEAR)

CLASS 2 NICS

If the annual pre-tax profit figure is £4,025* or more, then the amount of notional class 2 NICs is £104**.

CLASS 4 NICS

(a) Start with the annual pre-tax profit figure (unless this is greater than £30,420†, in which case start with £30,420).

(b) Subtract £4,615†.

(c) If there is a remainder, multiply it by 7%. The result is the amount of notional class 4 NICs.

**Notes**

The person may have class 2 notional NICs alone, or may have both class 2 and class 4 notional NICs.

* £4,025 is the lower threshold for class 2 NICs. If the person's pre-tax profit is lower, then the notional class 2 NICs figure is nil (regardless of whether he or she has in fact applied to the Inland Revenue for exemption).

** £104 is 52 times £2.00 (the weekly rate of class 2 NICs), there being 52 Sundays in the 2002-03 tax year.

† £4,615 is the lower threshold, and £30,420 the upper threshold, for class 4 NICs.

**15.35** The allowance applies only whilst the claimant is making such payments. So if a claimant starts or ceases making such payments whilst he or she is on HB or CTB (or the amount of the payments changes), this is taken into account as a change of circumstances and HB and/or CTB must be reassessed.

**15.36** To find the annual equivalent of pension contributions:

- for contributions payable calendar monthly, multiply the monthly contribution by 12;
- in any other case, divide the contribution by the number of days it covers (e.g. in the case of a weekly contribution, divide by 7) and multiply by 366.

> **Example: Pension contributions**
>
> When a claimant claims HB and CTB, he is paying pension contributions of £50 per month. The annual equivalent is 12 x £50 = £600. Half of this (£300) is allowable in calculating his annual net profit.
>
> After making three monthly payments, he reduces his payments to £40 per month. The annual equivalent is 12 x £40 = £480. Half of this (£240) is allowable in calculating his annual net profit. His claim must be reassessed taking his new annual net profit into account from the Monday after the day on which the first payment of £40 was due.

## Net profit

**15.37** The final step is to work out the claimant's net profit. It is always advisable to work this out initially on an annual basis. HBR 31(1)-(3) CTBR 22(1)-(3)

Pre-tax profit (paras. 15.26-30)

MINUS

- notional income tax and notional NI contributions (paras. 15.31-33)
- half of pension contributions (paras. 15.34-36)

= net profit.

### CONVERSION TO A WEEKLY FIGURE

**15.38** The result must be converted to a weekly figure. Divide the annual figure by 365 and then multiply the result by 7. This weekly figure is the one used in calculating entitlement to HB and main CTB (subject to the earned income disregards: chapter 12). HBR 25(2) CTBR 17(2)

> **Example: Notional tax and NI contributions and net profit: 2002-03**
>
> A married woman's annual pre-tax profit is £9,000. She contributes £480 per year to a personal pension scheme. Her husband has no source of earned income.
>
> NOTIONAL INCOME TAX (TABLE 15.2)
>
> (a) Start with the annual pre-tax profit figure. This is £9,000.
>
> (b) Subtract £4,615. This leaves £4,385.

(c) Of this,

multiply the first £1,920 by 10%

| | |
|---|---|
| 10% of £1,920 is: | £192.00 |
| multiply the rest (£4,385 – £1,920 = £2,465) by 22% | |
| 22% of £2,465 is | £542.30 |
| Adding these together gives: | £734.30 |
| (d) So her notional tax is: | £734.30 |

NOTIONAL CLASS 2 NICS (TABLE 15.3)

The annual pre-tax profit figure (£9,000) is greater than £4,025, so the amount of her notional class 2 NICs is £104.00.

NOTIONAL CLASS 4 NICS (TABLE 15.3)

(a) Start with the annual pre-tax profit figure (which is not greater than £30,420). This is £9,000.

(b) Subtract £4,615.

(c) Multiply the remainder (which is £4,385) by 7%.
This is £306.95 – which is the amount of her notional class 4 NICs.

NET PROFIT

| | |
|---|---|
| Annual pre-tax profit | £9,000.00 |
| minus notional income tax | £734.30 |
| minus notional class 2 NICs | £104.00 |
| minus notional class 4 NICs | £306.95 |
| minus half of annual contributions to pension scheme | £240.00 |
| Equals annual net profit: | £7,614.75 |
| On a weekly basis this is (£7,614.75 ÷ 365 x 7 =) | £146.04 |
| She qualifies for an earned income disregard of | £10.00 |
| So her weekly net profit (after the disregard) is | £136.04 |

# People on the self-employed route of the New Deal

**15.39** The following rules apply to people on the 'self-employed route' of the 'Employment Option' of the New Deal, and to people assisted with pursuing self-employment on an Employment Zone programme or on the 'intensive activity period' of the New Deal (para. 13.41 and table 13.2). Most such people should be entitled to income support or income-based jobseeker's allowance: in their case, all their income and capital is disregarded for HB and main CTB purposes. The following rules apply in the uncommon cases in which such people are not on either of those benefits: in their case, their income and capital is assessed, for HB and main CTB purposes, in a special way (which differs from the rules in the other parts of this chapter).

## BACKGROUND

**15.40** A person on the self-employed route gets assistance from the Jobcentre with his or her 'commercial activity'. The Jobcentre keeps a 'special account' for that commercial activity, the main features of which are as follows:

- any income he or she makes on the commercial activity is payable into the special account;
- payments may be taken from the special account to meet business expenses or the repayment of business loans relating to the commercial activity;
- the amounts in the special account are treated as capital for IS and JSA(IB) purposes;
- when he or she reaches the end of the self-employed route, the balance in the special account is assessed for IS and JSA(IB) purposes in a special way as income for the future.

## ASSESSMENT FOR HB/MAIN CTB PURPOSES

**15.41** The following rules apply in the assessment of HB and main CTB for people on the self-employed route (for references to 'commercial activity' and 'special account', see above):

HBR 40(7)
HBR sch 4
paras 64,66,
sch 5
paras 7, 53, 55
NIHBR sch 4
paras 66, 67,
sch 5 paras 7,
51, 53
CTBR 31(7),
sch 4 paras 64,
sch 5 paras 7,
53, 55

- the gross receipts of the commercial activity are treated as capital for HB and main CTB purposes – but only to the extent that they are payable into the special account;
- payments the person takes from the special account are disregarded as unearned income for HB and main CTB purposes – but only if they are to meet expenses wholly and necessarily incurred in the commercial activity; or are used or intended to be used to maintain repayments on a loan taken out to establish or carry on the commercial activity;

- any capital acquired by the person for the purposes of establishing or carrying on the commercial activity (from whatever source) is disregarded for HB and main CTB purposes for 52 weeks from the date on which it was acquired;
- any business assets acquired by the person for establishing or carrying on the commercial activity (from whatever source) are disregarded as capital for HB and main CTB purposes for as long as the person remains on the self-employed route and then for as long as is reasonable in the circumstances to allow for their disposal (or, if he or she remains self-employed, see para. 15.5).

In broad terms, the effect of these rules is that, so long as the self-employment is run through the Jobcentre's 'special account', the monies have no impact on the claimant's JSA(IB), HB or CTB.

# 16 Decisions, notification and payment

**16.1** This chapter considers the process of decision-making, notification and payment. It covers the following:

- how quickly the authority should deal with claims and changes of circumstances;
- who must be notified of the authority's decision;
- information that must be provided to the claimant and others;
- how, and when, HB/CTB should be paid;
- when a payment on account should be made in a rent allowance case;
- how often a rent allowance should be paid;
- when a landlord is paid direct;
- when a payment of HB/CTB is suspended;
- who else may receive payment of a rent allowance/CTB.

## How quickly should the claim be dealt with and benefit paid?

**16.2** Once the authority has received a claim and all the information and evidence it reasonably requires from the claimant it must:

- HBR 76(3) CTBR 66(3) reach a decision on entitlement within 14 days or as soon as possible after that;
- HBR 77(1)(a) CTBR 67(1)(a) notify persons affected (para. 16.7) as soon as the claim is decided; and
- HBR 88(3) in the case of HB, make payment within 14 days of the receipt of the claim or as soon as possible after that.

Authorities are required to 'fast track' (give administrative priority to) 'in-work' claims made by people who have notified the relevant change that gives rise to the extended payment entitlement within 14 days of starting work etc, and claimed the in-work related HB/CTB either before IS/JSA(IB) stops or within 14 days from the day after it stops. The aim of this rule is to ensure that the ongoing entitlement to benefit is available at the end of the four week extended payment period.

In all rent allowance cases if the authority is unable to meet the 14 day decision-making timetable it must normally make a payment on account (para. 16.16).

## EXCEPTIONS TO THE REQUIREMENT TO DECIDE

**16.3** The authority does not have to meet the above time limits however where a claim: HBR 76(2) CTBR 66(2)

- is not made in the proper time and manner (para. 7.33); or
- is not supported by reasonably required information or evidence from the claimant (para. 7.37); or
- has been withdrawn (para. 7.51); or
- is made more than 13 benefit weeks prior to the expiry of the claimant's current benefit period (para. 7.70).

## TIME PERIOD IN WHICH OTHER DECISIONS SHOULD BE MADE

**16.4** From time to time authorities have to make other decisions on a claim, e.g. to supersede an original decision following a change of circumstance. Notification of such decisions must be made within 14 days or as soon as possible after that. Notification is not required, however, where a change in CTB entitlement relates solely to a reduction in the council tax where government 'tax-capping' or a delayed award of transitional relief, disability reduction or discount leads to an overpayment of CTB. HBR 77(1)(b) CTBR 67(1)(b)

## REMEDIES FOR DELAYS

**16.5** Authorities are expected to meet the time limits in the majority of cases. Delays are normally only justifiable, for example, in periods of peak pressure such as the annual up-rating or while handling a high level of enquiries following a take-up campaign. Many authorities fail to meet the time limit and it may be necessary for outside agencies and individuals to place pressure upon such authorities via campaigns and legal and other remedies to ensure that they meet this obligation in the future. Such remedies include:

- complaints to the local government ombudsman;
- action in the High Court or Court of Session in Scotland for judicial review to require authorities to make a determination; and
- action in the County Court or Sheriff Court to require authorities to make a payment if they have agreed that the claimant is entitled.

**16.6** *R v Liverpool City Council ex parte Pauline Linda Johnson and others,* QBD, 23rd June 1994 considered a sample of the many applications made for judicial review of the authority's failure to meet its statutory duties. The judge said that 'in their discretionary decisions as to allocation of resources, authorities must, in making their arrangements for carrying the housing benefit regulations into effect, have specific regard to the time limits'. In response to the authority's assertion that it should not be singled out because the Audit Commission had found that many authorities were in breach of the regulations, the judge said 'if the legal rights of disadvantaged people to expeditious determination of their claims for benefit are being denied across the country, the need for the court's intervention is all the greater'.

## Who should be notified and how?

### PERSONS AFFECTED

HBR 77, 2(1)
CTBR 67, 2(1)
DAR 3

**16.7** The authority is required to notify all persons affected by a decision. A 'person affected' means any of the following where their rights, duties or obligations are affected by a decision:

- the claimant;
- where a claimant, or would-be claimant, is unable to act on his or her own behalf:
  - a receiver appointed by the Court of Protection;
  - an attorney with a general power or a power to claim or as the case may be receive benefit appointed under the Powers of Attorney Act 1971 or the Enduring Powers of Attorney Act 1985;
  - a person appointed by the Council to act on behalf of someone who is unable to act on his or her own behalf;
  - a person appointed by the Secretary of State (in practice a manager at the Benefit Agency office) to act on behalf of someone who is unable to act on his or her own behalf;
- the landlord – but only in relation to a decision (not) to make direct payments (where the payment is made to an agent acting for the landlord the agent is the person affected); or
- anyone – including the landlord – from whom the Council has decided that an overpayment is recoverable.

**16.8** There may be more than one person affected by any decision made by the authority. For example, where the authority decided to recover an overpayment from the claimant's landlord both the landlord and the claimant are 'persons affected' and both should be notified of the relevant decisions. The 'person affected' label is not confined to natural persons; it also applies to legal entities such as housing associations and letting companies.

### INFORMATION TO BE PROVIDED

HBR 77, sch 6
CTBR 67, sch 6

**16.9** The authority must send a written notification to a person affected by a decision. Table 16.1 illustrates the minimum amount of information that an authority must make available automatically following its decisions on a claim.

In practice, it is a regrettable fact that many notification letters contain insufficient information and/or are very hard to understand. It is also regrettable that many authorities do not keep copies of their own notification letters, thereby placing their own staff in the impossible position of being unable to explain to claimants what they have said to them.

**16.10** Notifications are also required, for instance, where rent allowances are paid direct to the landlord (para. 16.27); where, in the case of HB or main CTB the income of a non-dependant is treated as the claimant's (para. 15.4); and in any case where a recoverable overpayment exists. HBR 77, sch 6 CTBR 67, sch 6

**16.11** All notifications must include statements explaining the right of the person affected to: HBR sch 6 part 1 CTBR sch 6 part 1

- obtain a written statement of the authority's reasons for the decision; and
- make an application for a revision (para. 19.6) and, where appropriate, to appeal against that decision (i.e. where it is an appealable decision – paras. 21.13-21.14).

**Table 16.1 INFORMATION TO BE NOTIFIED FOLLOWING DECISIONS ON A CLAIM**

*(HB AND CTB NOTIFICATIONS SHOULD BE SEPARATE)*

A. WHERE THE CLAIMANT IS ENTITLED TO HB/MAIN CTB

*Claimant on income support (IS)/income-based JSA (JSA(IB))*

- Weekly eligible rent/weekly amount of council tax.
- HB – amount and explanation of fuel deductions from eligible rent where they have been estimated using the standard figures in table 13.2, together with the fact that the amount may be varied if the claimant supplies reasonable evidence.
- Amount and category of any non-dependant deductions.
- Normal weekly amount of benefit.
- Rent allowances – date of payment and period for which payment is made.
- First day of entitlement.
- End of benefit period.
- The claimant's duty to notify the authority of changes of circumstance and examples of the kinds of change that should be reported.
- CTB – details of any 'rounding' of figures.

*Claimant not on IS/JSA(IB)*

- The information given where the claimant is on IS/JSA(IB).
- The applicable amount and how it is worked out.
- Weekly earnings.
- Weekly unearned income.

## B. WHERE THE CLAIMANT IS NOT ENTITLED TO HB/MAIN CTB BECAUSE OF INCOME OR THE MINIMUM HB PAYMENT RULE

*IS/JSA(IB) claimants*

- Weekly eligible rent/weekly amount of council tax.
- HB – amount and explanation of fuel deductions from eligible rent where they have been estimated using the standard figures in table 13.27, together with the fact that the amount may be varied if the claimant supplies reasonable evidence.
- Amount and category of non-dependant deductions.
- HB – normal weekly amount of benefit and the fact that it is not payable because it is below the minimum.

*Claimants not on IS/JSA(IB)*

- The information given where the claimant is on IS/JSA(IB).
- The applicable amount and how it is worked out.
- Weekly earnings.
- Weekly unearned income.

## C. WHERE THE CTB CLAIMANT IS BETTER OFF ON SECOND ADULT REBATE

- The fact that the claimant is better off on second adult rebate and the amount.
- The lesser amount of main CTB.

## D. WHERE THE CTB CLAIMANT IS ENTITLED TO SECOND ADULT REBATE

- Normal weekly amount of council tax rounded to nearest penny.
- Normal weekly amount of second adult rebate rounded to nearest penny.
- Rates of second adult rebate and related gross income levels.
- First day of entitlement.
- End of benefit period.
- Gross income of any second adult or the fact that the second adult is on IS/JSA(IB).

- The claimant's duty to notify the authority of changes of circumstance and examples of the kinds of change that should be reported.
- Details of any 'rounding' of figures.

E. ITEMS TO BE NOTIFIED WHERE SECOND ADULT REBATE IS NOT PAYABLE

*Where gross income of second adult(s) too high*

- Normal weekly amount of council tax rounded to nearest penny.
- Rates of second adult rebate and related gross income levels.
- Gross income of any second adult or the fact that the second adult is on IS/JSA(IB).

*Where claimant better off on main CTB*

- The fact that the claimant is better off on main CTB.
- The lesser amount of second adult rebate.

F. CLAIMANT NOT ENTITLED FOR SOME OTHER REASON

- The reason why the claimant is not entitled.

G. ITEMS TO BE NOTIFIED IN ALL CASES

- The right, time and manner in which to request a written explanation of a determination.
- The right, time and manner in which to apply for a revision (para. 19.6) and, where appropriate, to appeal against the decision (i.e. where it is an appealable decision – paras. 21-13-21.14).
- Any other appropriate matters.

## Time and manner of payment

### PAYMENT OF HB

**16.12** Authorities may decide on the time and manner in which to make payments of HB on the basis of the circumstances of the individual case. They are expected to have regard to the reasonable needs and convenience of the person they are paying, as well as the time and frequency with which the liability to make payments arises. From 2nd July 2001 decisions on payment method/frequency are not appealable but a person affected can request the authority to revise its decision at any time. HBR 88

**16.13** The requirement that the authority must have regard to the reasonable needs and convenience of the person receiving payment means that they should not make unreasonable demands, such as collection from a place not easily accessible, or insistence upon crossed cheques or credit transfer arrangements when the payee does not have a bank account (GM para. A6.27).

**16.14** In the case of rent rebates, payment is usually in the form of a rebate applied to the rent account. Where the claimant has already made payments for the benefit period, for example where rent has been paid four months in advance, benefit should normally be paid direct to the claimant unless he or she is in arrears or agrees to the amount being credited to his or her rent account (GM para. A6.30).

HBR 88(1), 92(1) **16.15** Where the claimant is a private tenant, he or she is normally paid direct, though in certain circumstances a rent allowance may be paid to the landlord (paras. 16.27-33).

## PAYMENTS ON ACCOUNT (INTERIM PAYMENTS)

HBR 91(1) **16.16** A payment on account, (sometimes known as an interim payment), must be paid within 14 days if the following circumstances are met:

- the authority is unable to make a decision on the amount of benefit payable within 14 days of receipt of the claim; and
- that inability has not risen out of the claimant's failure to provide necessary information or evidence (which the authority has requested from the claimant in writing) without good cause.

The authority must pay an amount it considers reasonable on the basis of whatever information is available to it about the individual claimant's circumstances, such as sources of income, and any relevant determination made by a rent officer (para. 23.25).

**16.17** Payments on account are not discretionary and must be paid if the circumstances set out in paragraph 16.16 apply. In the case of *R v London Borough of Haringey ex parte Azad Ayub,* (1992) 25 HLR 566 QBD, the judge confirmed that a rent allowance claimant 'who has done all that he should is to be paid something within 14 days of a claim being made'. The judge also confirmed that no separate claim or request need be made in respect of a payment on account. The DSS (GM A6.38) considers it important for authorities to note that the duty to make a payment on account rests entirely with the authority. 'It is not the responsibility of the claimant to ask for such a payment and authorities should not wait for him to do so.' It should also be emphasised that the rule applies to all rent allowance claims including those from housing association tenants.

AR sch para 1(b) **16.18** Many authorities fail to make payments on account or only make such payments when the claimant's tenancy is at risk. Such authorities are acting illegally. The DSS (HB/CTB(93)37) expresses its 'concern about continuing reports of delays by some authorities in processing rent allowance claims, and their failure to make payments on account where appropriate'. The authority's decisions relating to payments on account, (except subsequent adjustments to take account of an under or overpayment) are not appealable but may be the trigger for an application for judicial review or a complaint to the local government ombudsman. A high proportion of complaints to the local government ombudsman concern failure to make payments on account. The ombudsman is likely to find maladministration with injustice and make a recommendation that compensation be paid in such cases.

**16.19** Good cause for the claimant failing to provide necessary information and evidence would include, for example, a landlord's unwillingness to provide evidence of rent payments. The DSS (GM A6.40) points out that a claimant cannot be held responsible for delays in receiving confirmation of IS entitlement from the local Benefits Agency office unless asked to provide evidence of entitlement independently and any delay in doing so is directly attributable to the claimant. The DSS also reminds authorities (HB/CTB(93)37) that a claimant cannot be held responsible for a failure to supply evidence and information which he or she has not been asked specifically to provide. The claimant must also be given a reasonable time to provide any information which has been asked for before he or she can be judged to have failed to have done so. For example, if the authority does not write to the claimant asking for verification of, say, his or her earnings until the 13th day after the date on which the claim was made and the verification is supplied a few days later, the authority cannot then reasonably argue that it was impractical to decide the claim within 14 days because of the claimant's failure to provide the necessary information. The DSS advises that, in such a case, the claimant would clearly have good cause for failing to provide the information within the 14-day period. The authority is obliged to make initial payment on account on the 14th day following receipt of the claim based on the information originally available to it. This is the case even when the new payment rules (para. 16.21) apply.

**16.20** If the authority finds, when it makes its formal decision on the claim, that HB entitlement is different from the amount it has paid on account, further rent allowance payments will be adjusted to allow for under- or overpayments. The authority's decisions regarding adjustments to payment on account of rent allowance to take account of an under or overpayment are appealable to an independent appeal tribunal. The letter advising of a payment on account must include a statement informing the claimant that if the payment is in excess of actual entitlement it will be recoverable from the person to whom the payment is made.

HBR 91(2),(3)

DAR sch para 1(b

## FREQUENCY OF RENT ALLOWANCE PAYMENTS BEFORE AND FROM 7TH OCTOBER 1996

HBR 90(1),(2), 88(3)

**16.21** Following any 'payment on account', or first payment, the authority may choose to pay a rent allowance at intervals of two or four weeks or one calendar month or, with the consent of the person entitled to payment, at intervals greater than one month.

Prior to 7th October 1996 authorities had a duty, as far as possible, to make payments two weeks before the end of the period covered. So a fortnightly rent liability should be paid in advance, while four-weekly or monthly liabilities should be met midway through the period. However, where rent is paid in arrears the authority has the discretion to make payments at the end of the period.

From 7th October 1996, for claimants who are not exempt from the new rules (para. 16.22), the authority must make payments to claimants at the end of the period to which they relate. Where payment is being made direct to the landlord, and the claimant is not exempt from the October 1996 rules (para. 16.22), it should be made every 4 weeks (or, at the authority's discretion, monthly where there is a monthly rent liability) at the end of the period to which it relates. If, however, the authority is paying benefit direct to a landlord for more than one claimant a first payment may be made at a shorter interval than four weeks if the authority thinks that it is in the best interest of the efficient administration of housing benefit.

SI 1996 No. 965
SR 1996 No. 181

**16.22** The 7th October 1996 payment rules do not apply to claimants who were (or who were treated as) entitled to and in receipt of housing benefit before 7th October 1996 so long as they remain continuously entitled to and in receipt housing benefit for the same dwelling. People who claim benefit as a result of a partner's death are also not affected by the October 1996 rules if the partner is in receipt of benefit up to the date of death, *and* benefit is paid under the pre-October 1996 rules (or, if the death occurred between 30th September and 6th October 1996, would have been). For this exemption to apply, however, the new claim must be made, or treated as made, within four weeks of the death.

## THE CLAIMANT'S RIGHT TO FORTNIGHTLY PAYMENTS

HBR 90(3)

**16.23** Subject to the rules described in paras 16.21 and 16.22 (but excluding cases where HB is paid direct to a landlord), anyone who has a weekly entitlement to a rent allowance of more than £2 can require the authority to pay fortnightly.

## AUTHORITY'S DISCRETION TO PAY WEEKLY

HBR 90(4)

**16.24** Subject to the rules described in paras. 16.21 and 16.22 (but excluding cases where HB is paid direct to a landlord), authorities have discretion to pay HB weekly if they consider that:

- paying HB over a longer period would lead to an overpayment; or
- the claimant pays rent weekly and it is in his or her interest (or that of the family) to receive weekly payments.

The former instance covers cases where there is only a short period of entitlement to HB, or where a change of circumstance is anticipated in the near future. The latter instance may be helpful in cases where claimants have difficulty in budgeting over a longer period.

### PAYMENT OF CTB

**16.25** Normally authorities pay CTB by means of a rebate (credit) to the individual's council tax account and thus reduce the liability for the tax. Where the rebate is greater than the tax liability the authority may reduce the liability for the tax in subsequent years. However, where the tax has been paid for the financial year, and the claimant requires it, or the claimant is jointly and severally liable for the tax and the authority considers it appropriate, the balance of any CTB must be paid direct to the claimant. Also where a person has met the tax liability in full and the tax account has been closed, e.g. because he or she has left the area or is no longer liable, the authority must pay the outstanding amount of CTB direct to the claimant. In all cases where the payment is direct to the claimant rather than to the claimant's council tax account, payment should normally be made within 14 days or as soon as reasonably practicable after that. CTBR 77

### PAYMENT OF RATE REBATES IN NORTHERN IRELAND

In Northern Ireland the rate rebate can be paid with the claimant's rent allowance provided they are not billed directly by the rates collection agency (i.e. they pay their rates as part of their rent). NIHBR 89

## To whom should the payment be made?

**16.26** The normal requirement of the schemes is that the benefit is paid to the claimant though with HB for council tenants and CTB for council tax payers this is normally by way of a rebate to their account. However, in particular circumstances: HBR 92 CTBR 78

- a rent allowance is paid to the claimant's landlord, or someone else to whom rent is payable, e.g. a lettings agent, or a nominee; and
- a rent allowance or CTB is paid to an appointee or, in the case of a claimant who has died, a personal representative or next of kin aged 16 or over.

When an amount of rent allowance is paid to a landlord or lettings agent this discharges the claimant's liability to pay that amount of rent, unless and to the extent that the authority recovers any such amount as a recoverable overpayment from that landlord or lettings agent (para. 20.37).

## RENT ALLOWANCE PAYMENTS DIRECT TO A LANDLORD OR LETTINGS AGENT

HBR 94(1A) **16.27** The authority has the discretion to make the first payment of a new or renewed rent allowance claim by sending the claimant a cheque or other instrument of payment payable to the landlord for part or all of the amount due. The DSS suggests that 'this will help remove the temptation for some claimants to abscond with the first payment of housing benefit without paying the landlord' (DSS Press Release *Housing Benefit Regulations Laid Before Parliament,* 2nd April 1996). The authority is, however, only able to make the first cheque, etc, payable to the landlord where:

- the authority is of the opinion that the claimant has not already paid the landlord for the period in respect of which any payment is to be made; and
- it is in the interests of the efficient administration of housing benefit.

The DSS has advised authorities (HB/CTB A9/96 para. 24) to consider using this power where:

- the amount due is £100 or more; or
- it has reason to think that the claimant might default; or
- there is a rent debt but the case is not appropriate for longer term direct payment arrangements.

## MANDATORY DIRECT PAYMENTS

HBR 93 **16.28** The authority must make direct payments of a rent allowance to a landlord where:

- an amount of income support or either kind of JSA payable to the claimant, or partner, is being paid direct to the landlord to meet arrears; or
- the claimant has rent arrears equivalent to eight weeks or more, except where the authority considers it to be in the overriding interest of the claimant not to make direct payments.

3R 93(3), 94(1B), The exception to the above rules requiring direct payment is where the authority is not satisfied that the landlord is a 'fit and proper person' to receive direct payments. The DSS advises (HB/CTB A48/97) that a landlord should be assumed to be a 'fit and proper person' in the absence of evidence to the contrary. The test enables the authority to refuse direct payments in cases where the landlord is involved in fraudulent acts related to HB. The DSS suggest that the authority might also consider whether the landlord has habitually failed to:

- report changes in tenants circumstances which he or she might reasonably be expected to know might affect entitlement; or
- repay an overpayment which the authority has decided is recoverable –

despite the fact that a proper notification was issued and that the rights of review had been exercised or made available.

The authority should not base its judgment on:

- the landlord's undesirable activity in non-HB matters; or
- the fact that the landlord makes use of the right to request a revision or appeal before repaying any recoverable overpayment; or
- the fact that the landlord has made complaints of maladministration to the local government ombudsman.

Where the authority is satisfied that the landlord is not a 'fit and proper person' but it appears to be in the overriding interest of the claimant to pay the landlord direct – then direct payments may still be considered under the discretionary direct payment rules (para. 16.32).

**16.29** In the case of *R v London Borough of Haringey ex parte Azad Ayub*, (1992) 25 HLR 566 QBD the judge found that the duty to pay a landlord direct once the claimant is eight weeks or more in rent arrears only arises if the landlord or someone else informs the authority that there are eight weeks or more arrears. It is not up to the authority to find this out for itself. If the tenant disputes that there are eight weeks arrears the authority must consider the available evidence and come to a finding of fact on the balance of probability. Either party (the claimant or landlord) can appeal about the authority's decision.

**16.30** If the claimant dies but the authority has already determined to make payment direct to the landlord, any amount of benefit outstanding at the time of the claimant's death must be paid to the landlord if a written application has been made for it.

Where deductions are being made from income support/JSA to meet rent arrears, direct payments of HB to the landlord should continue until such time as the Benefits Agency ceases to make the relevant deductions. Benefits Agency local offices should advise authorities of appropriate cases (GM para. A6.47).

**16.31** Where the authority is making direct payments because the claimant is eight or more weeks in rent arrears, the direct payment should cease once the arrears fall below the eight-week level unless one of the circumstances in paras. 16.29 or 16.30 apply.

## DISCRETIONARY DIRECT PAYMENTS

**16.32** An authority may implement direct payment arrangements where: HBR 94

- the claimant requests, or consents to, such an arrangement; or
- the authority considers it to be in the interest of the claimant and family; or
- benefit is owing to a claimant who has left a dwelling with rent arrears.

In the last circumstance direct payment is limited to an amount equivalent to the rent owing.

As with mandatory direct payments, the authority may decide not to make direct payments where the landlord is not a 'fit and proper person' to receive such payments. However, where it appears to be in the overriding interest of the claimant for the landlord to be paid direct, and there are no practicable alternatives, the authority may make direct payments. This would apply, for example, where the risk to the claimant of not paying the landlord outweighs any risk associated with direct payment.

**16.33** Authorities might use their power to pay direct in the interest of the claimant and family where, for example, the claimant has a history of rent arrears at a previous address or where social or medical problems (such as mental illness or drug addiction) indicate that help with budgeting is needed.

### INFORMATION TO BE PROVIDED TO CLAIMANTS AND LANDLORDS OR LETTINGS AGENTS

HBR 77, sch 6 part IV

**16.34** When a decision has been made that HB is to be paid direct to the landlord both the claimant and landlord should be notified of that fact within 14 days (para. 16.2). The notification must include the date from which the arrangement will commence and their right to obtain a written statement of reasons and make written representations. The notification must also inform both the landlord and claimant that where:

- an overpayment is recoverable from the landlord; and
- is recovered from direct payments made on behalf of a tenant to whom the overpayment does not relate,

that tenant's rent must be treated as paid to the value of the amount recovered.

The landlord must also be informed of his or her duty to report any change of circumstances which might affect the claimant's amount of, or right to, HB and the kind of change which should be notified.

## Suspending HB/CTB

SI 2001 No. 1605
SR 2000 No. 215
DAR Part III

**16.35** Rules on the withholding and suspending of HB/CTB are changed from 2nd July 2001 onwards. In particular the authority's power to withhold benefit is removed. The authority may suspend payment in the circumstances set out in the following paragraphs.

### DOUBT REGARDING ENTITLEMENT

DAR 11(1),(2),12

**16.36** The authority may suspend, in whole or in part any payment of HB/CTB; where there is doubts as to whether the conditions for entitlement are or were fulfilled. The authority may also suspend, in whole or in part any HB/CTB payment where it is considering whether a decision as to an award should be revised or superseded. Obviously where a revised or superseded decision would result in an increase in entitlement, there is no need for the authority to consider suspension.

**16.37** Payments should be made in both cases once the authority is satisfied that the suspended benefit is properly payable and no outstanding issues remain to be resolved. This should be done so far as practicable within 14 days of the decision to make or restore the payment.

## SUSPENSION WHERE AN APPEAL IS PENDING

**16.38** The authority may suspend, in whole or in part any payment of HB/CTB where an appeal is pending against a decision of an appeal tribunal, a Commissioner or a court. DAR 11(1),(2)(b), 1

**16.39** An appeal is pending where an appeal against the decision has been made, but not determined or an application for leave to appeal against the decision has been made, but not yet determined.

**16.40** Payments should be made when the appeal is no longer pending and the suspended benefit remains payable following the decision of the appeal. This should be done so far as practicable within 14 days of the decision to make or restore payment.

## SUSPENSION WHERE AN APPEAL IS PENDING AGAINST A DECISION IN A DIFFERENT CASE

**16.41** The authority may suspend, in whole or in part any payment of HB/CTB where an appeal is pending against a decision given by a Commissioner or a court in a different case, and it appears to the authority that if the appeal were to be determined in a particular way an issue would arise as to whether the award of HB/CTB in the case under consideration ought to be revised or supersede.

**16.42** Payments should be made when the appeal is no longer pending and the benefit suspended remains payable following the determination of the appeal. This should be done so far as practicable within 14 days of the decision to make or restore payment.

## POSSIBLE OVERPAYMENTS

**16.43** The authority may suspend, in whole or in part any payment of HB/CTB when an issue arises as to whether an amount of HB/CTB is recoverable. Again once resolved payment of any outstanding amount should be made. Again, so far as practicable, this should be done within 14 days of the decision to make or restore payment.

### SUSPENSION FOR FAILURE TO FURNISH INFORMATION ETC

DAR 13 **16.44** The authority may suspend in whole or in part any payment of HB/CTB that relates to someone who fails to comply with the requirements to provide information or evidence needed by the authority in deciding whether a decision should be revised or superseded.

**16.45** The authority must notify the person concerned of this power. The person concerned must:

- furnish the information or evidence required within:
  - one month beginning with the date on which the notification was sent to them; or
  - such longer period as the authority considers necessary to enable them to comply with the requirement; or
- satisfy the authority within the relevant period that:
  - the information or evidence required does not exist; or
  - it is not possible for them to obtain the required information or evidence.

Where a person satisfies the requirements the authority must, so far as practicable, make, or restore, payment within 14 days of making the decision to make or restore payment.

## Termination in cases of a failure to furnish information

DAR 14 **16.46** Where someone has had payment suspended and they subsequently fail to comply with the information requirement they are no longer entitled to the benefit from the date on which the payments were suspended, or such earlier date on which entitlement to benefit ceases.

## Other people who may receive a rent allowance or CTB

### APPOINTEE

HBR 92(2) CTBR 78(2) **16.47** Where an appointee acts on behalf of a claimant who is incapable of managing his or her own affairs (para. 7.6) then payment may be made to that person. In most cases, however, CTB will be paid by rebating the claimant's tax liability.

## NOMINEE

**16.48** In the case of HB if the claimant requests in writing that the authority makes payment to another person (who must be 18 or more), the authority may make payments to that person. The DSS incorrectly refers to this person as an agent and advises that the claimant must be unable to collect the money himself or herself (GM para. A6.40). This is not the case. HBR 92(3)

## A DEAD CLAIMANT'S PERSONAL REPRESENTATIVE OR NEXT OF KIN

**16.49** Following a claimant's death, the authority must, if a written application is received within 12 months (or such longer period as the authority may allow), pay a rent allowance – or any CTB above the dead claimant's residual council tax liability – to his or her personal representative or, if there is none, the next of kin. The next of kin take priority in the following order: spouse, issue (children, grandchildren), other relatives (parents, brothers, sisters or their children); and must be aged 16 or over. HBR 96(1)-(3) CTBR 81(1)-(3)

# 17 Changes to entitlement

**17.1** This chapter explains what happens when there is a change in the claimant's circumstances (or in any other circumstances which affect HB or CTB). It gives the rules as they have applied since 2nd July 2001, taking into account the new rules about decisions, revisions and supersessions applying from that date. It covers:

- how a decision may be changed;
- when and how a decision may be revised or superseded;
- the claimant's duty to notify a change of circumstances;
- when changes of circumstances take effect from; and
- the rules about 'extended payments'.

## HOW A DECISION MAY BE CHANGED

CSPSSA sch 7 paras 2, 11

**17.2** Once an authority has decided a claim, the claim is not regarded as subsisting thereafter and so the claimant is not entitled to HB/CTB on the basis of circumstances not obtaining then (unless he or she makes a further claim). Decisions on claims are final, except as follows. Once a decision has been made, it may be changed in the following circumstances:

- if the authority revises a decision;
- if the authority supersedes a decision;
- if an appeal tribunal, Commissioner or tribunal of commissioners, or court alters the decision on appeal.

The first two are described in this chapter; appeals are described in chapter 19.

## REVISIONS AND SUPERSESSIONS: SUMMARY

**17.3** This section explains how revisions and supersessions affect entitlement to HB and CTB; in other words, how the authority may of its own initiative, or as a result of a request by a 'person affected', alter decisions it has made. 'Decisions' and 'persons affected' were defined in chapter 16.

## THE DIFFERENCE BETWEEN REVISIONS AND SUPERSESSIONS

**17.4** Generally speaking the distinction is as follows:

- revisions go back to the beginning (i.e. to the date of the decision in question);
- supersessions do not go right back: there will always be a 'before' and an 'after'.

Table 17.1 summarises the circumstances in which each of the above may be done and the date from which it applies. Although the terminology can seem complicated, it usually does not matter if a claimant or other person affected gets the name of what he or she is asking for wrong. For example a request for a revision can be treated as a request for a supersession, and so on: this is dealt with in more detail below. Examples are given after table 17.1. Note: table 17.1 is a summary of the main points only. Further information is in the text. The table does not deal with decisions relating to work-focused interviews, to decisions which have been appealed to or beyond an appeal tribunal, nor with restrictions on entitlement following certain errors of law.

## Revisions and conditions for revising a decision

**17.5** The authority may revise or further revise any decision it has made (including a decision superseding an earlier decision of the authority, an appeal tribunal, a Commissioner or a tribunal of Commissioners) in the circumstances described in the next few paragraphs. CSPSSA sch 7 paras. 1(2), 3(1)

### PERSON AFFECTED REQUESTS A REVISION

**17.6** The authority may revise a decision if the person affected applies for a revision within one calendar month of the date of the notification of the original decision. In calculating the one month time limit, any time is ignored from the date the authority received the request for a written statement (chapter 19) to the date the authority provided the statement (both dates inclusive). DAR 4(1),(4),(8),(9 NIDAR 4(1),(3),(7),

**17.7** Applications must be in writing and delivered by any means to the authority (or, in relevant cases to a One office). The person does not have to remember to use the word 'revision' in his or request: even if the person asks for a supersession, the authority may treat the request as a request for a revision. In practice, it is more common to describe asking for a revision as asking the authority to 'reconsider' or to 'look again'.

**17.8** This time limit may be extended by the authority as described below (para. 17.16). If the authority requires further information or evidence it must request this (para. 17.29). If the time limit is not extended, the authrotiy should nonetheless supersede (para. 17.35).

### MISTAKE OF FACT: GENERAL CASES

**17.9** The authority may revise a decision if, within one month of the date of notifying it, the authority has information sufficient to show that it was made in ignorance of, or was based on a mistake as to, some material fact. Note that under this provision, the time limit cannot be extended (though the person affected could write in as in the previous paragraph and ask for an extension.) DAR 4(1)

## TABLE 17.1 REVISIONS AND SUPERSESSIONS: MAIN POINTS

| Situation | Revision or Supersession? | Date it takes effect |
|---|---|---|
| *Changes of circumstances* | | |
| Change of circumstances notified to the authority more than one month after it occurred (this time limit can be extended) and the claimant qualifies for more HB/CTB | Supersession | Monday following day when authority receives notification (or in certain cases up to a week earlier) |
| Any other change of circumstances | Supersession | Following Monday etc (using the standard rules) |
| *Official error* | | |
| Official error arising at any time (whether resulting in an overpayment or an underpayment) | Revision | Date original decision took effect (or should have) |
| *Overpayments (other than as above)* | | |
| Mistake of fact meaning the claimant was overpaid | Revision | Date original decision took effect (or should have) |
| *Requests by person affected* | | |
| The person affected requests the authority to reconsider its decision within one month (which can be extended) | Revision | Date original decision took effect (or should have) |
| The person affected requests this outside the above time limits | Supersession | Monday of week in which authority received the request |
| The person affected appeals and the authority chooses to revise instead | Revision | Date original decision took effect (or should have) |
| *Rent officer appeal re-determinations* | | |
| Rent officer re-determination is in the claimant's favour | Revision | Date original decision took effect (or should have) |
| Rent officer re-determination is against the claimant's favour | Supersession | Monday following rent officer re-determination |
| *Other mistakes of fact or law* | | |
| Other mistake of fact arising within one month of the decision | Revision | Date original decision took effect (or should have) |
| Any other mistake of fact or law | Supersession | Monday of week in which authority was notified of it or became aware of it |

**Examples: Claims, changes, revisions and supersessions**

A CLAIM AND A REVISION

A claimant has been awarded HB/CTB on the basis that the maximum non-dependant deduction is to apply in respect of her son (because he works full-time but she has been unable to provide evidence of his income). Within one month of notification of the decision on her claim, she writes in with acceptable evidence of his true (low) income.

The authority should revise its decision, so that the lower non-dependant deduction applies from the beginning of her claim.

A CLAIM AND A SUPERSESSION

The same as the above story, except that the claimant took eight months to provide the evidence (and has no reason for her delay).

The authority should make a superseding decision, so that the lower non-dependant deduction applies from the Monday of the week it received the evidence from her.

A CHANGE AND A SUPERSESSION

A claimant writes to tell the authority that her wages went down some months into her HB/CTB benefit period. Her letter gets to the authority within one month of the change, and she provides acceptable evidence.

The authority should make a superseding decision, so that the increase in her HB/CTB is awarded from the Monday following the date her wages went down.

ANOTHER CHANGE AND SUPERSESSION

The same as the last story, except that the claimant took six months to inform the authority (and has no reason for her delay).

The authority should make a superseding decision, so that the increase in her HB/CTB is awarded from the Monday following the date it received the information from her.

*An example involving two changes is given later in this chapter.*

## MISTAKE OF FACT RESULTING IN A DECISION THAT WAS TOO FAVOURABLE

DAR 4(2)

**17.10** The authority may revise a decision at any time if the decision was made in ignorance of, or was based on a mistake as to, some material fact – and the decision was, as a result, more favourable than it would otherwise have been. This and the following paragraph cover most overpayments.

## FOLLOWING AN OFFICIAL ERROR

CSPSSA sch 7 paras 1(1), 23(1) DAR 1(2), 4(2)

**17.11** The authority may revise a decision at any time if the decision arose from an 'official error'. An 'official error' means an error by an authority; a contractor to the authority; an officer of the DWP (including the benefits agency and the jobcentre) or the Commissioners of Inland Revenue, acting as such; or an employee of an authority designated to undertake work-focused interviews. However, an error does not count as an 'official error' if it was caused wholly or partly by any person or body other than the above; or is an error of law which is shown to have been an error only by a subsequent decision of a Commissioner or tribunal of Commissioners. The official error in question could mean too much or too little HB/CTB was awarded.

## RENT OFFICER RE-DETERMINATIONS, ETC. IN THE CLAIMANT'S FAVOUR

DAR 4(3) NIDAR 4(2)

**17.12** The authority may revise a decision about a rent officer determination at any time if (following an appeal to the rent officer by the claimant or the authority) there is a rent officer re-determination, substitute determination or substitute re-determination, and the result would be to increase the amount of the claimant's eligible rent.

In Northern Ireland, decisions to restrict rents are just ordinary decisions of the Executive so a decision can be revised or superseded in the normal way.

## FOLLOWING A REQUEST FOR AN APPEAL

CSPSSA sch 7 para. 3(6) DAR 4(1)

**17.13** The authority may revise a decision if an appeal to an appeal tribunal is made against it within the relevant time limits, and the appeal has not yet been determined. Generally speaking, if the authority does revise a decision in these circumstances, the appeal lapses. More information is in chapter 19.

## FOLLOWING THE OUTCOME OF AN APPEAL

DAR 4(7) NIDAR 4(6)

**17.14** The authority may revise a decision at any time to take account of an appeal decision in the same case (by an appeal tribunal, Commissioner, tribunal of Commissioners or court) which the authority was not aware of at the time it made the decision and which would have affected how the authority made its decision.

OTHER DECISIONS

**17.15** The Secretary of State may prescribe that certain decisions may be revised at any time, but has not yet used this power. CSPSSA sch 7 para 6(2)(e),(4)(a) NICSPSSA sch 7 para 6(2)(c), 4(a) DAR 4(6)

## Late applications for revisions

**17.16** A person affected may, if he or she is outside the time limits described earlier (paras. 17.6-8) write applying for an extension of time. The application must be in writing and must: DAR 5(1)-(3)

- give sufficient details identifying the decision which is sought to be revised; and
- specify that an extension of time is being sought and state the grounds on which it is sought; and
- be delivered (by any means) to the authority (or, in relevant cases to a One office) within 13 months of the date of notification of the decision.

**17.17** The authority must not grant an extension of time unless it is satisfied that: DAR 5(4)

- it is reasonable to grant the application (as described below); and
- the application for revision 'has merit'; and
- special circumstances are relevant to that application as a result of which it was not practicable to make it within the time limit.

**17.18** In determining whether it is reasonable to grant the application, the authority: DAR 5(5),(6)

- may not take account of the following:
  - the fact that the person was unaware of the law (including the law about time limits);
  - that a Commissioner or tribunal of Commissioners or court has taken a different view of the law from that previously understood and applied; and
- must take account of the fact that the longer the delay, the more compelling the special circumstances need to be.

**17.19** Once refused, an application for a late revision may not be renewed. DAR 5(7)

## Dealing with a revision

**17.20** When revising, the authority need not consider any matter which was not raised in the application or did not cause them to act on their own initiative (however, see below). Authorities may ask experts for help when considering any decision it has made (in order to decide whether, for example, it should be CSPSSA sch 7 paras 3(2), 5, 16 revised). The authority may 'stay' (i.e. not make) a revision when an appeal is pending against a Commissioner or tribunal of Commissioners or court in another similar case – or, in certain circumstances, make that revision by following special rules: further details are in chapter 19.

### REQUESTS FOR FURTHER INFORMATION OR EVIDENCE

AA 5(1)(hh), 6(1)(hh) NIDAR 4(4) DAR 4(5)

**17.21** When a revision is being entertained as a result of an application by a person affected, and the authority requires further evidence or information in order to consider all the issues raised, the authority has a duty to request this in writing from the person affected. Then:

- if the information or evidence is provided within one calendar month of the date of the authority's request – or within such longer period as the authority may allow – the authority must consider the revision taking it into account;
- if the information or evidence is not provided within the above time limits, the authority must consider the revision on the basis of the original application.

### EFFECT OF CHANGES OF CIRCUMSTANCES

DAR 4(10) NIDAR 4(9)

**17.22** In considering revising a decision, the authority must ignore any change of circumstances which has occurred since the decision was made and must ignore any future change of circumstances which may be about to occur. (In relation to these, the authority must consider supersession instead, as described below.)

## When a revision takes effect

CSPSSA sch 7 para. 3(3)-(5), 18 NICSPSSA sch 7 para 4(1),(3),(6) DAR 6

**17.23** A revision takes effect when the original decision took effect (or was to take effect), but with the following exceptions:

- If on a revision the authority decides that the original decision took effect from a wrong date, the revision must take effect from the right date.
- For the purposes of time limits relating to appeals, the decision is regarded as having taken place at the date it is revised.
- There are further limitations when there has been a test case which means that claimants generally could qualify for more money (para. 21.84).

# Supersessions and the conditions for superseding a decision

**17.24** The authority may supersede any decision it has made (including a revised decision or a superseded decision or a decision by an appeal tribunal or Commissioner or tribunal of Commissioners), in the circumstances described in the next few paragraphs – which in each case also explain when the supersession takes effect from.

CSPSSA sch 7 para 4(1)-(2),(4)
DAR 7(1)

**17.25** In each of the following cases, the authority may supersede either because a person affected has applied for this or on the authority's own initiative. There is no time limit in either case.

CSPSSA sch 7 para 4(1)

**17.26** Generally, if a decision may be revised it may not be superseded – unless circumstances arise which would require both a revision and a supersession, in which case the supersession wins out and deals with both matters. For example, a claimant may request a revision so late that it can only be dealt with as a supersession (para. 17.8), but the authority realises it has made an official error (para. 17.11) which has to be treated as a revision: the revision 'wins'.

DAR 7(4)

## HOW APPLICATIONS FOR A SUPERSESSION ARE MADE

**17.27** Applications (when they are made) must be in writing and delivered by any means to the authority (or, in relevant cases to a One office). The person does not have to remember to use the word 'supersession' in his or request: even if the person asks for a revision, the authority may treat the request as a request for a supersession; and the authority may also treat the notification of a change of circumstances as a request for a supersession.

DAR 7(6),(7)

# Dealing with a supersession

## WHAT MATTERS ARE TAKEN INTO ACCOUNT

**17.28** When superseding, the authority need not consider any matter which was not raised in the application or did not cause them to act on their own initiative (however, see below). Authorities may ask experts for help when considering any decision it has made (in order to decide whether, for example, it should be superseded. The authority may stay (i.e. not make) a supersession when an appeal is pending against a Commissioner or tribunal of Commissioners or court in another similar case – or, in certain circumstances, make that supersession by following special rules (para. 19.82).

CSPSSA sch 7 para 4(3), 5, 16
NICSPSSA sch 7 para 4(2), 5, 16

### REQUESTS FOR FURTHER INFORMATION OR EVIDENCE

AA 5(1)(hh), 6(1)(hh) DAR 7(5)

**17.29** When a supersession is being entertained as a result of an application by a person affected, and the authority requires further evidence or information in order to consider all the issues raised, the authority has a duty to request this in writing from the person affected. Then:

- if the information or evidence is provided within one calendar month of the date of the authority's request – or within such longer period as the authority may allow – the authority must consider the revision taking it into account;
- if the information or evidence is not provided within the above time limits, the authority must consider the revision on the basis of the original application.

## Conditions for supersession and when supersessions take effect

### GENERAL RULE

CSPSSA sch 7 paras 4(5),(6), 18 NICSPSSA sch 7 paras 4(4), (5), 18 DAR 8(1),(8) NIDAR 8(1),(7)

**17.30** In general terms, a supersession takes effect when it is made (or, if appropriate, when the application for it was made). The following paragraphs give the variations to this rule. There are further limitations when there has been a test case which means that claimants generally could qualify for more money (para. 19.84).

### CHANGE OF CIRCUMSTANCES

DAR 7(2)(a),(3)

**17.31** The authority may supersede a decision if there has been a change of circumstances or one is anticipated. This includes changes which the claimant has no duty to notify (as well as those he or she must notify): paras. 17.50-56.

DAR 8(2)

**17.32** Except as mentioned below, supersessions due a change of circumstances take effect when that change of circumstances takes effect as described later in this chapter (paras. 17.62 onwards).

### CHANGES NOTIFIED LATE TO THE AUTHORITY

DAR 8(3),(5)

**17.33** The exception is that the change is deemed to have occurred on the date of notification to the authority (i.e. the claimant loses money) if:

- the change of circumstances is one which is required to be notified to the authority (other than a change related to whether a person has taken part in a work-focused interview in an area where the 'One' project applies); and

- the change is notified more than one month after it occurs (or after such longer period as may be allowed as described in para. 17.43, and
- the superseding decision is 'advantageous' to the claimant.

Note that the above rule applies only to changes which the claimant has a duty to notify, and therefore does not apply to the changes mentioned in paragraph 17.53. It also appears reasonable that a claimant cannot be held to have a duty to notify something which he cannot know. For example, a claimant waiting for the outcome of a lengthy appeal about entitlement to (say) disability living allowance surely cannot have a duty to notify a successful outcome until it turns out to be successful. If that is the case, then he or she has a month to notify the authority (which can be extended) from being informed of the outcome of the appeal, and should not therefore lose his or her arrears of HB/CTB. Finally, the effect of late notification of an advantageous change is sometimes mitigated by the rules about underlying entitlement (para. 18.16) as illustrated in the following example.

**Example: Late notified advantageous change and underlying entitlement**

A woman on HB/CTB (but not on JSA(IB) or income support) had a baby in May 2002 and did not inform the authority of this until September 2002 (when she made a renewal claim). Nor did she inform the authority of her award of child benefit till then. She makes it clear that she has no special circumstances for failing to notify these things.

The increase in her HB/CTB due to the addition to her family would not normally be awarded for the period from May to September: for that period it is 'underlying entitlement'. However, it must be used to reduce the HB/CTB overpayment that has arisen due to the award of child benefit. Typically the underlying entitlement in a case like this would be greater than the overpayment. So no overpayment would be recoverable (but also no increase would be awarded for the period).

## MISTAKES OF FACT

**17.34** Supersessions which would be 'advantageous' to the claimant, and which are due to ignorance or a mistake of fact take effect from the Monday at the beginning of the benefit week in which: DAR 8(4),(5)

- the application for the supersession was made (if an application was in fact the cause of the authority considering supersesssion); or
- the authority first had information to show that the original decision was made in ignorance or mistake of fact (in any other case).

## ERRORS OF LAW OR FACT WHICH CANNOT RESULT IN A REVISION

DAR 7(2)(b) **17.35** The authority may supersede a decision if:

- the original decision was erroneous in point of law, or was made in ignorance of or based on a mistake as to a material fact; and (in each of those cases)
- the law does not permit it to be revised under any of the rules described earlier.

CSPSSA sch 7 para 4(5),(6) NICSPSSA sch 7 paras 4(4),(5) **17.36** In such a case, the supersession takes effect from the date on which it is made (or, if appropriate, from the date the application for it was made). This rule would apply, for example, to applications for a revision made outside the time limit where there are no special circumstances permitting a late application (para. 17.8).

## RENT OFFICER RE-DETERMINATIONS, ETC. AGAINST THE CLAIMANT'S FAVOUR (GB ONLY)

DAR 7(2)(c) **17.37** The authority may supersede a decision about a rent officer determination if there is a rent officer re-determination, substitute determination or substitute re-determination, and the result would be to reduce the amount of the claimant's eligible rent.

DAR 8(6) **17.38** In such a case, it takes effect as though the date of the rent officer's determination or redetermination was the date of a change of circumstances.

## ERRORS OF FACT FOLLOWING AN APPEAL

DAR 7(2)(d) NIDAR 7(2)(c) **17.39** The authority may supersede a decision by an appeal tribunal or Commissioner or tribunal of Commissioners which was made in ignorance of, or based on a mistake about, a material fact.

DAR 8(7) NIDAR 8(6) **17.40** When the supersession supersedes such an appeal decision, and that appeal decision was made in ignorance or mistake of fact and was more advantageous to the claimant as a result, the supersession takes effect from when the appeal decision took effect.

## WHEN THE 'ONE' PROJECT NO LONGER APPLIES

DAR 7(2)(f) NIDAR 7(2),(e) **17.41** The authority may supersede a decision that a person has not taken part in a work-focused interview if:

- the person has now reached 60;
- the person has moved to an area where taking part in a work-focused interview is not a requirement of getting HB/CTB; or
- a fresh determination or decision as to whether he or she took part in a work-focused interview has now been made.

### OTHER DECISIONS

**17.42** The Secretary of State (in Northern Ireland the Department) may prescribe that certain other decisions may be superseded, but has as yet used this power only for technical purposes. CSPSSA sch 7 para 6(2)(e),(4)(a) NICSPSSA sch 7 para 6(2)(c), 4(a) DAR 7(2)(e) NIDAR 7(2)(d)

## Late notification of changes of circumstances

DAR 9(1),(2)

**17.43** A notification of a change of circumstances may be made later than described above (and the claimant not lose money) if the person affected writes applying for this. The application must:

- give particulars of the change; and
- state the reasons for the failure to notify the change earlier; and
- be made within 13 months of the date on which the change occurred. DAR 9(3)

**17.44** The authority must not grant an extension of time unless the authority is satisfied that:

- it is reasonable to grant the application; and
- the change of circumstances is relevant to the decision; and
- special circumstances are relevant to that application as a result of which it was not practicable to notify the change within the one month time limit. DAR 9(4),(5)

**17.45** In determining whether it is reasonable to grant the application, the authority:

- may not take account of the following:
- the fact that the person was unaware of the law (including the law about time limits);
- that a Commissioner or tribunal of Commissioners or court has taken a different view of the law from that previously understood and applied; and
- must take account of the fact that the longer the delay (beyond the time limit), the more compelling the special circumstances need to be. DAR 9(6)

**17.46** Once refused, an application for a late supersession may not be renewed. However, since there must be a supersession (from the later date – to take account of the change), that supersession (and the date it is to apply from) becomes a decision itself, carrying the rights in this chapter and subject to appeal (chapter 19).

## Duty to notify a change of circumstances

**17.47** With one exception, the claimant has a duty to notify the authority's 'designated office' (para. 5.31), in writing, of any relevant change of circumstances. HBR 75(1), (4) HBR 75 (1A) (GB only) CTBR 65(1), (1A)

**17.48** The exception is that if the claimant sent or delivered his or her HB/CTB claim to a 'One office' (para. 7.11), he or she may alternatively notify changes of circumstances to that office or to any other 'gateway office' mentioned on or with the claim form.

**17.49** The duty to notify begins on the date the claim is made and continues for as long as the person is in receipt of HB or CTB (except in relation to 'extended payments': para. 17.88).

HBR sch A1

**17.50** In the special case of refugees who were formerly asylum seekers (para. 20.51), the claimant has a duty to notify relevant changes of circumstances which occurred in any previous period for which they have become entitled to HB/CTB. If HB/CTB is payable to someone other than the claimant (e.g. a landlord or an appointee), that person is also required to notify relevant changes.

**17.51** These duties apply to all HB and CTB claims including both main CTB and second adult rebate.

HBR 75(1)
CTBR 65(1)

**17.52** For these purposes a relevant change is one which the claimant (or other person) could reasonably be expected to know might affect:

- entitlement to HB/CTB; or
- amount of HB/CTB; or
- method of payment.

Examples are given below. Whether a claimant (or other person) could reasonably be expected to know a change might affect HB or CTB, is of importance if failure to notify a change results in an overpayment, and the question of recovering the overpayment arises (chapter 16).

## WHICH CHANGES MUST BE NOTIFIED?

HBR 75(2)
CTBR 65(2)

**17.53** The claimant need not inform the authority of:

- changes in rent if he or she is a council tenant;
- changes in council tax liability;
- changes in the age of any member of the family or non-dependant;
- changes in the HB or CTB regulations;
- changes which affect his or her entitlement to income support or income-based jobseeker's allowance but do not affect his or her HB/CTB.

In the first two cases, the authority has made the changes, and so should not need to be informed of them. In the third case, the authority should be able to implement the change automatically.

**Example: Two changes – overpayments and underlying entitlement**

WHAT HAPPENED FIRST

A claimant first claimed HB/CTB from September 2002. In January 2003 the authority gets a letter from her saying her non-dependant moved out in October 2002. There is full supporting evidence that this is true. She gives no reason for the delay in informing the authority. The authority was (correctly) making a non-dependant deduction of £7.40 in HB and £2.30 in CTB.

This is a late-notified change of circumstances which would (if she had told the authority in time) have resulted in an underpayment. So it is dealt with as a supersession with effect from the Monday following the date the authority got the letter from her.

*As a result of her delay she has 'lost' HB of £7.40 per week and CTB of £2.30 per week between the relevant dates in October and January.*

WHAT HAPPENED NEXT

In March 2003 the authority finds out that the same claimant's income from maintenance went up by £20 per week (a permanent increase) in December 2002. She did not tell the authority till now.

This is a change of circumstances resulting in an overpayment. So it is dealt with as a supersession with effect from the Monday following the date her maintenance went up in December 2002.

*If this was the only change, it would mean she was overpaid HB of (65% of £20) £13.00 per week and CTB of (20% of £20) £4.00 per week between the relevant dates in December and March. But...*

LOOKING AT THE OVERPAYMENT

...the rules about underlying entitlement must be taken into account (para. 18.16).

Her underlying entitlement (due to the removal of the non-dependant deduction) must be set against the amount of the overpayment (due to the increase in maintenance) – making the amount of the recoverable overpayment (between the relevant dates in December and January):

- HB (£13.00 – £7.40 =) £5.60 per week;
- CTB (£4.00 – £2.30 =) £1.70 per week.

Between the relevant dates in January and March, the overpayment is the full amount shown earlier (£13.00 and £4.00) as there is no underlying entitlement during that period.

## DIAGRAM ILLUSTRATING THE EXAMPLE

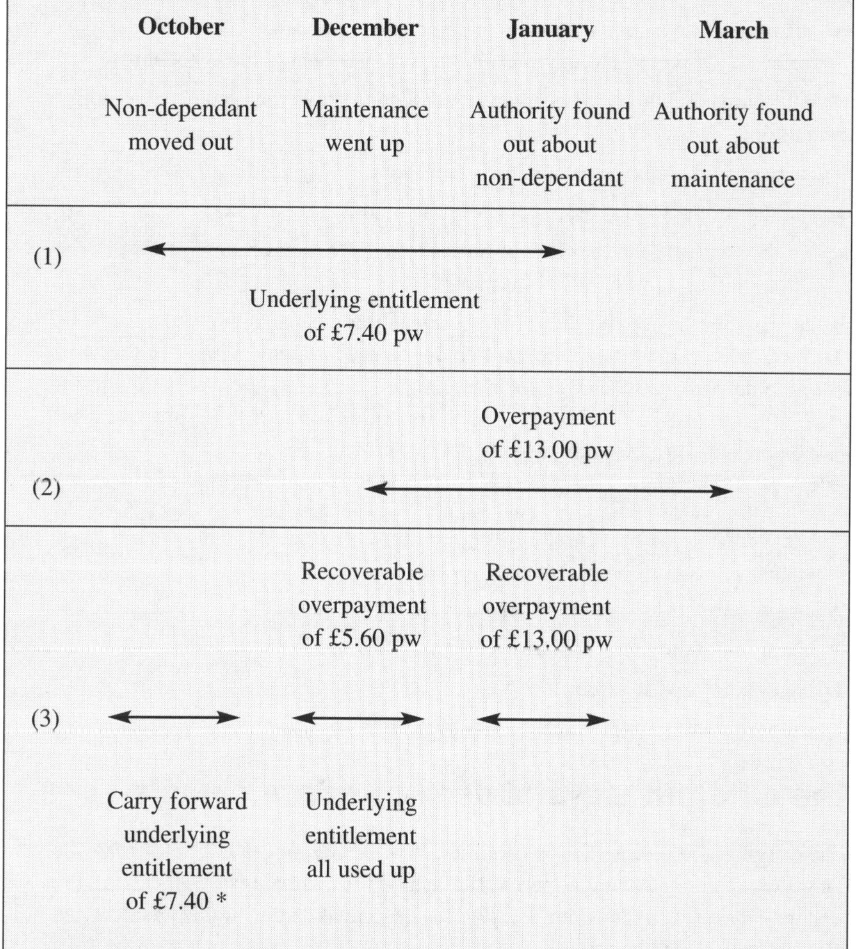


**Notes:**

*The diagram shows just the HB figures for simplicity.*

(1) This indicates 'what happened first'.

(2) This indicates 'what happened next'.

(3) This indicates the outcome of (1) and (2).

* This would be used if a further overpayment were discovered for this period.

**17.54** The claimant must inform the authority of: HBR 75(2)(e),(3) CTBR 65(2)(e),(3)

- the end of his or her (or any partner's) entitlement to income support or income-based jobseeker's allowance;
- changes where a child or young person ceases to be a member of the family: for example, where a young person reaches 19 or leaves the household.

**17.55** Claimants who have been awarded second adult rebate must also notify the authority of: CTBR 65(4)

- changes in the number of adults in their home;
- changes in the total gross incomes of the adults in their home;
- the date any adult in their home ceases to receive income support or income-based jobseeker's allowance.

In the first two cases, the duty arises only if the change might reasonably be expected to alter the claimant's entitlement to second adult rebate. In the third case, the duty arises whenever such a change occurs – regardless of whether it could affect entitlement. The word 'adult' is not defined for these purposes, but may be presumed to mean anyone aged 18 or more.

**17.56** Examples of other matters which must be notified to the authority include:

- changes of address;
- changes in rent if the claimant is not a council tenant;
- changes in the status of non-dependants/second adults;
- changes in family circumstances affecting the applicable amount;
- changes in capital and/or income;
- changes relating to payment of HB direct to a landlord.

## The different ways of dealing with a change

**17.57** When there is a change of circumstances affecting HB/CTB during the course of a claimant's benefit period (i.e. whilst the claimant is on HB/CTB), the authority makes a superseding decision (as described earlier in this chapter), the effect of which may be to:

- end the benefit period early; or
- alter the claimant's entitlement to HB/CTB.

### ENDING A BENEFIT PERIOD EARLY

**17.58** In the case of some changes of circumstances, the authority must end the benefit period early (in other words, stop awarding the claimant HB/CTB). In the case of other changes of circumstances, the authority may choose to end the benefit period early. HBR 67 CTBR 58

**17.59** In such cases, authorities should invite claimants to make a renewal claim or, when this is clearly inappropriate (e.g. if a claimant has capital valued for HB/CTB purposes at over £16,000 and has no second adults), remind claimants that they may make a further claim if their circumstances change again.

### ALTERING ENTITLEMENT TO HB/CTB

DAR 7(2) **17.60** Except in cases when the benefit period must be ended early, an authority may alter the claimant's entitlement to HB/CTB if there is a relevant change of circumstances during the course of a benefit period.

HBR 77(1)(b) CTBR 67(1)(b) **17.61** The claimant and any other person affected must be notified in writing of the change, within 14 days or as soon as reasonably practicable.

## The different types of change

### THE GENERAL RULE

**17.62** The following general rule applies for all changes other than those mentioned in the remainder of this chapter. Typical examples are changes in income, capital, age or household composition – including cases where a claimant who has been awarded main CTB becomes entitled to second adult rebate instead, or *vice versa;* and including cases where a claimant becomes entitled to income support or income-based jobseeker's allowance.

HBR 26, 68(1) DAR 8(2) CTBR 18, 59(1) **17.63** If the result of a change is that the claimant's entitlement reduces to nil, the authority must end the benefit period early. If the result of a change is that entitlement continues, the most common practice is to revise HB/CTB; but the authority may end the period early in appropriate cases – e.g. if a change is very complicated.

**17.64** It is up to the authority to determine the date on which such a change actually occurs. This can be straightforward (e.g. in the case of a claimant's birthday) or difficult (e.g. in the case of varying capital). In three cases there are specific rules:

- If entitlement to any social security benefit ends, the date the change actually occurs is defined as being the day after the last day of entitlement to that benefit.
- If there is a change in tax or national insurance caused by a change in the law (e.g. the Budget) it may be disregarded (i.e. treated as not occurring) until up to 30 benefit weeks later. This applies to the income of a claimant, partner, non-dependant or second adult (whether in employment or self-employment).
- There are special rules about arrears of income (para. 11.18).

**17.65** When the authority alters HB/CTB in general cases, the new amount of HB/CTB is awarded from the Monday after the date the change occurs, even if the change occurs on a Monday. (So for the benefit week including the change, benefit is calculated as if the change had not occurred.) HBR 68(1) CTBR 59(1) DAR 8(2)

**17.66** When the authority ends the benefit period early in general cases: HBR 67(1)(c), 79(3)(a) CTBR 58(c), 69(3)(a)

- the last week of HB/CTB entitlement is the benefit week (para. 5.53) in which the claimant's circumstances change; and
- in the last week, the claimant is entitled to a full week's HB/CTB (i.e. calculated as if the change had not occurred).

**Example: A claimant's birthday**

A claimant receiving HB and CTB (but not income support or JSA(IB)) reaches the age of 75 on Wednesday 10th July. The effect is that her HB and CTB increase.

Normally, it would be inappropriate to end the benefit period early in such a case. instead, the authority should revise HB and CTB.

The new amounts of HB and CTB are awarded from the benefit week after the change, i.e. benefit week commencing Monday 15th July.

## WHEN INCOME SUPPORT OR JSA(IB) ENTITLEMENT ENDS

**17.67** Entitlement to income support (IS) or income-based jobseeker's allowance – JSA(IB) – may end for a variety of reasons. As described below, there are three rules about how this affects the person's HB/CTB.

## END OF INCOME SUPPORT OR JSA(IB): GENERAL RULE

**17.68** If the claimant's (or any partner's) entitlement to IS or JSA(IB) ends for any reason other than those described below (for example, if the claimant takes up work), the authority must end the benefit period early and must invite a renewal claim. HBR 67(1)(a), 68(1) CTBR 58(1)(a), 59(1)

In such cases, the change actually occurs on the day after the last day of entitlement to IS or JSA(IB) (para. 17.64). The HB/CTB benefit period ends at the end of the benefit week containing the day the change actually occurs.

## TRANSFERRING BETWEEN INCOME SUPPORT AND JSA(IB)

**17.69** If the claimant's (or any partner's) entitlement to IS ceases but the claimant (or partner) immediately becomes entitled to JSA(IB) – or the reverse occurs – there is no change in the claimant's entitlement to HB or main CTB (unless some other change occurs at the same time). This is because receipt of HBR 67(2), 68(1) CTBR 58(2), 59(1) either of those benefits entitles the claimant to maximum HB/CTB (para. 9.9). The claimant is nonetheless required to notify the authority of such a change.

**17.70** In such cases, the authority should usually simply continue awarding HB/CTB (and notify the claimant of the new reason why he or she qualifies for maximum HB/CTB). It may alternatively bring the benefit period to an early end, but this would normally be appropriate only in exceptional cases. If the authority does end the benefit period, it should do so according to the rule described in paragraph 17.68 and must invite a renewal claim.

## TRANSFERRING FROM INCOME SUPPORT OR JSA(IB) TO ANOTHER SOCIAL SECURITY BENEFIT

HBR 67(1)(b), 68(1) CTBR 58(1)(b), 59(1)

**17.71** If the claimant's (or any partner's) entitlement to IS or JSA(IB) ceases because any other social security benefit (e.g. contribution-based jobseeker's allowance, incapacity benefit, etc.) is awarded instead, the authority must end the benefit period early and must invite a renewal claim.

In such cases, the HB/CTB benefit period ends at the end of the benefit week which contains the last day on which IS or JSA(IB) is *paid* (regardless of the date on which *entitlement* to IS or JSA(IB) ends or ended).

**17.72** This rule can apply in cases where claimants were awarded IS or JSA(IB) while they were waiting to find out whether they qualify for some other social security benefit. As illustrated in the following example, the point of the rule is to ensure that they are able to satisfy the four weeks time limit for renewal claims (para. 5.80). Authorities sometimes have difficulty administering this rule since, when the Benefits Agency notifies them of a change of this kind on form NHB(IS) or NHB(JSA), it can be difficult to distinguish the date IS or JSA(IB) entitlement ended from the last date on which IS or JSA(IB) was paid.

**17.73** The rule is only about when the claimant's benefit period ends – not about the amount of his or her HB/CTB. Therefore authorities may revise entitlement to HB/CTB retrospectively to take account of the social security benefit from the date entitlement to it began. This may result in an overpayment for that period. Except in certain cases where there has been an official error or delay, such overpayments are recoverable.

## CERTAIN CHANGES INVOLVING RENT OFFICER REFERRALS (GB ONLY)

HBR 66(3),(5)

**17.74** The following applies only in cases referred to the rent officer (chapter 8). In such cases, if the rent officer makes a determination following a 'relevant change of circumstances' (as listed in table 6.2), the law expects the authority to extend the claimant's benefit period (for HB only) by a period of at least one benefit week and no more than 60 benefit weeks. Within those limits, it is for the authority to choose how long to extend it by. In practice, this rule (which was introduced in April 2000) is all but unworkable and most authorities appear to ignore it.

## WHEN RENT LIABILITY CHANGES OR ENDS

**17.75** If a claimant's rent increases (or decreases), the authority may either revise his or her HB or (less commonly) bring the HB benefit period to an early end. If the claimant is a private tenant, the authority may in some cases need to refer the rent to the rent officer (chapter 8).

**17.76** If a claimant moves within an authority's area, it is possible for his or her HB to be revised, though authorities may alternatively end the benefit period early in such a case (in which case the rules about renewal claims apply: chapter 5). If a claimant moves out of the authority's area, the authority must end the benefit period early (unless a relevant agency arrangement exists: para. 1.18).

**Examples: When income support entitlement ends**

In (a) and (b) the claimants income support entitlement has stopped – but not because he or she has been awarded another social security benefit. The authority must end the HB/CTB benefit period early in such cases (and invite a renewal claim).

(a) Last day of income support entitlement: Thursday 6th June. Change occurs: Friday 7th June. HB/CTB benefit period ends: Sunday 9th June.

(b) Last day of income support entitlement: Sunday 9th June. Change occurs: Monday 10th June. HB/CTB benefit period ends: Sunday 16th June.

**17.77** When HB is revised as a result of a change in liability for rent, this is done from the benefit week in which the date of the change falls: HBR 68(2), 69(4),(5)

- if rent is expressed on a weekly basis (or in multiples of weeks), a whole week's new entitlement is awarded in that benefit week;
- if rent is expressed on a non-weekly basis (e.g. daily or calendar-monthly), entitlement for that benefit week is assessed on a daily basis for both the old and new entitlements.

**17.78** When the HB benefit period is brought to an early end as a result of rent liability ending: HBR 67(1)(c), 69(4),(5)

- if rent is expressed on a weekly basis (or in multiples of weeks), no HB is awarded in the last benefit week; unless the claimant is liable for rent up to and including the Sunday, in which case a whole week's HB is awarded for that benefit week;

- if rent is expressed on a non-weekly basis (e.g. daily or calendar-monthly), entitlement in the last benefit week is calculated on a daily basis.

**Example: Rent increase**

A claimant receiving HB pays rent weekly on Saturdays. It increases on Saturday 13th July. In her case, the effect is that her HB increases.

It would be inappropriate to end the HB benefit early in such a case. Instead, the authority should revise HB entitlement.

The new amount of HB is awarded from the benefit week in which the change occurs, i.e. from benefit week commencing Monday 8th July.

## WHEN COUNCIL TAX LIABILITY CHANGES OR ENDS

CTBR 59(2)

**17.79** If a claimant's liability for council tax increases or decreases, the authority should revise his or her CTB from the benefit week in which the date of the change falls (on a daily basis in all cases: para. 17.83). It may alternatively bring the benefit period to an early end, but this would normally be appropriate only in exceptional cases.

CTBR 59(3)

**17.80** If the change is in the amount of entitlement to a council tax transitional reduction (para. 2.30), the change must be taken into account from the date on which it takes effect (usually 1st April). If the change is due to the authority setting revised council taxes due to council tax 'capping', the change must be taken into account from the beginning of the financial year (1st April).

CTBR 59(3)

**17.81** If the change is in entitlement to, or the amount of, a council tax discount (para. 2.35) or a reduction for disabilities (para. 2.32), the change must be taken into account from the date on which it actually occurs.

**17.82** If a claimant moves within an authority's area, it is possible for his or her CTB to be revised, though authorities may alternatively end the benefit period early in such a case. If a claimant moves out of an authority's area, the authority must end the benefit period early.

CTBR 57(2), 58(c), 59(2),(3)

**17.83** In all the above cases:

- when CTB is revised: in the benefit week including the date of the change, CTB is calculated on a daily basis for both old and new entitlements;
- when the CTB benefit period is brought to an early end: entitlement for the last benefit week is calculated on a daily basis.

## CHANGES RELATING TO COUPLES

**17.84** In CTB only, a specific rule deals with cases in which: CTBR 57(2), 58(c), 59(5),(6)

- a claimant acquires a partner; or
- a claimant's partner dies; or
- a claimant and partner separate.

In all these cases the change is taken into account on the day on which that event occurs. The authority may revise the claimant's entitlement to CTB in such cases, or may bring the benefit period to an early end. In either case this is done on a daily basis following the rules in paragraph 17.83.

**17.85** There is no specific rule in HB, where such changes fall within the general rule (para. 17.62), and are therefore taken into account from the Monday following the event in question. The reason for the discrepancy between the CTB and HB rules is that in CTB these types of change are often associated with a change in liability for council tax whereas in HB they are unlikely to be associated with a change in liability for rent.

## CHANGES IN THE REGULATIONS; AND LOCAL GOVERNMENT REORGANISATION (GB ONLY)

**17.86** When the regulations are amended, the authority revises HB/CTB from the date on which the amendment takes effect. In the case of the annual April HB/CTB up-rating, this means 1st April. The one exception applies in HB only, and only for claimants whose rent is due weekly or in multiples of weeks: in their HB claims, the up-rating instead takes effect from the first Monday in April (in 2001, this is 2nd April); and furthermore any other change of circumstances occurring in the week beginning with that Monday also takes effect from the same day. HBR 68(3),(5) CTBR 59(4)

Following local government reorganisation, a newly-constituted authority may, within six months of reorganisation (or, in Scotland, twelve months), end the benefit period of any claimant whose claim was formerly administered by a different authority. A determination to do this is not appealable. SI 1995 No. 531 SI 1996 No. 548 SI 1996 No. 549

## WHEN THERE IS MORE THAN ONE CHANGE

**17.87** Apart from the cases described in paragraph 17.86, if two or more changes occur in relation to the same claim, they are dealt with in turn, following the above rules. The exception to this is when changes which actually occur in the same benefit week would have an effect (under those rules) in different benefit weeks. In these cases: HBR 68(4) CTBR 59(6)

- for HB if one of the changes is in the amount of rent liability, the other changes in entitlement instead apply when that applies;

- for HB in any other case, work out the various days on which the changes have an effect (under the above rules): all the changes instead apply from the earliest of these;
- for CTB in all cases, work out the various days on which the changes have an effect (under the above rules): all the changes instead apply from the earliest of these.

**Example: More than one change**

The circumstances in two earlier examples (claimant's birthday and rent increase) apply to the same claimant.

The authority decides to revise HB and CTB (rather than bring the HB and CTB benefit periods to an early end).

Both the changes affect HB. They actually occur in the same benefit week, but would have an effect in different benefit weeks. So HB is revised to take into account both the claimant's birthday and the rent increase from benefit week commencing Monday 8th July.

Only the first change affects CTB, so CTB is revised to take into account the claimant's birthday from benefit week commencing Monday 15th July.

## Extended payments

HBR 2(1), 62A, 76(4), sch 5A
HBR 69(8)(GB)
NIHBR 69(9)
CTBR 2(1), 51(6), 53A, 66(4), sch 5A
SI 1988 No. 662

**17.88** The rest of this chapter describes the rules designed to help long-term unemployed people who are returning to work. This section describes how they can get an 'extended payment' of two or four weeks extra HB/CTB and gives the rules as they apply (after very welcome simplification) from 9th April 2001.

### ENTITLEMENT TO EXTENDED PAYMENTS

**17.89** A claimant is entitled to an extended payment ('EP') if:

- the claimant or partner starts employment or self-employment, or increases his or her hours or earnings; and
- this is expected to last for at least 5 weeks; and
- the claimant or partner has been entitled to IS or JSA continuously for 26 weeks and this entitlement ceases as a result; and
- the claimant or partner has been on HB/CTB and this ceases as a result of the end of IS/JSA or as a result of moving home; and
- the claimant or partner remains liable (or treated as liable) for rent or liable for council tax (at the same or new address).

In the case of a couple, it no longer matters which partner fulfils any or all of the conditions.

## CLAIMS, ETC.

**17.90** There is no longer a requirement for a written claim. Instead, a person who fulfils the conditions is treated as having claimed an EP so long as he or she notifies the authority or the Benefits Agency of the first three matters in the list in paragraph 17.89. This must be done within four weeks of the day the new job, new hours or new rate of pay, began. Although it could be done by telephone, it is wise for claimants to follow this up with written confirmation. This notification is not, however, required at all in 'lone parent run-on cases' (described later), in which cases the Benefits Agency should notify the authority automatically of entitlement to EPs.

**17.91** The authority has a duty to determine EP claims and notify the outcome – even if a claimant does not qualify for an EP – and even if the only reason is that the Benefits Agency has said that the claimant does not satisfy the '26-week condition'. Unlike the other conditions (in para. 17.89), it is for the Secretary of State (via the Benefits Agency) to'certify' whether or not the claimant fulfils this condition – and this is binding on the authority. If the claimant disagrees with this particular matter he or she may negotiate with the Benefits Agency, but the only formal method of appeal would be to seek judicial review.

**17.92** As regards whether the claimant satisfies the other conditions (in para. 17.89) the DWP's advice is that authorities should normally accept what the claimant has said – though, of course, an authority may well not accept it if a claimant said, in late December, that his new job impersonating Father Christmas would last five weeks.

## PERIODS AND AMOUNT OF EXTENDED PAYMENTS

**17.93** Except in lone parent run-on cases (described below), an EP is awarded for the four weeks following the Sunday on which the authority ends the HB/CTB benefit period as a result of the claimant ceasing to be entitled to IS/JSA(IB) or (if relevant) moving. Although an EP is not technically an extension of the HB/CTB benefit period, it is treated as though it was ordinary HB/CTB for other purposes (such as whether the claimant falls within the New Scheme or Old Scheme for eligible rent purposes: chapter 10). Also it may be replaced, later, by a new ongoing HB/CTB benefit period as described later.

**17.94** In each of those four weeks, the amount of HB/CTB EP equals the amount awarded in the last benefit week of the (recently ended) HB/CTB benefit period – ignoring any part-week of entitlement and ignoring any rent-free period in that week. The one exception is that (from this year) no HB EP is awarded in a rent-free week. (For example, if the normal four week EP period contains one rent free week, the claimant will get only three weeks' worth of EPs.) Otherwise all changes of circumstances are ignored.

## 'LONE PARENT RUN-ON' CASES

**17.95** In broad terms, 'lone parent run-on' is available for certain lone parents who have been on income support and who start work after being out of work for 26 weeks or more. It means they get two weeks' extra income support after they start the job. During these two weeks they continue to qualify for HB/CTB in the ordinary way. Their entitlement to an EP is for only two weeks (rather than the usual four). (The idea behind this is that they get the 'other' two weeks during their lone parent run-on.) The rules about the amount of the EP are the same as in other cases. The EP runs:

- from the day after the last day of entitlement to IS (i.e. the day after the last day of the IS 'lone parent run-on');
- to the end of the HB/CTB benefit week which contains the day four weeks after the day on which the claimant started remunerative work (unless the person's liability for rent or council tax ceases earlier, in which case entitlement to the EP also ceases at the same time).

In most cases, this is a two-week period (para. 17.94). The BA notifies the authority of both the last day of entitlement to IS and the date on which the claimant started remunerative work, in order that the authority can calculate the above period.

## EXTENDED PAYMENTS AND RENEWAL CLAIMS

**17.96** Claimants may remain entitled to HB/CTB despite their (or their partner's) new job or increase in hours or earnings. A renewal claim (by the claimant or partner) for ongoing HB/CTB runs consecutively from the end of the old HB/CTB benefit period if it is made during the EP period or during the four weeks after it.

- If the claimant is entitled to less ongoing HB/CTB than the amount of the EP (or exactly the same amount), the new amount is awarded from the benefit week immediately following the end of the EP period.
- If the claimant is entitled to more ongoing HB/CTB than the amount of the EP, the balance is awarded for the EP period, and the whole amount is awarded thereafter. (This could arise, for example, if a non-dependant left the household and the increase in entitlement due to this was greater than the decrease in entitlement due to the new income of the claimant or partner.)

If the authority fails to end the old HB/CTB benefit period for any reason, the amount awarded to the claimant is offset against the amount of the EP, i.e. the amount awarded during the EP period is treated as though it was the EP.

**Examples: Extended payments**

GENERAL CASE

A claimant – who satisfies all the conditions for an EP – gets a new job on Monday 8th April. He is not a lone parent. The Benefits Agency decides that his last day of entitlement to income support is Sunday 7th April.

(a) The end of his HB/CTB entitlement under the usual rules (para. 17.68) is Sunday 14th April.

(b) His EP period runs from Monday 15th April to Sunday 12th May (four weeks).

'LONE PARENT RUN-ON' CASE

A claimant – who satisfies all the conditions for an EP – gets a new job on Monday 8th April. Because she turns out to qualify for a 'lone parent run-on', the Benefits Agency decides that her last day of entitlement to income support is Sunday 21st April.

(a) The end of her HB/CTB entitlement under the usual rules (para. 17.68) is Sunday 28th April.

(b) Her EP period runs from Monday 29th April to Sunday 12th May (two weeks).

## MISCELLANEOUS MATTERS

**17.97** The following are the main further matters relating to EPs.

- A separate determination should be made (and notified) about whether to pay HB to a landlord during an EP period.
- A separate determination should be made (and notified) about whether to recover recoverable overpayments of HB by deduction from an EP for HB.
- The question of whether an EP has been overpaid depends on who has to notify and/or determine what. For example, if a claimant said that his new job would last at least 5 weeks and then the employer (unforeseeably) closed down, the extended payment was correctly paid: there has been no overpayment.
- A claimant who is entitled to an EP and who has been entitled to HB on two homes (para. 3.67) appears to qualify for an EP on both homes.

## EXTENDED PAYMENTS FOR MOVERS

**17.98** Claimants who are entitled to an EP are entitled to it even if they move home during the week before, or the week in which, they or a partner take up employment or self-employment – but not in cases of increasing hours or earnings. In practice, in nearly all cases, the claimant will be at the new address for the whole of the EP period.

**17.99** The amount of the EP for HB at the new address (during the EP period) depends on whether the claimant's entitlements at the old and new addresses are to a rent allowance or a rent rebate, as shown in table 17.2, which also shows the amount of the EP for CTB at the new address.

**17.100** In any case when the claimant moves to a new authority area, the law allows authorities to exchange information relevant to extended payments. The DSS advises that the old authority should keep all the documentation and write to the new authority confirming the details.

## FAST-TRACKING

HBR 76(4), (5)
CTBR 66(4), (5)

**17.101** An authority must 'give priority… over other claims' to a claim made by any claimant who:

- makes a claim for an EP within the time limit (para. 17.90) – regardless of whether he or she actually qualifies for it; and makes a claim for ongoing HB/CTB (on the basis of his or her new circumstances) no later than seven days after that – regardless of whether he or she actually qualifies for it; or
- is entitled to an EP because of qualifying for a 'lone parent run-on' (para. 17.95); and makes a claim for on-going HB/CTB no later than seven days after the date he or she started the work in question; and the BA certifies that the person qualifies no later than 14 days after that date.

**17.102** This is known as 'fast-tracking'. In addition to the above requirement, there are subsidy incentives and penalties for authorities related to 'fast-tracking' as described in chapter 22.

**Table 17.2: EXTENDED PAYMENTS FOR MOVERS**

HB: A MOVE FROM RENT ALLOWANCE TO RENT ALLOWANCE

The amount of HB at the new address is exactly equal to the amount of HB at the old address.

If the move is to a new authority area, the old authority makes this payment.

HB: A MOVE FROM RENT ALLOWANCE TO RENT REBATE

The amount of HB at the new address is calculated using:

- the eligible rent at the new address, but
- the non-dependant deduction(s) (if any) at the old address.

If the move is to a new authority area, the new authority makes this payment.

HB: A MOVE FROM RENT REBATE TO RENT REBATE

The amount of HB at the new address is calculated using:

- the eligible rent at the new address, but
- the non-dependant deduction(s) (if any) at the old address.

If the move is to a new authority area, the new authority makes this payment.

HB: A MOVE FROM RENT REBATE TO RENT ALLOWANCE

The amount of HB at the new address is exactly equal to the amount of HB at the old address.

If the move is to a new authority area, the new authority makes this payment.

CTB: ALL CASES

The amount of CTB at the new address is calculated using:

- the eligible council tax liability at the new address, but
- the non-dependant deduction(s) (if any) at the old address.

If the move is to a new authority area, the new authority makes this payment.

# 18 Overpayments

**18.1** This chapter explains:

- what an overpayment is;
- why the cause of an overpayment is important;
- when an overpayment is recoverable;
- how the amount of the overpayment is worked out;
- when, from whom, how, and at what rate an overpayment should be recovered;
- the information that should be provided to the claimant and any other person affected;
- how far recovery of an overpayment may be pursued; and
- when an administrative penalty may be added to a fraudulent overpayment.

AA 75(1),76(1) NIAA 73(1) HBR 98 CTBR 83

**18.2** Where more HB is paid than a claimant is entitled to, this is referred to as an 'overpayment'. The term includes not only overpayments made by way of instruments of payment such as cheques but also any overpayment by way of a rebate to a rent account. Where more CTB is allowed (by way of a rebate to a council tax account or otherwise) than a claimant is entitled to, this is referred to as 'excess benefit'. As most of the rules relating to 'overpayments' and 'excess benefit' are the same, the term overpayment is used in this chapter to refer to both.

**18.3** The overpayment and recovery of benefit has created major difficulties for claimants, landlords and authorities. Claimants and landlords have had their rights denied and unnecessary debts created. Many authorities have failed to follow the correct process of determination, notify claimants, keep adequate records, or account for overpayments properly. As a consequence they have made inaccurate subsidy claims and created rent and council tax arrears for themselves and debts for landlords.

## What is an overpayment?

HBR 98 CTBR 83

**18.4** Overpayments are established through revision of benefit entitlement. They are amounts of benefit which have been paid but to which there is no entitlement under the regulations. They include any overpayment of:

- a rent allowance paid on account;
- CTB due to a backdated award of a council tax discount (para. 3.35), council tax disability reduction (para. 3.32) or council tax transitional relief (para. 3.30).

> **Example: An overpayment**
>
> The claimant receives HB and CTB from 9th April 2001. On 14th May 2001 her adult son comes to live with her. the claimant has a duty to inform the authority of this change of circumstances but does not do so until 6th August 2001. The authority determines that a non-dependant deduction should have been made for the son from the benefit week commencing Monday 21st May 2001 (the date from which the change of circumstances should have taken effect). The claimant has received benefit up to and including the benefit week commencing 13th August 2001. An overpayment of benefit has occurred for 19 weeks.

**18.5** Having identified that an overpayment has occurred the authority must:

- establish the cause of each overpayment;
- decide whether or not the overpayment is recoverable;
- identify the period and calculate the amount of the overpayment;
- consider whether or not recovery should be sought;
- decide from whom the recovery should be sought.

and, within 14 days (para. 18.42), notify the claimant and other persons affected, for example the landlord where recovery is sought from him or her, accordingly.

**18.6** In the case of HB overpayments of rebates to an authority's rent account or overpaid CTB allowed to its council tax accounts, the regulations must not be circumvented by the automatic creation of debits applied retrospectively with the resulting creation of arrears for the claimant. The authority must perform the duties imposed by the regulations and make each decision required.

## Establishing the cause of the overpayment

**18.7** The authority must establish the cause of an overpayment in order to:

- decide whether or not it is recoverable;
- correctly notify the claimant, the person the authority is seeking to recover from (if not the claimant), and any other person affected;
- claim the correct amount of subsidy.

**18.8** An overpayment might arise due to:

- local authority error, e.g. the authority fails to act on notification of a change of circumstances provided by the claimant;

- Benefits Agency or employment service error, e.g. the Benefits Agency makes a mistaken award of income support or income-based JSA;
- claimant error or claimant fraud, e.g. the claimant fails to inform the authority of a change in circumstance which he or she has a duty to report, such as the end of entitlement to income support or income-based JSA; or
- other reasons, e.g. the claimant obtains a retrospective award of a council tax discount and this reduces the council tax liability for that period.

Technical and advance overpayments are amounts of CTB or rent rebates (but not rent allowances) that are paid in advance by way of a rebate to an account.

**18.9** Consecutive overpayments may result from different causes. For example, the claimant may fail to notify the authority that his or her earnings have increased. The authority may then delay acting on that information once it is informed. In such a case the cause and amount of each overpayment must be separately identified.

## Recoverable overpayments

HBR 91(3), 99(1),(2) CTBR 84(1),(2),(3)

**18.10** An overpayment of a rent allowance payment on account may, where there is ongoing benefit once entitlement has been decided, be recovered whatever the cause of the overpayment. An overpayment of CTB may be due to a retrospective reduction in the claimant's council tax as a result of a delayed award of transitional relief, a discount or a disability reduction. Such overpayments are recoverable in all cases. All other amounts that have been overpaid are recoverable except where they are due to official error. Even an official error overpayment is recoverable if:

- the claimant, someone acting on his or her behalf, or the person to whom the payment was made, could reasonably have been expected to realise that an overpayment was taking place at the time of payment or upon receipt of any notification relating to the payment; or
- it is an amount of rent rebate or CTB that has been overpaid in respect of a period following the date of the review that identified overpayment.

HBR 99(3) CTBR 84(3)

**18.11** An official error is a mistake, whether in the form of an act or omission made by the authority, an external contractor acting for the authority, the Department of Social Security; the Department for Education and Employment; or the Commissioners of the Inland Revenue, or a person providing services to either Department or to the Commissioners. The definition of an official error does not include circumstances where the claimant, or someone acting on the claimant's behalf, or the person to whom payment has been made, caused or materially contributed to that error. In *R v Cambridge City Council, ex parte Sier,* QBD, 28/2/2001, it was argued that the Benefit Agency's failure to notify the authority that IS had ceased meant that there was a non-recoverable 'official error' overpayment. The Court held that whilst it was an official error it was the claimant's failure to inform the authority of a change in his circumstances that caused the overpayment. Such overpayments are categorised as claimant or third party error and are recoverable. An official error occurs, for example, where there is a mistaken award of IS by the Benefits Agency or where the authority put the wrong information into its computer or delayed acting upon information it had received.

**18.12** Where the claimant, a person acting on his or her behalf, or the person to whom the payment has been made, could reasonably have been expected to realise that it was an overpayment at the time of payment, or of any notice relating to that payment, an official error overpayment is recoverable. In *R v Liverpool City Council ex parte Griffiths,* (1990) 22 HLR 312 QBD, it was held that this rule requires the reasonable expectation, not that a payment might be an overpayment, but that it was an overpayment. A decision regarding recoverability requires examination of all the relevant facts. If, for example, the claimant has learning difficulties it may be that he or she could not reasonably have been expected to realise that it was an overpayment.

**18.13** If the claimant, etc, did not have the information necessary to know that benefit was being overpaid at the time of payment or notification relating to the payment, then an official error overpayment is not recoverable. The DSS (HB/CCB(90)23) advises that when in rent rebate cases credits are made to the landlord's rent accounts before the claimant receives a written notification of the award, the claimant cannot know if he is being overpaid unless or until he receives written notification of the rebate. This will also be the case, for example, where HB is paid direct to a landlord (unless the landlord could reasonably have been expected to realise it was an overpayment) or CTB is paid into a council tax account. The claimant and/or any other person affected may apply for a revision of the authority's decision that an overpayment is recoverable or appeal the decision.

**18.14** The rules regarding HB/CTB overpayments differ from those applicable to the other major welfare benefits. With the latter the power to recover rests on the adjudicating authority being satisfied that a material misrepresentation or non-disclosure has been proved.

## Working out the amount of a recoverable overpayment

HBR 104 **18.15** The current rules setting out how the amount of a recoverable overpayment is calculated were introduced from 2nd October 2000. They apply to all recoverable overpayments:

- identified on or after that date; or
- identified prior to that date but not calculated until on or after that date.

**18.16** The amount of a recoverable overpayment is the difference between the benefit the claimant was actually paid and the amount they should have been paid had a claim for benefit been determined on the basis of the correct application of the law to the true facts of the case over the same period. An example follows para. 19.46.

**18.17** To arrive at the amount of the recoverable overpayment, the authority works out:

- the amount of benefit actually paid over the period of the overpayment; LESS
- any amount of benefit which should have been decided to be payable over any or all of that same period:
  - on the basis of the claim as presented to the authority; or
  - on the basis of the claim as it would have appeared had any misrepresentation or non-disclosure been remedied before the authority made a decision on it; or
  - on the basis of the claim as it would have appeared if any change of circumstances had been notified at the time that change occurred.

**18.18** Where the change in question is the cessation of income support or income-based jobseeker's allowance the amount of HB/CTB that should have been paid will be taken as the amount that would have been payable as if that change had not brought the HB/CTB period to an end. The claimant must provide evidence of their actual circumstances during the overpayment period before the authority can deduct any underlying entitlement when calculating the net amount of the recoverable overpayment for that period. These rules only apply for the purpose of calculating the amount of a recoverable overpayment. They do not apply for any other purpose whatsoever.

**Example: The amount of a recoverable overpayment**

For simplicity of explanation the following example refers only to HB. The same rules apply to the calculation of a CTB overpayment.

At the beginning of November 2000 the claimant was on JSA(IB) and receiving HB of £120 per week. She failed to tell the Council when she went into full-time work and came off JSA(IB) on the 23 rd November 2000.

When her JSA(IB) ended this should have brought her HB period to an end on the 26th November 2000.

The authority did not discover that the claimant's JSA(IB) had ended until advised by the Benefits Agency some time after the event. As a result, the claimant continued to receive £120 per week HB for a further 10 weeks after her HB claim had legally ended. This resulted in a total gross overpayment for the ten weeks of £1200. Having been notified that JSA(IB) had ended on a particular past date the authority needed to:

- end the current HB period;
- calculate the gross overpayment of £1200;
- invite a new claim for HB; and
- request the required additional information from the claimant in conjunction with issuing the new claim form.

The authority needs to establish the relevant facts during the period of the overpayment, e.g. claimant's earnings from paid employment, paid child care arrangements, etc, in order to calculate any possible underlying entitlement during the period of the overpayment.

If the claimant had not responded or had failed to supply the relevant information and evidence for the period covered by the overpayment then the authority would have calculated and determined the overpayment based on the information available to it. In this case this would have meant that there was no underlying entitlement and that the gross overpayment of £1200 would have been recoverable.

The claimant, however, submits her new claim form together with the information and evidence that the authority had requested to enable it to calculate the underlying entitlement during the period of the overpayment.

In calculating the recoverable overpayment the authority has to deduct the amount of HB the claimant would have received on the basis of her

> changed circumstances had her benefit period not been brought to an end by the cessation of her income-based job-seeker's allowance.
>
> The authority determined that during the 10 weeks overpayment period the claimant would have been paid £100 per week HB on the basis of her low income from work. This gave her a total underlying entitlement of £1000 for this period.
>
> The authority deducts the £1000 underlying entitlement from the £1200 gross overpayment, resulting in a total recoverable overpayment of £200.

HBR 104(b)
CTBR 90(b)

**18.19** During the period of the overpayment the claimant may have paid money into a local authority rent or council tax account above his or her erroneous liability. If this is the case such payments may be deducted for the purpose of working out the amount of the recoverable overpayment.

> **Example: Claimant has continued to pay rent**
>
> A council tenant's eligible rent is £45. From week 1, he is unemployed, claiming JSA(IB) and in receipt of maximum HB of £45. The claimant starts work in week 5 and is no longer entitled to any HB from week 6. The claimant fails to inform the authority of the change of circumstance but starts to pay full rent from week 6. However, HB continues to be paid at £45 per week until week 10.
>
> For the purpose of working out the amount of the recoverable overpayment (from weeks 6 to 10) the authority may deduct the amount of the additional rent paid (£45 per week) over the erroneous liability (nil per week) from the overpaid HB.

## DIMINISHING CAPITAL RULE

HBR 103(1)
CTBR 89(1)

**18.20** Where the overpayment arose as:

- a result of a misrepresentation or failure to disclose relevant information relating to the claimant's capital, or that of a child or young person; or
- an error relating to capital (other than a non-recoverable official error, paras. 18.10-11); and in either case
- the overpayment is in respect of more than 13 weeks;

the authority must treat the amount of the capital as having been reduced by the amount overpaid during the first and each subsequent period of 13 benefit weeks for the purpose of working out the overpayment.

**Example: Diminishing capital rule**

The claimant has been in receipt of a £5.73 rent allowance each week since 25th May 1998. She visits the authority's housing benefit office on 15th October 1998, to query the amount of benefit she is receiving.

During the course of her interview it emerges that she had accidentally forgotten to include on her original application form £250 which she has retained throughout the period in a building society account. When this amount is added to her previously declared and still existing capital of £15,783 it brings the amount that counts for HB purposes to £16,033. With capital above the maximum limit there has been no entitlement to benefit from the start of the claim.

The overpayment arose due to the claimant's failure to disclose a material fact relating to capital and is recoverable. The overpayment has taken place over 21 benefit weeks so the diminishing capital rule applies. There is only one complete 13-week period.

The amount of HB overpaid by the end of 13 benefit weeks is: £5.73 x 13 = £74.49

With the application of the diminishing capital rule for the rest of the period of payment – and for the sole purpose of calculating the overpayment – the claimant's capital is assumed to be £15,958.51, i.e.

| | |
|---|---|
| Claimant's capital | £16,033.00 |
| MINUS amount of overpaid HB during 13-week period | £74.49 |
| Claimant's assumed capital for purpose of calculating overpaid HB = | £15,958.51 |

The original calculation of HB had taken into account the declared capital of £15,783. The tariff income from the actual and 'diminished' capital amount is the same. Therefore, under the diminishing capital rule, no overpayment has occurred between the 14th and last week in which the benefit has been paid. The total amount of recoverable overpayment is £74.49.

The claimant still actually has capital of £16.033. She is not entitled to HB until such time as the amount of her capital falls below £16,000.01 (as would be the case if, for example, she repaid the overpayment).

**18.21** The reasoning behind this rule is that if the capital had been taken into account, so that the benefit was reduced or not awarded, the claimant's capital would in all probability have been reduced to meet his or her housing costs, council tax liability, or day-to-day living expenses.

HBR 103(2)
CTBR 89(2)

**18.22** This notional reduction of capital does not count for any other purpose, e.g. calculating entitlement.

## When should a recoverable overpayment be recovered?

**18.23** A recoverable overpayment may be recovered at the Council's discretion. The law says that such overpayments are recoverable and not that they must be recovered. The Department of Social Security advises:

> *'Authorities should note that a determination that an overpayment is recoverable must be quite separate from a decision to recover it. Due regard should be given to the circumstances relating to individual cases when deciding whether or not recovery is appropriate.' (DSS Guidance Manual, para. A7.23)*

**18.24** The authority is not obliged to make recoveries. The exercise of the discretionary power contained with the legislation is governed by a number of legal principles that are long established. Each and every individual case must be decided on its merits. This means that the authority must be satisfied that it is reasonable to make a recovery in the individual case. A person affected can ask the authority to revise its decision to recover a recoverable overpayment but the are no appeal rights against a decision as to the exercise of discretion to recover an overpayment. An authority which acted unreasonably or irrationally would be susceptible to judicial review.

## From whom may recovery be sought?

AA 75
NIAA 73
HBR 101
CTBR 86

**18.25** A recoverable HB/CTB overpayment may always be recovered from the claimant and/or the person to whom it was paid except in the circumstances set out below. It may, for example, be recovered from a landlord to whom HB has been paid direct. The Court of Appeal, in Warwick District Council v Freeman, 31st October 1994 (27 HLR 616), confirmed that a recoverable overpayment may be recovered from a landlord where the overpayment was paid directly to the landlord, even where the landlord did not contribute to, or have any knowledge of, the overpayment. Nonetheless, in exercising its choice whether to recover the overpayment from either the claimant or the landlord, the authority must act reasonably and take into account all relevant factors (paras. 1.48-49). Since October 1st 2001, however, HB overpayments should not be recovered from the landlord who has received the benefit direct where:

- the landlord has notified the authority or the DWP/Benefits Agency in writing that s/he suspects that there has been an overpayment;

- it appears to the authority that:
  - there are grounds for instituting proceedings against any person for an offence under section 111A or 112(1) of the Administration Act (dishonest or false representations for obtaining benefit);
  - there has been a deliberate failure to report a relevant change of circumstances and the overpayment occurred as a result of that deliberate failure
- the authority is satisfied that the landlord has not:
  - colluded with the claimant so as to cause the overpayment
  - acted, or neglected to act, in such a way so as to contribute to the period, or the amount, of the overpayment.

**18.26** Where an overpayment of HB has arisen due to a misrepresentation or failure to disclose a relevant fact by: HBR 101(1)(a)

- the claimant; or
- someone on his or her behalf such as an appointee or agent; or
- the person to whom a payment may be made such as a landlord;

then it may also be recovered from that person. This does not apply in the case of overpaid CTB.

**18.27** Where an HB overpayment has been made to a claimant who has a partner it may be deducted from HB payable or, in the case of a CTB overpayment, CTB allowed to the partner. This may only occur if the claimant and partner are members of the same household (para. 6.11) both at the date of the overpayment and the date it is recovered. HBR 101(2) CTBR 86(2)

**18.28** If a recoverable overpayment has been made to a deceased person recovery may be sought from the estate.

## Method of recovery

**18.29** Authorities may recover a recoverable overpayment via any lawful method but an overpayment of HB cannot be recovered from a payment of CTB or *vice versa.* The following are the main methods adopted by authorities: HBR 102, 105

(a) by deduction from on-going benefit;

(b) from arrears of HB or CTB which become payable while there is an outstanding overpayment;

(c) by deduction from certain social security benefits;

(d) by setting up a sundry debtors' account and billing for the overpayment;

(e) in the cases of CTB only, by adding the overpaid CTB on to the claimant's council tax account as an amount of council tax owing.

Only method (a) is available where the authority has chosen to recover the overpayment from the claimant's partner (para. 18.27).

## RECOVERY FROM THE CLAIMANT BY DEDUCTIONS FROM BENEFIT PAID DIRECT TO A LANDLORD OR TO A COUNCIL TENANT'S RENT ACCOUNT

**18.30** Where the authority has determined to recover an overpayment from the claimant and is recovering it by deduction from his or her on-going benefit paid direct to a landlord or, in the case of a council tenant, in the form of a reduction to the rebate to the rent account, this counts not as recovery from the landlord but from the claimant. The landlord is not a 'person affected' and does not have any right to apply for a revision of the decision or appeal it. The claimant must make up the subsequent shortfall in HB to avoid rent arrears accruing (GM para. A7.39 Example 1). Any such arrears are arrears of rent and the landlord should pursue recovery as such.

**18.31** Authorities should not recover overpaid rent rebates by debiting the rent account of the claimant so that he or she is placed in rent arrears. Such arrears cannot, for example, be recovered by possession proceedings as they are not amounts of rent lawfully due and the tenant-claimant would have a defence against any such action. Authorities may, however, use their rent accounting systems to control recovery of overpayments. The DSS advises that authorities should be able to distinguish 'recovered' overpaid HB from arrears of rent. Authorities should also make it clear to claimants that the payments being sought represent overpaid HB (GM paras. A7.40-43) and should be able to distinguish payments the claimant makes to cover the overpayment and payments of rent.

## RECOVERY FROM THE LANDLORD BY DEDUCTIONS FROM BENEFIT PAID DIRECT TO THE LANDLORD

AA s 75(5)
NIAA 73(5)

**18.32** In a rent allowance case the authority may, in appropriate circumstances, decide to recover the overpayment from the landlord. In such a case two of the methods of recovery available are:

- deduction from HB paid to the landlord on behalf of other tenants/claimants to whom the overpayment does not relate; and.
- deduction from HB paid to the landlord on behalf of the claimant to whom the overpayment relates.

## RECOVERY FROM THE HB OF TENANT(S) UNRELATED TO THE OVERPAYMENT

**18.33** Where the authority recovers an overpayment by making deductions from the HB paid to the landlord for a tenant to whom the overpayment does not relate, that tenant is always deemed to have paid rent to the value of the recovered sum.

In these circumstances the landlord is a 'person affected' but the tenant/claimant from whose benefit the deductions are being made is not. Consequently such tenant/claimants should not receive an overpayment notifications on this matter. Nor do they have the right to apply for a revision of the decision or appeal it. The authority should, however, have notified all claimants and landlords at the time direct payments commenced that:

- it had the power to make deductions from the amount paid to the landlord in order to recover an overpayment of benefit relating to another tenant; and
- that in such a case the claimant's rent liability will have been discharged to the full value of his or her HB entitlement.

## RECOVERY FROM THE LANDLORD BY DEDUCTIONS FROM THE HB OF THE CLAIMANT TO WHOM THE OVERPAYMENT RELATES

**18.34** Where the authority has decided to recover an overpayment from the landlord, but has chosen to do this by deduction from HB paid to the landlord on behalf of the claimant to whom the overpayment relates, then both the landlord and claimant are persons affected. In other words, in such a case the landlord and claimant may apply for a revision of the decision or appeal it. Again, normally the claimant must make up the subsequent shortfall in HB to avoid rent arrears. It is unlikely that an authority would adopt this method in these circumstances except in cases of landlord fraud. Where the landlord: AA s 75(6) NIAA 73(6)

- has agreed to pay a 30 per cent penalty (para 18.57) as an alternative to prosecution; or
- has been prosecuted in relation to that overpayment,

the claimant to whom the overpayment relates is deemed to have paid the rent to the value of the recovered sum.

**18.35** In the above circumstances the authority must write to the claimant and landlord: SI 1997 No. 243 NISR 1997 No. 4

- explaining the process; and
- stating that the landlord has no right to that sum from the tenant and that the tenant's obligation to the landlord is deemed to have been met by the amount recovered.

**18.36** The DSS points out (HB/CTB A1/98, para. 16) that the legislation imposes no penalty upon landlords who attempt to recover such overpayment or evict a tenant due to non-closure of the tenant's liability but that the Courts have been advised that landlords would be in breach of the relevant legislation if they attempted this action.

### METHODS BY WHICH THE LANDLORD MAY RECOVER THE REPAID OVERPAYMENT FROM THE CLAIMANT

HBR 93(2)
NIHBR 93(1A)

**18.37** The landlord may seek to recover the sum repaid to the authority from the claimant to whom the overpayment relates. The exception to this rule is where the claimant's obligation to the landlord is deemed to have been discharged (paras. 18.33-36). Where the claimant is a current tenant the non-local authority landlord is able to treat the sum it has repaid to the authority as rent arrears and has the ultimate sanction of eviction to secure payment. Where the claimant to whom the overpayment relates is no longer the landlord's tenant the landlord may invoice the former tenant and then pursue the debt through normal civil debt recovery procedures.

### RECOVERY FROM OTHER SOCIAL SECURITY BENEFITS

HBR 105
CTBR 91

**18.38** Where methods (a), (b) or (e) in para 18.29 are not possible, the authority may request the Benefits Agency to recover any overpayment from most social security benefits payable to any person identified in para. 18.26. It may not be recovered from guardians allowance, child benefit, war pensions or tax credits. The Benefits Agency will recover overpayments from social security benefits where it is:

- requested by the authority to do so; and
- satisfied that the overpayment arose as a result of a misrepresentation or failure to disclose a material fact by, or on behalf of, the claimant; or by some other person to whom a payment of HB/CTB has been made; and
- that person is receiving sufficient amounts of one or more benefits to enable deductions to be made.

## Rate of recovery

**18.39** The current rules, which prescribe the maximum permitted rate of recovery where deductions are to be made from a claimant's on-going housing benefit, came into effect from 2 October 2000. The amounts were uprated in April 2001. There are two maximum permitted rates of deduction depending on whether or not the overpayment has arisen as a result of fraud.

HBR 102(2)-(5)

**18.40** Where the claimant has been found guilty of fraud; or admitted fraud after caution; or agreed to pay a penalty (para. 18.58) the maximum permitted weekly deduction is £10.80 plus 50% of any of the earned income disregards shown in table 16.1 or any disregarded regular charitable or voluntary payments (para. 15.80) or war disablement pension or war widows pension (para. 15.28) if they apply to the claim. In any other case the maximum permitted weekly deduction is £8.10 plus 50% of the income disregards previously identified if they apply to the claim. In both cases the amounts are subject to an overall maximum deduction which does not reduce the balance of benefit payable to less than 50p. The Council should deduct less than the maximum permitted amount in any case where, after considering the claimant's all of the claimant's circumstances this is justified in order to avoid undue hardship.

**18.41** In deciding the rate of recovery from organisations the authority has the power to effect large recoveries in a single lump sum but it will often not be appropriate to do so. The authority should act reasonably in deciding a rate of recovery. In particular, as a matter of good practice, the authority should discuss the rate of recovery with the organisation concerned to ensure the rate of recovery does not undermine that organisation's financial stability or essential activities.

## Information to be provided to claimants, landlords, etc

**18.42** When the authority decides that a recoverable HB/CTB overpayment has occurred, and exercises its discretion to recover it, a letter should be sent to the person from whom recovery is sought and any other person affected by the decision. So, for example, if the authority decides to recover from the landlord, it must send letters to both the claimant and the landlord. This should happen within 14 days of the decision being made or as soon as reasonably practicable thereafter. HBR 77(1)(b) CTBR 67(1)(b)

**18.43** Overpayment letters to claimants, landlords and other persons affected must state: HBR sch 6 part V CTBR sch 6 part

- the fact that there is a recoverable overpayment;
- the reason why there is a recoverable overpayment;
- the amount of the recoverable overpayment;
- how the amount was calculated;
- the benefit weeks to which the recoverable overpayment relates;
- where recovery of HB is to be made by deduction from future HB, the amount of that deduction;
- in the case of overpaid CTB, the method of recovery to be adopted;
- the person's right to request a written statement setting out the authority's reasons for its decision on any matter set out in the letter and the manner and time in which to do so; and
- the person's right to apply for a revision of the decisions or appeal them and the manner and time in which to do so; and
- any other appropriate matter, e.g. the opportunity to make representations with regard to hardship.

HBR 77(1)
sch 6 para 14(2)

**18.44** Where the authority is seeking to recovery an overpayment from another claimant's direct payments to the landlord, the decision notice to that landlord must also identify both:

- the original claimant on whose behalf the recoverable amount was paid to that landlord; and
- the other claimant from whose benefit recovery is going to be made.

SI 1997 No. 2435
NISR 1977 No. 454

**18.45** Where the authority has decided to recover a recoverable overpayment from a rent allowance paid direct to the landlord in respect of any tenant; and the landlord in that case has either:

- been convicted of fraud; or
- agreed to pay a penalty as an alternative to prosecution in relation to the overpayment in question,

the authority must also notify both the landlord and the tenant that:

- the overpayment which it has recovered, or decided to recover, is one for which the landlord has been convicted of fraud or has agreed to pay a penalty; and
- any tenant from whose benefit the recovery is made must be deemed to have paid his or her rent to the value of the amount recovered.

**18.46** The DSS advises (GM para. A7.51) that overpayment notifications should include an invitation to the person in question to either make a full repayment or negotiate some other arrangement within 28 days. A more appropriate period in fact is the six weeks normally allowed for a request for an internal review to be made.

## DEFECTIVE NOTIFICATION

**18.47** Failure by authorities to notify persons affected clearly and correctly of decisions about overpayments has caused problems for claimants, landlords and authorities. Experience has shown that overpayment notification letters, particularly those to landlords, are often defective in a number of ways. A significant number, for example, fail to give an adequate and intelligible reason why there is a recoverable overpayment or advise landlords of their appeal rights. In *R v Thanet District Council, ex parte Warren Court Hotels Ltd,* QBD, 6.4.2000, for example, it was held that the phrase 'change of circumstances' was not itself a statement of the reason why there was a recoverable overpayment, since it covered a multitude of possible reasons. The failure to provide the required information constitutes maladministration. Additionally authorities that have deficient notifications should be aware that they are undermining the legal basis of their debt recovery action (*Warwick District Council v Freeman* (1994) CA 27 HLR 616). There is no legally recoverable debt until such time as the authority makes the appropriate determinations and issues the required notification.

**18.48** A more recent Court of Appeal decision (*Haringey London Borough Council v Awaritefe,* CA, [1999] All ER (D) 540), while agreeing with the approach taken in Warwick and Freeman, ruled that where the failure to provide a valid notification was only trivial, and no substantial harm was caused as a result, the authority was still entitled to pursue recovery of the overpaid amount.

**18.49** *Jones v Waveney District Council* (1999) CA 1/12/99 concerned a case where the authority failed to follow the statutory procedures provided and had recovered an alleged overpayment from the landlord by making deductions from benefit due to him on other properties. The Court, applying Warwick and Freeman, held that the landlord was entitled to bring a county court action to recover from the authority the amount that the authority had recovered illegally. This point may be contrasted with the decision in *Norwich City Council v Stringer,* CA, (2001) 33 HLR 15, where the Court held that the landlord could not seek restitution of the sums paid to the Council on the basis that if the landlord had not repaid the money the Council would have been unable to recover it.

## The pursuit of recovery

**18.50** The DSS advises (GM para. A7.28) that 'it is for authorities to decide how far to pursue recovery…' In the past many authorities have failed to pursue recovery actively if legal proceedings were required. Where an authority has decided an overpayment is recoverable, exercised its discretion and decided to recover, the DSS expects it to make a serious attempt at recovery. The GM (para. A7.28) advises that at least two letters requesting payment should be issued, that an interview will often be appropriate and that a home visit might be cost-effective. As a matter of good practice authorities should include, in their recovery work, procedures that ensure that the claimant is receiving all the HB/CTB and other benefits to which he or she may be entitled, with the aim of reducing the overpayment and increasing resources to meet the debt. AA 75(7), 76(6)

**18.51** The authority may take civil proceedings for debt in an appropriate court. The DSS advises that authorities should consider civil proceedings 'where attempts to achieve recovery by other means have failed and there is good reason to believe that the debtor can afford to make repayments' (GM para. A7.39iv).

### SIMPLIFIED DEBT RECOVERY PROCEDURE

**18.52** The authority has the power to recover HB overpayments by execution in the County Court in England and Wales as if under a court order; and in Scotland as if it were an extract registered decree arbitral. AA 75 (7) NIAA 73(7)

**18.53** In England and Wales this procedure allows an HB overpayment determination to be registered directly as an Order of the Court without the need to bring a separate action. This procedure remains intact under the Civil Procedure Rules 1998 introduced in April 1999. The authority applies to the Court on a standard County Court form (N 322A), attaching a copy of the overpayment determination notice and accompanied by the relevant fee. The DSS advise (DSS A 59/98, para 8) that the overpayment notification can only be used as proof of debt where it complies fully with the requirements for such notifications under Schedule 6 of the benefit regulations (para. 18.43). An Officer of the Court then makes an Order and a copy is sent to the authority and the debtor. Once an Order has been made the normal methods of enforcement are available to the authority, i.e. attachment of earnings, a garnishee order allowing the authority to obtain money owed to the debtor by a third party, a warrant of execution against goods executed by the County Court bailiff or a charging order normally against land.

**18.54** There is no provision for any appeal against an Order made by the 'proper officer' of the Court. Consequently where the claimant or landlord disputes the determination that there is a recoverable overpayment or from whom it should be recovered this is a matter which can only be taken up by applying for a revision of, or appealing, the relevant decision(s) (Chapter 19). However, where, for example overpayment notification is defective or appeal rights ignored by the authority an application for the setting aside of the Order can be made to the Court.

**18.55** In Scotland the HB determination is immediately enforceable as if it were an extract registered decree arbitral. There is no requirement to register the overpayment determination with the Sheriff Court. The usual methods of enforcement are available, i.e: arrestment of earnings; poinding and warrant sale; arrestment of moveable property and inhibition of heritable property.

## Overpayments and fraud

**18.56** The subject of HB/CTB fraud and the authority's response goes beyond the remit of this chapter. The interested general reader is referred to the Audit Commission's *Countering housing benefit fraud: a management handbook* (1997) whilst officers working for an authority should also refer to the DSS's *Local authority fraud investigators manual* and the DSS Fraud Circulars. Overpayments are, however, often related to charges of fraud. The effective recovery of overpayments is one tool in the authority's anti-fraud strategy and as anti-fraud work increases, in the short term at least, the number and amount of overpayments that are identified by the authority increases. Additionally the authority's discretion to levy an administrative penalty (a fine), as an alternative to bringing a prosecution for fraud, is directly related to the question of overpayments.

## THE ADMINISTRATIVE PENALTY

**18.57** The penalty is equivalent to 30 per cent of the recoverable overpayment due from the person concerned and is recoverable by the same methods available to the authority as when seeking recovery of the overpayment. AA 115A NIAA 109A

## WHEN WILL A PENALTY APPLY?

**18.58** The authority has the discretion to levy the penalty as an alternative to bringing a prosecution for fraud. Prosecutions for HB/CTB offences are in fact extremely rare. In 1995/96 over 50 per cent of authorities failed to secure one successful prosecution for fraud. In 1998-99 there were approximately 800 successful prosecutions for HB fraud in the UK. *(Hansard, Commons Written Answers, 04/07/2000, 353 c156W.)*

**18.59** The question of a penalty cannot arise until the authority has decided that an overpayment is recoverable under the regulations and the person from whom recovery is sought has been properly notified. The authority then has the discretion to invite a person to pay a penalty where it is satisfied that: AA 115A (1) NIAA 109A(1)

- the overpayment was caused by an 'act or omission' on the part of that person; and
- there are grounds for bringing a prosecution against that person for fraud relating to that overpayment under the Social Security Administration Act or any other enactment.

**18.60** Where the conditions for a penalty apply it can only be levied with the agreement of the person concerned. However, if that person refuses to agree to pay a penalty they could be liable to have fraud proceedings brought against them instead. AA 115A(2)(a) NIAA 109(2)(a)

## CALCULATION OF THE PENALTY

**18.61** The penalty is equivalent to 30 per cent of the recoverable overpayment due from the person concerned. Where an ongoing overpayment started before the penalty provision came into force, a penalty can only be calculated on the amount of recoverable overpayment that accrued after 18 December 1997. (See also section 25(7) of the Social Security Administration (Fraud) Act 1997.) AA 115A(3) NIAA 109A(3)

## AGREEING TO PAY A PENALTY

**18.62** It is up to the authority to decide how any agreement to pay a penalty will be made. However, where the authority considers that a penalty may be appropriate in any particular case it must give a written penalty notice to the person liable for prosecution.

**18.63** This notice advises them:

- that they may be invited to agree to pay a penalty; and
- that if they make the agreement to do this in the manner specified by the authority (e.g. by signing a standard written undertaking) no fraud proceedings will be brought against them for the overpayment in question.

SI 1997 No. 2813
NISR 1997 No. 514

**18.64** The penalty notice must, by law, contain the following points of information about the penalty system:

- the manner specified by the authority by which the person may agree to pay a penalty;
- that the penalty only applies to an overpayment which is recoverable under section 75 or 76 of the Social Security Administration Act 1992 (s73 of the Northern Ireland Act);
- that the penalty only applies where it appears to the authority that the overpayment was caused by an act or omission by the person and that there are grounds for commencing criminal proceedings for an offence relating to the overpayment;
- the penalty is 30 per cent of the overpayment, is payable in addition to repayment of the overpayment and is recoverable by the same methods as those by which the overpayment is recoverable;
- a person who agrees to pay a penalty may withdraw the agreement within 28 days (including the date of the agreement) by notifying the authority in the manner specified by the authority (i.e. in writing or by using a notice provided by the authority for this specific purpose, etc);
- where the person withdraws their agreement, any amount of the penalty which has already been recovered will be repaid and the person will no longer be immune from proceedings for an offence;
- where it is decided on revision or appeal (or in accordance with regulations) that the overpayment is not recoverable or due, any amount of the penalty which has already been recovered will be repaid;
- where the amount of the overpayment is revised on revision or appeal, except as covered by a new agreement to pay the revised penalty, any amount of the penalty which has already been recovered will be repaid and the person will no longer be immune from proceedings for an offence; and
- the payment of a penalty does not give the person immunity from prosecution in relation to any other overpayment or any offence not relating to an overpayment.

# 19 Appeals

**19.1** New arrangements for changing and appealing HB and CTB decisions were introduced from 2nd July 2001. These arrangements are similar and in many instances identical to the arrangements that apply to other social security benefits. Chapter 17 describes the related decision-making arrangements. This chapter describes what can be done if a claimant (or in certain cases other people such as a landlord or a landlord's agent) disagrees with the authority's decision or simply does not understand it. The system contains a right of appeal from the authority's decisions to an independent legally qualified appeal tribunal. This tribunal replaces the former HB/CTB review board. See Chapter 21 of the 2001-2002 edition of the Guide for a description of the transitional rules and saving rules that made provision for the transfer of outstanding cases in the former system of review/ further review on the 1st July 2001.

## The legislative framework

**19.2** Section 68 and Schedule 7 of the Child Support, Pensions and Social Security Act, 2000 (abbreviated to CSPSSA) provides for:

- a right of appeal from the authority's HB/CTB decisions to an appeal tribunal administered by the Appeals Service agency;
- a right of appeal from a decision of the tribunal, on a point of law, to a Social Security Commissioner.

**19.3** The Housing Benefit and Council Tax Benefit (Decisions and Appeals) Regulations 2001 (SI 2001 1002, in Northern Ireland SR 2001 No. 213) (abbreviated to DAR, NIDAR) set out in detail the procedures to be followed in the making of an appeal. The regulations cross-refer to the Social Security and Child Support (Decisions and Appeals) Regulations 1999 (SI 1999 No. 991, in Northern Ireland SR 1999 No. 162) (abbreviated to DAR99, NIDAR99) where they relate to the powers and procedures of appeal tribunals. The Housing Benefit and Council Tax Benefit (Decisions and Appeals) (Transitional and Savings) Regulations 2001 (SI 2001 No. 1264, in Northern Ireland SR 2001 No. 214) deal with the treatment of any business outstanding on the 2nd July. Social Security Commissioners (Procedure) Regulations 1999 (S.I. 1999/1495, in Northern Ireland SR 2001 No. 225) have been amended by the Social Security Commissioners (Procedure) (Amendment) Regulations 2001 (SI 2001 No. 1095) to extend them to cover HB/CTB appeals.

# Overview of the appeal process

## APPEAL TRIBUNALS AND THE APPEALS SERVICE

**19.4** The appeal tribunal that decides HB/CTB appeals is part of an independent tribunal body responsible for hearing appeals on decisions on social security, child support, vaccine damage, tax credit and compensation recovery. Appeal tribunals are one arm of the Appeal Service (TAS). This also consists of an executive agency responsible for the administration of appeals.

## THE DISPUTES PROCESS

**19.5** Whilst not a term contained in the legislation the matters described in this chapter are often referred to as part of a 'disputes process'. In the first instance a person affected (para. 19.11) may seek to have a disputed decision changed via one of two routes:

- by requesting the authority to look at it again (i.e. apply for a revision); or
- by making an appeal against it.

**19.6** In both cases applications must be made in writing and sent to the authority normally within one calendar month of the date the authority notified the relevant decision. If the first route is taken, once the person affected has the result of their application for revision they normally have one calendar month from the date that was sent out in which to appeal. If the second route is taken the authority will normally take the opportunity provided by receipt of an appeal to reconsider the disputed decision.

**19.7** There are three ways in which the authority may change a disputed decision. It can be:

- revised – see Chapter 19);
- superseded – where it cannot be revised (see Chapter 19);
- changed on appeal.

**19.8** As mentioned above when an appeal is received, the authority may consider whether the decision can be revised. If it can be revised to the advantage of the person affected, the authority should revise the decision and the appeal lapses. This applies even though the person affected may not receive all that has been asked for in the appeal. The person affected then has a fresh decision with a fresh dispute period, and fresh rights to apply for a revision or appeal.

**19.9** From the person affected's perspective the appeal should automatically proceed to an independent appeal tribunal if:

- the decision is not revised by the authority, or
- the decision is revised, but not in the person affected's favour, or
- the decision is superseded by the authority.

**19.10** There are no statutory performance standards relating to how quickly the appeal tribunal should hear a case. Appeals take on average 14 weeks from the time the Appeal Service receives the completed enquiry form (TAS 1) from the person affected (paras 19.31-32) to the date of the tribunal hearing (The Appeals Service: 'Putting Service First': A Statement of the Appeals Service Aims and Standards).

## Who may appeal?

DAR Reg 3

**19.11** The people who have a right to appeal an HB/CTB decision are referred to as 'persons affected'. Someone is a 'person affected' by a decision where their rights, duties or obligations are affected by it. Additionally, to be a 'person affected' they must be:

- a claimant;
- in the case of a person who is unable for the time being to act:
  - a receiver appointed by the Court of Protection with power to claim, or as the case may be, receive benefit on his behalf,
  - in Scotland, a tutor, curator or other guardian acting or appointed in terms of law administering that person's estate, or
  - an attorney with a general power or a power to receive benefit appointed by the person liable to make those payments under the Powers of Attorney Act 1971 or the Enduring Powers of Attorney Act 1985;
- a person appointed by the authority to act for the claimant;
- the landlord (or agent where a decision has been made by the authority under regulation 93 (circumstances in which payment is to be made to a landlord) or 94 (circumstances in which payment may be made to a landlord) of the Housing Benefit Regulations (where payment of benefit is to the landlord's agent – the agent is the person affected); or
- a person from whom the authority decides that an HB/CTB 'overpayment' is recoverable.

DAR Reg 20(7)(b)

**19.12** An appeal made by someone who is not a 'person affected' is not 'duly made' and should be identified as such by the authority. It will be turned down by the tribunal member because it fails to satisfy the legal requirement. The tribunal member should inform the appellant and the authority of the determination.

## Decisions that may be appealed

CSPSSA Sch 7, para. 6(1)(a), (b)

**19.13** A person affected has a right of appeal (via the authority) to an independent appeal tribunal against any relevant decision (whether as originally made or as revised or superseded) the authority makes on a claim for, or on an award of, HB/CTB; and certain other prescribed decisions.

**19.14** Table 19.1 sets out other decisions that cannot be appealed. CSPSSA Sch 7, para 6, DAR reg. 16(1) and Sch

## TABLE 19.1: DECISIONS WHICH CANNOT BE APPEALED

- Any decision terminating or reducing the amount of a person's HB made in consequence of a decision made in relation to a work-focused interview in a ONE pilot area;
- Any decision made by the authority as to the application or operation of a local scheme (i.e. disregard of war disablement and war widows' pensions);
- Any decision made by the authority that adopts a decision of a rent officer (i.e. the authority's decision regarding the maximum rent where the authority is bound by the figures produced by the rent officer);
- Any decision as to the amount of benefit to which a person is entitled in a case in which the amount is determined by the rate of benefit provided for by law;
- A decision made by virtue of, or as a consequence of any of the provisions in Part X of the main HB Regulations or Part VIII of the main CTB Regulations (claims) *except* a decision regarding:
  - the date of claim (including backdating);
- A decision made under any of the provisions in Part XII (Payments) *except* a decision regarding:
  - adjustments to payment on account of rent allowance to take account of an under or overpayment;
  - the circumstances in which payment is to be made to a landlord;
  - the circumstances in which payment may be made to a landlord;
- A decision made by virtue of, or as a consequence of any of the provisions in Part XIII (overpayments) of the main HB Regulations or Part XI (excess benefit) of the main CTB Regulations *except* a decision regarding:
  - recoverable overpayments;
  - person from whom recovery may be sought;
  - diminution of capital;
  - sums to be deducted in calculating recoverable overpayments;
- A decision as to the exercise of discretion to recover an 'overpayment';
- A decision involving issues that arise on appeal to the Commissioners or the courts in other cases;
- A decision relating to the suspension of benefit or payment following a suspension.

**19.15** In appropriate cases certain of the non-appealable decisions set out in Table 19.1 can be revised or superseded. For example the claimant or landlord could request the authority to revise its discretionary decision to recover a recoverable overpayment in a case of hardship. If an appeal is made against one of the decisions set out in Table 19.1 it should be identified as 'out of jurisdiction' by the authority and struck out by the appeal tribunal clerk or member. Were the authority to act irrationally, unreasonably or in bad faith in relation to many of these non-appealable decisions it would be susceptible to judicial review or a complaint of maladministration.

## Notification of appealable decisions to persons affected

DAR Reg 10 **19.16** The authority has an obligation to notify its appealable decisions (para. 19.13) to all persons affected. The notification should set out

- the decision against which the right of appeal lies;
- the right to request the Council to provide them with a written statement of the reasons for that decision – in a case where the notice does not include a statement of reasons;
- the right of appeal against that decision.

### OBTAINING A WRITTEN STATEMENT EXPLAINING THE DECISION

If no written statement is included in the notification of the decision, a person affected may request one at any time. The authority must then, 'so far as practicable', provide one within 14 days.

## Making an appeal

**19.17** Authorities are expected as a matter of good practice to make available forms on which an appeal may be made. An appeal may also be accepted in a letter. To be properly made an appeal should meet the conditions set out in Table 19.2 and normally made within one month of the date of notification of the decision against which it is made. Out of time appeals may be made in special circumstances but must be made at the latest within 13 calendar months of the date of notification of the decision. Such out of time applications should describe the special circumstances that caused the delay. Where an appeal form is not used the person seeking the appeal is advised to head their letter 'Appeal' and use the phrase 'I wish to appeal against…' in the body of the letter. In this way the authority should not mistake it for an application for revision (para. 19.5).

**TABLE 19.2: NECESSARY ATTRIBUTES FOR A VALID APPEAL** DAR Reg 20(1)

The appeal must:

- be in writing on a form approved for the purpose by the authority or in such other form (e.g. letter) as the authority may accept; *and*
- be signed by the person who has a right of appeal; *and*
- be delivered, by whatever means (e.g. post, fax, e-mail) to the authority, or in a case to which the work-focused interviews rules apply – a ONE office; *and*
- contain details of the grounds on which it is made (it is not enough, for example, for the claimant to say that they are unhappy with the decision – he or she must state why they think the decision is wrong); *and*
- contain sufficient particulars of the decision to enable that decision to be identified.

**19.18** An appeal made by someone who is not a 'person affected' is not 'duly made' and should be identified as such by the authority. It will be turned down by a legally qualified tribunal member because it fails to satisfy the legal requirement. The tribunal member should inform the appellant and the Council of their determination. DAR Reg 20(7)(b)

## WITHDRAWING AN APPEAL

**19.19** An appeal may be withdrawn by an appellant in writing at any time before it is decided. If the authority has not sent the appeal to the Appeal Service any request to withdraw can be accepted by the authority. If the authority has referred the appeal to the Appeal Service any request from the appellant to withdraw the appeal must be sent to the Appeal Service. Reg 20(9)

## WHAT HAPPENS IF THE APPELLANT DIES DURING THE APPEAL PROCESS?

**19.20** If the appellant dies during the appeal process the authority may appoint anyone it thinks fit to proceed with the appeal in the place of the deceased. DAR Reg 21(1)

## Out of time appeals

DAR Reg 18(1) **19.21** An appeal must normally be made to the authority within one month of the date of notification of the decision against which it is made or in special circumstances 13 months. The decision is notified when it is posted or handed to the person affected.

DAR Reg 18(2) **19.22** In calculating the one month period, if the appellant has requested a written statement of reasons for the decision, no account is taken of the time the authority takes to provide that statement. The time taken begins with the day on which the authority received the request and ends with day on which that statement is provided.

DAR Reg 19(12) **19.23** It is a tribunal member who determines an application for an extension of the time limit. The authority should identify 'out of time' appeals and advise the Appeal Service as to whether or not it supports the 'out of time' appeal. As soon as practicable, a copy of the decision on the out of time appeal made by the tribunal member must be sent or given to principal parties to the proceedings.

### IN WHAT CIRCUMSTANCES SHOULD AN OUT OF TIME APPEAL BE ACCEPTED BY THE TRIBUNAL?

DAR Reg 19(4) **19.24** An effective application for an out-of-time appeal must:

- contain the grounds on which the extension of time is sought, and
- include details of any relevant special circumstances.

### NECESSARY CONDITIONS FOR AN OUT OF TIME APPEAL

DAR Reg 19(5) (a)-(b) **19.25** An application cannot be granted unless the tribunal member is satisfied that:

- there are reasonable prospects that the appeal will be successful; and
- it is in the interests of justice for the application to be granted.

DAR 19(6)(a) and 19(7) **19.26** It is not in the interests of justice to grant an application unless the tribunal member is satisfied that one of the following circumstances exists and is relevant to the application:

- the applicant or a spouse or dependant of the applicant has died or suffered serious illness; or
- the applicant is not resident in the United Kingdom; or
- normal postal services were disrupted; or
- some other special circumstances exist which are wholly exceptional and relevant to the application.

Additionally it must be as a result of those special circumstances, that it was not practicable for the application to be made within the time limit.

GUIDING PRINCIPLE

**19.27** In determining whether it is in the interests of justice to grant the application, the tribunal member must have regard to the principle that the later the application for the extension of time the more compelling the special circumstances for lateness must be. DAR Reg 19(8)

FACTORS THAT CANNOT BE TAKEN INTO ACCOUNT

**19.28** In determining whether it is in the interests of justice to grant an application, the tribunal member cannot take account of the following factors: DAR Reg 19(9)(a)-(b)

- that the applicant was unaware of or misunderstood the law or the time limits; or
- that a Commissioner or a court has taken a different view of the law from that previously understood and applied.

## The authority's action on receipt of an appeal

**19.29** On receipt of an appeal the authority should:

- consider revising the decision appealed against (para. 19.6);
- classify the appeal (i.e. not duly made, out of time, misconceived and/or involves a third party) if not revised to the person affected's advantage;
- send the appropriate forms (the pre-hearing enquiry form (TAS1) to the appellant and the notification of appeal (AT37) to the Appeal service) and its submission to:
    - the appellant; and
    - the Appeal Service.

**19.30** The authority must send all appeals to the Appeals service unless the appeal lapses following revision or is withdrawn by the appellant. The authority should indicate on the notification of appeal form (AT37) sent to the Appeal Service if it knows that eviction proceedings have begun. Such cases can be heard urgently by tribunals.

## The pre-hearing enquiry form (TAS1)

**19.31** The pre-hearing enquiry form the authority send to the person affected includes questions as to whether that person:

- wants to withdraw their appeal;
- wants an oral hearing (at which they and/or their representative can be present) or paper hearing (which does not require their attendance);

- agrees to having less than 14 days notice where they have opted for an oral hearing;
- has an outstanding appeal against another benefit decision; and/or
- needs an interpreter or signer.

### NORMALLY 14 DAYS TO RETURN ENQUIRY FORM TO THE APPEAL SERVICE

DAR99 Reg 39(2)-(3)

**19.32** The person affected should normally return the pre-hearing enquiry form (TAS1) to the appropriate regional office of the Appeal Service within 14 days of the date it was sent out by the authority. If it is not returned within 14 days the Appeal Service will assume that the person affected does not wish to continue with the appeal and the appeal will be struck out. The tribunal clerk may give a longer period for reply, for example where the appellant is in hospital or some other reasons exists which would prevent the appellant from replying on time if the form cannot be returned within 14 days the regional office of the Appeal Service should be advised. If the authority is aware of any reason that might prevent the appellant from replying on time, this must be clearly marked on the notification of appeal (AT37) it sends to the Appeal Service.

## The appeal hearing

### MEMBERSHIP OF TRIBUNAL

DAR Reg 22(1)-(2)

**19.33** All tribunal members are independent of the authority. In the case of an appeal concerning HB/CTB the tribunal normally consists of just one person who will be legally qualified. In rare instances where financial questions are raised, e.g. regarding a difficult question relating to a self-employed claimant's accounts, there may also be a financially qualified tribunal member. An additional member may also be present to provide that member with experience or to assist with the monitoring of standards.

### VENUES

**19.34** The hearing normally takes place at a tribunal venue near to the appellant. The Appeal Service has a network of around 140 tribunal venues that it uses to hear cases across England, Wales and Scotland.

# The oral hearing

## NOTICE

**19.35** At least 14 days before the hearing (beginning with the day on which the notice is given and ending on the day before the hearing of the appeal is to take place) notice of the time and place of any oral hearing must be given to every party to the proceedings. If such notice has not been given to someone who should have been given it, the hearing may proceed only with the consent of that person. DAR99 Reg 49(2)

## POSTPONEMENT

**19.36** A tribunal member or the clerk may at any time before the beginning of the hearing postpone the hearing. Where a person affected wishes to request a postponement of the hearing they should do so in writing to the Clerk stating the reasons for the request. If it is too late to request a postponement an adjournment may be requested at the hearing. The Clerk or tribunal member may grant or refuse the request as they think fit. DAR99 Reg 51(1)

## PUBLIC OR PRIVATE HEARINGS

**19.37** The initial presumption is that a hearing will be in public. A private hearing may be held, however, where: DAR99 Reg 49

- the appellant requests a private hearing; or
- the Chair is satisfied that intimate personal or financial circumstances may have to be disclosed; or that considerations of national security are involved.

**19.38** Certain persons such as trainee panel members or trainee clerks are entitled to be present at an oral hearing (whether or not it is otherwise in private) but are not able to take part in the proceedings. DAR99 Reg 49(9)

## DECIDING TO PROCEED IN THE ABSENCE OF ANY OF THE PARTIES

**19.39** If a party to the proceedings to whom notice has been given fails to appear at the hearing the Chair may, having regard to all the circumstances including any explanation offered for the absence: DAR99 Reg 49(4

- proceed with the hearing notwithstanding the absence, or
- give such directions with a view to the determination of the appeal as they think proper.

**19.40** If a party to the proceedings has waived the right to be given 14 days notice of the hearing the Chair may proceed with the hearing notwithstanding the absence. DAR99 Reg 49(5

## THE PARTIES' RIGHTS AT THE HEARING

DAR99 Reg 49(1), (7)

**19.41** Whilst the procedure for an oral hearing is determined by the Chair the parties to the proceeding have certain rights which the Chair must respect. Any party to the proceedings is entitled to:

- be present; and
- be heard at an oral hearing.

DAR99 Reg 49(8)

**19.42** A person who has the right to be heard at a hearing:

- may be accompanied; and
- may be represented by another person whether having professional qualifications or not.

DAR99 Reg 49(8)

**19.43** For the purposes of the proceedings at the hearing, any representative has all the rights and powers to which the person represented is entitled.

DAR99 Reg 49(11)

**19.44** Any person entitled to be heard at an oral hearing may:

- address the tribunal,
- give evidence,
- call witnesses; and
- put questions directly to any other person called as a witness.

## ORDER OF THE HEARING

DAR99 Reg 49(1), 38(2)

**19.45** The procedure for an oral hearing is determined by the Chair. The Chair may at any stage of the proceedings, either of their own motion or on a written application made to the clerk by any party to the proceedings:

- give such directions as they consider necessary or desirable for the just, effective and efficient conduct of the proceedings; and
- may direct any party to the proceedings to provide such particulars or to produce such documents as may be reasonably required.

**19.46** The way in which the tribunal actually hears the appeal will vary according to the issue that the tribunal has to decide. For those familiar with review board hearings the tribunal hearing is likely to appear less 'structured'. Each Chair has their own way of conducting a hearing. Nevertheless the appellant should expect to have those present in the room introduced and their function explained at the start. The Chair should also explain the procedure they wish to follow and seek the agreement of the parties to going ahead in that way. The Chair may wish the appellant to start by explaining why they think the decision is wrong. If there is a Presenting Officer for the authority in attendance, they will be asked to explain the reasons for the authority's decision. At some point the Chair is likely to ask questions of the parties. Usually the appellant will be offered the opportunity of having the final word before the tribunal goes on to consider its decision.

### ADJOURNMENT

**19.47** An oral hearing may be adjourned by the Chair at any time on the application of any party to the proceedings or of their own motion. This might be case, for example, to allow new evidence to be looked at. Where a hearing has been adjourned and it is not practicable, or would cause undue delay, for it to be resumed before a tribunal with the same tribunal member(s) the appeal must be heard by a differently constituted tribunal. In these cases there must be a complete rehearing. DAR99 Reg 51(4), Reg 51(5)

### WITHDRAWING AN APPEAL

**19.48** An appeal may be withdrawn by the appellant at the oral hearing. If this happens the clerk must send a notice in writing to any party to the proceedings who is not present when the appeal or referral is withdrawn, informing them that the appeal has been withdrawn. DAR99 Reg 40(1)(a),(2)

## The tribunal's decision

**19.49** The tribunal reaches a decision once it has considered all the evidence from an oral or paper hearing. If the appellant attends an oral hearing they may be given the decision on the day but it will be confirmed in writing as soon as it may be practicable by the chair.

### THE WRITTEN DECISION NOTICE

**19.50** Every decision of an appeal tribunal must be recorded in summary by the Chair. The decision notice must be in the written form approved by the President of appeal tribunals. The Chair must sign it. Where there was a legally qualified member and a financially qualified member the decision notice should state if the decision is unanimous or not. DAR99 Reg 53(1)&(2)

### COMMUNICATION OF THE DECISION

**19.51** As soon as may be practicable after an appeal has been decided a copy of the decision notice must be sent or given to every party to the proceedings. They must also be informed of: DAR99 Reg 53(1)&(2), 53(3)

- the right to apply for a statement of reasons; and
- the conditions governing appeals to a Commissioner.

**19.52** The decision notice is the legal document that enables the authority to correct and pay benefit in line with the tribunal's decision.

## WHAT IS A 'STATEMENT OF REASONS'

**19.53** A statement of reasons sets out the findings of fact and the reasons for the decision. If an appeal to the Social Security Commissioners is being considered a statement of reasons must be asked for.

## TIME LIMIT FOR APPLICATION FOR STATEMENT OF REASONS

DAR99 Reg 53(4)

**19.54** A party to the proceedings may apply to the tribunal member for a statement of the reasons for the tribunal's decision. A statement of reasons can be asked for at the tribunal. Otherwise the application must normally be made within one month of the date the decision notice was given or sent. If this is not asked for in time the chance of appealing may be lost.

DAR99 Reg 54

**19.55** Late applications for the statement of reasons can only be accepted if the application is made in writing to the Clerk within three months of the date the decision note was sent. In calculating this three month period no account is to be taken of time that elapses before the day on which notice was given of:

- a correction of a decision or the record of a decision, or
- a decision to refuse to set aside.

Where a correction is made, or where set-aside is refused, the three month period will be counted from the day notice of the correction or refusal is given.

**19.56** The application must explain why the application is late, including details of any relevant special circumstances. A legally qualified panel member will consider the application and decide the matter. Similar considerations apply as to those that apply to late appeals.

## REQUIREMENT TO SUPPLY WRITTEN STATEMENT OF REASONS

**19.57** Following receipt of an accepted application for a written statement of reasons the tribunal member must:

- record a statement of the reasons; and
- send or give a copy of that statement to every party to the proceedings as soon as may be practicable.

## RECORD OF TRIBUNAL PROCEEDINGS

DAR99 Reg 55(1)-(2)

**19.58** A record of the proceedings at an oral hearing, which is sufficient to indicate the evidence taken, must be made by the tribunal member. This record must be preserved by the Appeal Service for six months from the date of the decision. Any party to the proceedings may within that six month period apply in writing for a copy of that record. The copy must be supplied.

# What actions can be taken if a tribunal's decision is wrong?

**19.59** Once a tribunal has made and communicated its decision it may be altered if:

- the authority supersedes the decision;
- corrected – where there is an accidental error;
- set aside on certain limited grounds;
- appealed to the Social Security Commissioners.

## WHEN MAY THE AUTHORITY SUPERSEDE THE TRIBUNAL'S DECISION?

**19.60** A decision of a tribunal may be superseded, either on application or on the authority's own initiative where:

DAR Reg 7(2)(a), 7(2)(d)
NIDAR 7(2)(b), 7(2)(c)

- the decision was made in ignorance of a material fact; or
- the decision was based on a mistake as to a material fact; or
- there has been a relevant change of circumstances since the decision was made.

## WHEN MAY A TRIBUNAL'S DECISION BE CORRECTED?

**19.61** The clerk, or a tribunal member, may at any time correct accidental errors such as a mistake in a date or an amount in any decision, or the record of any such decision. A correction made to, or to the record of, a decision is deemed part of the decision or record of that decision. Any of the parties to the appeal can ask for a correction to be made. A written notice of the correction must be given as soon as practicable to every party to the proceedings. There is no right of appeal against a correction or a refusal to make a correction.

DAR99 Reg 56(1)-(2)

## SETTING ASIDE DECISIONS ON CERTAIN GROUNDS

**19.62** If a tribunal decision is 'set aside' this means that the decision is cancelled and a new tribunal must be arranged. Any party to the proceedings may apply for a decision of an appeal tribunal to be set aside by a legally qualified tribunal member. The member may set the decision aside where it appears just on the ground that:

DAR99 Reg 57(1)-(2)

- a document relating to the proceedings was not sent to, or was not received at an appropriate time by, any of the parties to the proceedings or their representatives or was not received at an appropriate time by the person who made the decision;
- any party to the proceedings or their representative was not present at the hearing.

**19.63** In determining whether it is just to set aside a decision on the ground that someone was not present the tribunal member must consider whether the party making the application gave notice that they wished to have an oral hearing. If that party did not give such notice the decision cannot be set aside unless the tribunal member is satisfied that the interests of justice obviously support acceptance of the set aside application.

**19.64** An application for a set aside must:

- be made within one month of the date on which:
  - a copy of the decision notice is sent or given to the parties; or
  - the statement of the reasons for the decision is given or sent in,

  whichever is the later;
- be in writing; and
- signed by a party to the proceedings or, where the party has provided written authority to a representative to act on their behalf, that representative;
- contain particulars of the grounds on which it is made; and
- be sent to the clerk to the appeal tribunal.

## EXTENSION OF THE TIME LIMITS IN WHICH TO APPLY FOR A SET ASIDE

**19.65** Late applications for set aside may be accepted up to one year after the end of the one month time limit.

**19.66** An application for an extension of time must include details of any relevant special circumstances. It must be determined by a legally qualified panel member.

**19.67** An application for an extension of time cannot be granted unless the panel member is satisfied that:

- if the application is granted there are reasonable prospects that the application to set aside will be successful; and
- it is in the interests of justice for the application for an extension of time to be granted.

**19.68** It is not in the interests of justice to grant an application for an extension of time unless the panel member is satisfied that:

- the applicant or a spouse or dependant of the applicant has died or suffered serious illness;
- the applicant is not resident in the United Kingdom; or
- normal postal services were disrupted; or

- some other special circumstances exist which are wholly exceptional and relevant to that application,

and as a result of those special circumstances, it was not practicable for the application to set aside to be made within the one month time limit.

**19.69** In determining whether it is in the interests of justice to grant an application for an extension of time, the panel member must have regard to the principle that the greater the amount of time that has elapsed between the expiry of the time within which the application to set aside is to be made and the making of the application for an extension of time, the more compelling should be the special circumstances on which the application for an extension is based.

**19.70** Where an application to set aside a decision is entertained every party to the proceedings must be sent a copy of the application. They must also be afforded a reasonable opportunity of making representations on it before the application is determined.

### COMMUNICATION OF THE DECISION ON THE APPLICATION TO SET ASIDE

**19.71** Every party to the proceedings must receive a written notice of the decision on an application to set aside as soon as may be practicable. The notice must contain a statement giving the reasons for the decision.

**19.72** There is no right of appeal against the outcome of a set aside request. If the request is refused, however, the time limit for appealing to the Commissioner does not start until the notification of the set aside decision has been issued.

**19.73** An application under this regulation for an extension of time which has been refused may not be renewed.

## Appeals to Social Security Commissioners

**19.74** The Social Security Commissioners are appointed to decide appeals on questions of law from appeal tribunals. The Commissioner's role is to give interpretations of the law which are binding on all decision makers and appeal tribunals The Commissioners are barristers, solicitors or advocates of not less than ten year's standing who are specialists in social security law. Commissioners have a legal status comparable to that of a High Court judge in their specialised area. Any appeals from their decisions are to the Court of Appeal or the Inner House of the Court of Session, and from there to the House of Lords. Cases involving European Union law are referred by the Commissioners direct to the European Court of Justice.

**19.75** DSS Circular A25/2001 provides detailed guidance on appeals to Commissioners. Most appeals are determined on paper without a hearing. Parties make their submissions in writing. However, parties may ask for an oral hearing. Hearings take place at the Commissioners' offices in London (Harp House, 83-86 Farringdon Street, London EC4A 4DH – correspondence should be sent to 5th Floor, Newspaper House, 8/16 Great New Street, London EC4A 3NN) and Edinburgh (23 Melville Street, Edinburgh EH3 7PW). Hearings may take place at other locations in particular circumstances.

### WHEN CAN AN APPEAL BE MADE TO THE COMMISSIONERS?

**19.76** An appeal can only be made to the Social Security Commissioners where the following criteria are satisfied:

- the ground for seeking an appeal is that the appeal tribunal made an error in a point of law in arriving at its decision;
- the appeal is being made by someone entitled to make it;
- the appellant has applied to the tribunal, within one month of the decision notice relating to the disputed decision being sent, for a statement of the reasons for the decision in question;
- the appellant has applied to the tribunal for leave to appeal to the Commissioner and has made this application within one month of being sent the tribunal's statement of reasons; and
- the appellant has submitted the appeal, together with all the necessary accompanying documents, to the Commissioner within one month of the date the tribunal's decision granting leave was sent and, in response, the Commissioner has also granted leave to appeal.

## What is an error in a point of law?

**19.77** An appeal to a Commissioner can only be made on an error in a point of law.

**19.78** An error in a point of law is where, for example, the appeal tribunal:

- failed to apply the correct law;
- wrongly interpreted the relevant Acts or Regulations;
- followed a procedure that breached the rules of natural justice;
- took irrelevant matters into account, or did not consider relevant matters, or did both of these things;
- did not give adequate reasons in the full statement of its decision;
- gave a decision which was not supported by the evidence;
- decided the facts in such a way that no person properly instructed as to the relevant law, and acting judicially, could have come to the decision made by the tribunal.

## Who can apply for leave to appeal?

**19.79** Where the disputed decision relates to housing benefit, the following can apply for leave to appeal to the Commissioners: CSPSSA 68 sch 7 para 8 (2) NICSPSSA 59, sch 7 para 8(2)

- the claimant;
- anyone who has been found liable to repay an amount of overpaid housing benefit (i.e. a landlord in a direct payment case);
- the Council against whose decision the appeal to the appeal tribunal was brought;
- the Secretary of State.

## Overview of other matters

### STAYING A DECISION WHEN AN APPEAL IS PENDING

**19.80** The rules about 'staying' a decision apply when: CSPSSA sch 7 para 16 DAR 15

- a decision, revision or supersession falls to be made in a particular HB/CTB case; and
- an appeal is pending against a Commissioner or court (including both judicial review and leave to appeal) in another case about HB or CTB (but not any other social security benefit).

In such cases, the authority:

- need not make the decision (or supersession or revision) while the appeal is pending; or
- may make the decision (etc) as if the appeal had already been determined in the way most unfavourable to the claimant.

Once the appeal itself is determined, the authority must, if appropriate, revise its decision in accordance with the result of the appeal.

### STAYING AN APPEAL WHEN AN APPEAL IS PENDING

**19.81** The rules about 'staying' an appeal apply when: CSPSSA sch 7 para 17

- an appeal ('A') to a tribunal or Commissioner is pending in a particular HB/CTB case (including leave to appeal); and
- an appeal ('B') is pending against a Commissioner or court in another case about HB or CTB (but not any other social security benefit), and the authority considers that the possible result of appeal 'B' would affect the outcome of appeal 'A'.

In such cases, the authority may write requiring the tribunal or Commissioner:

- to return appeal 'A' to the authority without determining it. In this case, once appeal 'B' is determined, the authority must revise its case 'A' decision (if it is a stayed appeal to a tribunal) or supersede the tribunal's case 'A' decision (if it is a stayed appeal to a Commissioner) in accordance with the result of appeal 'B'; or
- to decide what to do. In this case, the tribunal or Commissioner must either:
  - stay appeal 'A' until appeal 'B' has been determined; or
  - if it is in the interests of the appellant to do so, determine appeal 'A' as if appeal 'B' had been determined and the issues decided in the way that was most unfavourable to the appellant. In such a case, once appeal 'B' is determined, the authority must, if appropriate, supersede the tribunal's or Commissioner's case 'A' decision in accordance with the result of appeal 'B'.

## ERRORS OF LAW: RESTRICTIONS ON ENTITLEMENT

CSPSSA sch 7 para 18

**19.82** The rules about this apply when:

- the result of an appeal to a Commissioner or court (i.e. the High Court, Court of Appeal, Court of Session, House of Lords or Court of Justice of the European Community) is that the authority's decision was erroneous in point of law (including cases where all or part of a Regulation or Order has been held to be invalid); and
- after the date of the determination of that appeal, that authority or another authority has to make a decision in accordance with it; and
- the authority's decision would be about:
  - a claim (regardless of whether the claim was made before or after the appeal determination), or
  - a revision (and if this is as a result of an application to do so, regardless of whether the application was made before or after the appeal determination), or
  - a supersession following an application for one (regardless of whether the application was made before or after the appeal determination).

In such cases, in respect of the period before the appeal determination, the authority must make the decision as though it had not been found to be wrong in law. This does not, however, apply where the decision would have been made before the appeal determination apart from the fact that it was stayed as described above.

# 20 Immigration status and habitual residence

**20.1** Certain claimants are not entitled to HB or CTB if they are:

- 'subject to immigration control'; or
- considered not habitually resident in the United Kingdom, the Channel Islands, the Isle of Man or the Republic of Ireland.

The question of habitual residence is separate from the issue of immigration control.

**20.2** This is a complex area of the HB/CTB schemes where the law has been amended and radically altered over a number of years. Transitional provisions also apply. Certain persons who under current rules are excluded from entitlement nevertheless remain entitled because of the date they first claimed HB/CTB.

## The relevant legislation

**20.3** Section 115 (which applies to Great Britain and Northern Ireland) of the Immigration and Asylum Act 1999 which came into force on 3 April 2000 excludes persons subject to immigration control from HB/CTB entitlement (and most other forms of assistance).

**20.4** Exceptions to this general exclusion, and transitional provisions, are prescribed in the Social Security (Immigration and Asylum) Consequential Amendment Regulations (SI 2000 No. 636, in Northern Ireland SR 2000 No. 71).

**20.5** HB regulation 7A and the equivalent CTB regulation 4A additionally exclude from HB/CTB entitlement certain persons who are not habitually resident in the United Kingdom, the Channel Islands, the Isle of Man or the Republic of Ireland. These regulations which purport to relate to 'persons from abroad' now only contain the habitual residence test and the claimants exempt from it.

## Persons 'subject to immigration control'

**20.6** Section 115(9) of the Act defines 'a person subject to immigration control' as someone who is not an EEA national and who:

- requires leave (permission) to enter or remain in the United Kingdom but does not have it (i.e. an illegal entrant or someone who has overstayed his or her leave);

- has leave to enter or remain in the United Kingdom which is subject to a condition that he does not have recourse to public funds (such as a visitor or student);
- has leave to enter or remain in the United Kingdom given as a result of a maintenance undertaking (i.e. a resident has formally agreed to sponsor him or her);
- has had leave extended to allow an appeal against a decision on the grounds that he or she is an asylum seeker;
- has leave to enter or remain in the United Kingdom only as a result of a pending appeal against:
- a decision to vary, or to refuse to vary, any limited leave to enter or remain in the United Kingdom; or
- a requirement to leave the United Kingdom because he or she is an asylum seeker.

## Persons 'subject to immigration control' who remain entitled

**20.7** Claimants who fall into any of the categories identified in the following paragraphs are exempt from the general exclusion from HB/CTB contained in the Immigration and Asylum Act 1999. SI 2000 No. 636 NISR 2000 No. 71

### CLAIMANTS WITH LIMITED LEAVE – FUNDS DISRUPTED

**20.8** Claimants with limited leave to remain in the UK (and thus normally ineligible for HB/CTB) but whose funds from abroad have stopped temporarily. They cease to be excluded from HB/CTB for up to 42 days in any one period of leave where they are temporarily without funds from abroad and there is a reasonable expectation that the funds will resume with three months.

### SPONSORED IMMIGRANTS – SPONSOR(S) DIE

**20.9** A person given leave to enter or remain in the UK on the condition that one or more sponsors have given a formal, written undertaking under the 1971 Immigration Act to be responsible for maintaining and accommodating them during their stay, but where all such sponsors have subsequently died.

### SPONSORED IMMIGRANTS – RESIDENT FOR FIVE YEARS OR MORE

**20.10** People admitted to the UK as sponsored immigrants who have been resident in the UK for five years or more.

### EUROPEAN ECONOMIC AREA NATIONALS

**20.11** The EEA states are: Austria, Belgium, Denmark, Finland, France, Germany, Greece, Iceland, Ireland, Italy, Liechtenstein, Luxembourg, Netherlands, Norway, Portugal, Spain, and Sweden.

### ECSMA/CESC NATIONALS

**20.12** A person who is a national of a state which has ratified the European Convention on Social and Medical Assistance (ECSMA) or a state which has ratified the Council of Europe Social Charter (CESC) and who is lawfully present in the United Kingdom.

**20.13** In addition to EEA countries the countries that had ratified the ECSMA as at May 2001 are: Malta and Turkey. In addition to EEA countries, Malta and Turkey the countries that had ratified the CESC as at May 2001 are: Republic of Cyprus, Czech Republic, Hungary, Poland, and Slovakia. Turkish Cypriots are not considered to be nationals of either Turkey or Cyprus.

**20.14** Prior to 3rd April 2000 national of countries that are not members of the EEA but which had signed (but not ratified) the ECSMA or CESC were eligible for HB/CTB. The DSS advised authorities that these cases should have been closed at the next review after 3 April 2000 (DSS A18/2000, para. 24).

## Asylum Seekers

**20.15** An asylum seeker is someone normally subject to immigration control who seeks to enter or remain in the UK by applying for asylum as a refugee, or who otherwise indicates a fear of being required to return to his or her country of origin or habitual residence.

**20.16** Asylum applications can be made:

- on arrival at the port when the person first enters the UK (port applicants), or
- later after the person has been allowed into the UK subject to immigration control (in-country applicants).

**20.17** Applications are referred by Immigration Officers for determination by the Home Secretary. Applications may be subject to a process of appeal involving several stages via a special adjudicator, Immigration Appeal Tribunal and, ultimately, Judicial Review in the courts.

**20.18** The final determination of an asylum application either:

- recognises the applicant's refugee status; or
- grants the applicant exceptional leave to enter/remain in the UK; or
- refuses the asylum application and expels the applicant.

**20.19** For immigration purposes, an asylum application is not finally determined until all avenues of appeal are exhausted. No action is taken to require the applicant's departure from the UK in the meantime.

## Port applicant asylum seekers – from 3 April 2000

**20.20** One of the main consequences of the Immigration and Asylum Act 1999 is that new port applicant asylum seekers who prior to 3rd April 2000 would have been eligible for HB/CTB are no longer entitled when they first claim on or after that date. Instead support is provided under the arrangements managed by the National Asylum Seekers Service (NASS).

### THE ASYLUM SUPPORT SCHEME

**20.21** A detailed description of the April 2000 support arrangements for asylum seekers and their dependants is beyond the scope of this Guide. Briefly, section 95 of the Immigration and Asylum Act enables the Home Secretary (through the National Asylum Support Service) to provide support to an asylum seeker and any dependants if he or she appears to be either:

- destitute; or
- likely to become destitute within a period of 14 days beginning with the date on which the application for support is made.

**20.22** Destitution is defined as the lack of adequate accommodation or the means to obtain it, and/or the lack of resources to meet other essential living needs.

**20.23** Under the support arrangements asylum seekers and dependants may be provided with:

- accommodation on a 'no choice' basis in clusters throughout the country; and/or
- support for day to day living costs mainly by vouchers but with a small cash element.

**20.24** Unaccompanied children seeking asylum will continue to be supported by local authority Social Services Departments under the provisions of the Children Act 1991.

**20.25** As at the end of February 2001, 11,630 asylum seekers (including dependants) were allocated subsistence only support by NASS and 21,400 asylum seekers (including dependants) were allocated accommodation and subsistence support by NASS. As at the 26 January 2001 there were 5,540 unaccompanied minors being supported in England by local authorities. The figures for unaccompanied minors being supported in Scotland and Wales are not held centrally (Hansard, Written Questions, 10th April 2001, 366 c570W; 366 c556-7W).

**20.26** Asylum seekers supported by NASS attract a non-dependant deduction if they choose to stay with people who are receiving HB or CTB, rather than take up accommodation offered by NASS.

## In-country asylum seekers – from 3 April 2000

**20.27** The new arrangements for asylum seekers have been phased in. In-country asylum seekers were not immediately eligible for NASS support in April 2000 and instead were supported by local authorities under interim arrangements that were introduced in December 1999. Under these interim provisions support for asylum seekers has been provided by Social Services Departments of the local authority to whom they apply for support. Support provided under this scheme replaces that previously available under the National Assistance Act 1948 and (for asylum seekers with children aged under 18) the Children Act 1991. NASS has extended its support arrangements to include certain in-country applicant asylum seekers in different geographical areas since April 2000.

## Refugees and those given exceptional leave to remain

**20.28** As was the case prior to April 2000, an asylum seeker who is:

- accorded refugee status (i.e. recorded by the Home Secretary as a refugee within the meaning of the Refugee Convention), or
- given exceptional leave,

is eligible for HB/CTB from the date the decision is recorded.

**20.29** Where the National Asylum Support Service is providing support the support continues for a period of 14 days after the successful asylum seeker is notified of the decision.

### RETROSPECTIVE AWARDS OF BENEFIT FOR REFUGEES

**20.30** As was the case prior to April 2000 if an asylum seeker is recorded by the Home Secretary as a refugee and before that date he or she, or a dependant, was a person subject to immigration control and excluded from benefit entitlement then the refugee may apply for a backdated payment of income support, HB and CTB for the period of exclusion.

## Transitional protection for asylum seekers potentially entitled to HB/CTB prior to 3 April 2000

**20.31** The previous edition of this Guide identified the asylum seekers eligible for HB/CTB prior to April 2000. There is transitional protection for those asylum seekers who were entitled (or who would have been entitled had they claimed) HB/CTB before 3rd April 2000. They continue to receive HB/CTB until the first negative decision on their asylum application. The one exception to this is the so called 'loophole' cases i.e. illegal entrants, who were subsequently given temporary admission; and made in-country applications for asylum. They were no longer entitled to HB/CTB from 3rd April 2001. SI 2000 No. 636 NISR 2000 No. 71

## The habitual residence test

**20.32** If the claimant is not exempt from the 'habitual residence' the authority should decide that they are a 'person from abroad' and not entitled to HB/CTB where it considers that they are not habitually resident in the United Kingdom, the Channel Islands, the Isle of Man or the Republic of Ireland (formerly referred to as the Common Travel Area). The rule applies to all claimants who are not exempt from the test irrespective of nationality. HBR 7A CTBR 4A

### EXEMPT CLAIMANTS

**20.33** The following claimants are exempt from the habitual residence test:

- Claimants who have lived in the relevant area for more than two years unless there is other evidence which clearly indicates the need for further enquiries about terms of entry, etc (DSS Circular A22/2000 part 1);
- Recipients of income support or income-based jobseeker's allowance;
- EEA nationals who are 'workers' for the purposes of Council Regulation (EEC) No. 1612/68 or (EEC) No. 125 1/70;
- EEA nationals who have a right to reside in the UK under Council Directive No. 68/360/EEC or No. 73/148/EEC (e.g. the self-employed);
- Refugees;
- Claimants given exceptional leave to enter the UK;
- Claimants given exceptional leave to remain in the UK;
- Claimants who left the territory of Montserrat after 1st November 1995 because of the effect on that territory of volcanic eruption;

- Claimants not subject to immigration control who have been deported, expelled or otherwise removed by compulsion of law from another country to the United Kingdom.

## EEA WORKER

**20.34** The EEA states are identified in para. 20.11. The definition of an EEA worker has become ambiguous due to a growing body of case law. To be classed as an 'EEA worker' a person must be currently, or in certain circumstances (see below) have been, engaged in remunerative work in the UK which is both:

- 'effective and genuine'; and
- not 'on such a small scale as to be purely marginal and ancillary'.

**20.35** European case law has established that no-one should be denied EEA worker status simply because they are working part-time or because they are low paid and need to supplement their income with social security benefits. The DSS suggests that a number of factors should be considered before the authority decides whether any work done by the claimant is 'effective and genuine'. These include:

- the period of employment;
- the number of hours worked;
- the level of earnings; and
- whether the work is regular or erratic.

These factors are meant to be considered as a whole. The presence or absence of any one factor is not, by itself, conclusive.

**20.36** The definition of an EEA worker does not include a UK citizen who is working in the UK. Such individuals do not need to exercise rights under European law in order to be able to work in their home state. However British citizens can obtain the status of EEA worker by living and working in another EEA country and then returning to the UK.

**20.37** A former worker who retains EEA worker status is one who has worked in the UK in the past and who is:

- actively seeking to rejoin the workforce; or unemployed and undergoing retraining; or
- voluntarily unemployed in order to take up vocational training linked to a previous job; or
- retired after working in the UK for at least 12 months before pensionable age (60 for a woman, 65 for a man) and who has either resided continuously in the UK for more than three years or whose spouse is (or was at the time of marriage) a British national; or

- incapable of work through illness or injury sustained while working in the UK and who either:
  - is entitled to UK invalidity or disablement benefit, or
  - previously resided in the UK for two years or more, or
  - has a spouse who is (or was at the time of marriage) a British national; or
- seeking reinstatement or re-employment with the same employer after being temporarily laid off.

**20.38** Self-employed people have a right to reside in the UK under specific EEC directives and are therefore also exempt.

### PERSONS WITH EXCEPTIONAL LEAVE TO ENTER OR REMAIN

**20.39** Exceptional leave to enter or remain in the UK is a form of leave given by the Home Secretary outside the normal immigration rules. It is granted to people when it is considered that they should be allowed to enter or remain in the United Kingdom on humanitarian grounds.

**20.40** This form of leave is mostly given to asylum seekers who have not been recognised as refugees but have been allowed to remain in the UK.

## The meaning of 'habitual residence'

**20.41** The term 'habitual residence' is not defined in the regulations. The DSS (HB/CTB A7/94 annex 3, para. 4) described the term as 'intended to convey a degree of permanence in the claimant's residence in the Common Travel Area'. The term 'habitual residence' arises in European legislation, in particular EEC Regulation 1408/71 dealing with social security for migrant workers and in family law.

### 'HABITUAL RESIDENCE' IN EUROPEAN SOCIAL SECURITY LAW

**20.42** In *Angenjeux v. Hakenberg* [1973] ECR 935 the Court ruled that 'the place where one habitually resides must be understood in the case of a business representative… as the place in which he has established the permanent centre of his interests and to which he returns in the intervals between his tours'. In *Di Paolo v. Office National de l'Emploi* [1977] ECR 315 the Court ruled that where a person habitually resides also corresponds with where the habitual centre of his interests is situated. The Court also ruled that account should be taken of the length and continuity of residence before the person concerned moved, the length and purpose of his absence, the nature of the occupation found in the other member state and the intention of the person concerned as it appears from all the circumstances.

**20.43** The judgment in the Di Paolo case emphasised that whenever a worker has stable employment in a member state there is a presumption that he resides there, even if he has left his family in another state.

**20.44** The authority must establish the relevant facts on which it can make a decision as to whether or not someone is 'habitually resident'. Drawing on the relevant European case law, the DSS suggests (HB/CTB A7/94) that the authority, in deciding this question, should consider the following factors:

- length and continuity of residence;
- future intentions;
- employment prospects;
- reasons for coming to the UK; and
- centre of interest.

## 'HABITUAL RESIDENCE' IN FAMILY LAW

**20.45** The prime authority on the ordinary and natural meaning of 'habitual residence' is the speech of Lord Brandon in *Re J (A Minor) (Abduction)* [1990] 2 AC 562. This was a case on the Convention on the Civil Aspects of International Child Abduction. Lord Brandon emphasised that: 'there is a significant difference between a person ceasing to be habitually resident in country A, and his subsequently becoming habitually resident in country B. A person may cease to be habitually resident in country A in a single day if he or she leaves it with a settled intention not to return to it but to take up long-term residence in country B instead. Such a person cannot however, become habitually resident in country B in a single day. An appreciable period of time and a settled intention will be necessary to enable him or her to become so.'

## PERSUASIVE COMMISSIONER'S DECISIONS

**20.46** There are a number of Commissioner's decisions relating to the test of habitual residence within the income support scheme that must be considered persuasive for HB/CTB purposes. These decisions have adopted the key criteria of 'an appreciable period of time' and a 'settled intention'. The following key points arose from CIS 1067/1995:

- residence implies a more settled state than mere physical presence, thereby excluding short stay visitors;
- to be a resident the claimant must be seen to be making a home here;
- the home need not be his or her only home, nor need it be intended to be a permanent one, but it must be a genuine home for the time being;
- the length, continuity and general nature of a claimant's actual residence are more important than his or her intentions as to the future;

- a person may abandon habitual residence in a single day but this does not mean that he or she becomes a habitual resident of another country to which he or she intends to move;
- an appreciable period of time, as well as a settled intention, is necessary to enable the claimant to become habitually resident; and
- what counts as an 'appreciable period of time' must depend on the facts in each case it must, however, be the kind of period which demonstrates a settled and stable pattern of living as a resident.

**20.47** Commissioner's Decision CIS/2326/1995 agreed with the main points of CIS 1067/1995. It emphasised, however, that no particular periods should be mentioned as amounting to an appreciable period of time except in relation to actual cases that arise for decision. The Commissioner considered that the question in each individual case must be whether, in all the circumstances, including the settledness of the person's intentions as to residence, the residence has continued for a sufficient period for it to be said to be habitual.

## RECENT UK COURT DECISIONS

**20.48** The House of Lords upheld the Commissioner decision in CIS 2326/1995. It found that an appreciable period of time of actual residence is needed to establish habitual residence for people coming to the UK for the first time (Nessa v CAO, [1999] 1 WLR 1937). Meanwhile the European Court of Justice in Case C-90/97 Swaddling v CA0 (ECJ 25 February 1995) has ruled that a UK claimant who had returned to Britain after living and working in France for several years could not have his right to benefit made subject to any period of actual residence here after his return by the 'habitual residence' test.

**20.49** The DSS has accepted that people returning to the UK from an EU member state and re-establishing their ties here should be treated as habitually resident immediately upon their return (see DSS Press Release 99/132, 14 June 1999). Authorities should do the same. Indeed the DSS has gone further than the principle established in the European Court case. Circular A12/99 (para. 5) advises authorities to extend the effect of the judgment to people of any nationality returning from any country overseas and re-establishing their ties in the UK, Republic of Ireland, Channel Islands or Isle of Man. In other words, they should be treat as habitually resident immediately on return.

# 21 Students

**21.1** The general rules in the rest of this guide apply to students, but with a number of variations. This chapter explains all these variations. It covers:

- the terminology used in student cases;
- which students can get HB and CTB;
- how HB and CTB are assessed for students; and
- the rules for assessing students' income and rent.

**21.2** The student figures given in this chapter apply from 1st September 2001 to 31st August 2002. These and other relevant figures for the 2001-02 academic year are summarised in DSS circular HB/CTB A31/2001. Figures for the 2002-03 academic year were not available in time for this edition of the guide.

**21.3** As described in this chapter, the student rules vary between HB and CTB, and also between main CTB and second adult rebate. Also, the rules have changed frequently in the past few years – and, many would argue, are absurdly and unnecessarily complex. All students are advised to check carefully that their claims have been dealt with correctly – perhaps by requesting a written statement from the authority (chapter 19).

## Who counts as a 'student'?

**21.4** For the HB/CTB student rules to apply, the person in question must be a 'student'. The definition is given below. Other important terms are defined after that. Paragraph 21.22 compares these with the definitions used in council tax law – which are different.

### DEFINITION OF 'STUDENT'

HBR 2(1), 46, 47, 52
CTBR 2(1), 38, 39

**21.5** For HB and CTB purposes, a student is defined as any person 'who is attending or undertaking a course of study at an educational establishment… [or a New Deal qualifying course]'. This includes:

- study at any level (from school onwards) whether full-time or part-time;
- students with or without grants;
- both state-funded and private establishments; and
- both term-times and vacations.

Some special cases are mentioned below.

**21.6** Once a course has started, a person carries on counting as a student until his or her course finishes or he or she abandons it or is dismissed from it. So someone does count as a student during the Christmas and Easter vacations and any summer vacation(s) occurring within the course, even if he or she takes up full-time work then. But someone does not count as a student during the summer vacation after the end of a course or between two different courses.

## STUDENTS WITH PARTNERS

**21.7** In the case of a couple, the HB and CTB rules vary depending on whether one or both are students and which partner makes the claim. Details are given as each rule is described.

HBR 47, 52
CTBR 39

## INTERCALATED PERIODS

**21.8** Although the general rule is that a person must be 'attending or undertaking' the course to count as a 'student', a person continues to count as a 'student' during 'intercalated periods'(*O'Connor v Chief Adjudication Officer,* CA, *The Times,* 11.3.99). An intercalated period is one during which a student temporarily suspends attendance, for example because of sickness or for personal reasons, but still remains registered with his or her educational establishment.

## SANDWICH COURSES

**21.9** People on sandwich courses do count as students – both when they are studying and during their periods of work experience.

HBR 46
CTBR 38

## HEALTH CARE STUDENTS

**21.10** The following count as students if (which is almost always the case) they fit the definition given above (para. 21.5):

- students undertaking nursing and midwifery diploma courses, formerly known as the Project 2000 training scheme;
- NHS-funded students undertaking degree programmes.

## QUALIFYING COURSES UNDER THE NEW DEAL

**21.11** Studying on a 'qualifying course' is one of the options under the New Deal (table 13.2) for certain people. Such people count as students. All the student rules apply to them, apart from following variations:

HBR 35(3),(3A), 43(3),(3A), 46
HBR sch 4 para sch 5 para 56
NIHBR sch 4 pa 69, sch 5 para
CTBR 26(3),(3A) 34(3),(3A), 38, 4 para 67, sch para 56

- they carry on counting as a student until either the last day of their course or the date of their last examination, whichever comes later (and the points in para. 21.6 do not apply);
- discretionary payments made to them under the New Deal (table 13.2) are disregarded:

- as income: the one exception is that no discretionary payment for travel is disregarded if the normal student disregard for travel applies to them (tables 21.3 and 21.4 );
- as capital in all cases – but only for 52 weeks from the date of payment;
- as notional income and as notional capital in all cases.

**21.12** However, most people on a 'qualifying course' continue to receive income-based jobseeker's allowance: in their case, all their income and capital is disregarded for HB and main CTB purposes (and they are eligible for HB and CTB: table 21.1).

### TRAINING SCHEMES

HBR 46 CTBR 38 **21.13** People on the New Deal (except as described above) do not count as students; nor do people on other government training schemes. The question of whether anyone else on a training scheme counts as a student is decided by reference to the definition of 'student' quoted above: they usually do not count as a student.

## 'Full-time' vs 'part-time' students

**21.14** Some of the HB and CTB rules apply to both full-time and part-time students; some apply only to full-time students. Details are given as each rule is described.

### GENERAL CASES

HBR 46 CTBR 38 **21.15** There is no general-purpose definition of 'full-time' (or 'part-time'). Some special cases do have definitions (as in the next few paragraphs). But in any other case, the DWP suggests (GM para. C5.03) that, if doubt arises, the educational establishment should be consulted about whether a course is full-time, and that the nature of the student's grant (if any) may also be a useful indication.

### FURTHER EDUCATION COURSES

HBR 46 CTBR 38 **21.16** A student studying at a further education college counts as a full-time student if (and only if) his or her course involves:

- in England, more than 16 hours per week of 'guided learning', as set out in the 'learning agreement' obtainable from his or her college;
- in Wales, more than 16 hours per week of 'guided learning', as set out in a college document;

- in Scotland:
  - more than 16 hours of classroom-based or workshop-based 'guided learning', or
  - more than 21 hours per week of a combination of that and additional hours using structured learning packages,

as set out (in either case) in a college document.

### SANDWICH COURSES

**21.17** All students on sandwich courses count as full-time. HBR 46 CTBR 38

### MODULAR COURSES

**21.18** A modular course is one which contains two or more modules, a specified number of which have to be completed in order to complete the course. They often permit full-time, part-time or mixed attendance. The question of whether a student on a modular course counts as full-time for HB/CTB purposes can be difficult. It now appears clear, however, despite DWP guidance (circular HB/CTB A32/2000) that a student counts as full-time only during the parts of the course for which he or she is registered as full-time (so a student in fact changing from full-time in (say) her second year to part-time in her third would count for HB/CTB purposes as part-time in her third year). HBR 46(2),(4) CTBR 38(2),(4)

### RETAKES ON MODULAR COURSES

**21.19** The following applies only to the parts of modular courses that count as full-time for HB/CTB purposes. If someone fails a module or an exam in such a case, he or she continues to count as full-time for any period in which he or she continues to attend or undertake the course for the purposes of retaking the exam or module (including any vacations within that period other than vacations after the end of the course). HBR 46(3) CTBR 38(3)

## Other definitions

### HIGHER EDUCATION

**21.20** Whether a student is in higher education or not, is one of the main descriptions used in HB and CTB to distinguish different levels of education. Higher education is defined as meaning: HBR 46, 48A CTBR 38, 40

- first degree, postgraduate and higher degree courses;
- courses for the further training of teachers and youth and community workers;

- courses for the Diploma of Higher Education, the BTEC/SVEC Higher National Diploma (HND) or Higher National Certificate (HNC), the Diploma in Management Studies, or the Certificate in Education;
- any other courses at a level higher than GCE A level or BTEC/SVEC Ordinary National Diploma (OND) or Ordinary National Certificate (ONC), whether or not leading to a qualification.

## PERIOD OF STUDY AND SUMMER VACATION

HBR 46(1)
CTBR 38

**21.21** Some of the HB and CTB rules apply only in a student's period of study, others only in the summer vacation (if he or she has a summer vacation), others in both:

- the period of study for any course requiring more than 45 weeks study in a year (e.g. for many postgraduate courses) runs from the first day of the academic year to the day before the first day of the next academic year. The course is treated as not having a summer vacation;
- for courses of less than one year, the period of study is the whole of the course;
- in all other cases, the period of study runs from the first day of the academic year to the last day before the summer vacation (or in the final year of a course of more than one year, to the last day of the course). This usually means three terms plus the Christmas and Easter vacations;
- subject to the above points, for students on sandwich courses, periods of work experience are included in the period of study.

## HB AND CTB DEFINITIONS vs COUNCIL TAX DEFINITIONS

**21.22** For council tax purposes, four groups of people – including certain foreign language assistants and student nurses – are defined in the law as being 'students' (categories 5 to 8 in appendix 6). These council tax definitions are relevant for considering whether a dwelling is completely exempt from council tax (para. 2.12) and whether a council taxpayer can get a discount (para. 2.35). The council tax definitions rather than the HB and CTB definitions are also used for certain purposes to do with second adult rebate (paras. 10.6, 10.17-18). But for all the HB and CTB rules described in this chapter, the council tax definitions are irrelevant: only the definitions given earlier are relevant.

**21.23** There is some overlap between the council tax definitions and the HB and CTB definitions. For example, a person who counts as a 'student' in council tax law (apart from a foreign language assistant) is usually a 'student' in HB and CTB law. However, this does not guarantee that he or she will count as a 'full-time student' (category 10 in appendix 6). (For example, there are small but growing numbers of further education students who count as full-time for council tax purposes but not for HB/CTB purposes – usually because of the nature of their studies.) Matters such as these depend on the individual circumstances of the case.

## Which students can get HB and CTB?

**21.24** To be eligible for HB a student must satisfy all of the following rules. To be eligible for main CTB a student need satisfy only the first rule. None of the rules affects eligibility for second adult rebate. The three rules are dealt with in turn below:

- the primary rule – which prevents full-time students from getting HB or main CTB (but not second adult rebate) unless they fall within certain groups;
- the rule preventing full-time and part-time students from getting HB on halls of residence, etc, but which is irrelevant in CTB;
- the rule preventing full-time students from getting HB (but not main CTB or second adult rebate) on their term-time accommodation if they are absent during their summer vacation.

### THE PRIMARY RULE: SUMMARY

**21.25** This primary rule prevents full-time students from getting HB or main CTB unless they fall within certain groups. This rule does not apply to second adult rebate. The rule works as follows: HBR 6(1)(e), 48A CTBR 40

- Students who are single claimants are eligible for HB and main CTB only if they are in one (or more) of the groups in table 21.1.
- Students who are lone parents are in all cases eligible for HB and main CTB.
- Couples are eligible for HB and main CTB in all cases unless both are students and neither of them is in any of the groups in table 21.1. (Information about which partner should claim is given below.)

### THE PRIMARY RULE: WHICH PARTNER IN A COUPLE SHOULD CLAIM?

**21.26** Table 21.2 explains which partner in a couple is eligible to claim HB and main CTB on behalf of both. In all cases where a claim may be made, it takes into account the income, capital and applicable amount relating to them both. Authorities who receive claims from the 'wrong partner' (i.e. in the cases in the second and fifth rows of the table) should return the application form with an explanation and a suggestion that the other partner should be the claimant. HBR 6(1)(e), 48A CTBR 40

## TABLE 21.1 HB AND MAIN CTB ELIGIBLE GROUPS: THE PRIMARY RULE

(a) All students who are currently receiving income support or income-based jobseeker's allowance (but student eligibility for IS and JSA(IB) is also restricted).

(b) All part-time students.

(c) Students under 19 not in higher education.

(d) Students (men or women) aged 60 or more.

(e) Students (couples or lone parents) who are responsible for a child or young person.

(f) Students who are responsible for a foster child.

(g) Students who qualify for a disability premium (chapter 14).

(h) Students who are disqualified from incapacity benefit.

(i) Students who have been incapable of work for 28 weeks or more.*

(j) Students whose grant assessment (if made by an English, Welsh, Scottish or Northern Ireland grant-awarding body) includes a disabled student's allowance for deafness – even if they get a grant for fees only.

(k) Students who were absent, with the consent of their educational establishment, due to illness or because of providing care for another person, and who have now ceased to be ill or providing care, and who are now not eligible for a grant or loan – but in this case only from the date of ceasing to be ill or providing care until the day before resuming the course (or until the beginning of the new academic year if earlier).

**Note**

* 'Incapable of work' means what it does for incapacity benefit purposes. The student is not eligible during the first 28 weeks of incapacity for work – referred to here as a 'waiting period'.

In calculating the 'waiting period', periods of incapacity for work are added together if they are separated by gaps of eight weeks or less.

Once the waiting period is completed, the student is eligible. After a gap (i.e. a period in which the student is capable of work or is disqualified from incapacity benefit) of eight weeks or less, the student does not have to start a new waiting period: he or she becomes eligible again straightaway. But after a gap of more than eight weeks, the student is not eligible until he or she has completed a fresh waiting period.

**Table 21.2 SUMMARY: STUDENT COUPLES: HB AND MAIN CTB**

| Partner A | Partner B | Who can claim HB and main CTB? | HB on two homes? |
|---|---|---|---|
| ◆ Student in the eligible groups | Student in the eligible groups | Either | Yes on both, if reasonable, and if maintaining two is unavoidable |
| ◆ Student in the eligible groups | Student not in the eligible groups | Partner A only | Only on the home occupied by partner A |
| ◆ Student in the eligible groups | Non-student | Either | Yes on both, if reasonable, and if maintaining two is unavoidable |
| ◆ Student not in the eligible groups | Student not in the eligible groups | Neither | Not on either |
| ◆ Student not in the eligible groups | Non-student | Partner B only | Only on the home occupied by partner B |
| ◆ Non-student | Non-student | Either | Student rules do not apply |

*The 'eligible groups' referred to in this table are those listed in table 21.1*

## THE PRIMARY RULE: STUDENTS WHO MAINTAIN TWO HOMES

**21.27** Some students have to maintain two homes, one near their educational establishment and one elsewhere. There are special rules for students in these circumstances which apply for HB purposes only: HBR 5(3),(5)(b)

- students without partners (i.e. single claimants and lone parents) can, if they are in one of the eligible groups in table 21.1, get HB on only one home (paras. 3.59-60);
- for couples, the rules are given in table 21.2.

There are other rules about HB on two homes (para. 3.65) which apply in addition to these. For CTB there are no special rules for students maintaining two homes.

## HALLS OF RESIDENCE, ETC.

HBR 46, 50 **21.28** In addition to the previous rules, students (whether full-time or part-time, and including couples whether one or both are students) are not eligible for HB on halls of residence or any other accommodation where the rent is payable to the educational establishment they attend. This rule only applies in the period of study, so such students are eligible for HB during their summer vacation (if they have one).

**21.29** This rule applies to any accommodation which the establishment owns, leases under a lease granted for more than 21 years, or rents from another educational establishment or an education authority. It does not apply (i.e. the students are eligible for HB) if the establishment itself rents accommodation on a temporary basis from a council, housing association or private landlord and then sublets it to its students – unless it has arranged this in order to take advantage of the HB scheme.

**21.30** There is no equivalent rule in CTB. This is because halls of residence are exempt from council tax (para. 2.12).

## ABSENCE DURING THE SUMMER VACATION

HBR 48 **21.31** Finally, full-time students are not eligible for HB on their term-time accommodation if they are absent from it during the summer vacation. The rule does not apply unless the student is absent for at least one Sunday/Monday midnight. Once the rule applies, it continues to apply (but only during the summer vacation) until the end of the benefit week in which the student returns to the accommodation. (This is because of the ordinary rules about start of entitlement to HB: chapter 5.) This rule never applies to part-time students, and for couples it applies only if both are full-time students.

**21.32** Furthermore the rule applies only if the student's main purpose in occupying the accommodation during his or her period of study is to facilitate attendance on the course. The DWP advises that the rule would not therefore apply (GM para. C5.26) if the student:

- has a child or young person living with him or her; or
- is aged 25 or over and has no other accommodation; or
- is under 25 and has no parent or guardian and no other accommodation.

Authorities should also take into account any other relevant factor in reaching a decision. For example, if the student lived in the accommodation before starting the course, or moved to the area to be near relatives, or is a council or housing association tenant, it is unlikely that the main purpose of occupying the home is to attend the course.

**21.33** There is no equivalent rule in CTB. There may therefore be cases in which a student is eligible only for CTB during a period of absence from his or her term-time accommodation.

## Assessing HB and main CTB for students

**21.34** For students who are eligible, the calculation of their HB and main CTB follows the same rules as for anyone else. But for students not on income support or income-based jobseeker's allowance there are two main variations:

- in HB only, part of a full-time student's rent and income is not counted; and
- in HB and main CTB, there are special rules for assessing students' income.

Examples of calculations for students are given at the end of this chapter. There are no special rules about calculating second adult rebate for students. The ordinary rules in chapter 10 apply.

### 'NEW RULES' vs 'OLD RULES'

**21.35** During the 2001-02 academic year (which ends in summer 2002) most students fall within the 'new rules' introduced in stages over recent years. In this year, the only students who fall within the old 'rules' are fourth year students who deferred their studies for a year when they began them and fifth and later year students. The remainder of this chapter gives the new rules, with a summary of the old rules (and a fuller definition of who they apply to) at the end (para 21.62).

**21.36** Most undergraduate students who fall within the new rules can get a student loan (the figures are given in table 21.3); but they cannot get a government grant – unless they have specific needs (such as for a disability or for dependants).

### THE RENT DEDUCTION AND INCOME DISREGARD FOR FULL-TIME STUDENTS CLAIMING HB

**21.37** This rule results in students getting less HB. It does not apply in main CTB. However, in HB it applies regardless of whether the student has a loan or a grant or indeed any form of income at all. The details of the rule follow.

**21.38** With the exceptions mentioned below, a full-time student's eligible rent is reduced by the following amount in every week during his or her period of study (in the 2001-02 academic year). In those weeks, the same amount is disregarded from his or her income, whether from a grant or any other source, in the assessment of HB. HBR 51(1),(2A)

- £28.40 in London (the City of London and the former Metropolitan Police District); or
- £19.65 outside London including Northern Ireland.

For a student who attends an educational establishment in London but lives outside London, the London figure applies, and vice versa.

**21.39** The rule applies for couples (with the exceptions mentioned below), whether one or both are full-time students, and regardless of which partner claims. Even if both are full-time students, there is only one rent deduction and only one income disregard. Technically, the income disregard is applied as follows:

- if only one partner is a full-time student: first to the full-time student's income, then (if that does not use up the disregard) to the other partner's income;
- if both partners are full-time students: first to the claimant's income, then (if that does not use up the disregard) to the other partner's income.

## EXCEPTIONS

HBR 46, 51(2) **21.40** There is no rent deduction or income disregard in any of the following cases:

- if the student or any partner is on income support or income-based jobseeker's allowance; or
- if the student or any partner receives an allowance (covering the needs of any member of the family) for attendance on a government training scheme; or
- during any period of work experience for a student on a sandwich course (para. 21.11); or
- the student was formerly ill or providing care and falls within the eligible group described in entry (k) in table 21; or
- if the low income rule applies (described below).

## THE 'LOW INCOME RULE'

HBR 51(2)(c) **21.41** There is no rent deduction or income disregard if making the student income disregard would mean that the student had weekly income (assessed for HB purposes) below his or her applicable amount, and

- the student is a lone parent, or
- the disability premium applies (chapter 12), or the student is disqualified from incapacity benefit, or the student has been incapable of work for 28 weeks or more (as described in the note to table 21.1), or
- the student has a partner who is not also a full-time student.

Note that the 'low income rule' applies only to the above three groups of student. It does not apply to, say, a foster parent or a student over 60 (unless they also fall into one of the three groups).

**21.42** The above is one way of describing the low income rule. The other method would be to more closely mimic the regulations themselves by saying: 'There is no rent deduction or income disregard if the student's weekly income (as assessed for HB purposes) is less than the sum of his or her applicable amount and the amount of the rent deduction (and the student falls into one of the three groups).' This and the description in the previous paragraph are identical in every way.

### TERMLY PAYMENT OF HB

**21.43** The authority may pay a student's HB once a term. However, if the student is entitled to more than £2.00 HB per week, he or she can insist on being paid under the normal rules about frequency of payment (chapter 16). This rule applies to full-time and part-time students, and to couples where either or both are students. In practice it is never used. HBR 90(5)

## Student loan income

### WHO CAN GET A STUDENT LOAN?

**21.44** With the exceptions mentioned in the following paragraph, all full-time students in higher education are eligible to apply for a student loan. Parents, spouses and students themselves may, depending on the circumstances, be assessed as having to make a contribution to a student loan.

**21.45** The following are not eligible for a student loan:

- part-time students;
- students undertaking nursing and midwifery diploma courses (para. 21.10);
- most postgraduates – except that students studying for a Postgraduate Certificate of Education (PGCE) are eligible for a student loan;
- certain students aged 50 or more.

The situation is complex for students aged 50 or more, and it is advisable for an authority to enquire of the student himself or herself as to whether he or she can get a student loan, and to seek supporting documentation as appropriate.

### AMOUNTS

**21.46** In the 2001-02 academic year, for students living away from home, the maximum student loan is shown in table 21.3. The figures for NHS-funded students are lower (and may be found in DWP circular HB/CTB A31/2001).

### ASSESSMENT

**21.47** In calculating HB and main CTB, all students who are eligible to apply for a student loan are treated as receiving one at the maximum level applicable to them (as shown in table 21.3) if they 'could acquire [a student loan] in respect of that year by taking reasonable steps to do so'. This is done regardless of whether HBR 57A CTBR 47 they actually apply for a student loan and/or actually receive one. In the case of a couple this means taking up to two student loans into account as appropriate. Note, however, that hardship loans are dealt with differently (para. 21.58).

HBR 46, 53, 57A
CTBR 38, 43, 47

**21.48** This academic year (2001-02), the student loan is then assessed for HB and main CTB purposes as shown in table 21.3: an example also follows. This is different from the previous academic year (which is turn was different from the one before that, as was that from the one before it).

**21.49** Table 21.3 covers all the main types of student course. Further variations are given in paragraphs 21.65 onwards, covering students who fall within the old rules, courses that start other than in autumn and students who leave part way through their course.

**21.50** In all cases, when in future years former students begin repaying student loans, they will not be able to offset them against earnings or other income for HB or main CTB purposes; and the repayment will not count as a change of circumstances for HB/CTB purposes.

HBR 58(1), 58A
CTBR 48, 48A

**21.51** If a student loan is assessed on the assumption that the student, or his or her partner, will make a contribution, the amount of that contribution is disregarded from the student's or partner's other income. (There may also be circumstances in which a parent who makes a contribution can have that amount disregarded in the assessment of his or her own HB and main CTB: para. 13.85.)

## Student grant income

HBR 53(1)
CTBR 42(1)

**21.52** The rules for assessing grant income apply to any kind of educational grant, award, scholarship, studentship, exhibition, allowance or bursary, whether paid by an education authority or anyone else.

**21.53** Except for students who fall within the old rules (para. 21.35), education authority grants are not available for basic maintenance but may be awarded for specific needs such as adult dependants, disability, extra travel costs and school meals. In the 2001-02 academic year, the main grant figures for education authority grants may be found in DWP circulars HB/CTB A31/2001.

### ASSESSMENT

R 46,53,57,57A
BR 38,42,46,47

**21.54** This academic year (2001-02) grant income is assessed for HB and main CTB purposes as shown in table 21.4. This is different from the previous academic year.

HBR 58(1), 58A
CTBR 48, 48A

**21.55** If a student's grant is assessed on the assumption that the student, or his or her partner, will make a contribution, the amount of that contribution is disregarded from the student's or partner's other income. (Similarly, a parent who makes a contribution has that amount disregarded in the assessment of his or her own HB and main CTB: para. 13.85.)

## TABLE 21.3 STUDENT LOANS: 2001-02 ACADEMIC YEAR

| **AMOUNTS** | **Final year** | **Other years** | **Per extra week** |
|---|---|---|---|
| Courses in London: | £4,075 | £4,700 | £88 |
| Courses outside London: | £3,310 | £3,815 | £67 |

*Note:* Figures are for English, Welsh and Scottish students living away from home in the 2001-02 academic year. In each case, they are the maximum amount a student could obtain. The figures do not apply to NHS-funded courses or to nursing and midwifery diploma students. Figures are taken from DWP circular HB/CTB A31/2001.

### TREATMENT FOR HB/MAIN CTB PURPOSES

(a) Take the whole amount into account as income (even though it is in fact a loan). Include any amount from extra weeks. Treat any parental or spouse's (or student's own) assumed contribution to it as being received (even if not actually paid).

(b) Disregard £579 in all cases. This is a standard amount including £260 towards travel and £319 towards books and equipment. (From this year, there are no exceptions.)

(c) Average the resulting amount over the period described below.

(d) Then disregard £10 from the weekly figure (in the case of a couple, disregard £10 from each one's weekly figure), subject to the over-riding £20.00 limit on certain disregards (para. 13.109).

### PERIOD OVER WHICH THE LOAN IS AVERAGED

**General rule**

Average over the period from the first Monday in September to the last Sunday in June. (In 2001-02 this is 43 weeks: 3.9.01 to 30.6.02. In 2002-03 it will also be 43 weeks: 2.9.02 to 29.6.03.)

**Exceptions**

*First years only:* If the course begins after the first Monday in September, still average over the period described above, but then ignore it as income for the week(s) before the course begins.

*Final years and one-year courses only:* Average over the period from the first Monday in September to the last Sunday in the course.

*All years (but likely to apply only in Scotland):* If any year of the course starts before the first Monday in September, average over the period from the first Monday in the course to the last Sunday in June (or, in the final year, the last Sunday in the course).

*Further exceptions and special cases are given in paras. 21.65 onwards.*

**Example: A student loan**

In the 2001-02 academic year, a student in his second year of a degree course in Wales could get a student loan of £3,815. (He is not in receipt of a grant of any kind.) His wife is not a student and has claimed HB and CTB for them both. His student loan is assessed as follows in the assessment of his wife's HB/CTB claim.

Whether or not he applies for or receives it, he is treated as receiving it and it is assessed as follows (see also table 21.3):

(a) Treat the whole £3,815 as income (even though it is in fact a loan).

(b) Disregard £579 for books and equipment and travel, leaving £3,236.

(c) Average this over the 43 weeks from 3.9.01 to 30.6.02, which is £75.26 per week.

(d) Disregard £10, which gives £65.26 per week.

So this student has student loan income of £65.26 per week from 3.9.01 to 30.6.02. This is the case even if his second year did not start until a date in October 2000. (But if he had been a first year, the £65.26 per week would have been ignored as income until the first Monday in his first year.)

## TABLE 21.4: STUDENT GRANTS: 2001-02 ACADEMIC YEAR

TREATMENT FOR HB/MAIN CTB PURPOSES

(a) Treat any parental or spouse's (or student's own) assumed contribution to it as being received (even if not actually paid).

(b) No standard disregard is made for travel or for books and equipment – unless the student neither receives nor is treated as receiving a student loan, in which case disregard £579. (But see also step (c).)

(c) Disregard any amount included in the grant for:

- additions for books and equipment (in addition to the standard £579 if appropriate);
- the extra £500 awarded in some cases for travel, books and equipment;
- child care additions;
- the extra £250 awarded for the only, elder or eldest child in some cases;

- tuition or examination fees;
- school meals grants;
- additions because the student has a disability;
- expenses for term-time residential study;
- two homes grant;
- additions for anyone outside the UK so long as the student's applicable amount does not include an amount for that person.

(d) Average the resulting amount over the period described below.

PERIOD OVER WHICH THE GRANT IS AVERAGED

**Awards for (adult or child) dependant(s) from an education authority or government department**

Average over the same period as the student loan (table 21.3: the general rule and exceptions all apply).

**Any other amount (other than the disregarded amounts)**

*If it is attributable to the student's period of study (para. 21.21):* Average over the period of study excluding, for sandwich students, any period of work experience.

*If it is attributable to any other period:* Average over that period.

**Exceptions**

*Nursing and midwifery diploma students:* They get a bursary towards their maintenance (and cannot get a student loan). Their bursary (after any appropriate disregards) is averaged over the full calendar year (52/53 weeks).

*NHS-funded students on degree courses:* They get a bursary towards their maintenance (and can get a student loan at a lower rate than other students). Their bursary (after any appropriate disregards) is averaged over the full calendar year (52/53 weeks) – and their loan is dealt with as in table 21.3.

*NHS dependant grants:* If the student is receiving instruction as an officer of a hospital authority, average these over 12 months.

*Students to whom the old rules apply:* See paragraph 21.62.

## Other income

### ACCESS FUND PAYMENTS

**21.56** 'Access fund payments' are administered by educational establishments. (They are sometimes also called 'hardship fund payments' – but they are not the same as hardship loans: see below.) The establishments may make such payments to:

- students who fall within the student loan scheme (para. 21.44);
- postgraduates (of all kinds); and
- students aged 19 or more in further education.

HBR 46, 57B, 59(2),(3)
HBR sch 4 para 33
HBR sch 4 para 35
CTBR 38, 47A, 49(2),(3), sch 4 para 34

**21.57** Access fund payments are treated as follows:

- if they meet costs which are not met through a grant, but would be disregarded if they were met through a grant (as in table 21.4), they are disregarded in full;
- any other regular payments towards certain necessities (defined below) are:
  - disregarded in full as income if they are made before the student's course begins and are made in anticipation of the person becoming a student;
  - disregarded in full as income if they are made on or after 1st September (or the first day of the course if later) to tide a student over till receipt of his or her student loan;
  - in any other case, treated as income (averaged over the period they cover), then £20 per week is disregarded (subject to the over-riding £20.00 limit on certain disregards (para. 13.109).
- regular payments towards any other amount are completely disregarded;
- single lump sum payments are treated as capital; but if they are for certain necessities (defined below), the capital is disregarded for 52 weeks from the date of payment.

The 'certain necessities' mentioned above are food, ordinary clothing and footwear, household fuel, eligible rent (apart from any amount attributable to non-dependant deductions), council tax or water charges – of the claimant or any member of the family.

### HARDSHIP LOANS

HBR 57A(1),(1A)
CTBR 47(1),(1A)

**21.58** These are different from access fund payments. They may be loaned to students who have received at least part of their student loan. Even though they may be administered with student loans, they are not counted as income. As loans, they are capital not income. The DWP advises they should be disregarded as such (HB/CTB A32/2000).

## COVENANT INCOME

**21.59** In the past, many parents paid their student son or daughter income through a covenant (a legally enforceable promise to pay money). The tax advantages of creating a covenant ended on 15th March 1988, and so such covenants probably do not exist. There remain, however, special rules for assessing any covenant paid to a full-time student by his or her parent. The details are in GM chapter C5. HBR 46, 54-56 CTBR 38, 43-45

## OTHER INCOME

**21.60** If a full-time or part-time student receives earned or unearned income other than (or as well as) grant or covenant income or a student loan, the ordinary earned and unearned income disregards apply to it (chapters 13-15).

## THE EXTRA STUDENT INCOME DISREGARD

**21.61** In addition to the above points, there is a further disregard for student expenditure, which works as follows. If the student has loan or grant income, certain amounts are disregard from it, as shown in tables 21.3 and 21.4. If the student necessarily spends more on those items than the amounts indicated in the tables, the excess is disregarded from his or her other income (as illustrated in the diagram). This important disregard is often overlooked: students are advised to check that it has been applied properly. HBR 57 CTBR 46

**Example: The extra student income disregard**

A student receives a student loan. In the assessment of the loan for HB/CTB purposes, £319 is disregarded towards books and equipment and £260 towards travel. She is not in receipt of any grant for travel, but can satisfy the authority that her actual travel costs for the year will be £690 (£430 more). She uses money from a part-time job to pay for this.

The additional £430 per year for travel is disregarded in assessing her income from her part-time job (as well as any other earned income disregards which may apply: chapter 14). There is no particular rule for which weeks to allow this in. Since her loan income has to be averaged over 43 weeks, it may be fair to average this £430 over those 43 weeks.

## Special cases

### VARIATIONS FOR STUDENTS WHO FALL WITHIN THE OLD RULES

**21.62** A student falls within the 'old rules' (para. 21.35) if he or she:

- started his or her course of study before 1st September 1998 (1st August 1998 in Scotland); or
- started his or her course of study before 1st September 1999 (1st August 1999 in Scotland) but only if he or she had the formal agreement (usually this means written agreement) of the educational establishment concerned to defer starting a course from the previous year.

So, during this 2001-02 academic year, this means a fifth (or later) year student; or a fourth year who deferred starting his or her course for a year.

**21.63** Most undergraduate students who fall within the old rules can get a student loan (but at a rate lower than the figures given in table 21.3) plus some government grant towards their maintenance (plus additions for specific needs such as for a disability or for dependants).

HBR 53(3A), 60
CTBR 42(4A), 50

**21.64** With two variations, all the student rules in this chapter apply to students who fall within the old rules in the same way as they do to students who fall within the new rules. The two variations for students who fall within the old rules are to do with how grants are assessed (table 21.4) and are as follows:

- awards or additions for (adult or child) dependants are averaged over the full calendar year (52/53 weeks); and
- once grant income has been assessed, any change in the standard maintenance grant occurring during the summer vacation is ignored until the end of the summer vacation. The standard maintenance grant is up-rated with effect from 1st September each year. So for a student whose autumn term begins on a date in October, the change is ignored until then.

### COURSES THAT START OTHER THAN IN AUTUMN

HBR 46(1), 57A(2)
CTBR 38(1), 47(2)

**21.65** From this (2001-02) academic year, new rules are introduced to cater for courses that do not start in the autumn. They use the concepts 'academic year' (as defined in para. 21.69) and 'quarter' (as defined in para. 21.68) in ways that do not always match day-to-day expectations.

**21.66** For students whose 'academic year' (para. 21.69) begins on 1st September, their loan is averaged over the benefit weeks falling wholly within the ten months from 1st September to 30th June both dates inclusive (as described in table 21.3).

**21.67** But for students whose 'academic year' (para. 21.69) begins on 1st

January, 1st April or 1st July, their loan is averaged over the benefit weeks falling wholly within:

- the whole academic year beginning on that date;
- but excluding the whole of the 'quarter' (para. 21.68) in which, 'in the opinion of the Secretary of State', the longest of any vacation is taken.

### DEFINITION OF 'QUARTER'

**21.68** For purposes of the above rules, the following (despite the fact that they are of different lengths in two cases) are the four 'quarters':

- 1st January to 31st March (3 months);
- 1st April to 30th June (3 months);
- 1st July to 31st August (2 months);
- 1st September to 31st December (4 months).

### DEFINITION OF 'ACADEMIC YEAR'

**21.69** For the purposes of the above rules, 'academic year' means the twelve months beginning on:

- 1st January if the course begins in the winter;
- 1st April in the course begins in the spring;
- 1st July if the course begins in the summer – *but see below for an exception;*
- 1st September in the course begins in the autumn.

But if a student is required to begin attending a course during August or September and continue attending through the autumn, his or her academic year is the one beginning on 1st September.

**21.70** The seasons are not in turn defined in the law, but the following is believed to be correct (indeed the last two lines in para. 21.69 would not work in law if the following were wrong):

- winter starts on the winter solstice in late December;
- spring starts on the spring equinox in late March;
- summer starts on the summer solstice in late June;
- autumn starts on autumn equinox in late September.

## LOAN INCOME AND DEPENDANT INCOME OF STUDENTS LEAVING PART WAY THROUGH A COURSE

HBR 33(3A)-(3C), CTBR 24(4A)-(4C)

**21.71** New rules are introduced this (2001-02) academic year, changing the way these forms of income are dealt with.

**21.72** A student who leaves part way through his or her course is treated for HB and main CTB purposes as having income from a student loan or dependant grant – but only if a payment of a student loan and/or a dependant grant has actually been paid to the student in the 'academic year' (defined as in para. 21.69) in question. In such cases there are four steps:

(a) Take the total amount of student loan and/or grant for dependants which he or she would have received if he or she had remained till the end of the academic term in which he or she left. Then deduct the standard amount for travel and books and equipment (£579). In the law (and guidance), the result is '**A**'.

(b) Calculate how much student loan income has been taken into account already in that academic year (up to – and including – the benefit week in which he or she left) under the normal rules (table 21.3) but pretending that there was no £10 disregard. In the law (and guidance), the result is '**B x C**' (**B** being the number of weeks and **C** the weekly amount in those weeks).

(c) Subtract **B x C** from **A**. Average the result over the benefit weeks from (and including) the benefit week following that in which the student abandoned or was dismissed from the course up to (and including) the final benefit week in the last 'quarter' (as defined in para. 21.68) for which the student loan and/or dependant grant was paid to that student. In the law (and guidance) the number of weeks in this period is '**D**'; and the amount taken into account as income in each of those weeks is the formula:

$$\frac{\mathbf{A - (B \times C)}}{\mathbf{D}}$$

(d) This counts as the ex-student's income only from (and including) the benefit week following that in which the student abandoned or was dismissed from the course up to (and including) the final benefit week in the last 'quarter' (para. 21.68) for which a student loan or a grant for dependants was paid to the student.

**Example: Student assessment: New rules: 2001-02 academic year**

INFORMATION

| | |
|---|---|
| Student claimant | Single woman, student aged 20, lives alone. She is eligible for HB because of her disability (table 21.1) |
| Course | 2001-02, outside London, first year of course, full-time, undergraduate. |
| Period of study | Tuesday 2.10.01 to Thursday 21.6.02 inclusive. |
| Student loan | She receives £3,815 (the maximum amount available in her case). |
| Grant | She gets a disabled student's grant only. |
| Other income | Net earnings (after all appropriate disregards) of £50 per week at all material times; no capital. |
| Applicable amount | Includes a disability premium and is £64.60 to 31.3.02, £65.70 from 1.4.02. |
| Eligible rent | Would be £60.00 per week if she was not a student. |
| Council tax | Her home is exempt. |

INCOME FROM LOAN

She qualifies for a student loan, and is treated as receiving one at the maximum level available – which in her case is £3,815. (In fact she actually receives this amount.)

Disregard £579 for books and equipment and travel, leaving £3,236.

Average this (£3,236) over the 43 weeks from 3.9.01 to 30.6.02, giving £75.26 per week.

Disregard £10.00, giving £65.26 per week.

INCOME FROM GRANT

Her disabled student's grant is disregarded completely.

### HB: IS THERE AN INCOME DISREGARD AND RENT DEDUCTION?

During her period of study, her total income is £115.26 per week (which is £65.26 from the student loan plus £50.00 from her net earnings). Making the income disregard (£19.65) leaves £95.61.

£95.61 is more than her applicable amount (£65.70) so the student income disregard and rent deduction must be applied during her period of study (para. 21.41).

### HB: ASSESSED INCOME AND ELIGIBLE RENT

*Monday 3.9.01 to Sunday 7.10.01:* She is not yet a student and the income from her loan is ignored. So her assessed income is £50.00 per week (from the job alone) and her eligible rent is £60 per week (with no deduction).

*Monday 8.10.01 to Sunday 30.6.02:* Her assessed income is £95.61 per week (as above) and her eligible rent is £40.35 per week (£60.00 minus £19.65).

*Monday 1.7.02 to Sunday 1.9.02:* This is outside the period over which her loan is averaged. So her assessed income is £50.00 (from the job alone) and her eligible rent is £60 per week (with no deduction).

# 22 Subsidy

**22.1** This chapter examines how HB and CTB are expected to be paid for in 2002-03. It applies to Great Britain only. It considers:

- the different types of expenditure;
- government objectives in establishing who pays for what;
- the different types of central government subsidy;
- subsidy penalties and incentives for authorities to control certain types of HB and CTB expenditure;
- the HB element of the housing revenue account (HRA) subsidy that applies in England and Wales; and
- subsidy to meet HB and CTB administration costs.

The special subsidy arrangements that apply to new towns or Scottish Homes are not described in this chapter.

**22.2** The importance of an appropriate level of central government subsidy has sometimes been overlooked by authorities and advisers. An absence of correct procedures in some authorities has meant that they have lost a significant amount of subsidy from central government. The DWP has identified in circular S1-2002 that the majority of cases giving rise to overpayments of subsidy related to a failure to refer cases to the Rent Officer, the inability to substantiate the subsidy claim, claims being unlawfully decided by contractors or agency staff and claims which were allowed to run beyond the end of the benefit period. Not only do these payments form a significant proportion of most authorities' total income, they are also a vital factor in determining the quality, effectiveness and style of HB and CTB administration. Studies of HB and CCB administration have highlighted the tension between proper decision-making (para. 1.21) and some of the 'perverse' penalties and incentives built into the subsidy systems (see, for example, *Remote Control: The National Administration of Housing Benefit,* Audit Commission, HMSO 1993).

## Legislation

**22.3** Benefit subsidy, except the subsidy relating to HRA benefit expenditure in England and Wales, is governed by amendments to SI 1998 No. 562, the Income-Related Benefits (Subsidy to Authorities) Order. These are normally issued at the end of the year to which it applies. The rules covering subsidy relating to HRA benefit expenditure in England and Wales for 2002-03 are contained in the

Housing Revenue Account Subsidy Determination 2002-03. Separate determinations are issued by the DETR and the Welsh Office. DWP guidance on the details of the subsidy arrangements for 2002-03 had yet to be issued at the time of writing.

## Expenditure and government objectives

**22.4** Money spent on the different aspects of the HB and CTB schemes consists of:

- benefit payment costs, i.e. the money paid out in the form of HB or CTB; and
- on-going administrative costs, which include salaries, accommodation, postage, computer running costs and giro charges.

**22.5** Money to meet these costs comes from three different sources:

- central government subsidy;
- the authority's own general fund; and
- (in England and Wales in the case of HRA rent rebates) the authority's own housing revenue account.

The government's stated objective for the subsidy arrangements is to provide 'incentives for local authorities to monitor and control costs whilst providing a fair level of support for expenditure which they properly incur' (*Hansard,* 25th June 1986, col. 210). AA 135

## Types of central government subsidies

**22.6** The following central government subsidies are paid to meet the costs of the schemes:

- rent allowance subsidy to meet the cost of rent allowances;
- rent rebate subsidy to meet the cost of non-HRA rent rebates, and in Scotland only, the cost of HRA rent rebates;
- CTB subsidy to meet the cost of CTB expenditure; and
- HRA subsidy – which may help meet the cost of HRA rent rebate expenditure in England and Wales (but not in Scotland).

HB and CTB subsidies are described in paras. 22.8-30. The rent rebate element of HRA subsidy is described in paras. 22.31-38. Subsidy arrangements are summarised in table 22.1.

## Table 22.1 SUMMARY OF BENEFIT EXPENDITURE SUBSIDY ARRANGEMENTS 2002-2003

| | *Benefit expenditure (except HRA rent rebate expenditure in England and Wales)* | *HRA rent rebate (England and Wales)* |
|---|---|---|
| **Basic rate of subsidy** | 95% | 100% taken into account in subsidy calculation where an authority's rent increases have kept to government guidelines |
| **Backdated benefit** | 50% | nil |
| **Overpayments** | | |
| ◆ authority error | nil | nil |
| ◆ claimant/third party error | 40% | nil |
| ◆ claimant/third party fraud | 80% or 40% where authority has adoped new anti-fraud incentive scheme | nil |
| ◆ rebate credited in advance of entitlement | nil | nil |
| ◆ DSS error | 95% | 100% |
| ◆ CTB overpaid due to delayed award of council tax discounts, disability reductions, transitional relief or budget capping | nil | N/A |
| ◆ other | 40% | nil |
| Duplicate rent allowance payment where original lost/ stolen/not received and later found to have been encashed | 25% | N/A |
| **HB attributable to disproportionate increase in authority's rent** | nil on HB attributable to disproportionate increase (Scotland) | nil on HB attributable to disproportionate increase |

| | *Benefit expenditure (except HRA rent rebate expenditure in England and Wales)* | *HRA rent rebate (England and Wales)* |
|---|---|---|
| **Unreasonably high private rents not covered by the January 1996 rules** | | |
| ◆ regulated tenancies | 25% of HB attributable to rent above the specified threshold, 95% of rest | N/A |
| ◆ deregulated tenancies (where authority unable to restrict the claimant's eligible rent) | 60% on HB attributable to rent above rent officer determination and any support charges under the transitional housing benefit scheme, 95% of rest | N/A |
| ◆ deregulated tenancies | nil on HB attributable to rent above rent officer determination and any support charges under the transitional housing benefit scheme, 95% of rest | N/A |
| **Homeless people in board and lodging accommodation** | 12.5% on HB attributable to rent above the specified threshold up to level of newly introduced cap, nil above, 95% of rest | N/A |
| **Accommodation licensed by authority** | 12.5% on HB attributable to rent above the specified threshold up to level of newly introduced cap, nil above, 95% of rest | N/A |
| **Short-term leased accommodation** | 12.5% on HB attributable to rent above the specified threshold up to level of newly introduced cap, nil above, 95% of rest | N/A |
| **Short-term leased accommodation in Scottish authorities' HRA** | nil on HB attributable to rent above the specified threshold, 95% of rest | N/A |
| **Period overruns** | | |
| *Overrun weeks as a % of benefit weeks in year* | *% of total qualifying expenditure to be deducted from net subsidy claimed* | *See formula in Subsidy Determination* |
| ◆ 81 to 100% | 5% | |
| ◆ 61 to 80.99% | 4% | |
| ◆ 41 to 60.99% | 3% | |
| ◆ 21 to 40.99% | 2% | |
| ◆ 5 to 20.99% | 1% | |
| ◆ less than 5% | nil% | |

### HRA AND NON-HRA RENT REBATE EXPENDITURE

**22.7** HRA rent rebate expenditure includes all rent rebates paid in respect of dwellings which are accounted for within the authority's HRA. They include mainstream council housing to council tenants. Non-HRA rent rebates include those paid for:

- homeless people housed by the authority in bed and breakfast accommodation;
- accommodation leased by the local authority from a private landlord, e.g. hotel annexes; and
- occupants of accommodation that has been leased to the authority for a period which does not exceed three years (short-term leased accommodation).

## HB and CTB subsidies

### QUALIFYING EXPENDITURE

**22.8** Benefit expenditure that counts for subsidy purposes is known as qualifying expenditure. The following are the main items of benefit expenditure that do not count as qualifying expenditure and that therefore are not eligible for HB or CTB subsidy as appropriate:

- any old scheme (pre-April 1988) overpayments;
- any benefit expenditure attributable to a local scheme (para. 9.39).

### PERMITTED TOTALS

**22.9** An authority's discretionary expenditure on modified schemes to enhance the mandatory disregards of Navy and Army war widows' pensions (para. 9.40) should be contained within the relevant permitted total.

### MODULAR IMPROVEMENT SCHEMES

**22.10** In Scotland, for the purpose of rent rebate subsidy (and also in England and Wales, for the purpose of HRA subsidy), rent rebate expenditure attributable to modular or menu improvement schemes for council tenants are not eligible for subsidy. These are schemes where tenants choose to pay increased rents in return for additional rights, services or facilities such as a door entry system or improved heating. Authorities are exempt from the reduction, however, where the rights, services or facilities:

- were made available with the sole purpose either of improving the physical condition of the dwellings or of meeting the needs of tenants or both; and
- were available for tenants to choose regardless of whether the tenants were or were not in receipt of rebates; and

- were not an influence on the authorities' letting policies and practices in the current and two proceeding financial years in relation to tenants eligible to receive rebates; and
- were made available at reasonable cost.

**22.11** In Scotland, for the purpose of rent rebate subsidy rent rebate expenditure attributable to rent-free weeks not taken account of in calculating the rent rebate does not count as qualifying expenditure. Qualifying rent rebate expenditure is also reduced by the amount of any cash payments or payments in kind made to a local authority tenant by the authority except: SI 1996 No 677 SI 1996 No 678 SI 1998 No 566 SI 1999 No 642

- payments made that are unrelated to the fact that the claimant is a tenant of the local authority, e.g. educational bursaries;
- awards required by law;
- discretionary payments made under section 137 of the Local Government Act 1972;
- reasonable compensation for repairs or redecorating carried out by the tenant which would normally have been carried out by the landlord; and
- one-off compensation payments for the loss, damage or inconvenience caused because the tenant occupies a particular property. This provision catches, for example, certain rent payment incentive schemes.

### SUBSIDY ON QUALIFYING HB/CTB BENEFIT EXPENDITURE

**22.12** The normal subsidy rate on benefit expenditure, except HRA benefit in England and Wales, is 95 per cent. A lower rate is payable in specific circumstances (para. 22.13). Different rules apply to HRA rent rebate expenditure in England and Wales in the same circumstances (para. 22.31).

## Penalised benefit expenditure

**22.13** To provide authorities with a firm incentive to monitor and control costs, the following areas of benefit expenditure are penalised:

- the backdating of claims (para. 22.15);
- identified overpayments (para. 22.16);
- disproportionately high increases in rents for local authority tenants (para. 22.19);
- rent allowances paid in respect of unreasonably high rents on most pre-1988 Housing Act tenancies without a registered or reasonable rent (para. 22.21);
- rent allowances paid under the rules introduced on 2nd January 1996 (para. 22.22);

- rent allowances which do not fall to be calculated under the rules introduced on 2nd January 1996 (para. 22.26), paid in respect of most rents of, in Scotland, post-2nd January 1989 lettings, and in England and Wales, post-15th January 1989 lettings; which are above reasonable market rents determined by the rent officer or which the rent officer determines to be exceptionally high, or accommodation which the rent officer considers unreasonably large;
- non-HRA rent rebates paid for certain homeless families in bed and breakfast accommodation and occupants of certain short-term leased accommodation where the rent payment is above a certain level (para. 22.20);
- cases that have overrun the maximum benefit period without a review taking place (benefit period overruns) (see GM paras. C10.50-57).

The same areas of English and Welsh HRA benefit expenditure are penalised (paras. 22.31 onwards).

**22.14** Authorities must apply the rules of the scheme fairly, objectively and impartially. They must not allow the subsidy penalties to interfere with this duty though where the authority has a discretion one factor it may take into account is its own financial position.

## BACKDATING OF CLAIMS

**22.15** A 50 per cent subsidy is payable on amounts of benefit, except HRA benefit in England and Wales, that have been backdated where the claimant has good cause for a late claim (para. 7.93). In general, where an overpayment was backdated and is subsequently found to be overpaid, it should be treated as a backdated payment. The exception is where a backdated amount is later identified as a fraudulent overpayment. In such a case the fraudulent overpayment category (table. 22.1) takes priority.

## OVERPAYMENTS

**22.16** The subsidy payable on benefit overpayments, except HRA benefit in England and Wales, varies with the cause shown in table 22.1.

**22.17** In the case of overpayments the subsidy arrangement acts, at least in part, as an incentive to authorities. Subsidy is paid on the identified overpayments. Amounts recovered, except in the case of Benefits Agency error overpayments, are not deducted from the authority's subsidy entitlement. For example, if the authority recovers a fraudulent overpayment or claimant error overpayment it receives 40 per cent subsidy and keeps the money it has recovered.

**22.18** The nil rate of subsidy on authority error overpayments, which are often non-recoverable, acts as a severe penalty on the authority and as an incentive to misclassification.

## HOMELESS PEOPLE IN B & B, LICENSED AND SHORT-TERM LEASED ACCOMMODATION OUTSIDE THE HRA

**22.19** Threshold figures cover rent rebates awarded to homeless people placed in bed and breakfast accommodation by the local authority under the Housing Act 1985 or Housing (Scotland) Act 1987 as well as other licensed accommodation, e.g. hotel annexes, and also for short-term leased accommodation. Subsidy of 12½ per cent is paid on any HB equal to or less than the amount by which the eligible rent exceeds the threshold figure up to the level of a cap with nil entitlement above the capped figure. Benefit attributable to that part of the eligible rent which does not exceed the threshold attracts direct subsidy at the usual rate of 95 per cent.

## UNREASONABLY HIGH RENTS ON OLD STYLE TENANCIES

**22.20** If the claimant occupies a regulated tenancy without a registered rent, or is a restricted contract holder without a reasonable rent determined by a rent tribunal, and his or her eligible rent exceeds the local threshold, the amount of any HB equal to or less than that excess figure only qualifies for a 25 per cent subsidy. The local threshold is a figure equivalent to a multiple of the average registered rent in the relevant registration area for each authority. This subsidy penalty does not apply where the claimant's rent (though above the threshold) is registered or (in the case of a restricted contract) is a reasonable rent determined by a rent tribunal.

## RENT ALLOWANCES PAID UNDER THE RULES THAT OPERATE FROM 2ND JANUARY 1996

**22.21** From 2nd January 1996 new rules have applied to certain rent allowance claims. Under the arrangements that existed prior to that date and which continue for some claimants, the rent officer's determinations restrict the amount of subsidy paid by central government (paras. 22.26-22.30) but do not necessarily restrict the rent on which HB is assessed. Under the new arrangements, the rent officer's determinations are used directly to calculate the maximum rent on which HB can be assessed. 95 per cent subsidy is normally payable on the HB calculated under the new rules. This entitlement to maximum subsidy includes those cases where the authority cannot restrict the rent because there has been a bereavement in the household or where the rent could be afforded when the tenancy was taken up and the claimant has not been in receipt of HB for 52 weeks prior to the current claim.

**22.22** The one exception to the full subsidy entitlement under the new rules is where the authority uses a lower value for ineligible services than the ineligible service figure provided by the rent officer. In such cases any additional HB attributable to the use of the lower ineligible service figure does not qualify for subsidy.

**22.23** Discretionary payments made in exceptional hardship cases do not count as qualifying expenditure for HB subsidy purposes (para. 22.8) and must be contained within the permitted totals figure (para. 22.9).

## INDICATIVE RENT LEVELS

**22.24** From 2nd January 1996 rent officers have supplied authorities with indicative rent levels (IRLs) which replace the former interim determinations. These are supplied on the first working day of each month for eight types of property (table 8.5). As the authority is unable to determine rent allowance entitlement under the January 1996 rules until the rent officer has made a full determination, IRLs can be used by the authority in working out the amount of a payment on account (para. 18.16). Where the authority is unable to recover all or part of an overpaid payment on account caused by the difference between the final determination (and consequent maximum rent) and the IRL, full subsidy is payable on the unrecovered amount providing the IRL used was the correct one and provided the authority applies the final determination in the HB assessment by the Monday following the date it was received.

**Examples: Old style tenancies**

The claimant's eligible rent (after any restriction) is £65. The rent is not registered. The weekly threshold figure notified to the authority by the DSS is £50. The claimant's eligible rent exceeds the threshold figure by £15.

If the claimant's rent allowance is £15 or less it only attracts a 25 per cent subsidy.

If the claimant's rent allowance is £30, £15 attracts a 25 per cent subsidy and £15 a 95 per cent subsidy,
i.e. subsidy = £3.75 + £14.25 = £18.00.

If the claimant's rent allowance is £65, £15 attracts 25 per cent subsidy and £50 attracts a 95 per cent subsidy,
i.e. subsidy = £3.75 + £47.50 = £51.25.

## SUBSIDY ON HB PAID ON NEW STYLE TENANCIES NOT PAID UNDER THE JANUARY 1996 RULES

**22.25** In most cases falling under the pre-January 1996 rules, no DWP subsidy is payable on any HB equal to or less than the amount by which the eligible rent exceeds the rent officer's significantly high rent figure or exceptionally high rent determination less the rent officer's valuation for certain services. The exception is where the authority is unable to treat a claimant's eligible rent as reduced (para. 22.27).

**22.26** In certain cases falling under the pre-January 1996 rules, the authority is unable to restrict the claimant's eligible rent, or a rent increase. This applies, for example, where the claimant falls into a 'protected' category, e.g. the claimant is 60 or over and there is no suitable alternative accommodation available.

**22.27** In such cases subsidy at the rate of 60 per cent is payable on any HB equal to or less than the amount by which the eligible rent exceeds the rent officer's determination and any support charges eligible under the transitional HB scheme.

**22.28** The aim of these subsidy penalties is to encourage authorities to use their powers to restrict eligible rents under the pre-January 1996 rules where they consider them unreasonable.

**22.29** The subsidy threshold figure and the rent officer's determinations represent the point above which the DWP are not prepared to pay subsidy or only prepared to pay a reduced amount of subsidy. These two figures do not represent the level above which authorities should not meet rents. Authorities are required to consider the individual circumstances of each case before deciding whether or not to meet the rent in full.

## HRA subsidy

**22.30** A housing authority's housing revenue account (HRA) records its income and expenditure on local authority housing. In England and Wales, but not Scotland, HRA subsidy was introduced under part VI of the Local Government and Housing Act 1989.

**22.31** The amount of HRA subsidy that an English or Welsh authority is entitled to is calculated under a formula laid down by the Secretary of State to make up the assumed deficit on the authority's HRA.

**22.32** The formula takes account of nine items of debit and credit of which qualifying rent rebate expenditure is only one. An English or Welsh authority's HRA subsidy entitlement equals its government assumed expenditure minus its government assumed income. If the assumed income is greater than the assumed expenditure then an amount equivalent to the excess income must be debited to the authority's HRA and transferred to its general fund.

**22.33** Items of expenditure consist of:

- government-set allowances for the management and maintenance of council property;
- allowance for major repairs;

- charges for capital;
- 100 per cent of most qualifying rent rebate expenditure;
- other items of reckonable expenditure;
- allowance for tenant participation compacts;
- allowance for resource accounting.

**22.34** Items of income consist of:

- its rental income assumed by government;
- interest on certain capital receipts invested by the authority.

**22.35** Whilst most qualifying rent rebate expenditure scores 100 per cent for HRA subsidy purposes, rent rebate expenditure itself is only one element in a deficit subsidy equation and consequently the HRA subsidy received by an authority may be significantly less th an its qualifying rent rebate expenditure.

### QUALIFYING HRA BENEFIT EXPENDITURE

**22.36** The categories of expenditure which are deducted from the total of HRA rent rebates granted in calculating qualifying HRA benefit expenditure are those described in paras. 22.8-10, and 100 per cent of the spending in the appropriate penalised areas described in para. 22.13. A fixed allowance of 1.7 per cent of rent rebate expenditure is also allowed in each authority's HRA subsidy entitlement to cover the cost of overpayments and backdating.

### LIMITING HRA SUBSIDY ON RENT REBATES TO GUIDELINE RENT INCREASES

**22.37** For 1996-97 onwards HRA subsidy is not paid on any additional rent rebate expenditure which results from an authority increasing its average actual rents by more than its central government guideline rent increase. An authority may, however, apply for special determinations to disapply the new rule where it can show that it faces exceptional circumstances outside its control. The details of the revised rules are described in *Rent Rebate Subsidy Limitation: Derogations in 2002-2003* (DTLR/LAH December 2001).

### SHORT-TERM LEASED ACCOMMODATION IN THE HRA

**22.38** From April 1995 there is no longer any short-term leased accommodation within English authorities' HRAs (HB/CTB S2/95 para. 5.1).

## Subsidy on administrative costs

**22.39** Authorities are reimbursed for their administrative costs via a cash-limited specific grant. 50 per cent of this grant is added to their HB and CTB subsidy entitlement. The remaining 50 per cent is reflected in the revenue support grant (RSG) for English and Welsh authorities and the grant aided expenditure (GAE) arrangements in Scotland. In the case of English and Welsh authorities no addition is made to their HRA subsidy entitlement, as the costs of rent rebate administration are met outside the HRA and subsidised via the specific administration grant.

**22.40** The non-RSG/GAE element of administration subsidy is allocated amongst authorities on the basis of assumed workload rather than actual expenditure. The assumed workload is determined by a formula that takes into account type of case, caseload, turnover data and tenure.

**22.41** This unit cost subsidy fails to take account of 'quality of service' objectives such as the percentage of claims processed within the 14-day time period and error rates. As well as penalising inefficient authorities, a unit cost subsidy penalises those authorities that have sought to administer HB in a positive manner, for example by providing home visits to maximise take-up or by making their offices more accessible.

## ABOLITION OF WEEKLY BENEFIT SAVINGS AND THE NEW INCENTIVE SUBSIDY ARRANGEMENTS

**22.42** The New Incentive Arrangements takes over from the previous arrangements that sought to encourage the Council to identify fraudulent payments of benefit – primarily the Weekly Benefits Savings scheme (WBS). The New Arrangements are mandatory for all authorities from 1st April 2002. These new arrangements are set out in DSS/DWP Circulars F12/2000, F15/2000, F10/2001 and F19/2001.

**22.43** One element of the new arrangements – the Weekly Incorrect Benefit (WIBs) reward scheme – enables the authority to obtain additional subsidy where it attracts rewards above its DWP set target by:

- identifying overpayments arising from 'fraud', 'claimant' and 'other' error as well as 'BA departmental error' discovered by the authority;
- reducing improperly paid benefit if it is unable to establish an overpayment where the claimant is not occupying the dwelling as a home (non-residency); or has failed to declare that they are living with a partner as husband and wife; and/or
- identifying incorrect details for Benefits Agency benefit claims where the recipient is in receipt of HB and/or CTB but no overpayment of HB/CTB has occurred.

**22.44** Unlike the previous WBS scheme there are currently no financial penalties for authorities that fail to meet their DWP set target. Under a separate sanctions and prosecutions reward scheme authorities attract additional subsidy where they:

- raise an administrative penalty – £1000),
- issue a formal caution – £1000;
- information is laid with a court and a summons is issued – £1000; and
- £2000 for each successful prosecution.

**22.45** The rules above apply for each claim. This means that for combined HB and CTB cases any subsidy gain or loss will be £20. In the case of rent allowances, any subsidy gain or loss is decided by the date the claim is correctly determined and not by the date a payment on account is made.

## 'Fast-tracking' subsidy arrangements for 'in-work' HB/CTB claims

**22.46** Authorities are required to give priority to 'in-work' claims made by people who have been awarded extended payments (para. 18.2). This requirement is reinforced through a system of time limits and subsidy rewards and penalties known as 'fast-tracking' (HB/CTB A6/96).

### HOW DO THE 'FAST-TRACKING' SUBSIDY RULES WORK?

**22.47** The subsidy rules are summarised in table 22.2.

**Table 22.2 'FAST-TRACKING' SUBSIDY**

| *Claim correctly determined within the specified 7/14 day time limit?* | *Claim correctly determined within the extended payment period?* | *Subsidy gained or lost* |
|---|---|---|
| YES | YES | Authority gains £10 extra subsidy |
| YES | NO | Authority incurs no subsidy gain/loss |
| NO | YES | Authority incurs no subsidy gain/loss |
| NO | NO | Authority loses £10 subsidy |

**22.48** The rules above apply for each claim. This means that for combined HB and CTB cases any subsidy gain or loss will be £20. In the case of rent allowances, any subsidy gain or loss is decided by the date the claim is correctly determined and not by the date a payment on account is made.

# Appendix 1: Main and recent statutory instruments

Here we list the main statutory instruments that contain the detailed rules of the HB and CTB schemes and also all amending and related statutory instruments issued since the beginning of 2000.

## MAIN STATUTORY INSTRUMENTS

(see also note on sources of Northern Ireland legislation, page xiii)

| | |
|---|---|
| SI 1987 No. 1971 | The Housing Benefit (General) Regulations (as amended) |
| SI 1988 No. 662 | The Housing Benefit (Supply of Information) Regulations |
| SI 1992 No. 1814 | The Council Tax Benefit (General) Regulations |
| SI 1995 No. 1644 | The Housing Benefit (General) Amendment Regulations |
| SI 1997 No. 1984 | The Rent Officers (Housing Benefit Functions) Order |
| SI 1997 No. 1995 | The Rent Officers (Housing Benefit Functions) (Scotland) Order |
| SI 1997 No. 2435 | The Housing Benefit (Recovery of Overpayments) Regulations |
| SI 1997 No. 2436 | The Housing Benefit (Information from Landlords and Agents) Regulations |
| SI 1997 No. 2813 | The Social Security (Penalty Notice) Regulations |
| SI 1998 No. 562 | The Income-related Benefits (Subsidy to Authorities) Order |
| SI 2001 No. 1002 | The Housing Benefit and Council Tax Benefit (Decisions and Appeals) Regulations |

## RECENT STATUTORY INSTRUMENTS

(see also table 1.1 which includes Northern Ireland)

| | |
|---|---|
| SI 2001 No. 22 | Social Security Amendment (Capital Disregards) Regulations |
| SI 2001 No. 207 | Social Security Benefits Up-rating (No. 2) Order |
| SI 2001 No. 487 | Housing Benefit (General) Amendment Regulations |
| SI 2001 No. 518 | Social Security Amendment (Joint Claims) Regulations |
| SI 2001 No. 537 | Housing Benefit and Council Tax Benefit (Extended Payments) Regulations |
| SI 2001 No. 652 | Social Security (Miscellaneous Amendments) (No. 2) Regulations |

| | |
|---|---|
| SI 2001 No. 724 | Local Government (Best Value) Performance Indicators and Performance Standards Order |
| SI 2001 No. 859 | Social Security (Miscellaneous Amendments) (No. 3) Regulations |
| SI 2001 No. 970 | New Deal (Miscellaneous Provisions) Order |
| SI 2001 No. 1002 | Housing Benefit and Council Tax Benefit (Decisions and Appeals) Regulations |
| SI 2001 No. 1029 | Social Security Amendment (New Deal) Regulations |
| SI 2001 No. 1095 | Social Security Commissioners (Procedure) (Amendment) Regulations |
| SI 2001 No. 1118 | Social Security Amendment (Capital Disregards and Recovery of Benefits) Regulations |
| SI 2001 No. 1129 | Housing Benefit (Permitted Totals) (Amendment) Order |
| SI 2001 No. 1130 | Council Tax Benefit (Permitted Totals) (Amendment) Order |
| SI 2001 No. 1167 | Discretionary Financial Assistance Regulations |
| SI 2001 No. 1190 | Housing Benefit (General) Amendment (No.2) Regulations |
| SI 2001 No. 1252 | Child Support, Pensions and Social Security Act 2000 (Commencement No 8) ) Order |
| SI 2001 No. 1264 | Housing Benefit and Council Tax Benefit (Decisions and Appeals) (Transitional and Savings) Regulations |
| SI 2001 No. 1324 | Housing Benefit (General) Amendment (No. 3) Regulations |
| SI 2001 No. 1325 | Rent Officers (Housing Benefit Functions) (Amendment) Order |
| SI 2001 No. 1326 (S.4) | Rent Officers (Housing Benefit Functions) (Scotland) (Amendment) Order |
| SI 2001 No. 1605 | Housing Benefit and Council Tax Benefit (Decisions and Appeals and Discretionary Financial Assistance) (Consequential Amendments and Revocations) Regulations |
| SI 2001 No. 1711 | Social Security (Breach of Community Order) (Consequential Amendments) Regulations |
| SI 2001 No. 2317 | Rent Officers (Housing Benefit Functions)(Amendment)(No.2) Order |
| SI 2001 No. 2318 | Rent Officers (Housing Benefit Functions)(Scotland) (Amendment)(No.2) Order |
| SI 2001 No. 2333 | Social Security Amendment (Discretionary Housing Payments) Regulations |
| SI 2001 No. 2340 | Discretionary Housing Payments (Grants) Order |
| SI 2001 No. 2350 | Income-related Benefits (Subsidy to Authorities) Amendment Order 2001 |

| | |
|---|---|
| SI 2001 No. 2915 | New Deal (Lone Parents) (Miscellaneous Provisions) Order 2001 |
| SI 2001 No. 2980 | Social Security Amendment (Personal Allowances for Children and Young Persons) Regulations 2001 |
| SI 2001 No. 3070 | Children (Leaving Care) Act 2000 (Commencement No 2 and Consequential Provisions) Order 2001 |
| SI 2001 No. 3252 | Social Security (Notification of Change of Circumstances) Regulations 2001 |
| SI 2001 No. 3481 | Social Security Amendment (Capital Disregards) (No 2) Regulations 2001 |
| SI 2001 No. 3561 | Rent Officers (Housing Benefit Functions) (Amendment) Order 2001 |
| SI 2001 No. 4022 | Social Security (Loss of Benefit) Regulations 2001 |

# Appendix 2: Table of selected cases

The following list includes selected cases decided since the beginning of 2001. See the 2001-02 edition of the Guide for a list covering preceding years.

| NAME, COURT AND DATE OF JUDGMENT | REPORT | SUBJECT |
|---|---|---|
| R v City of Westminster Housing Benefit Review Board ex p Mehanne, House of Lords, 8.3.01 | (2001) 33 HLR 46 Independent, April 30, 2001 | The House of Lords upheld the Court of Appeal's decision (same case name, 21.12.98). In an 'exempt case', despite the word 'shall' in reg. 11(2) of the main HB Regs, the Review Board has a discretion to decide the amount of any reduction in HB to be applied; and, although the regulation refers to the cost of suitable alternative accommodation as one factor to be taken into account, it is not the only one: other reasonably relevant facts have to be taken into account and their importance must be weighed up by the Review Board (or, at earlier stages, the authority). |
| R (on the application of Saxby) v Milton Keynes Housing Benefit Review Board, CA, 3.4.01 | 33 HLR 82; [2001] Times, June 7, 2001 | Elders of a Christian community home were entitled to claim HB in respect of payment attributable to the occupation of all residents living in the home sharing all outgoings even though the elders occupied only part of the house. |
| R (on the application of Painter) v Carmarthenshire County Council Housing Benefit Review Board QBD, 4.5.01. | [2001] All ER (D) 59 (May) Times, May 16, 2001; Independent, June 18, 2001 | A person who ceased a cohabitating relationship with his partner but continued to occupy the same property as her lodger was not entitled to HB. |
| R. (on the application of Waite) v Hammersmith and Fulham LBC QBD, 20.8.01 | [2001] All ER (D) 284 (Jul) | The authority's decision that the claimant, a prisoner, released on life licence but later recalled, was not entitled to HB for the period up until the parole board had confirmed his recall to prison, did not infringe the claimant's rights under the Human Rights Act 1998. |

| | | |
|---|---|---|
| R. (on the application of Bewry) v Norwich City Council QBD, 31.8.01 | [2002] HLR 2 | The fact that the Review Board was made up of councillors of the administering authority meant that there was a real risk of bias. Case remitted to an appeal tribunal. |
| R. (on the application of Sier) v The Housing Benefit Review Board of Cambridge County Council CA, 8.10.2001 | [2001] All ER (D) 85 (Oct) | DSS's failure to pass on details to authority was not the cause of an overpayment. |
| R. (on the application of Saadat) v Rent Service CA, 26.10.01 | [2001] EWCA Civ 1559 Times, November 6, 2001 | In setting the local reference rent for HB, 'locality' was to signify an area no greater than would enable the rent officer reliably to make the specified calculations and judgments depending on the character of the area in which the dwelling was located. (The law in Great Britain has since been amended to undo the effect of this case: see para. 6.18.) |
| R. (on the application of Tucker) v Secretary of State for Social Security, CA, 8.11.01 | [2001] All ER (D) 109 (Nov) Daily Telegraph, November 13, 2001 | The assumption underlying Regulation 7(1)(d) was that where the tenant was a parent and carer of the landlord's child, the landlord would not generally consider the tenancy in the usual commercial manner. There was no contravention of the claimant's rights under the Human Rights Act 1998. |
| R. (on the application of Bibi) v Rochdale Metropolitan Borough Council Housing Benefit Review Board, QBD, 27.11.01 | [2001] All ER (D) 394 (Nov) | The connection between the councillors on the Board and the authority had not tainted the board's decision. |

# Appendix 3: Current HB and CTB circulars

The following list includes all DSS and DWP circulars issued since the beginning of 2001. See the 2001-02 edition of this Guide for a list covering 1996 to 2000.

## ADJUDICATION AND OPERATIONS CIRCULARS

| | |
|---|---|
| HB/CTB A1/2001 | Disregard of special payments for Far Eastern Prisoners of War that we expect will be made from the beginning of February |
| HB/CTB A2/2001 | The Housing Benefit and Council Tax Benefit (Decision and Appeals) Regulations 2001 |
| HB/CTB A3/2001 | Correction to circular HB/CTB A2/2001 |
| HB/CTB A4/2001 | Verification Framework – Continuing & Set up funding for 2001-02 |
| HB/CTB A5/2001 | 1. The Social Security Commissioners<br>2. Decision making and Appeals Leeds – Local Authority Information unit |
| HB/CTB A6/2001 | I. Contact List<br>II. Guidance Manual Update |
| HB/CTB A7/2001 | Joint Claims for JSA |
| HB/CTB A8/2001 | Changes to the HB and CTB Extended Payment Scheme to come into effect from 9 April 2001 |
| HB/CTB A9/2001 | 1) Alignment of rules on self-employment route<br>2) Amendments consequential to the Learning and Skills Act 2000<br>3) Further information about HB/CTB A7/2001<br>4) Information about the Children Tax Credit (CTC)<br>(NB: this circular contained an error on the rate of Children Tax Credit – see the correction provided in Circular A14/2001) |
| HB/CTB A10/2001 | Service Charges in Supported Accommodation |
| HB/CTB A11/2001 | Decision Making and Appeals |
| HB/CTB A12/2001 | 1. Summary<br>2. Liability to Pay Regulation 7(1)(h) Ex-Owners<br>3. Rent rules and Rent Officer referrals:<br>(i) Calculation of Eligible Rent<br>(ii) Deductions for meals<br>(iii) Exceptional Hardship Payments<br>(iv) Referrals to the Rent Officer |
| HB/CTB A13/2001 | Verification Framework – modified requirements for the period of the Foot and Mouth outbreak in 'temporarily laid off from work' cases |

| | |
|---|---|
| HB/CTB A14/2001 | Amendment to Circular HB/CTB A9/2001 |
| HB/CTB A15/2001 | The Housing Benefit Improvement Programme: update on information provided in Circular A45/2000 |
| HB/CTB A16/2001 | Verification Framework: April 2001 amendments |
| HB/CTB A17/2001 | The Housing Benefit and Councils Tax Benefit (Decision and Appeals) (Transitional and Savings Regulations) 2001 |
| HB/CTB A18/2001 | Decision Making and Appeals |
| HB/CTB A19/2001 | 1. Disregard for special payments to vCTD sufferers and their families<br>2. Treatment of personal injury payments |
| HB/CTB A20/2001 | Broadening the Single Room Rent from 2 July 2001 |
| HB/CTB A21/2001 | Participation in a pilot to involve RSLs in HB verification work |
| HB/CTB A22/2001 | Foot and mouth outbreak |
| HB/CTB A23/2001 | HB/CTB Decisions and Appeals: Applications made before 2 July 2001 for further review by a Review Board, or for an appeal to an appeal tribunal. |
| HB/CTB A24/2001 | Enhanced Model National Service Level Agreement between the Benefits Agency and the Local Authority Associations. |
| HB/CTB A25/2001 | Appeals to the Commissioners. Chapter 6 of the rewritten guidance manual |
| HB/CTB A26/2001 | I Help with childcare costs<br>II The main rates of Income Tax and National Insurance Contributions for the year 2001-02<br>III Increases in Working Families' Tax Credit (WFTC) and Disabled Person's Tax Credit (DPTC) from 5 June 2001<br>IV Children (Leaving Care) Act 2000<br>V Revised Contact point |
| HB/CTB A27/2001 | Amendment to Circular HB/CTB A25/2001. Amendment to Circular HB/CTB A26/2001. Claim Forms on the old DSS Web Site. |
| HB/CTB A28/2001 | HB/CTB Decisions and Appeals (Savings and Transitional Provisions) Regulations 2001 – Transitional Arrangements |
| HB/CTB A29/2001 | The Housing Benefit Improvements Programme: update on information provided in HB/CTB Circular 15/2001 |
| HB/CTB A30/2001 | Amendments to HB/CTB Overpayments/Excess Benefit Regulations: Further Guidance |
| HB/CTB A31/2001 | 1. Rates of loans/disregards<br>2. Treatment of student income<br>3. NHS funded students<br>4. Postgraduate students<br>5. Rent deductions, incentive payments and new allowances/disregards<br>6. Former students<br>7. Contact point |
| HB/CTB A32/2001 | 1. National Savings Certificates – July 2001<br>2. New Disregards<br>3 Changes to the local reference rent<br>4. Contact List – update |

| | |
|---|---|
| HB/CTB A33/2001 | Secondment opportunities to the Department for Work and Pensions |
| HB/CTB A35-2001 | To invite bids for the Help Fund – an initiative that has been set up to support LAs in improving their administration of HB. |
| HB/CTB A36/2001 | 1. Expenses paid to volunteers<br>2. Corrections to circular HB/CTB A32/2001<br>3. Valuation of capital assets liaison with Valuation Office Agency (VOA) |
| HB/CTB A37/2001 | Increase in personal allowance of children under and over age 16 |
| HB/CTB A38/2001 | Questions frequently asked on the DWP CCB HB Appeals Project Helpline |
| HB/CTB A39/2001 | Students – Clarification and Enhancement of Circular A31/01 |
| HB/CTB A40/2001 | Closure of the DWP WAG CCB HB Appeals Project |
| HB/CTB A41/2001 | Children (Leaving Care) Act 2000 |
| HB/CTB A42/2001 | The Housing Benefit Improvements Programme: update of information |
| HB/CTB A43/2001 | Update on Circular A21/2001 regarding participation in a pilot to involve Registered Social Landlords (RSLs) in HB verification work |
| HB/CTB A44/2001 | Amendments to the HB Regulations about overpayments |
| HB/CTB A45/2001 | New Entrepreneur Scholarship |
| HB/CTB A46/2001 | Jobcentre Plus industrial action within Pathfinder Areas: contingency plans |
| HB/CTB A47/2001 | The Transitional Housing Benefit Scheme |
| HB/CTB A48/2001 | 1.Victims of atrocities during the Second World War<br>2. Judicial Review |
| HB/CTB A50/2001 | Community Sentences and Benefits |
| HB/CTB A51/2001 | New Deal for Disabled People Extension |
| HB/CTB A52/2001 | Decision Making and Appeals and Overpayments |
| HB/CTB A53/2001 | Uprating 2002 |
| HB/CTB A1/2002 | 1. New-look HB/CTB Circulars and distribution arrangements<br>2. Amendments to Circulars A48/2001 and A53/2001<br>3. Estimating earnings<br>4. Participation in the pilot to involve Registered Social Landlords (RSLs) in HB verification work |
| HB/CTB A2/2002 | Industrial action in DWP offices – contingency plans |
| HB/CTB A3/2002 | Guidance on Performance Indicator relating to recoverable overpayments provided in:<br>• DTLR's 'Best Value Performance Indicators for 2001/02' (BV 79b in England)<br>• National Assembly Wales (NAW) circular 8/2001<br>• Local Government Act 1992 Statutory Performance Indicators<br>• (Accounts Commission – Scotland) |

## FRAUD CIRCULARS

| | |
|---|---|
| HB/CTB F1/2001 | Housing Benefit Matching Service (HBMS) Data Take on and Processing Schedule |
| HB/CTB F2/2001 | Obtaining information from the Inland Revenue |
| HB/CTB F3/2001 | 1. BA/LA Joint Working<br>2. Amendment to HB/CTB F2/2001 |

| | |
|---|---|
| HB/CTB F4/2001 | The New Authorised Officer Powers (Inspector's Powers) (NB: this Circular contained an error in paragraph 6 – see the correction supplied in Circular F7/2001) |
| HB/CTB F5/2001 | Training for Counter Fraud Officers |
| HB/CTB F6/2001 | 2001-02 Counter Fraud operational Agreement (SLA) |
| HB/CTB F7/2001 | Amendment to Circular HB/CTB F4/2001 |
| HB/CTB F8/2001 | Applying the New Authorised Officer Powers |
| HB/CTB F9/2001 | Data Sharing Aide-Memoire |
| HB/CTB F10/2001 | Further guidance on the new incentive scheme & the modified WBS scheme for 2001-02: Sanctions & Prosecution |
| HB/CTB F11/2001 | List of named Authorised Officers |
| HB/CTB F12/2001 | Training for Counter Fraud Officers |
| HB/CTB F13/2001 | 1. Housing Benefit Matching Service (HBMS) Data Take on and Processing Schedule |
| HB/CTB F14/2001 | The Social Security Fraud Act 2001 |
| HB/CTB F15/2001 | Joint Regional Board Bids |
| HB/CTB F16/2001 | Section 19 |
| HB/CTB F17/2001 | Targeting Fraud |
| HB/CTB F18/2001 | HBMS Data Take on and Processing Schedule |
| HB/CTB F19/2001 | Further guidance on the new anti-fraud incentive scheme. |
| HB/CTB F20/2001 | The impact of the Regulation of Investigatory Powers (RIP) Act 2000 |
| HB/CTB F21/2001 | Funding of Joint Working Initiatives via Joint Regional Boards |
| HB/CTB F22/2001 | Updated contact list |
| HB/CTB F23/2001 | Authorised Officer Powers |
| HB/CTB F24/2001 | Not Issued |
| HB/CTB F25/2001 | Verification Framework Modules and Changes from 2002 Funding Arrangements |
| HB/CTB F26/2001 | Housing Benefit Matching Service (HBMS) Data Take on and Processing Schedule |

## SUBSIDY CIRCULARS

| | |
|---|---|
| HB/CTB S5/2001 | Details of the distribution of the government contribution and overall limit for discretionary housing payments (DHPs). Claiming for re-imbursement of DHPs Disregarding DHPs in the assessment of entitlement to HB/CTB |
| HB/CTB S6/2001 | Completion of 2000-01 Final Subsidy Claims for the year 2000-01 |
| HB/CTB S7/2001 | The Rents Act (Maximum Fair Rent Order) 1999 – treatment of overpaid benefit and subsidy |
| HB/CTB S8/2001 | HB/CTB subsidy 2002-03: details of the specific grant for administration costs |
| HB/CTB S1/2002 | Outcome of the policy review on the recovery of overpaid benefit subsidy |

# Appendix 4: HB and CTB figures (from April 2002)

## MAXIMUM BENEFIT AND TAPER PERCENTAGES (chapter 7)

| | HB | Main CTB |
|---|---|---|
| Maximum benefit | 100% | 100% |
| Taper | 65% | 20% |

## NON-DEPENDANT DEDUCTIONS (chapter 7)

| | HB | Main CTB |
|---|---|---|
| Non-dependants in remunerative work (16 or more hours per week) whose gross income is | | |
| £281.00 pw or more | £47.75 | £6.95 |
| £225.00 to £280.99pw | £43.50 | £5.80 |
| £170.00 to £224.99pw | £38.20 | £4.60 |
| £131.00 to £169.99 pw | £23.35 | £4.60 |
| £88.00 to £130.99 pw | £17.00 | £2.30 |
| below £88.00 | £7.40 | £2.30 |
| Non-dependants in other work – regardless of income | £7.40 | £2.30 |

## AMOUNT OF SECOND ADULT REBATE (chapter 8)

| | |
|---|---|
| Second adult(s) on income support or JSA(IB) | 25% |
| Second adult(s) whose gross income is below £125.00 pw | 15% |
| £131.00 to £169.99 pw | 7½% |
| £170 pw or more | nil |

## APPLICABLE AMOUNTS
(chapter 12)

### PERSONAL ALLOWANCES

| | | |
|---|---|---|
| Single claimant | aged under 25 | £42.70 |
| | aged 25 or over | £53.95 |
| Lone parent | aged under 18 (HB only) | £42.70 |
| | aged 18 or over | £53.95 |
| Couple | both aged under 18 (HB only) | £64.45 |
| | at least one aged 18 or over | £84.65 |
| Child/young person addition | lower rate | £33.50 |
| | higher rate | £34.30 |
| Polygamous partner addition | | £30.70 |

### PREMIUMS

| | | |
|---|---|---|
| Family premium | protected rate (certain lone parents) | £22.20 |
| | basic rate (couples and other lone parents) | £14.75 |
| Pensioner premium *or* Enhanced pensioner premium *or* Higher pensioner premium | single claimant or lone parent | £44.20 |
| | couple (one or both qualifying) | £65.15 |
| Disability premium | single claimant or lone parent | £23.00 |
| | couple (one or both qualifying) | £32.80 |
| Disabled child premium | child/young person | £35.50 |
| Enhanced disability premium | child/young person | £11.25 |
| | single claimant or lone parent | £11.25 |
| | couple (one or both qualifying) | £16.25 |
| Severe disability premium | single rate | £42.25 |
| | double rate | £84.50 |
| Carer premium | claimant or partner or each | £24.80 |
| Bereavement premium | single claimant | £21.55 |

## CAPITAL
(chapter 13)

| | | |
|---|---|---|
| Capital limit | | £16,000 |
| Lower capital limit: | | |
| | claimant and any partner under 60 | £3,000 |
| | claimant or partner aged 60 or more | £6,000 |
| | certain special cases (para. 13.11) | £10,000 |
| Tariff income between these | | £1 per £250 or part thereof |

## EARNED INCOME DISREGARDS
(chapters 13-15)

| | |
|---|---|
| *Earnings of claimant or partner* | |
| lone parents | £25.00 |
| certain disabled or elderly people, certain carers and certain occupations | £20.00 |
| couples in other cases | £10.00 |
| single claimants in other cases | £5.00 |
| *Earnings of certain children and young persons* | |
| certain disabled children/young persons | £15.00 |
| other cases | £5.00 |
| *Childcare earnings disregard for certain couples/lone parents* | |
| care for one child | £94.50 |
| care for two or more children | £140.00 |

## MAXIMUM RATE OF RECOVERY OF OVERPAID HB FROM ONGOING HB
(chapter 18)

| | |
|---|---|
| General rate | £8.10 |
| Certain fraud cases | £10.80 |

## STUDENT RENT DEDUCTION AND INCOME DISREGARD (HB ONLY) (chapter 21)

| | **2001-02 academic year** |
|---|---|
| Courses in London | £28.40 |
| Courses elsewhere | £19.65 |

## NOTIONAL TAX AND NI FIGURES (chapter 15)

These are used for claims for HB/CTB made in the 2002-03 tax year, in calculating net profit from self-employment (tax and classes 2 and 4 NI).

### TAX

*Personal allowance*

| | |
|---|---|
| single person/each partner in a couple | £4,615 |
| (other allowances are ignored) | |

*Rate of tax*

| | |
|---|---|
| first £1,920 above personal allowance | 10% |
| remainder | 22% |
| (the 40% rate is not used) | |

### NATIONAL INSURANCE

*Class 2 contributions for chargeable income of*

| | |
|---|---|
| under £4,025 per year | nil |
| £4,025 or more per year | £104 per year |

*Class 4 contributions for chargeable income*

| | |
|---|---|
| first £4,615 per year | nil |
| balance to £30,420 per year | 7% of this balance |

# Appendix 5: Other benefit rates (from April 2002)

| | |
|---|---|
| *Contribution-based jobseeker's allowance* | |
| claimant aged under 18 | £32.50 |
| claimant aged 18 to 24 | £42.70 |
| claimant aged 25 or more | £53.95 |
| *Child benefit* | |
| only or older/oldest child (general rate) | £15.75 |
| only or older/oldest child (protected lone parent rate) | £17.55 |
| each other child (couple or lone parent) | £10.55 |
| *Incapacity benefit* | |
| *Long-term rate* | |
| single person | £70.95 |
| couple | £113.40 |
| *Short-term higher rate* | |
| single person | £63.25 |
| couple | £96.35 |
| *Short-term lower rate* | |
| single person | £53.50 |
| couple | £86.60 |
| *Retirement pension standard rate* | |
| single person | £75.50 |
| couple | £120.70 |

*Disability living allowance*

*Care component*

| | |
|---|---|
| highest rate | £56.25 |
| middle rate | £37.65 |
| lowest rate | £14.90 |

*Mobility component*

| | |
|---|---|
| higher rate | £39.30 |
| lower rate | £14.90 |

| | |
|---|---|
| *Special payment for pre-1973 war widows* | £59.95 |

# Appendix 6: Categories of people for non-dependant deduction and second adult rebate purposes

There are many categories of people relevant for non-dependant deductions in HB, for non-dependant deductions in main CTB, and for second adult rebate. The categories are not always the same for these three purposes.

This appendix defines all the categories relevant for these purposes (as they have applied since 1st April 2000, there having been no changes since then), and answers the following questions for each category:

- Is there a non-dependant deduction for them in HB and main CTB (paras. 9.23, 9.26)?
- Are they 'disregarded persons' for second adult rebate purposes?

The second question is relevant because a 'disregarded person' cannot be a second adult (para. 10.6); and because the rules about whether couples and joint occupiers can qualify for second adult rebate refer to 'disregarded persons' (paras. 10.17-18). It is also relevant to the rules about council tax discounts (para. 3.35).

People may fall into more than one category. If a particular category (e.g. category 1) indicates that a non-dependant deduction applies (or that they are not 'disregarded persons'), this is over-ridden if they fall into another category (e.g. category 13) where no non-dependant deduction applies (or where they are 'disregarded persons').

The category numbers have no significance except to aid cross-referencing.

## 1. PEOPLE ON INCOME SUPPORT OR JSA(IB)

| | |
|---|---|
| HB | No non-dependant deduction if aged under 25. Otherwise a non-dependant deduction applies. |
| Main CTB | No non-dependant deduction. |
| Second adult rebate | Not 'disregarded persons'. |

This means anyone in receipt of income support or income-based jobseeker's allowance – JSA(IB) – including people receiving these benefits whilst on government training schemes. It also includes people who would get JSA(IB) except that they are currently subject to a sanction.

## 2. PEOPLE UNDER 18

| | |
|---|---|
| HB and main CTB | No non-dependant deduction. |
| Second adult rebate | 'Disregarded persons' (because they do not count as 'residents'). |

This means anyone under 18 whether a member of the claimant's family or not.

## 3. 18-YEAR-OLDS FOR WHOM CHILD BENEFIT IS PAYABLE

| | |
|---|---|
| HB and main CTB | No non-dependant deduction. |
| Second adult rebate | 'Disregarded persons'. |

This means 18-year-olds for whom someone receives or could receive child benefit – e.g. at school and shortly after leaving school (see also category 4).

## 4. EDUCATION LEAVERS UNDER 20

| | |
|---|---|
| HB | A non-dependant deduction applies unless they fall within categories 2 or 3. |
| Main CTB | No non-dependant deduction. |
| Second adult rebate | 'Disregarded persons'. |

This only applies from 1st May to 31st October inclusive each year. It means anyone who leaves the type of education described in category 5 or 6 within that period. It lasts until that person reaches 20 or until 31st October, whichever comes first.

## 5. STUDENTS UNDER 20 AT SCHOOL OR COLLEGE

| | |
|---|---|
| HB and main CTB | Whether there is a non-dependant deduction depends on whether they fall within category 2, 3 or 10. |
| Second adult rebate | 'Disregarded persons'. |

The full definition is not given here. Its main elements are that the person:

- is under 20; and
- is studying up to (but not above) A level, ONC, OND or equivalent; and
- is on a course of at least 3 months' duration; and
- is normally required to study at least 12 hours per week in term times; and
- does not fall within categories 6 to 8.

## 6. FULL-TIME STUDENTS IN FURTHER OR HIGHER EDUCATION

| | |
|---|---|
| HB and main CTB | Whether there is a non-dependant deduction depends on whether they fall within category 10. |
| Second adult rebate | 'Disregarded persons'. |

The full definition is not given here. Its main elements are that the person:

- is attending a course of further or higher education (e.g. university); and
- is on a course of at least one academic or calendar year's duration; and
- is normally required to study at least 21 hours per week for at least 24 weeks per year.

## 7. FOREIGN LANGUAGE ASSISTANTS

| | |
|---|---|
| HB and main CTB | Whether there is a non-dependant deduction depends on whether they fall within category 10. |
| Second adult rebate | 'Disregarded persons'. |

They must be registered with the Central Bureau for Educational Visits and Exchanges.

## 8. STUDENTS ON NURSING AND RELATED COURSES

| | |
|---|---|
| HB and main CTB | Whether there is a non-dependant deduction depends on whether they fall within category 10. |
| Second adult rebate | 'Disregarded persons'. |

Students undertaking nursing, midwifery or health visitors' courses (if they also fall within category 6) count as students in this category.

## 9. STUDENT NURSES STUDYING FOR THEIR FIRST NURSING REGISTRATION

| | |
|---|---|
| HB and main CTB | Whether there is a non-dependant deduction depends on whether they fall within category 10. |
| Second adult rebate | 'Disregarded persons'. |

This means anyone studying for a first inclusion in Parts 1 to 6 or 8 of the nursing register.

## 10. FULL-TIME STUDENTS

| | |
|---|---|
| HB | No non-dependant deduction except during any period they take up remunerative work (16 hours per week or more) in a summer vacation. |
| Main CTB | No non-dependant deduction. |
| Second adult rebate | 'Disregarded persons'. |

A student at a further education college counts as 'full-time' if he or she is normally expected to undertake more than 16 guided learning hours per week. All students on sandwich courses count as 'full-time'. Otherwise 'full-time' is not defined.

## 11. YOUTH TRAINING TRAINEES

| | |
|---|---|
| HB and main CTB | No non-dependant deduction. |
| Second adult rebate | 'Disregarded persons' only if under 25. |

This means people on approved Youth Training or Youth Credit courses who are in receipt of an allowance as a trainee (not employees).

## 12. APPRENTICES ON NCVQ/SVEC COURSES

| | |
|---|---|
| HB | A non-dependant deduction applies. |
| Main CTB | No non-dependant deduction. |
| Second adult rebate | 'Disregarded persons'. |

This means someone who:

- is in employment; and
- is studying for a qualification accredited by the National Council for Vocational Qualifications (England and Wales) or Scottish Vocational Education Council (Scotland); and
- receives a reduced rate of pay because of being an apprentice; and
- receives gross pay which does not exceed £160 per week.

## 13. PEOPLE WHO ARE 'SEVERELY MENTALLY IMPAIRED'

| | |
|---|---|
| HB | A non-dependant deduction applies. |
| Main CTB | No non-dependant deduction. |
| Second adult rebate | 'Disregarded persons'. |

This means someone who has 'a severe impairment of intelligence and social functioning (however caused) which appears to be permanent'; and has a medical certificate confirming this; and is receiving one or more of the following (or would do so apart from the fact that he or she has reached pension age):

- the highest or middle rate of the care component of disability living allowance (DLA), or
- attendance allowance, constant attendance allowance or certain equivalent additions to industrial injuries and war pensions, or
- incapacity benefit (IB), or (for periods before April 2001) severe disablement allowance (SDA), or
- disability working allowance (DWA) but *only if* he or she was receiving IB or SDA in the eight weeks before claiming DWA or was receiving income support or JSA(IB) which included a disability premium before claiming SDA, or
- income support or JSA(IB) (or his or her partner is) – but *only if* it includes a disability premium awarded because of the person's incapacity for work.

## 14. CARERS OF PEOPLE RECEIVING CERTAIN BENEFITS

| | |
|---|---|
| HB | A non-dependant deduction applies unless they fall within category 17. |
| Main CTB | No non-dependant deduction. |
| Second adult rebate | 'Disregarded persons'. |

This applies to someone if:

- he or she is providing care or support for at least 35 hours a week; and
- he or she resides with the person receiving the care or support; and
- that person is not a child of his or hers under 18, nor his or her partner; and
- that person is entitled to the highest rate of the care component of disability living allowance, or a higher rate attendance allowance, or certain equivalent additions to industrial injuries and war pensions.

## 15. CARERS INTRODUCED BY AN OFFICIAL OR CHARITABLE BODY

| | |
|---|---|
| HB | A non-dependant deduction applies unless they fall within category 17. |
| Main CTB | No non-dependant deduction. |
| Second adult rebate | 'Disregarded persons'. |

This means someone who:

- is engaged or employed to provide care or support for at least 24 hours a week for no more than £36 per week; and
- is resident (for the better performance of this work) in premises provided by or on behalf of the person receiving the care or support; and
- is employed by that person; and
- was introduced to that person by a local authority, government department or charitable body.

## 16. CARERS RESIDENT IN OFFICIAL OR CHARITABLE PREMISES

| | |
|---|---|
| HB | A non-dependant deduction applies unless they fall within category 17. |
| Main CTB | No non-dependant deduction. |
| Second adult rebate | 'Disregarded persons'. |

This means someone who:

- is engaged or employed to provide care or support for at least 24 hours a week for no more than £36 per week; and
- is resident (for the better performance of this work) in premises provided by or on behalf of a local authority, government department or charitable body, on whose behalf the care or support is provided.

## 17. CARERS FOR WHOM THE CLAIMANT OR PARTNER IS CHARGED

| | |
|---|---|
| HB and main CTB | No non-dependant deduction. |
| Second adult rebate | 'Disregarded persons' only if they fall within categories 14 to 16. |

This means carers caring for the claimant or partner, who are provided by a charitable or voluntary body which charges the claimant or partner for this.

## 18. PEOPLE IN PRISON OR OTHER FORMS OF DETENTION

| | |
|---|---|
| HB | No non-dependant deduction. |
| Main CTB | No non-dependant deduction unless detained only for non-payment of a fine or (in England and Wales) council tax. |
| Second adult rebate | 'Disregarded persons' unless detained only for non-payment of a fine or (in England and Wales) council tax. |

The full definition is not given here, but this includes people in almost any kind of detention.

## 19. PEOPLE WHO HAVE BEEN IN AN NHS HOSPITAL FOR MORE THAN SIX WEEKS

| | |
|---|---|
| HB and main CTB | No non-dependant deduction. |
| Second adult rebate | 'Disregarded persons' only if they fall within category 20. |

This means someone who is in hospital and has been for more than six weeks – but only in the case of NHS hospitals (including NHS Trust hospitals) and not for wholly private patients. Two or more stays in hospital are added together if the break between them is four weeks or less.

## 20. PEOPLE ACTUALLY RESIDENT ELSEWHERE

| | |
|---|---|
| HB and main CTB | No non-dependant deduction. |
| Second adult rebate | 'Disregarded persons' (because they are not 'residents'). |

A person is 'resident' in his or her 'sole or main residence'. It does not matter what type of accommodation this is: it could be an ordinary home, a hospital, a care home, a hostel, or any other type of accommodation. This category could apply to a visitor or to a student returning just for the holidays.

## 21. PEOPLE NORMALLY RESIDENT ELSEWHERE

| | |
|---|---|
| HB and main CTB | No non-dependant deduction. |
| Second adult rebate | Not 'disregarded persons' unless they fall within category 20. |

The concept is not defined. In practice, it is very difficult to distinguish it from category 20.

## 22. RESIDENTS IN HOSPITALS, CARE HOMES AND CERTAIN HOSTELS

'Disregarded persons'.

Although a claim for HB is possible in some of these types of accommodation (and in rare cases a claim for CTB might be possible), it is unlikely that any claimant would have a non-dependant/second adult. This category is included because it affects council tax discounts in such accommodation. It applies to any of the following:

- patients with sole or main residence in an NHS hospital, military hospital, residential care home, nursing home or mental nursing home;
- people with sole or main residence in non-self-contained accommodation which provides them with personal care for old age, disablement, or past or present alcohol or drug dependence or mental disorder;
- people with sole or main residence in non-self-contained accommodation which provides licences (not tenancies) for people of no fixed abode and no settled way of life;
- people with sole or main residence in a bail hostel or probation hostel.

## 23. MEMBERS OF RELIGIOUS COMMUNITIES

| | |
|---|---|
| HB | A non-dependant deduction applies. |
| Main CTB | No non-dependant deduction. |
| Second adult rebate | 'Disregarded persons'. |

This means someone who:

- is a member of a religious community whose principal occupation is prayer, contemplation, education, the relief of suffering, or any combination of those; and
- has no income (other than an occupational pension) or capital; and
- is dependent on the community for his or her material needs.

## 24. (a) MEMBERS OF CERTAIN INTERNATIONAL BODIES OR OF VISITING FORCES, (b) THEIR NON-BRITISH SPOUSES, AND (c) CERTAIN NON-BRITISH SPOUSES OF STUDENTS

| | |
|---|---|
| HB | A non-dependant deduction applies. |
| Main CTB | No non-dependant deduction. |
| Second adult rebate | 'Disregarded persons'. |

The full definitions are not given here. Group (a) includes members of certain international headquarters and defence organisations and certain visiting forces (and in some cases their dependents). For groups (b) and (c), in broad terms, the spouse must be prevented from working or claiming. For group (c), 'student' means someone in category 4, 5 or 6.

## 25. ANYONE ELSE

| | |
|---|---|
| HB and main CTB | A non-dependant deduction applies. |
| Second adult rebate | Not 'disregarded persons'. |

This means anyone who does not fall into any of the previous categories.

# Index

*References in the Index are to paragraph numbers (not page numbers), except that 'A' refers to appendices and 'T' refers to tables in the text.*

## D



## E

## F



## G



## H



## I

## P



## Q



## R



## S